The end of populism

Manchester University Press

The end of populism

Twenty proposals to defend liberal democracy

Marcel H. Van Herpen

Manchester University Press

Copyright © Marcel H. Van Herpen 2021

The right of Marcel H. Van Herpen to be identified as the author of this work has been asserted by him in accordance with the Copyright, Designs and Patents Act 1988.

Published by Manchester University Press
Altrincham Street, Manchester M1 7JA
www.manchesteruniversitypress.co.uk

British Library Cataloguing-in-Publication Data
A catalogue record for this book is available from the British Library

ISBN 978 1 5261 5412 5 hardback
ISBN 978 1 5261 5413 2 paperback

First published 2021

The publisher has no responsibility for the persistence or accuracy of URLs for any external or third-party internet websites referred to in this book, and does not guarantee that any content on such websites is, or will remain, accurate or appropriate.

Typeset by
Servis Filmsetting Ltd, Stockport, Cheshire
Printed in Great Britain by
TJ Books Limited, Padstow

Contents

Acknowledgements — vii

Introduction — 1

Part I The populist wave: why did it happen?

1 What is populism? Constructing an ideal type — 21
2 A portrait of the populist voter — 33
3 Populism and the role of disgust — 48
4 The populist program: what do populists want? — 59
5 Populists in power — 68

Part II Do we have too much democracy or not enough?

6 Is democracy a question of supply or demand? — 79
7 Referendums and popular initiatives: can one have too much democracy? — 93
8 Open primaries: do they "give the power back" to the people? — 116
9 Reinforcing the independent agencies — 127

Part III Twenty proposals to defend liberal democracy: reforming politics and education

10 Not more, but less direct democracy is needed — 139
11 A plea for a *cordon sanitaire* — 145
12 Fight corruption, restore trust, and change party financing — 156

Contents

13	The Sisyphean task of making public life more moral	170
14	How to get rid of political castes	180
15	The need for democratic education	192

Part IV Twenty proposals to defend liberal democracy: reforming society

16	How to handle "fake news" and "alternative facts"	213
17	How to reduce economic inequality	225
18	Toward an economic democracy	240
19	Solving the knotty problem of migration	248

Conclusion 260

Bibliography 270
Index 283

Acknowledgements

In writing this book I owe a lot to discussions with members of the Board of the Cicero Foundation. I want to thank especially Albert van Driel, Peter Verweij, and Ernst Wolff, who read chapters of the book, for their interest in the project and for their continuous support. I also want to thank Rona Heald, who had a critical look at the English text, and the three anonymous peer reviewers who provided valuable feedback which led to important improvements. I want to thank the editorial staff of Manchester University Press, in particular the two commissioning editors Jonathan de Peyer and Robert Byron and copy-editor Diane Wardle, who, with great professionalism, shepherded the book through the editorial process. Finally, I want to thank my wife Valérie, who gave me her patient support during the years of research and writing, and my sons Michiel and Cyrille, who share my passion for this important topic. The book's flaws, omissions, and limitations are, of course, entirely mine.

Introduction

The text of this book was sent to the publisher on 31 December 2019. Although the COVID-19 virus was by then affecting many people in China, no one could suspect the global reach and the deep impact of this health crisis. It was only logical that in the following months this huge new problem captured the attention of the world. It was often said that "nothing would be again as it was before" and that the economic consequences would be felt for many years. One might therefore ask oneself whether this is the right moment to publish a book on populism. Isn't populism a problem of the old world, "the world before COVID-19"? And shouldn't one, therefore, focus rather on solving these new and more urgent problems? These are, indeed, legitimate questions. However, I do not think that populism is a problem of "the world before COVID-19." On the contrary, populism has not only deepened and exacerbated the COVID-19 crisis, but, additionally, it risks jeopardizing the solution of the crisis, surfing on the disaffection of large sections of the population.

The COVID-19 crisis and populism

Populist leaders may have reacted differently to different aspects of the crisis, but behind this one could discern a common pattern:

- Populist leaders tended first to *deny the facts* and, by reacting too late, increased the death toll.
- Instead of uniting the population, populist leaders tended to *divide* the population.
- Populist leaders invented *fake news* and spread disinformation.
- Populist leaders, known for their *anti-expert sentiments*, were reluctant to rely on medical experts.

Introduction

- Populist leaders, known for their authoritarian tendencies, did not hesitate to use the COVID-19 crisis as a cover for undermining the foundations of liberal democracy and for outright *power grabs*.

Some examples. At the end of February 2020, two months after the World Health Organization had reported the first coronavirus cases in Wuhan,[1] US president Donald Trump still denied the evidence and called the coronavirus epidemic the Democrats' "new hoax."[2] A whole month was lost and when the virus hit the US the country was unprepared. Boris Johnson, the British prime minister, was equally accused by critics of complacency and his government was criticized for having been "too slow to act."[3] Trump's remarks about injecting disinfectants in corona virus patients were an all-time low.[4] His remarks were unanimously condemned as dangerous to the health of US citizens. When they led to a spike in people using disinfectants, Trump refused to take any responsibility.[5] Brazil's Jair Bolsonaro, the "Trump of the Tropics," called the coronavirus "a small flu" and told reporters that Brazilians are "immune from diseases."[6] His behavior was no less erratic than that of Trump. He not only criticized state governors who imposed lockdowns, but fired also the health minister and touted the use of hydroxychloroquine, a malaria drug, despite a lack of scientific evidence.[7] Hungary's prime minister Viktor Orbán used the virus to make a new law, giving the government a mandate to rule by decree – without parliamentary oversight and without any sunset clause.[8] Rodrigo Duterte, the populist president of the Philippines, known for his infamous "war on drugs," equally acquired emergency powers.[9] Donald Trump followed suit. Despite being constrained by the checks and balances of the American Constitution, he wanted to pose as a "strongman" and claimed for himself "total authority" and "total control."[10] Far from being a phenomenon of the "pre-COVID-19" world, populism is here to stay. The COVID-19 crisis, as well as its dire economic consequences, will offer populists of all stripes plenty of opportunities to increase their influence. The proposals which I put forward in this book, which were suited to the "pre-COVID-19" world, are even more urgent for the "post-COVID-19" world.

Are our democracies doomed?

Are our democracies doomed? Only a few years ago this question would have been met with disbelief. Was our liberal democracy not a universal model to which the civilized middle classes of the emerging economies of what was still called "The Third World" aspired? And had not most countries of the former Soviet bloc recently embraced this political system? Wasn't the advance of liberal democracy unstoppable,

Introduction

and weren't we, therefore, destined to progress along the road to the best of all possible worlds, touted by Francis Fukuyama in his famous "End of History" article? Who, in the early 1990s, in those years of hope and optimism, would have predicted the populist wave which has engulfed Europe, the United States, and other parts of the world over the last decade and which has become a major challenge to our political system? History, instead of "ending," apparently has come back with a vengeance.

Claiming "more democracy" and pretending to represent "the people," populist leaders are attacking the liberal foundations of our societies. Despite their differences populist movements share two characteristics: their illiberalism and their authoritarianism. And one might well ask oneself if Ralf Dahrendorf wasn't right, when he wrote: "A century of authoritarianism is in no way the most improbable prognosis for the twenty-first century."[11] Some authors even compare our era with the post-First World War period, when liberal democracies came increasingly under attack from authoritarian – fascist and communist – movements.[12] This may be exaggerated and one should not cry wolf prematurely. However, there exist, indeed, some alarming similarities.

But what, exactly, is populism? The term itself gives us a clue. Populism comes from the Latin word *populus*, people. However, the ancient Romans had two words for people: *populus* and *vulgus*. The first indicated the people as a whole, the second only the lower classes of society. The word 'populism' refers to the first: to the people as a whole. Populist leaders do not profess to represent only one class or group of society, they profess to represent *the* people as such. This claim of representing the people in their entirety is accompanied by strong anti-elite attitudes. The elites – in particular the political elite but also the economic and media elites – are accused of not representing the people. Accused of being incompetent, corrupt, and self-serving, these elites are denied not only moral, but also democratic legitimacy. The populist leader becomes, thereby, the only honest and legitimate representative of the people. All others, in particular the political ruling class, tend to become illegitimate – even if they are elected according to existing democratic rules. It can only mean, in the eyes of the populists, that the rules have been broken by election fraud, that the rules are skewed in favor of the ruling class, or that the media, owned by the elite, have intentionally misled the public.

The claim to represent exclusively "the people" indicates a refusal to acknowledge that other parties equally can claim to represent classes or groups of the people. Populists do not consider that society consists of a plurality of groups with a plurality of interests, which, in a parliamentary process of debate, give-and-take, negotiations, and compromises, leads to the formulation of a national interest. They have a Manichaean, bipolar view, in which two groups are opposing each other:

Introduction

"the people" on the one side and "the elite" on the other. This bipolar view is not ethically neutral, noting that there are two groups in society with different interests. Populists, as a rule, idealize "the people." They consider the people – this is the "common man" and not the elite – to be gifted with inborn virtues. They contrast the natural morality of the people to the moral depravity of the allegedly self-seeking, corrupt elite.[13] This Manichaean view leads populists to have a rather negative attitude toward parliamentary democracy, which is denied its function of genuinely representing the people. Dutch populist Geert Wilders, for instance, called the Dutch parliament a *"nepparlement,"* a fake parliament. Rather than putting their trust in the slow wheels of parliamentary democracy populists trust in forms of direct democracy, in particular in referendums and popular initiatives, which are for them the optimal way for the will of the people to be expressed. This emphasis on direct democracy as a means to "express the people's will" leads to a simplification of the decision-making process: complex and intricate problems are reduced to simple yes-or-no questions.

Does this mean that we shouldn't take populist demands seriously? No, on the contrary, because populism is a sign of genuine disaffection and dissatisfaction of a section of the electorate. As such it has a signal function and it is unwise to neglect the message which is expressed by the populist vote. However, this does not mean that the solutions offered by populist parties are acceptable. Of course, there *are* corrupt politicians and yes, liberal democracy does not always function impeccably. This is a reason to improve democratic governance by fighting corruption, increasing transparency regulations, and holding politicians to account for their ethical conduct. But this does not mean that one should change the liberal foundations of our democracies by undermining the independence of the judiciary or attacking the freedom of the press. Neither should one suspend the protection of minorities, end human rights regimes, or close frontiers to refugees. Liberal democracies are fragile systems of checks and balances, which need to be strengthened rather than weakened.

The thesis of this book is that the populist wave is caused by real problems, which urgently need to be solved. At the same time the populist parties and their leaders who profit from the protest vote are a part of the problem. Not only are they incapable of solving these problems, but they also tend to compound them. This is true for populist parties both from the right and from the left. For this reason the democratic mainstream parties have a double mission: to stop the advance of the populist parties and to bring about the necessary political and economic reforms to save our liberal democracies. For this to happen we need not only a diagnosis of the problems, but also the political will to solve them.

Introduction

Populism: an international tsunami?

The populist crisis which is ravaging our political landscape resembles a tsunami rather than a storm. This is because the huge tidal wave which is hitting the shoreline does not come from nowhere. Like a tsunami, which is caused by invisible and powerful earthquakes deep under the surface of the ocean, the present wave of populism is caused by profound economic and cultural changes that are transforming our societies. The Great Recession, which started in 2008 with a banking crisis, certainly had a major impact. The COVID-19 health crisis of 2020 and its economic consequences will also leave their mark. However, fundamental changes had already started in the 1980s and 1990s, when globalization, automation, and growing migration flows fundamentally transformed the economies and the ethnic composition of our societies. It was these changes which increased economic insecurity and led to a growing anger and identity anxiety in sections of the population. The inability or unwillingness of the mainstream political parties to address these fears has certainly contributed to the emergence of the populist phenomenon.

The question is: can we still stop populism's advance? The prospects seem bleak. The number of governments in which populists are represented or in which they play a leading role is rapidly increasing. From Modi's India to Duterte's Philippines, from Maduro's Venezuela to Erdogan's Turkey, from Italy's Salvini to Brazil's Bolsonaro, populism has become a worldwide phenomenon. However, what is particularly alarming is the fact that populism is on the rise in the heartlands of modern liberal democracy, in the United States and Europe. Trump's presidency has declared war on the post-Second World War liberal international order, and the governments of Poland and Hungary openly adhere to a form of "illiberal democracy," while far-right populist parties have entered the governments of Austria and Italy. Italy followed the example of Greece in conducting a completely new experiment: the cooperation of far-right and far-left populist parties in government, an experiment which could be emulated elsewhere. When people find themselves in a situation of crisis they have the tendency to extrapolate this crisis into the future, expecting the crisis to deepen and to last.[14] In a crisis situation we have the unpleasant feeling that we are slowly losing the firm ground beneath our feet and that the floor on which we stand has been changed in a collection of moving ice floes. In such a situation there exists a great need for certainty and – in particular – for predictability, and we hope that history can offer us examples of how we can handle the situation in order to avoid calamities. In the case of populism there are some historic examples and it may be worthwhile to have a look at them.

Introduction

The origin of populism

Populism, it must be emphasized, is a *modern* political phenomenon. Certainly, there were popular revolts in ancient times, but these upheavals cannot be called populist. Peasants' revolts against feudal lords over imposed taxes often had a broad popular support. The Peasants' Revolt, for instance, which broke out in England in June 1381 and which came to the brink of overpowering the king's government, was, in the words of Barbara Tuchman, a result of a "weakened acceptance of the system, a mistrust of government and governors, lay and ecclesiastical, an awakening sense that authority could be challenged – that change was in fact possible."[15]

Central elements of modern populism are here already present: a weakened acceptance of the system, a mistrust of government and governors, and a sense that authority could be challenged by "those below." However, these revolts took place in a feudal, pre-democratic environment. And it is exactly the existence of a democratic political system with, at least, universal male suffrage, which is a necessary condition of the modern populist phenomenon. Therefore, even when they are labeled "populist," other movements do not necessarily fit in, such as the *narodniki* of early nineteenth century Tsarist Russia (from the Russian word *narod,* which means "people"). This was a movement of the young intelligentsia, who were alienated from the state and the existing political order. They "combined the deification of the masses with a conviction that they had a mission to save the people from suffering and show it the way to absolute and everlasting happiness on earth."[16] Some of them even "decided that it was improper for intellectuals to foist their ideas upon the masses. The toiling man was always right. Intellectuals should settle in the village and learn from the peasant instead of trying to teach him."[17] We find here the same "elite versus people" opposition as in modern populist movements, as well as the belief that "the people are always right." However, these movements lacked one important characteristic: they had no electoral impact, because they took place in a pre-democratic environment.

The American "People's Party"

One of the first modern populist movements took place in the United States in the last decades of the nineteenth century. The background of this movement was a profound agricultural crisis in the Great Plains and the South of the country, caused by falling prices, droughts, and extremely high levels of indebtedness. In the late 1880s the disgruntled farmers began to organize themselves into Farmers' Alliances. Not satisfied with either the Republican or the Democratic Party, in 1891 they founded their own political organization, the People's Party, also called "the Populists." In the presidential election of 1892 this party had an unexpected success. Its candidate, James B. Weaver, got 8.5 percent of the popular vote. In the 1894 election for the House of Representatives the party got as much as 10 percent.

The People's Party was a typical anti-establishment party. Its enemies were the tycoons and bankers living in the big cities, together with the politicians of the established parties, who allegedly served the interests of the "plutocrats."[18] The Populist platform was "leftist": Populists were in favor of a graduated income tax, a working day of eight hours, and government control of the railroads and banks.[19]

Despite their early electoral successes they were conscious of the fact that they would never be able to win a presidential election. This was the reason that they joined the Democratic Party and in 1896 endorsed the Democratic presidential candidate William Jennings Bryan (1860–1925),[20] who was ultimately defeated by the Republican candidate William McKinley. After 1896 the Populist movement gradually faded away. However, this did not mean that its ideas had disappeared. In fact the Populists made a major contribution to the ideas of the so-called "Progressive Era," the period from the 1890s to the 1920s, in which politicians such as Theodore Roosevelt and Woodrow Wilson would speak out for and implement radical reforms, which heralded Franklin D. Roosevelt's New Deal of the 1930s.

It was the great merit of the Populists that they had put the social question on the agenda. And this was far from superfluous. "That gross economic inequality has persisted among Americans for many generations is hardly an obscure or even highly contestable fact," wrote Robert A. Dahl. And he continued: "In the 1890s the Farmers' Alliance and the Populists publicized data showing great inequality in the distribution of wealth and income. Scholars also published estimates; in 1893 one political economist calculated that 0.33 percent of the population owned 20 percent of the national wealth, while 52 percent owned only 5 percent."[21] Contemporaries feared that the populists wanted to abolish private property, like the radical, new Marxist parties in Europe. "In the era of Bryan and McKinley many conservatives made the mistake of thinking that the agrarian populists were economic radicals who were against private property. [However] what the populists really wanted was not to abolish property, but to get some for themselves."[22] These fears were, therefore, clearly exaggerated. The American farmers, living with their families on isolated farms, were not only individualists but were also independent entrepreneurs and, as such, integrated into the capitalist world economy.

So should one consider the American Populists a positive force in the history of the United States? Partially, yes. But, as Peter Drucker reminds us:

Introduction

Historians tend to be kind to yesterday's radicals. They have a very good press with posterity – in striking contrast to the bad press they have with their contemporaries. For while the radicals rarely write the nation's songs, they write the nation's pamphlets. Also their measures – which usually are not so very radical at all – tend to be enacted into law long after their paranoid mood has faded away. One then remembers, for instance, that the Populists were in favor of an income tax and forgets that they believed in the conspiracy of bankers, Jews, and Catholics to destroy the republic and to enthrone the Pope in Washington.[23]

Contemporaries had, indeed, reasons to be skeptical. The Populists believed the most outrageous conspiracy theories and anti-Semitism was rampant. For them, the incarnation of the hated capitalist was a kind of modern Shylock: the Jewish banker. Because the international financial center was in London, anti-Semitism, personified in the Rothschild family, was mixed with Anglophobia. "One feature of the Populist conspiracy theory that has been generally overlooked is its frequent link with a kind of rhetorical anti-Semitism. The slight current of anti-Semitism that existed in the United States before the 1890s had been associated with problems of money and credit. During the closing years of the century it grew noticeably … it was chiefly Populist writers who expressed the identification of the Jew with the usurer."[24] The American Populists were fishing in the same murky waters as their modern counterparts, stirring up feelings of xenophobia, racism, and anti-Semitism. There is "something inherent in populism," wrote the historian John Lukacs, "which is that within its innate contempt for its opponents and outsiders there is that ever-present compound of hatreds and fears."[25] In the end, therefore, weighing the pros and cons, the assessment of this early Populist movement is mixed.

"Boulangism" in France

Some American authors tend to consider the People's Party as the beginning of modern populism, which later would spread into Europe. John B. Judis, for instance, speaks about "a kind of populism that runs through American history, and is transplanted to Europe."[26] However, Europe didn't need America to invent populism, and populism was certainly not "transplanted" to Europe. This is for the simple reason that Europe had its own, home-grown varieties of populism.

One of the most striking examples is the emergence of "boulangism" in France, which started three years before the foundation of the People's Party in the United States. It is interesting that this populist movement had the same socio-economic origin as that in the United States, because the agricultural crisis hit not only

Introduction

American farmers but also farmers in Europe. At that time 60 percent of the French working population consisted of farmers. They were not the only victims, however, because the agricultural crisis was part of a broader financial and economic crisis – a prolonged period of depression which lasted the whole last quarter of the century. Not only farmers were disgruntled, therefore, but also the industrial proletariat in the big cities such as Paris and Lyon who, if not unemployed, received low wages for long working hours in dirty and noisy factories. "The economic crisis of the 1880s," wrote Robert Paxton, "as the first major depression to occur in the era of mass politics, rewarded demagoguery. Henceforth a decline in the standard of living would translate quickly into electoral defeats for incumbents and victories for political outsiders ready to appeal with summary slogans to angry voters."[27]

Male adults in the French Third Republic had the right to vote. Conscious of their power, disgruntled voters were ready to use it as a weapon against a parliament and government which they considered incompetent and corrupt. All they needed was a leader who would express their rage. They found their providential man in General Georges Boulanger, a former war minister who was dismissed after his bellicose attitude almost led to an armed conflict with Germany. Boulanger began to organize a broad opposition to the government. A magnetic and charismatic personality, widely acclaimed by the public, his popularity grew as he positioned himself as the champion of the people by attacking the allegedly corrupt government and parliament. His campaign slogans were simple and rude. He called the 500 members of parliament *les 500 fainéants* – the 500 lazybones – and himself *Général nettoyage* – "General Clean-Up." The broom became the symbol of the movement.[28] Boulanger and his team made good use of new propaganda and communication methods, not restricting themselves to distributing pamphlets and pasting posters. They organized a modern campaign which was unique in its time: "Boulanger was the first politician who distributed his photo portrait on a massive scale among voters for his propaganda."[29] However, his program remained rather vague. It consisted of "the three Rs": Revanche (against Germany for the lost war of 1870), Revision (of the Constitution), and Restoration (of the monarchy). "Boulanger escapes from any dogmatic confinement. On the contrary, he is the end product of the confused values that became popular in the 1880s."[30] But it was just this vagueness which made it possible to attract a heterogeneous group of voters – from the left, as well as from the right.[31] When, in January 1889, he was elected as a member of parliament, his followers urged him to march on the Élysée palace and stage a *coup d'état*. Boulanger hesitated and refused to take the lead, after which the movement dissipated. Accused of organizing a complot against the republic he fled in April of that year to Belgium. It was the end of the movement.

Introduction

Boulangism had all the characteristics of a populist movement: it was anti-elite, it pretended to represent "the people" against the elite, it had a charismatic leader, it had a vague program, and its campaign slogans were simplistic. However, there was still *another* characteristic of the movement which should not be overlooked and which we have already met in the American People's Party: its xenophobia, and in particular its anti-Semitism. "Although Boulanger himself in his propaganda never made use of anti-Semitism," writes Michel Winock, "this did not prevent that notorious anti-Semites joined his movement."[32]

Populist movements develop when the state and its government lack legitimacy. This was clearly the case in France in the 1890s. The new, Third Republic, founded in 1870 after the collapse of the Second Empire of Napoleon III, still struggled to establish itself. Its legitimacy was challenged by both Bonapartists and monarchists, who were nostalgic for France's lost greatness. In the United States, populist movements have always found a fertile soil because of an American peculiarity: the ingrained suspicion of its citizens of the federal government. "Government as such has remarkably few defenders in the United States," writes Anthony King, "and 'the government' does seem to be perceived by a remarkably large number of people as an alien and hostile force."[33] For King it is a "mystery" "to account for the extreme intensity with which many Americans feel this distrust and to account for the fact that these extremely intense feelings – of anger, frustration, and betrayal – are directed to such a large extent at government, especially the federal government."[34]

When populism morphs into authoritarianism

Both the American "Populist Party" and the Boulangist movement in France are predecessors of modern populist movements. The first, with its rants against the abuses of capitalism and pleas for social justice, is an example of a left-wing movement, the second, aiming to restore the monarchy, is an example of a right-wing movement. Today there is a great variety of governments and movements – right wing and left wing – which are labeled "populist." There exists in this respect a certain confusion and one needs more clarity as to whether a regime or a government deserves to be labeled "populist." Can one, for instance, characterize Putin's regime in Russia as "populist"? Some authors do.[35] They point to Putin's behavior: using vulgar language and riding bare chested on horseback as a "strongman." It is indeed a fact that in his behavior Putin exhibits a populist style. However, this does not mean that one can characterize his regime as populist. Putin's regime is not an anti-establishment regime: it *is* the establishment. Neither can it pretend

Introduction

to fight the corruption of the elite, as the Kremlin itself is the center and embodiment of a deeply ingrained corruption. More importantly, Putin's regime can be labeled neither a "liberal democracy," nor even an "illiberal democracy," for the simple reason that the people do not have the possibility of changing the government at the ballot box. In Putin's system of "managed democracy" opposition parties are blocked from participating, election results are falsified, and there exists a deep distrust of "the people." There is no mobilization of support, but rather a demobilization and depoliticization. The fact that in Putin's Russia the possibility of democratic alternation of power through the ballot box does not exist means that Putin's regime is a fully fledged authoritarian regime. However, the absence of a populist regime in Russia does not mean that there couldn't in this country develop a populist *movement*, which would define itself as representing "the people" against the corrupt elite. Navalny's anti-corruption movement could be a candidate for this. In fact, the possibility of the formation of such a movement is anticipated by the Kremlin, which is introducing new repressive measures in order to prevent its emergence.[36]

Drawing the line between a populist and an authoritarian regime can be difficult. The litmus test is the possibility of the alternation of power. If a populist regime clings to power by preventing the organization of free and fair elections, populism is morphing into outright authoritarianism. Maduro's Venezuela is a case in point. Erdogan's government in Turkey also finds itself on a slippery slope in this respect. The tendency to slide into authoritarianism is one of the characteristics of populist regimes and populist movements, regardless of whether their ideological leanings are right wing or left wing. This means that they run the risk of derailing and – after having undermined the checks and balances and other foundations of liberal democracy – could be tempted to install an authoritarian regime.

Is it too late to stop the populist wave? That depends on us. The twenty proposals formulated in this book could make a difference. They are certainly not a magic wand and the implementation of only one or a few of them will not be enough to save our liberal political order. However, taken together they could fundamentally change the political landscape and ensure that our children and grandchildren can live in a free, democratic, and prosperous world.

Structure of the book

This book consists of four parts.

Introduction

Part I: The populist wave: why did it happen?

Chapter 1 presents "thin" and "thick" definitions of populism. A choice is made to elaborate a "thick" definition, which offers richer information on the phenomenon. This implies the construction of an "ideal type," as proposed by Max Weber. This ideal type of populism has three dimensions: organizational, ideological, and institutional. The *organizational dimension* is the subject of the first three chapters. In the first chapter a portrait is given of the populist leader, who is charismatic and has an authoritarian leadership style. In many cases he uses vulgar language, but this is interpreted as a sign that he is "one of us" and belongs to the people. This use of vulgar language, however, is not completely harmless, because it can be interpreted by adversaries as being threatening. Chapter 2 draws a portrait of the populist voter. His emotions are analyzed. What is the role played by negative emotions, such as fear, hate, and anger? The causes of his disaffection are explored. Should we seek the causes in economic anxiety? In personal dispositions, such as optimism versus pessimism, health, and personal wellbeing? In threatened identities? Or in a combination of these factors? In chapter 3 the role of disgust is discussed in connection with Donald Trump and the Trump voter, and how this emotion is related to authoritarianism.

Chapter 4 deals with the *ideological dimension* of the populist ideal type. The question here is: what do populists want? Populist programs are, in general, vague. However, a major trend can be distinguished: the populists' need for protection, which can take the form of economic protection for left-wing populist parties, and cultural/ethnic protection for right-wing populist parties. Chapter 5 deals with the *institutional dimension* of the ideal type. Here the question is: how do populist parties behave when in government? It is argued that populists in government have a preference for quick and simple measures and tend to attack the pillars of liberal democracy, such as the independent judiciary, independent central banks, the media, and independent anticorruption agencies. Another characteristic is their preference for forms of direct democracy, such as referendums and popular initiatives.

Part II: A burning question: do we have too much democracy or not enough?

In Part II the central question is: do we have too much democracy or not enough? Populists claim that we don't have enough democracy and want to introduce or enhance forms of direct democracy, such as referendums, popular initiatives, and

Introduction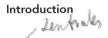

open primaries. Chapter 6 is a pivotal chapter. It discusses Joseph Schumpeter's thesis that democracy is a question of supply rather than of demand, a reason why the "people's will" – if such a will exists – is rather a "manufactured will." In chapter 7 practices of direct democracy are analyzed: the Brexit referendum in Britain, the Ukraine referendum in the Netherlands, popular initiatives in California, and referendums in Switzerland. It is argued that they did not lead to more democracy, nor to better decision-making, but became tools in the hands of populists. This leads in chapter 8 to an analysis of the system of open primaries in the United States, France, and the UK, weighing the positive and negative effects of this system, while chapter 9 examines the importance of independent agencies for the system of "checks and balances," a cornerstone of liberal democracy which is often attacked by populists.

Part III: Twenty proposals to defend liberal democracy: reforming politics and education

In this part sixteen proposals are formulated to defend liberal democracy. It is argued that it is not enough only to defend liberal democracy. The challenges today are such that returning to the post-war "golden age" of liberal democracy, which found its apotheosis in Huntington's "Third Wave" of democratization, is no longer possible. We have to find new solutions for the problems in our fast-changing societies. And populism is such a problem.

In chapter 10 proposals are discussed to restrict referendums, abolish open primaries, and defend the independent agencies. Chapter 11 discusses the installation of *cordons sanitaires* to keep populists out of government. It is argued that attempts "to tame populists" by giving them government responsibility, did not work. Chapters 12 and 13 present proposals to moralize public life by making party financing less dependent on rich donors, giving anti-corruption and ethics watchdogs more power, asking politicians to sign "moral charters," introducing term limits for politicians, and abolishing "revolving door" policies by making specific jobs off-limits for former office-holders.

Chapter 14 stresses the necessity of avoiding the creation of political castes, and analyzes the examples of the ENA elite school in France, the "Oxbridge" political elite in the UK, and the overrepresentation of billionaires in the US Congress. The question of whether parliaments should "mirror" the population is explored. Chapter 15 emphasizes the need for democratic education in secondary schools and what lessons we can learn from John Dewey. This chapter offers arguments for lowering the voting age to sixteen years in order to make voting an early habit.

Introduction

Part IV: Twenty proposals to defend liberal democracy: reforming society

Chapter 16 discusses methods for defending truth in a "post-truth" world, where social media have become a tool in the hands of populists, and warns against populists who act as agents of hostile foreign powers. Chapters 17, 18, and 19 focus on the macro-economic and societal roots of the populist phenomenon and how to tackle these.

Chapter 17 discusses growing economic inequality, resulting in the rise of the "1 percent," leading to a new "Gilded Age," and the necessity of inverting this trend. Proposals to reduce economic anxiety by the introduction of a universal basic income or a negative income tax are discussed. Chapter 18 formulates arguments to enhance economic democracy. Is the German system of co-determination ("*Mitbestimmung*") a possible model to emulate? In chapter 20 proposals are made for a humane and sustainable migration policy, pleading for a delicate balance between the populist "closed frontier" approach and a naive idealistic "open frontier" approach, taking into account the "absorption capacity" of our societies. Multiculturalism should be avoided, it is argued. Instead our ethnically diverse societies should formulate strict conditions for newcomers to integrate, which means accepting the basic values of our societies. The concluding chapter discusses the affinity between right-wing populism and fascism. The author argues that despite a number of similarities, right-wing populism is different from interbellum fascism, but he emphasizes that one should remain vigilant because of its innate authoritarianism and its illiberal tendencies.

Notes

1. "WHO timeline – COVID-19," World Health Organization, 27 April 2020. www.who.int/news/item/27–04–2020-who-timeline---covid-19 (accessed 2 May 2020).
2. Cf. Thomas Franck, "Trump says the coronavirus is the Democrats' 'new hoax'," CNBC, 28 February 2020. www.cnbc.com/2020/02/28/trump-says-the-coronavirus-is-the-democrats-new-hoax.html (accessed 2 May 2020).
3. Heather Stewart, Matthew Weaver, and Kate Proctor, "'Nonchament': Boris Johnson accused of COVID-19 complacency," *Guardian*, 27 March 2020. www.theguardian.com/world/2020/mar/27/nonchalant-boris-johnson-accused-of-covid-19-complacency (accessed 2 May 2020).
4. Matt Flegenheimer, "Trump's disinfectant remark raises a question about the 'very stable genius'," *New York Times*, 26 April 2020. www.nytimes.com/2020/04/26/us/politics/trump-disinfectant-coronavirus.html (accessed 2 May 2020).
5. Nikki Carvajal and Maegan Vazquez, "Trump said he takes no responsibility for any spike in people using disinfectants improperly," CNN, 28 April 2020. https://edition.cnn.com/2020/04/27/politics/donald-trump-disinfectants-coronavirus/index.html (accessed 2 May 2020).

Introduction

6   Isaac Chotiner, "The coronavirus crisis in Bolsonaro's Brazil," *New Yorker*, 27 April 2020. www.newyorker.com/news/q-and-a/the-coronavirus-crisis-in-bolsonaros-brazil (accessed 2 May 2020).

7   Cf. Shannon Sims, "Bolsonaro slams lockdowns amid rising virus death toll," Bloomberg News, 11 May 2020. www.bloomberg.com/news/articles/2020-05-11/bolsonaro-criticizes-lockdown-measures-as-brazil-becomes-hotspot (accessed 10 September 2020).

8   Dalibor Rohac, "Hungary's prime minister is using the virus to make an authoritarian power grab," *Washington Post*, 25 March 2020. www.washingtonpost.com/opinions/2020/03/25/hungarys-prime-minister-is-using-virus-make-an-authoritarian-power-grab/ (accessed 2 May 2020).

9   Julie McCarthy, "Concerns in Philippines after Duterte given emergency powers to fight COVID-19," NPR, 24 March 2020. www.npr.org/sections/coronavirus-live-updates/2020/03/24/820906636/concerns-in-philippines-after-duterte-given-emergency-powers-to-fight-covid-19-s?t=1588080049105 (accessed 2 May 2020).

10 Erin Burnett, "Trump falsely claims he has 'total' authority," CNN, 13 April 2020. https://edition.cnn.com/videos/politics/2020/04/13/trump-governors-total-power-bts-acosta-ebof-vpx.cnn (accessed 2 May 2020).

11 Ralf Dahrendorf, "Anmerkungen zur Globalisierung," in Peter Kemper and Ulrich Sonnenschein (eds), *Globalisierung im Alltag* (Frankfurt am Main: Suhrkamp, 2002), p. 23.

12 Cf. Richard Yeselson, "The return of the 1920s," *Atlantic*, 30 December 2015. www.theatlantic.com/politics/archive/2015/12/the-return-of-the-1920s/422163/ (accessed 10 September 2020).

13 Cf. Pierre-André Taguieff, *Le nouveau national-populisme* (Paris: CNRS Éditions, 2012), p. 81, where Taguieff speaks about "an idealization or transfiguration of 'the people'," which makes them the "sole bearer of human qualities and inborn virtues."

14 Eatwell and Goodwin express this uncertainty. "One interesting macro question," they write, "is whether political shocks like Brexit and Trump signal that the West is nearing the *end* of a period of political volatility, or instead is closer to the *beginning* of a new period of great change" (Roger Eatwell and Matthew Goodwin, *National Populism – The Revolt Against Liberal Democracy* (London: Pelican, 2018), p. xxv).

15 Barbara W. Tuchman, *A Distant Mirror – The Calamitous 14th Century* (Harmondsworth: Penguin, 1984), p. 374.

16 Alexander Chubarov, *The Fragile Empire – A History of Imperial Russia* (New York and London: Continuum, 2001), p. 88.

17 Richard Pipes, *Russia under the Old Regime* (London and New York: Penguin, 1995), p. 274.

18 These "plutocrats," however, were not devoid of their own ethic. Robert Bellah and his co-authors describe their "Establishment vision" as "primarily associated with those segments of the industrial and financial elites who at the end of the nineteenth century created and endowed a network of private institutions such as universities, hospitals, museums, symphony orchestras, schools, churches, clubs, and associations alongside their new corporations … The creators of these institutions sought to spread a cosmopolitan ethic of *noblesse oblige* and public service to give local magnates a sense of national responsibility" (Robert N. Bellah, Richard Madsen, William M. Sullivan, Ann Swidler, and Steven M. Tipton, *Habits of the Heart – Individualism and Commitment in American Life* (Berkeley, Los Angeles, and London: University of California Press, 1996), pp. 258–259). "Against the high-minded, genteel image of the Establishment," write the authors, "the

Populist vision accented the egalitarian ethos in the American tradition … The Populist vision asserted the claims of 'the people,' ordinary citizens, to sufficient wisdom to govern their affairs" (p. 259).

19 An important part in the movement was also played by the so-called "Silverites," who wanted to leave the gold standard and introduce a bimetallic monetary system based on gold and silver. They expected that this early version of "quantitative easing" would lead to inflation and thereby facilitate the payment of their debts.

20 Richard Hofstadter emphasizes that Bryan also had the profile of a populist leader. He quotes Oswald Garrison Villard, editor of the *New York Evening Post*, who wrote: "Of all the men I have seen at close range in thirty-one years of newspaper service, Mr Bryan seemed to me the most ignorant." Hofstadter continues: "The Commoner's heart was filled with simple emotions, but his mind was stocked with equally simple ideas. Presumably he would have lost his political effectiveness if he had learned to look at his supporters with a critical eye, but his capacity for identifying himself with them was costly, for it gave them not so much leadership as expression. He spoke for them so perfectly that he never spoke to them. In his lifelong stream of impassioned rhetoric he communicated only what they already believed" (Richard Hofstadter, *The American Political Tradition and the Men Who Made It* (New York: Vintage Books, 1948), p. 190). Bryan's speech to the Democratic Convention of 1895, titled "You Shall Not Crucify Mankind Upon a Cross of Gold," was a rhetorical masterpiece. It developed classical populist themes, such as the opposition between "the idle holders of idle capital" on the one side, and "the struggling masses" on the other, together with the message to take back sovereignty: "We declare that this nation is able to legislate for its own people on every question, without waiting for the aid or consent of any other nation on earth" (William Jennings Bryan, "You Shall Not Crucify Mankind Upon a Cross of Gold," in Brian MacArthur (ed.), *The Penguin Book of Historic Speeches* (London: Penguin Books, 2017), p. 383).

21 Robert A. Dahl, *Dilemmas of Pluralist Democracy – Autonomy vs. Control* (New Haven and London: Yale University Press, 1982), p. 172.

22 Don K. Price, "Science in the Great Society," in Bertram M. Gross (ed.), *A Great Society?* (New York and London: Basic Books, 1968), p. 230.

23 Peter F. Drucker, "New Political Alignments in the Great Society," in Gross (ed.), *A Great Society?*, p. 176. Robert Dahl shares this view. According to him, "Historians and intellectuals have, indeed, the idea that in the past populism has been an indigenous, peculiar American form of protest against some abuses of capitalism, and that for this reason it exerted a certain attraction. But American populism had in some areas even its dark side, which sometimes manifested itself also in racist hostilities" (Robert A. Dahl, *Intervista sul pluralismo: A cura di Giancarlo Bosetti* (Roma and Bari: Editori Laterza, 2002), p. 49). According to Alan Wolfe, "Older forms of populism, such as those associated with the three-time presidential candidate William Jennings Bryan … resonate with ideas of social justice and in that sense remain appealing to the left of this day. But even though populism shares something positive with liberalism, it is deeply illiberal temperamentally. Populism attempts to rouse people out of fear rather than to appeal to them through hope. It is strongly tempted to divide the world into friends and enemies. It has never been sympathetic toward those who live outside its rather restricted moral universe. It looks back with nostalgia toward a simpler past rather than anticipating a more complex future" (Alan Wolfe, *The Future of Liberalism* (New York: Vintage Books, 2010), p. 260).

24 Richard Hofstadter, *The Age of Reform – From Bryan to F.D.R.* (New York: Vintage Books, 1955), pp. 77–78.

Introduction

25 John Lukacs, *Democracy and Populism – Fear and Hatred* (New Haven and London: Yale University Press, 2005), p. 229.
26 John B. Judis, *The Populist Explosion – How the Great Recession Transformed American and European Politics* (New York: Columbia Global Reports, 2016), p. 14.
27 Robert O. Paxton, *The Anatomy of Fascism* (New York: Vintage Books, 2005), p. 46.
28 Cf. Michel Winock, *La Droite – Hier et aujourd'hui* (Paris: Perrin, 2012), p. 81. The image of the broom returns regularly in the populist vocabulary. In 1992 the Flemish Vlaams Blok (predecessor of Vlaams Belang) used in a campaign the slogan "*Grote Kuis*" ("Great Clean-Up"). The slogan was copied from the Belgian fascist REX organization, founded by Léon Degrelle in the 1930s. Donald Trump's slogans during the presidential campaign in 2016 – "Clean up this mess" and "Drain the swamp" – also belong in this category.
29 Pierre Rosanvallon, *La légitimité démocratique – Impartialité, réflexivité, proximité* (Paris: Éditions du Seuil, 2008), p. 307.
30 Michel Winock, *Histoire de l'extrême droite en France* (Paris: Éditions du Seuil, 1994), p. 74.
31 In an early French analysis, published in 1913, it was observed that the petty bourgeoisie was the recruiting ground for Boulanger's populism. "Crushed between the aggressive capitalism of the great companies and the increasing rise of the working people … they are in that state of discontent, from which the Boulangisms marshal their forces, in which reactionary demagogues see the best ground in which to agitate, and in which is born passionate resistance to certain democratic reforms" (André Siegried, *Tableau politique de la France de l'ouest sous la troisième république* (Paris: Librairie Armand Colin, 1913), p. 413. Quoted by Seymour Martin Lipset, in "Extremism of the centre," in Roger Griffin (ed.), *International Fascism: Theories, Causes and the New Consensus* (London: Arnold, 1998), p. 105).
32 Winock, *Histoire*, p. 75.
33 Anthony King, "Distrust of Government: Explaining American Exceptionalism," in Susan J. Pharr and Robert D. Putnam (eds), *Disaffected Democracies – What's Troubling the Trilateral Countries?* (Princeton: Princeton University Press, 2000), p. 77.
34 Ibid., pp. 97–98.
35 Natalia Mamonova, for instance, characterizes Putin's regime as "authoritarian populism." Cf. Natalia Mamonova, "Vladimir Putin and the rural roots of authoritarian populism in Russia," Open Democracy, 3 April 2018. www.opendemocracy.net/en/vladimir-putin-and-rural-roots-of-authoritarian-populism-in-russia/ (accessed 2 May 2020). Another example is a conference, organized on 19 October 2019 by Penn University, titled "Trump – Putin – Berlusconi – Orbán – Kaczyński – Farage: A populist cocktail," putting Putin into a group with notorious populist politicians.
36 Cf. Marcel H. Van Herpen, "Will populism come to Russia?" *The National Interest*, 20 September 2018. https://nationalinterest.org/feature/will-populism-come-russia-31602.

Part I

The populist wave: why did it happen?

1

What is populism? Constructing an ideal type

There are many ways to define populism. We saw in the introduction that a fundamental characteristic of populist movements is an anti-elite attitude and a pretension to represent and defend the "real people" against the allegedly corrupt and incompetent elites. This characteristic is shared by all populist movements, whatever their ideological content and eventual differences. I would like to call this a "thin" definition. It is the method of a physician who takes X-ray pictures of his or her patients. Ignoring their outward appearances he or she looks straight through the flesh of their bodies at what is behind: their skeleton. The "thin" definition is a method of ultimate abstraction until one arrives at the "essence" or "core" of a phenomenon. This "thin" definition, however, also has many constraints. In order to reveal the essence it has to ignore many relevant details and the richness of the phenomenon as it develops in different countries and cultures. A "thin" definition of populism could be formulated as follows:

> A political phenomenon in a modern liberal democratic society, in which a movement or a party claims to represent "the people" against the governing "elite" with the aim of replacing this elite and fundamentally changing the government's policy.

This "thin" definition leaves many questions open, such as: who are the followers? Who are the leaders? What do the populists want? What methods do they use? Are they a danger to liberal democracy or, on the contrary, an expression of democracy? And so on. For this reason the German sociologist Max Weber (1864–1920) developed a "thick" method, which he called "ideal types" (*Idealtypen*). An "ideal type" is not, strictly speaking, a definition, and neither is it a copy of reality. It is rather a virtual concept in which all the relevant properties, found in different manifestations of the phenomenon, are collected. Weber called it, therefore, "an artificial construct." In this construct the properties of different existent (or past) historical entities are gathered and accumulated.[1] The "thick" method can be compared to the work of an artist who makes a clay figure of a woman. The artist adds small details until the figure resembles the image of femininity that he has in his head. It may have the ears of his sister, the nose of his daughter, and the legs of the woman next door. It does not need to resemble any model which exists in reality. After the construction of the ideal type, existing historical phenomena can be compared with it to assess the distance between a historical phenomenon and the ideal type. This does not mean that the ideal type is, literally, an "ideal" or a norm. It is only a heuristic device to better understand the phenomenon. For Weber it is possible to construct an ideal type of religions, and equally of brothels. Ideal types are for sociologists heuristic instruments *par excellence* to analyze complex historical phenomena, such as "liberalism," "imperialism," or, in this case, "populism."

The "thick" definition: constructing an "ideal type" of populism

One can distinguish three dimensions of the ideal type:

- organizational;
- ideological;
- institutional.

In the organizational dimension we find the socio-economic and psycho-social profile of the followers ("the people") and their leaders. In the ideological dimension we find the explicit and implicit policy objectives of the movement, as well as its slogans and the way it uses the media for its propaganda. In the institutional dimension we find the ways of governance used by populist movements when they have gained power in their countries. In this chapter and the following two chapters we will analyze the organizational dimension of the ideal type, in particular the economic, psychological, and emotional profiles of the populist voter and the populist leader. In chapter 4 we will analyze the ideological dimension, and in chapter 5 the institutional dimension.

Blaming the government

Who are the voters of populist parties? There are many different kinds of populists, living in different countries, on different continents, often having different agendas. However, they all have one characteristic in common: they are *dissatisfied* with their situation. Of course, an individual can have many reasons for being dissatisfied. One can be passed over for a promotion, one can fail an exam, or one's marriage can be on the rocks. In these cases one can blame one's boss, one's professor, one's partner, or, eventually (reluctantly), oneself. In the case of a populist, the blame game primarily concerns the government. He or she blames the government for having lost a job, for being ripped off by the tax authorities, or for the fact that a business isn't doing well. This does not mean *per se* that the government bears whole or even partial responsibility for these problems. It is the perception that counts. In this perception the government plays a key role in society and it plays this role badly, because it does not listen to the citizens. Democracy, apparently, isn't working. "For the citizens," writes Pierre Rosanvallon, "lack of democracy means not being listened to, decisions being taken without consultation, ministers who don't assume their responsibilities, leaders who lie with impunity, a political class which is cut off from the world and is not sufficiently held accountable, [and] an administrative governance which remains opaque."[2]

The increasing criticism of government action which we are witnessing today is not only caused by failing politicians, but must be partially explained by a shift in the balance of power between parliaments and governments in favor of the latter. While in the nineteenth century parliaments dominated the executive, in the twentieth century power shifted increasingly to the executive. Although criticism of parliaments and parliamentarians did not disappear, it was the governments which became the main targets of popular dissatisfaction. "Whilst before all criticism concerned a sense of being badly represented, it is, therefore, a sense of being badly governed that also has to be taken into account."[3] The mounting critical attitude toward governments would seem to be the logical result of the dominating position governments occupy in modern states and of the many new tasks they have taken upon themselves with the introduction of the welfare state.

The charisma of the populist leader

The organizational dimension of populism implies the presence of populist leaders. The leader is the engine of the movement, the central person around whom the movement crystallizes. Without a leader there is no populist movement. This leader is, as a rule, a charismatic person, who is not (or no longer) a member of the ruling elite. He must be perceived as an outsider – just like his followers. According to Max Weber, "'Charisma' must be called … an uncommon quality of a personality, because of which he is considered as gifted with supernatural or superhuman or, at least, uncommon specific powers or qualities, or as sent by god or as exemplary and therefore as a *'leader'*."[4] Weber added that the objective proof of this charisma is not important: the main point is that it is believed by the followers. Charisma was originally a religious phenomenon. The charismatic person was a "man of god" endowed with an uncommon spiritual and psychological power, often including the power to heal. In modern times charisma is secular and the reference to religion or to a supernatural world has almost completely disappeared. Even the likes of Hitler and Mussolini were said to be "charismatic."

In his book *The Fall of Public Man* Richard Sennett has a chapter titled "Charisma becomes Uncivilized," in which he analyzes how in modern times charisma has become not only secular but also vulgar. "Secular charisma," he writes, "serves especially well the needs of a certain kind of politician … He, a politician of humble origins, founds a career on whipping up the public in attacks against the Establishment, the Entrenched Powers, the Old Order."[5] Sennett is clearly describing here the *populist* politician. Without using the term "charisma" Donald Trump is referring to this when he writes: "Even the most jaded journalists are realizing that Donald Trump is for real and that the people are responding to someone who is completely different from every other politician."[6] Trump presents himself here as someone who is "completely different" from the other politicians. Trump is a politician who seems to be led by his impulses. Sennett comments: "The politician who, in focusing our attention on his impulses … becomes a plausible leader by giving the appearance of spontaneously behaving according to these impulses, and yet being in control of himself. When this controlled spontaneity is achieved, the impulses seem real, therefore the politician is someone you can believe in."[7] Sennett rightly stresses the fact that the impulsiveness and the uncivilized behavior of the populist leader, which set him apart from other politicians, are perceived by his followers as a guarantee that he can be trusted. The fact that he does not use politically correct and woolly language, like the others, but expresses himself bluntly, but clearly, is seen as a sign of authenticity, and, therefore, of trustworthiness.[8]

The personalization of politics

The centrality of the charismatic leader further implies a *personalization* of politics. Apart from some simple slogans everything revolves around the personality of the leader.[9] One of the first populist leaders to start this trend toward personalization was General Boulanger at the end of the nineteenth century in France, who distributed his portraits on a wide scale. "Promotion of the claimed charismatic qualities of a party leader, and pictures and film footage of his or her person striking appropriate poses, increasingly take the place of debate over issues and conflicting interests," writes Colin Crouch. "Italian politics was long free of this until in the 2001 general

What is populism?

election Silvio Berlusconi organized the entire centre-right campaign around his own persona, using omnipresent and carefully rejuvenated pictures of himself, a strong contrast with the far more party-oriented style that Italian politics had adopted after the fall of Mussolini."[10]

Berlusconi called his party Forza Italia ('Go Italy'): not referring to an ideology or a political program, but to the slogan used by Italian supporters to encourage the national football team. In the Netherlands the populist leader Pim Fortuyn went so far as to call his party Lijst Pim Fortuyn (List Pim Fortuyn), using his own name as the party label. Donald Trump, who is building his "Trump Towers" all over the world, would certainly have called his party the Trump Party, if he hadn't been the official candidate of the Republican Party. The personalization of politics which takes place in populism inverts the relationship between the leader and the represented: no longer does the leader represent a movement or a social class, but, on the contrary, the whole movement is based on their personality. In France the Front National – rebaptized into Rassemblement National – became a "family business," daughter Marine Le Pen succeeding her father, with her niece Marion waiting in the wings. It is less their program than their individual person which counts, and with whom their followers identify themselves.

An authoritarian leadership style

The charismatic character of the populist leader implies still another characteristic: an authoritarian leadership style. Certainly, populist movements verbally pretend to champion "grassroot politics" and use slogans, such as "giving the power back to the people," but this does not reflect the practice within these movements. An extreme example of the populist leadership style is the Dutch populist Geert Wilders. His Freedom Party (Partij voor de Vrijheid) has only two members: Geert Wilders and the Foundation Group Wilders (Stichting Groep Wilders). Apart from Wilders and his private foundation this "political party" has no members. The party, therefore, has no local party branches and organizes no party congresses. Internal party democracy is lacking. "Wilders is considered as someone who wants to keep control over the party, surrounding himself with some trusted persons … and demanding absolute loyalty from his fraction."[11] In a TV interview his brother Paul Wilders said that Wilders "rules his kingdom like an emperor. Whoever contradicts him is finished, family or not."[12] The same phenomenon can also be observed in other populist movements, such as Le Pen's Rassemblement National or Matteo Salvini's Lega.

The populist wave: why did it happen?

The populist leader is charismatic, but "normal"

The ideal-typical populist leader is not only charismatic and authoritarian. He or she should have yet another quality, which is being perceived by the population as being "one of us." The leader must, therefore, distinguish himself from the members of the ruling political class and stand out as a "normal person," which means that he should not speak like the elite, behave like the elite, dress like the elite, or talk like the elite. When he is a *real* outsider, this isn't a problem. He can just play his normal role. An example of this is the founder of the Italian Five Star Movement, the populist Beppe Grillo, a clown and humorist. With his beard, wild hair, and casual dress, he could be the man sitting next to you in a bar. And he *speaks* to you like the man sitting next to you in a bar, attacking corrupt, inept politicians and complaining about high taxes. But sometimes the populist leader is a former member of the established political elite. Geert Wilders, for instance, before founding his own party, was a member of parliament for the Dutch liberal party VVD. Despite his verbal radicalism, the way he dresses and behaves is not so different from other politicians in his country. But Wilders found another way to look different: he dyed his hair. "Like Trump's combover," writes Ian Buruma, "it is an eccentricity that sets him apart from more conventional technocrats and professional politicians; and that is precisely the point. His fans want him to be as different from the mainstream as possible."[13] But it is not only his dyed blond hair that makes him an outsider, because

> there is something else in Wilders's makeup that is rarely mentioned. His mother's family is Eurasian, or Indo, as they say in Dutch. The Indos in the Dutch East Indies, today's Indonesia, looked down upon by the "pure" Dutch colonisers, were especially keen to distinguish themselves from native Indonesians, and identify themselves as more Dutch (that is to say, white) than the Dutch. Many joined the Dutch Nationalist Socialist Party (NSB) in the 1930s. After the second world war, when most of them settled in the Netherlands, after being kicked out of Indonesia by President Sukarno, Indos were often deeply conservative and hostile to Muslims.[14]

Wilders's extravagant, dyed blond hair, making him an icon of the identarian Dutch,[15] could thus be an overcompensation for doubts about his own "Dutchness."[16]

The need for the populist leader to be perceived "as one of us" can also have an impact on the *language* he uses. Already in 2015, early in the American campaign, journalists noticed the simple language used by presidential candidate Donald Trump. "Donald Trump isn't a simpleton, he just talks like one," wrote *Politico*'s Jack Shafer.[17] "Trump resists multisyllabic words and complex, writerly sentence constructions when speaking extemporaneously in a debate, at a news conference or in an interview. He prefers to link short, blocky words into other short, blocky words to create short, blocky sentences that he then stacks into short, blocky paragraphs."[18] Shafer observed that Trump's simplicity didn't chase his followers away. On the contrary.

> It's obvious that Trump's verbal deficit, as grating as it may be on the ears of the educated class, has not caused him much political pain. The media has noted the opposite: Trump's overreliance on sports and war metaphors in his public utterances, his reductionist, one-dimensional policy prescriptions … inspire trust in many rather than distrust. Trump's rejection of "convoluted nuance" and "politically correct norms" mark him as authentic in certain corners and advance his cred as a plainspoken guardian of the American way. By not conforming to the standard oratorical style, he distinguishes himself from the pompous politician. Less is more when you're speaking Trumpspeak.[19]

Shafer concluded: "Still, don't interpret Trump's low scores as a marker of low intelligence. Trump's professional history indicates a skill at dealing and deceiving, inspiring and selling, and such attributes would likely qualify as a type of intelligence … The role Trumpspeak has played in Trump's surging polls suggests that perhaps too many politicians talk over the public's head when more should be talking beneath it in the hope of winning elections."[20] This positive evaluation of Trump's vocabulary is confirmed by a Republican pollster, who on 9 December 2015 interviewed a Republican focus group of twenty-nine supporters in Alexandra, Virginia. Asking them if Trump acted presidentially when he said that he "would bomb the hell out of ISIS," "the 29 participants replied in unison 'yes, yes!' For these voters, Trump's transgression of conventional boundaries is a selling point, not a liability."[21] Another author equally observed Trump's "willingness to flout all the conventions of civilized discourse when it comes to the minority groups that authoritarians find so threatening. That's why it's a benefit rather than a liability for Trump when he says Mexicans are rapists or speaks gleefully of massacring Muslims with pig-blood-tainted bullets: He is sending a signal to his authoritarian supporters that he won't let 'political correctness' hold him back from attacking the outgroups they fear."[22] Even when Trump violated the basic rules of decency by mocking a disabled *New York Times* reporter during a rally in South Carolina, this did not damage him, although in normal times it would have disqualified him definitively from running for president.

The populist leader's vulgarity

Simple language "that makes him one of us," language that is understandable – and therefore attractive – to the "common man," is not the only tool used by the populist leader. The French psycho-analyst Elisabeth Roudinesco observed another aspect of Trump: his *vulgarity*. "He has," she wrote, "an obsession with his anatomy, because he said: 'I have long fingers and it is not only that part of my anatomy that is long' and he has not stopped making allusions at the size of the crowd which came to see him. Neither has he shown any restraint on the question of incest, he stated publicly the fact that he desired his daughter sexually ... Psychiatrists have also demanded, not without humor, that he take an IQ test because of his simplistic reasoning."[23] Florida senator and Republican presidential candidate Marco Rubio observed that Trump is "the most vulgar person to ever aspire to the presidency."[24] "Vulgarity" comes from the Latin word *vulgus*, referring to the lower classes of society. Using vulgar language or making vulgar allusions are among the strategies used by the populist leader to move closer to his electorate and to appear "as one of them."

The list of populist leaders accused of vulgar behavior or a vulgar way of expression is long. The French historian Michel Winock saw it already as a characteristic of the leaders of the Boulangist movement in nineteenth-century France: "The caustic wit, even the vulgarity of its protagonists are not indifferent characteristics. They are the expression of a political culture and maintain a threat of violence which is the soul of the movement."[25] In 2009 Maxime Verhagen, the Dutch minister of foreign affairs, felt obliged to distance himself openly from the "vulgar language" used by Geert Wilders, who compared the prophet Mohammed to a pig.[26] The Italian populist Beppe Grillo, founder of the Five Star Movement, organized nationwide "Vaffanculo" Days (F*ck Off Days) and was regularly accused of vulgar and aggressive language.[27] Norberto Bobbio, a respected Italian political scientist, gave the following characterization of Umberto Bossi, the leader of the radical right populist party which was then still known as Lega Nord: "Bossi seems to me a vulgar person, ignorant, and as concerns his attitude to different people, also racist."[28] The Lega Nord's "capacity to influence," wrote another author, "comes from the coarseness of the rallying cries that are used."[29] Miloš Zeman, the Czech Republic's populist president, said of the Czech Friends of the Earth, a respected NGO of nature conservationists, that he would treat them in a "good old medieval way: burn them, piss on them and salt them."[30] Ari Chaplin wrote how Venezuela's populist president Chávez applied "the principle of vulgarity. All propaganda needs to be popular and adapted to the people's intellectual level. Chávez follows this rule in its extreme form; it is not limited only to his colloquial language; it includes the insults of his enemies and lying with sarcasm."[31]

A special case is Vladimir Putin's use of populist methods. In the fall of 1999, even before he became president, Putin – at that time Boris Yeltsin's prime minister – famously threatened the Chechens with "wiping them out in the shit house."[32] Putin became known for using vulgar language. In November 2003, when a delegation of Italian journalists asked him a question about a Russian oligarch, "the interpreter's voice petered away into embarrassed silence. 'You must always obey the law, not just when they've got you by the balls' is a rough equivalent of what Mr Putin had said."[33] To be clear: it was an embarrassment for the interpreter, not for Putin. Robert Russell, the head of the Russian and Slavonic Studies at Sheffield University, commented: "Like Khrushchev, Putin has an earthy turn of phrase. It means people see him as one of their own. He's always controlled and usually rather unemotional but there's something else Russians respond to, something visceral. I think he does these things deliberately for that reason."[34] In 2003, when a French journalist asked Putin a critical question about the war in Chechnya, the Russian president said: "Come to Moscow. We can offer circumcision. I will recommend a doctor to carry out the operation in such a way that nothing else will ever grow there again."[35]

As a matter of fact, vulgar language not only refers to the language used by "the people below." It does more than just that. Often the common man – and even more so the common woman – is more decent in the choice of his or her words.

Vulgar language is threatening language

The populist leader's vulgar language contains an implicit and sometimes explicit reference to the language and invectives used by the underworld of criminals and prison inmates. It is, therefore, at the same time "popular" and menacing, a language by which the leader is showing off his toughness and ruthlessness.[36] It shows that he is a "strong" leader. However, the populist leader should manage his vulgarity intelligently, using it as a weapon against his adversaries. His behavior should be "statesmanlike" if necessary. Every populist leader has to manage a difficult balance between, on the one hand, the need to present himself as a "common man" who doesn't belong to the elite, and, on the other, the need to stand out as a special, charismatic person: "they must ostensibly be 'of the people' *as well as* simultaneously beyond 'the people'."[37] Hannah Arendt wrote that

> it is not really all that difficult to create an aura about oneself that will fool everyone – or just about everyone – who comes under its influence … It goes without saying that under these conditions the rule of a good upbringing that says one must not blow one's own horn has to be ruthlessly put aside. The more that the vulgar practice of unbridled self-praise spreads in a society which for the most part still adheres to the rules of good upbringing, the more powerful its effect will be and the more easily that society can be convinced that only a truly "great man" who cannot be judged by normal standards could summon the courage to break rules as sacrosanct as those of good breeding.[38]

It is a seeming contradiction that the populist leader, who violates all the rules of good behavior, is capable of posing as a "great man" *because* of his vulgarity.[39]

The populist wave: why did it happen?

Notes

English quotes of Dutch, French, German, Spanish, and Italian works were translated by the author.

1. Weber called this process of accumulation in an ideal type a *gedankliche Steigerung* (elevation through thinking). Cf. Max Weber, "Die 'Objektivität' sozialwissenschaftlicher und sozialpolitischer Erkenntnis," in Max Weber, *Gesammelte Aufsätze zur Wissenschaftslehre*, edited by J. Winckelmann (Tübingen: J. C. B. Mohr-Paul Siebeck, 1968), p. 190.
2. Pierre Rosanvallon, *Le bon gouvernement* (Paris: Éditions du Seuil, 2015), p. 10.
3. Ibid., p. 10.
4. Max Weber, *Wirtschaft und Gesellschaft*, first half-volume, edited by Johannes Winckelmann (Cologne and Berlin: Kiepenheuer & Witsch, 1964), p. 179.
5. Richard Sennett, *The Fall of Public Man – On the Psychology of Capitalism* (New York: Vintage Books, 1978), p. 277.
6. Donald J. Trump, *Great Again – How to Fix Our Crippled America* (New York and London: Threshold Editions, 2015), p. 5.
7. Sennett, *Fall of Public Man*, p. 270.
8. The language used by Geert Wilders is also perceived as "clear" and contrasted with the "woolly" language of a Dutch minister. Maarten van Leeuwen wrote that "Media reports conclude that Wilders' language use is very 'clear', while [Minister] Vogelaar is criticized for her 'unclear', 'veiled' or 'woolly' language use" (Maarten van Leeuwen, "Systematic Stylistic Analysis: The Use of a Linguistic Checklist," in Bertie Kaal, Isa Maks, and Annemarie van Elfrinkhof (eds), *From Text to Political Positions: Text Analysis Across Disciplines* (Amsterdam and Philadelphia: John Benjamins Publishing Company, 2014), p. 228).
9. Benjamin Moffitt observes that there exist some exceptions to the presence of a singular populist leader: "While in most cases this manifests in strong *singular* figures, there are a few cases of populism where there have been a number of concurrent strong populist leaders attached to a populist party or movement. For example, the US Tea Party has had a number of 'expressive leaders' … including Sarah Palin, Michele Bachmann, Glenn Beck, Herman Cain, Ron Paul and Rand Paul amongst others. The Belgian Vlaams Blok had a leadership 'triumvirate' of Frank Vanhecke, Filip Dewinter and Gerolf Annemans." He added: "However, these examples of multiple concurrent leaders remain exceptions to the rule" (Benjamin Moffitt, *The Global Rise of Populism – Performance, Political Style, and Representation* (Stanford: Stanford University Press, 2016), p. 168).
10. Colin Crouch, *Post-Democracy* (Cambridge: Polity Press, 2004), pp. 26–27.
11. Leonard Ornstein, "Wat is de PVV?" *NPO Focus*, no date. www.npofocus.nl/artikel/7505/wat-is-de-pvv (accessed 30 April 2018).
12. Michelle Sakkers, "Paul Wilders: Geert duldt geen tegenspraak," *AD*, 19 February 2017. www.ad.nl/binnenland/paul-wilders-geert-duldt-geen-tegenspraak~a6d82ac9/ (accessed 2 May 2018).
13. Ian Buruma, "Why Geert Wilders is taking over Dutch politics," *Spectator*, 28 January 2017. www.spectator.co.uk/2017/01/why-geert-wilders-is-taking-over-dutch-politics/ (accessed 2 May 2018).
14. Ibid.

15 According to Shahid Mahmood, "Mr. Wilders' blonde mane symbolizes a wave of nationalism that is sweeping Europe today. His hair, a revanchist symbol, is no different from Hitler's mustache or Mullah Omar's beard" (Shahid Mahmood, "A shock of peroxide-blonde hair," *Huffington Post*, 30 August 2011. www.huffingtonpost.com/shahid-mahmood/a-shock-of-peroxideblond-_b_887750.html (accessed 4 May 2018)).
16 This phenomenon, that an outsider, or even a non-national, becomes a hyper-nationalist, is common, as we can see in the examples of Napoleon (who came from Corsica), Stalin (who was Georgian), and Hitler (who was Austrian).
17 Jack Shafer, "Donald Trump talks like a third-grader," *Politico*, 13 August 2015. www.politico.com/magazine/story/2015/08/donald-trump-talks-like-a-third-grader-121340 (accessed 10 May 2018).
18 Ibid.
19 Ibid.
20 Ibid.
21 Thomas B. Edsall, "Purity, disgust and Donald Trump," *New York Times*, 6 January 2016. www.nytimes.com/2016/01/06/opinion/campaign-stops/purity-disgust-and-donald-trump.html (accessed 15 June 2018).
22 Amanda Taub, "The rise of American authoritarianism," *Vox*, 1 March 2016. www.vox.com/2016/3/1/11127424/trump-authoritarianism (accessed 11 May 2018).
23 Marie Lemonnier, "Ces fous qui nous gouvernent" (interview with Elisabeth Roudinesco), *L'Obs*, 23 February 2017.
24 Quoted in Josh Barro, "It matters that Donald Trump is very vulgar," *Businessinsider*, 18 July 2016.
25 Winock, *Histoire*, p. 74.
26 "Verhagen hekelt 'vulgaire taal' Wilders," *Reformatorisch Dagblad*, 18 September 2009.
27 "Blog Beppe Grillo attacca il Pd con un video violento e volgare," *L'Huffington Post*, 9 December 2013. www.huffingtonpost.it/2013/12/09/blog-beppe-grillo-attacca-il-pd_n_4411738.html (accessed 14 June 2018).
28 Norberto Bobbio, *Contro i nuovi dispotismi – Scritti sul berlusconismo*, with an introduction by Enzo Marzo (Bari: Edizione Dedalo, 2008), p. 59.
29 Rino Genovese, *Che cos'è il Berlusconismo – La democrazia deformata e il caso Italiano* (Rome: Manifestolibri, 2011), p. 66.
30 Jakub Patočka, "Miloš Zeman makes Nigel Farage look like a nice guy. It's even worse than that," *Guardian*, 15 September 2016. www.theguardian.com/commentisfree/2016/sep/15/milos-zeman-czech-republic-president-populists-post-communist (accessed 14 June 2018).
31 Ari Chaplin, *Chávez's Legacy: The Transformation from Democracy to a Mafia State* (Lanham, Boulder, and New York: University Press of America, 2014), p. 31.
32 Cf. Marcel H. Van Herpen, *Putinism - The Slow Rise of a Radical Right Regime in Russia* (Houndmills, Basingstoke, and New York: Palgrave Macmillan, 2013), p. 144.
33 Julius Strauss, "Putin's language is becoming the talk of the vulgar," *Telegraph*, 8 November 2003.
34 Quoted in ibid.
35 Ibid.
36 Cf. Bertrand Buffon, who considers vulgarity "a kind of continuous incivility. However, its wrongdoings don't stop there. In fact, the assumed rudeness of the language and the manners perverts the thinking and the emotions, which, transformed in this way,

quickly recommend and even cause uncivil or immoral acts" (Bertrand Buffon, *Vulgarité et modernité* (Paris: Gallimard, 2019), p. 208).

37 Moffitt, *The Global Rise of Populism*, p. 52.
38 Hannah Arendt, "At Table with Hitler," in Hannah Arendt, *Essays in Understanding 1930–1954: Formation, Exile, and Totalitarianism* (New York: Schocken Books, 1994), p. 292.
39 An Italian group, calling itself "sardines," which organizes local rallies against Lega leader Matteo Salvini, is fighting this vulgar and coarse behavior: "The movement demands a courteous and civilized tone, reason and moderation rather than passions and excesses. Therefore, on the Facebook pages of the movement, it is forbidden that the members resort to insults and abusive words." *Le Monde* comments that "In Italy in 2019 such claims have something extremely subversive" (Jérôme Gautheret, "En Italie, les 'sardines' s'en prennent à Matteo Salvini," *Le Monde*, 5 December 2019).

2
A portrait of the populist voter

The populist voter: increasingly disconnected from national politics

Above we have painted an ideal-typical portrait of the populist leader, which, to reiterate, means that each populist leader will not necessarily possess all the characteristics mentioned. But what about the populist voter? A populist leader cannot be successful without the presence of an electorate that is seduced by his appearance and rhetoric. To explain the emergence of a populist electorate we have to take into account the growing estrangement between governments and citizens. This may be due not only to changes on the government side. Changes on the citizens' side also have to be taken into account. Theda Skocpol, an American political scientist, observed, for instance, a steep decline in American civic voluntarism in the last third of the twentieth century. The nationwide associations which had dominated until the 1960s had a broad, cross-class membership and played an important role in bringing the public into contact with national politics. "In classic civic America," writes Skocpol, "millions of ordinary men and women could interact with one another, participate in groups side by side with the more privileged, and exercise influence in both community and national affairs. The poorest were left out, but many others were included. National elites had to pay attention to the values and interests of millions of ordinary Americans."[1] Skocpol deplores the fact that, "by contrast, early-twenty-first century Americans live in a diminished democracy, in a much less participatory and more oligarchicly managed civic world."[2] A similar criticism has been put forward by the American sociologist Robert Putnam, who, in his book *Bowling Alone*, analyzed the downward trend in civic participation in the United States, which had led to a diminution of "social capital"[3] and mutual trust. According to Putnam,

> The connection between high social capital and effective government performance begs an obvious question: Is there a similar link between declining social capital and declining trust in government? Is there a connection between our democratic discontent and civic disengagement? It is commonly assumed that cynicism toward government has

caused our disengagement from politics, but the converse is just as likely: that we are disaffected because as we and our neighbors have dropped out, the real performance of government has suffered.[4]

Whatever the causes of the citizens' disenchantment, in the populist blame game it is exclusively the supposed "elitist" government which is to blame. Skocpol and Putnam point also to the other side: the civic disengagement of the citizen as a possible cause of populist disaffection. However, this civic disengagement – not only from community life but even from relations with close relatives – is not only a question of changed lifestyles. It can also have objective, geographical causes. The French geographer Hervé Le Bras, for instance, in an interesting study analyzed the fact that the percentage of voters for the extreme right Front National increased proportionally with the distance they lived from city centers. This was at first sight counter-intuitive: the inhabitants of the city centers, where more immigrants lived, voted less for the Front National. Le Bras came to the conclusion that the Front National vote was an expression of social isolation, in particular the loss of family ties:

> Those who live in city centers can meet their close relatives more easily. Sometimes cities have been defined as a means for minimizing the cost and time of transport. On the other hand, for those who live in the faraway suburbs it is difficult to meet their close relatives, who often live scattered over the whole agglomeration. They and their neighbors have often arrived recently, they have poor knowledge of each other, work at distant places, and do their shopping in the big malls, which are also far away. A satisfactory social life is more difficult to get in the periphery than in the center."[5]

The populist voter and the "pessimism–optimism divide"

Hervé Le Bras pointed to social isolation as a possible explanation of the populist vote. Social isolation leads to feelings of malaise and impedes wellbeing. Six French analysts followed this track further and found that *optimism* and *pessimism* were important predictors of the vote, Front National voters being more pessimistic than the average voter. "The FN vote is not only the vote of the popular classes, but of the unhappy and pessimistic classes," they wrote.[6] "The probability of a vote for the Front National is very high, about 45 percent, for the most pessimistic French [voters], and this independent of their revenue. The results are similarly independent of employment situation and professional category. Whether one has a high or a low salary, whether one has a job, whether one is unemployed or pensioner, whether one is a worker, an employee, or a middle manager, the probability of voting for Le Pen increases with the level of pessimism."[7] The *gilets jaunes* movement, the spontaneous Yellow Vests rebellion which exploded in France in 2018–2019, confirms this analysis. The Yellow Vests came mainly from rural and peri-urban areas. In the 2019 elections for the European Parliament they voted twice as often for the Rassemblement National than the national average.

Similar results were found in a survey conducted in Flanders, the Dutch-speaking part of Belgium, in 2014. In this survey the hypothesis was tested that people in a weak and vulnerable economic position would be more likely to opt for populism. A second hypothesis was that one could also expect that people with a low level of education, due to their weak position in a knowledge society, would support populism. However, the results of the survey made clear that "political choices appear less influenced by 'egocentric motives' related to the personal life situation, more by 'sociotropic considerations' concerning the way society is evolving and is likely to evolve as a consequence of the political choices that are made."[8] The researchers concluded that "support for populism appears foremost as a consequence of a very negative view of the evolution of society – declinism – and of the feeling of belonging to a group of people that is unfairly treated by society."[9] Populism appears primarily to be a reaction to a diagnosis of societal decline. It expresses the wish to return to a situation that existed in the past "when everything was better." There is a nostalgic longing for a return to that idealized past, exemplified in Donald Trump's slogan "Make America Great *Again*."

One can observe a similar "pessimism–optimism divide" in Italy: while voters for the Democratic Party expressed a high level of trust in the future, voters for Beppe Grillo's populist Five Star Movement scored negatively on this question.[10] However, pessimism can be an inborn character trait, or it can be conjunctural. In the former it is simply there and an individual will remain pessimistic throughout his or her life. In the latter thepessimism has specific causes and these could be explained at least partially by poor governance, feelings of being ignored by the government and its bureaucracy, changes in society leading to social isolation, and depletion of trust. The pessimism of the populist voter, which expresses a deep dissatisfaction, seems rather to be of the second kind.

Winners versus losers

When attacking the government, even a populist, in order to have a minimal level of trustworthiness, has to be cautious. He can only blame the government for problems which are *persistent* and *grave*. A one-time event, for instance a terrorist attack or a natural catastrophe, does not, as a rule, lead to a populist response. On the contrary, in such a case one can observe rather that the population stands united behind the government. It is, therefore, particular situations of protracted economic crisis, such as recessions and depressions which negatively impact on the daily lives of the masses, which lead to populist upheavals. But they are not the only case. Another situation can be that of fast economic transformation and growth, which leads to winners and losers. The highly educated, who are employed in the new industries and service sectors, are doing well, while the workers in the old industries, usually the less educated and less able to adapt, are laid off or have to accept a deterioration of their working conditions. The rise of the French populist Pierre Poujade in the 1950s, for instance, is explained by Raymond Aron as follows:

> The number of Poujadists [who voted] in the last election can be explained primarily by the rapid economic growth of the last ten years. Each rapid economic expansion puts certain groups of the population, those who cannot adapt themselves, at risk. Rapid growth is unequal growth. There are regions, groups which profit more, others [which] profit less … in a country in expansion groups who don't have their share in the growth will revolt against society. Of course, they don't blame economic growth as such, they blame the tax regime (against which one always harbors resentment).[11]

Another case that can trigger a populist response might be a big corruption scandal in which government officials and politicians are involved. These scandals, attracting widespread media publicity, deplete trust in the mainstream parties and politicians and can lead to a reaction of "being fed up" with the system.

In general, therefore, where there's populist smoke, there is real fire: populist movements don't pop up out of nowhere. There is always a breeding ground leading to this phenomenon. This does not mean that populist movements always attract their followers from the same socio-economic category. The American Populists of the 1890s attracted mainly farmers. This was not surprising: not only were farmers the class which suffered most from the economic crisis, but at that time they still made up the majority of the American working population. The Poujadist movement in France in the 1950s, on the contrary, was a revolt of the middle classes, supported by shopkeepers and craftsmen and women who protested against the growing competition from malls and big supermarkets.

The populist voter and the role of economic anxiety

Socio-economic factors explain the populist phenomenon, but they do so only partially. In a Gallup survey conducted in the United States and based on 87,000 interviews,[12] one of the – counter-intuitive – results was that Trump followers, although mostly white men without college degrees, did not, on average, have lower incomes than other groups, nor were they disproportionately victims of globalization or competition from immigrants.[13] There were other explanatory factors, such as those already mentioned above: living in isolated, white neighborhoods where people had only little contact with minorities. Another interesting outcome was that Trump followers *did* differ in one important respect from other Americans: they worried more about money problems than other groups and this was the case no matter how rich they were. Forty-two percent of Trump supporters with a household income of more than $200,000 per year shared this economic anxiety, compared with 26 percent for others in this group. In the next highest income bracket ($100,000–$200,000) the percentage of Trump followers who felt this economic anxiety was even higher: 49 percent, compared with 34 percent for others in this group.[14] The Gallup analysis gave no explanation for this economic anxiety, but the fact that Trump-backers are more likely to be self-employed could be an indication: self-employed people are more exposed to the vagaries of the market and are less protected by the welfare state.

But the self-employed are not alone in being more exposed. A study by the US Financial Diaries Project[15] revealed that the basis of economic security – a job – is no longer a guarantee of a reliable income. This is because, for an increasing group of employees, the number of hours they work now changes from week to week – with direct consequences for their income and their family life. "This volatility helps unravel a persistent puzzle: why a below-average jobless rate in the United States – 4.4 percent in April [2017] – is still producing an above-average level of economic anxiety. Turbulence has replaced the traditional American narrative of steady financial progress over a lifetime," writes the author.[16] Field experiments showed that employees were willing to forego up to 20 percent of their weekly wage to avoid a schedule imposed by their employer at a week's notice. This same need for economic security was expressed by supporters of the populist Italian Five Star Movement. In a poll, supporters of this movement, in which young Internet-savvy people are overrepresented, gave as their first priority a reduction in the wage gap (54 percent), a score which was even higher than among supporters of the left-wing Italian Democratic Party (47 percent).[17]

The populist voter and poor health

Economic anxiety, however, is compounded by anxiety about other factors: in the US, for instance, *poor health* was also a predictor of a political preference for Trump. People living in places with higher disability rates and a higher prevalence of diabetes, places where middle-aged white men were dying younger,[18] were more inclined to vote for Trump.

Bad health and lower life expectancy, although long-term developments, can be triggered by large economic shocks. In a report, two American researchers came to the conclusion that a change in the American trade policy vis-à-vis China had led to a significant deterioration in the physical and mental health, and even mortality, of large sections of the American population. The change in policy concerned the granting, in October 2000, of Permanent Normal Trade Relations (PNTR) to China,[19] leading to a major trade liberalization, which exposed US counties to increased competition to differing degrees. According to the authors, "We find that counties more exposed to a plausibly exogenous trade liberalization exhibit higher rates of suicide and related causes of death, concentrated among whites, especially white males. These trends are consistent with our finding that more-exposed counties experience relative declines in manufacturing employment, a sector in which whites and males are disproportionally employed."[20] The authors focused on three causes of death: suicide, accidental poisoning (including drug overdoses), and alcohol-related liver disease. They found a significant relationship between the decline in employment and the increase in the three causes of mortality. About half of the sharp decline in US manufacturing employment between 2000 and 2007 was associated with rising imports from China.

Worried about the future of their children

In France a similar relationship was observed: regions with an above average vote for the Front National, such as Northern France, were characterized by a worse health status, a higher incidence of health disorders, and a lower life expectancy.[21] Bad health is a structural problem. Although it is dependent on the physical condition of the people involved and on their personal lifestyles, it is also a question of government policy.[22] Trump followers came disproportionately from places where there was also a lack of intergenerational mobility. In an interview, Jonathan Rothwell, one of the authors of the Gallup report mentioned above, suggested that the support for Trump

> [M]ight have something to do with parents and children. Trump voters tend to be older, blue-collar workers, and recent generations have had more difficulty getting well-paying jobs that didn't require much education. Those opportunities have largely dried up. And now, Trump supporters tend to live in places where the world has gotten visibly tougher for the kids on the block. It's easier to agree with Trump's narrative about American decline when you have seen your own child fall down the economic ladder ... It could be that Trump supporters aren't worried for themselves, but for their children.[23]

The recent wave of populism in the United States, but not only there, could therefore be partially explained by the fading away of the "American Dream" of social mobility: the idea that each generation has the possibility of "doing better" than their parents.

A portrait of the populist voter

The American political scientist Albert O. Hirschman gives yet another explanation. "Suppose my neighbor or acquaintance," he writes, "experiences a bad setback such as losing his job while I am keeping mine: Do I now experience … the satisfaction of relative enrichment? This is unlikely … I shall take what is happening to my neighbor as an indication of what the future might have in store for me, and hence I will be apprehensive and worried – less well off than before, just as he. This reaction is well-known from the onset and spread of depressions."[24] So it is not only real hardship or anxiety about the future of one's offspring, but also one's own *imagined* hardship which can lead to anxiety.

Threatened identities

The populist voter can be motivated – directly or indirectly – by economic motives. But in some cases other motivations might be even more compelling. This is particularly the case with anxieties that are based on perceived or imagined threats to one's national, social, gender, or sexual identity. Usually these threats come from outside: from the stranger, the immigrant, from those who have a different skin color, a different religion, or different habits. In Germany the phenomenon has been coined by the term *Angst für Überfremdung* – the fear of being "swamped by strangers." The theory of the "Great Replacement," for instance, is an expression of this fear. According to this theory, popularized by the French far-right author Renaud Camus, the political elites of Western countries would be instrumental in the replacement of the local white Christian population by an Arab and sub-Saharan African Muslim population.[25] In the United States this has an equivalent in the fear of a Latino invasion from the South, which is Donald Trump's driving motive to build a wall at the Mexican border.

This fear that one's identity is being threatened can also be observed in the case of the Dutch populist Pim Fortuyn. Fortuyn, a gay person, praised the tolerant attitude of Dutch society toward the LGBT community. He wrote that in the Netherlands "the emancipation of women and homosexuals … can be considered as almost being completed."[26] However, he observed that this tolerance was often absent in Muslim immigrants. "In the Islamic culture," he wrote, "homosexual men are already struggling, but lesbian women can totally forget it, they are completely non-existent."[27] Fortuyn wrote that "we have reached the limit … it is therefore time to come to practical and sober conclusions and to declare that the Netherlands is full – we should, therefore, really close the borders."[28]

Fortuyn became the apostle of anti-Muslim populism in the Netherlands. In his case his sexual identity played a major role. But identity – social, sexual, gender, racial, national, or other – need not be the predominant motivation of a populist voter. African Americans, for instance, had every reason to mistrust Trump, who did not conceal his sympathies for white supremacists. But did this mean that African Americans could not vote for him? Apparently not. In November 2019 *Vox* wrote that "a bunch of evidence suggests that support among black voters [for Trump] has in fact gone up and may rise further."[29] The reason for this would be that "under Trump the black unemployment rate has reached a record low – as has the gap between black and white unemployment rates."[30] In this case black Trump voters let economic considerations prevail over considerations of race identity.

Why the new rich support populist movements

Two Australian researchers, Frank Mols and Jolanda Jetten, have approached this phenomenon from a different angle. "What our research revealed," they write, "is that populist messages may not only stick among poor working class voters ... but also among more affluent voters ... The finding that populist parties can thrive in times of economic prosperity and among affluent voters is admittedly counterintuitive, and challenges the conventional wisdom that 'those doing it tough' are more likely to vote for populist parties and leaders."[31] They criticize the tendency to interpret the populist phenomenon exclusively through the prism of socio-economic class, because, they argue, this "is to overlook that it is not so much how much someone earns, but whether one has more or less *relative* to those immediately around them."[32] While Albert Hirschman emphasized the fact that comparing oneself with someone who was worse off could lead to anxieties, in this case the presence of people nearby who are doing better could trigger dissatisfaction and jealousy.

However, it is clear that populist parties are not necessarily exclusively "parties of the losers" or of those who fear that themselves or their children may be future losers. Not only high earners, but also the *new rich* can be attracted by these parties. The new rich, having made their fortunes recently, are regarded with a certain mistrust by "old money" and are not accepted in the exclusive circles and old boys' clubs of the established capitalist bourgeoisie. The new rich, therefore, share the resentment, felt by the broader population, caused by exclusion from the centers of power. According to Ian Buruma, "Trump, too ... appears to seethe with resentment against the elites who might look down on him as an uncouth arriviste, with his absurd golden skyscrapers and rococo mansions full of gilded chairs and massive chandeliers."[33] He continues:

> The Tea Party in the US would have been relatively marginal without powerful backers and ideologues. And these are often newly rich men who share their followers' bitterness.

A portrait of the populist voter

This was clearly the case in Italy, where former Prime Minister Silvio Berlusconi, whose background is almost identical to Trump's, managed to tap into the dreams and resentments of millions of people. Populist movements in other countries show a similar pattern ... In the Netherlands, a newly rich class of real-estate moguls backed the right-wing populist Pim Fortuyn and his cruder successor, Geert Wilders. The newly rich are as important a force in the rise of populism as the poorer and less educated people who feel neglected by the elites.[34]

The Dutch sociologist Koen Damhuis observed the same phenomenon in his book *Wegen naar Wilders* (Roads to Wilders), emphasizing also the importance of populist "ideologues":

Together with voters from the traditional left, worried about their future and considering immigrants as a menace, the sociologist has identified two other groups. Self-made men, small entrepreneurs and hardworking people, who think that they pay too much tax and financially support strangers. The third category, the newest, is that of the "ideologues", graduates and well-to-do people who reproach their leaders for caring more about indebted Greeks, refugees, or immigrant neighborhoods, than the interests of the Dutch people, [they are] seduced by an alternative and radical program which aims to overthrow the established order.[35]

In the Netherlands this last category is represented by the Forum voor Democratie (Forum for Democracy) of Thierry Baudet, a philosopher-ideologue whose anti-immigrant party, which adheres to the theory of the "Great Replacement," became in March 2019 the largest party in the election for the provincial parliaments. These "ideologues" and the new rich share the resentment and bitterness of the poorer people towards the elites.

But the new rich and the "ideologues" have yet another, second reason for supporting populist movements: a populist party is for them a means to gaining access to the levers of power. The new rich are often outraged by the many bureaucratic regulations and the (in their eyes too high) tax burden with which they are confronted. In their business dealings they do not want to be hindered by the laws of government bureaucracy. Populist movements, promising to "act quickly," to fight "the bureaucratic jungle," and "to make things easier," are the parties of choice for this category.

The inbuilt authoritarian tendency of populist parties is also attractive to the new rich. Foa and Mounk found that "the trend toward openness to nondemocratic alternatives is especially strong among citizens who are both young *and* rich."[36] While "in 1995 only 6 percent of rich young Americans" (those born since 1970) believed that it would be a 'good' thing for the army to take over, today this view is held by 35 percent of rich young Americans.[37] According to the authors, "their embrace of nondemocratic practices and institutions should not come as a surprise. If we widen the historical lens, we see that, with the exception of a brief period in the late twentieth century, democracy has usually been associated with redistributive demands by the poor and therefore regarded with skepticism by the elites."[38]

The importance of gender and age

However, this attraction of populist parties for the young rich is not shared by their peers who are less better off. They tend to be less attracted. The same is true for women. Polls conducted after the 2016 presidential election in the United States showed big differences in voting patterns. Young voters were less inclined to vote for Trump. In the age group 18–29 he got 28 percent of the vote, while this was 40 percent in the age group 30–49. In the age group 50–64 he got 51 percent and 53 percent in the age group over sixty-five.[39] Trump collected 52 percent of the male vote and only 39 percent of the female vote.[40] The reluctance of women to vote for Trump must be attributed to his misogynic behavior, but the results made clear that not all women were equally susceptible to this. It was, for instance, no surprise that 98 percent of black women and 67 percent of Hispanic women voted for Hillary Clinton. However, for white women this percentage was much lower: 45 percent, while 47 percent voted for Trump. The percentage of Trump voters was even higher for *married* white women. Why? Contrary to black women, who voted with the fate of their community in mind, white married women would be less influenced by the perception that their futures are connected to what happens to other women. According to a study they had "lower levels of gender-linked fate."[41] Kelsy Kretschmer, a social scientist at Oregon State University, one of the authors of the study, explained: "We know white men are more conservative, so when you're married to a white man you get a lot more pressure to vote consistent with that ideology."[42] She added that "single women tend to cast votes with the fate of all women in mind, while women married to men vote on behalf of their husbands and families."[43]

In the UK similar differences could be found between the voting patterns of men and women and of different age groups. In the Brexit referendum almost three-quarters of the age group 18–24 voted for Remain, while Leave was backed by a majority of people who were over forty-five, with those over sixty-five the most likely to vote for Leave.[44] This high percentage in favor of Remain remained stable for people who were too young to cast the ballot in the 2016 referendum. In a poll conducted in 2019, 74 percent of these new voters said they would vote Remain in an eventual second referendum.[45] In the Brexit referendum one could also observe a gender gap: while a majority of 55 percent of male voters voted to leave, this was only the case for a minority of 49 percent of female voters.[46] These voting patterns can also be observed elsewhere. In Germany, for instance, the right-wing populist AfD party is considered "a men's party for men."[47] Only 13 percent of its members are women. This "male character" of the party makes it particularly attractive for male voters. In the parliamentary election for the German Bundestag in September 2017 16 percent of the male electorate voted for this party, but only 9 percent of the female electorate.[48] In Finland we see the same tendency: 75 percent of the members of the populist Finns Party are men, so are the majority of its voters.[49]

In the Netherlands in March 2019 the right-wing populist party Forum voor Democratie became the largest party in the election for the provincial councils and the Dutch Senate. The great majority of its voters – 64 percent – were men. The age groups 35–64 and older were overrepresented. Young voters were underrepresented.[50] The question is why? One explanation is that young voters are more open and mobile than older voters. Because they adapt more easily to new situations they are less inclined to vote for parties that have a nostalgia for the past and want to close the frontiers. David Goodhart called this the difference between the *Anywheres* and the *Somewheres*. "The old distinctions of class and economic interest have not disappeared," he wrote, "but are increasingly over-laid by a larger and looser one – between the people who see the world from Anywhere and the people who see it from Somewhere. Anywheres dominate our culture and society … such people have portable 'achieved' identities … Somewheres are more rooted and usually have 'ascribed' identities … based on group belonging and particular places, which is why they find rapid change more unsettling."[51] Women may be less attracted to right-wing populist parties because they have a more positive view of the welfare state and its protection of the weak and the poor, while they themselves often work in sectors such as health care, education, culture, and social services, which are dependent on the state. The "greater tendency of women to hold egalitarian attitudes," write Susan Howell and Christine Day, is rooted in "the value of helping others … values learned early in life," and "being in an occupation affected by redistributive government policies," a reason why "they are more liberal on the issue of social welfare."[52]

Although there exists a clear tendency that young voters and women are less inclined to vote for right-wing populist parties, we should be careful not to consider this tendency an 'iron law', because these parties can conduct a policy aimed at changing their hard, masculine image. An example is the French Front National, a party which was always more attractive to male than female voters. In the parliamentary elections of 1997, for instance, 19 percent of the male electorate voted for this party, and only 12 percent of the female electorate.[53] Marine Le Pen, who succeeded her father Jean-Marie Le Pen in 2011, started a process of *dédiabolisation* (de-demonization), cutting the links with her father and with extreme right groups, in the end even changing the name of the party. This strategy was so successful that in the first round of the French presidential elections in 2017 she got 22 percent of the votes of *both* men and women.[54] As concerns left-wing populist parties: these seem to be more attractive to a young electorate. In the first round of the French presidential elections in 2017, for instance, La France Insoumise, led by Jean-Luc Mélenchon, got 30 percent of the votes of the 18–24 age group.[55]

Notes

1. Theda Skocpol, "United States – From Membership to Advocacy," in Robert D. Putnam (ed.), *Democracies in Flux – The Evolution of Social Capital in Contemporary Society* (Oxford and New York: Oxford University Press, 2004), pp. 135–136. Pierre Rosanvallon calls this tendency of American associations to lose their national focus and to concentrate increasingly exclusively on local affairs a *descente vers le local* (downward movement toward local affairs). Cf. Pierre Rosanvallon, *La contre-démocratie – La politique à l'âge de la défiance* (Paris: Éditions du Seuil, 2006), p. 303.
2. Theda Skocpol, *Diminished Democracy – From Membership to Management in American Civic Life* (Norman: University of Oklahoma Press, 2003), p. 11.
3. "Social capital" indicates high levels of civic participation and mutual trust. According to Putnam, "For the first two-thirds of the twentieth century a powerful tide bore Americans into ever deeper engagement in the life of their communities, but a few decades ago – silently, without warning – that tide reversed and we were overtaken by a treacherous rip current. Without at first noticing, we have been pulled apart from one another and from our communities over the last third of the century" (Robert D. Putnam, *Bowling Alone – The Collapse and Revival of American Community* (New York, London, and Toronto: Simon & Schuster, 2000), p. 27).
4. Ibid., p. 347.
5. Hervé Le Bras, *Une autre France – Votes, réseaux de relations et classes sociales* (Paris: Odile Jacob, 2002), pp. 35–36.
6. Yan Algan, Martial Foucault, Elizabeth Beasley, Daniel Cohen, Claudia Senik, and Paul Vertier, "Deux perceptions opposées de l'avenir," *Le Monde*, 4 May 2017.
7. Ibid.
8. Mark Elchardus and Bram Spruyt, "Populism, Persistent Republicanism and Declinism: An Empirical Analysis of Populism as a Thin Ideology," *Government and Opposition*, Vol. 51, No. 1, p. 115.
9. Ibid., p. 111.
10. Marco Revelli, *Populismo 2.0* (Turin: Giulio Einaudi Editore, 2017), p. 135.
11. Raymond Aron, *Démocratie et totalitarisme* (Paris: Gallimard, 1965), p. 213. The Poujadist movement was initiated in 1953 by Pierre Poujade. In the parliamentary election of 1956, under the slogan *Sortez les sortants* (Chase the government away), his party, Union et Fraternité Française, obtained 12.62 percent of the vote (fifty-two seats). One of the young parliamentarians was Jean-Marie Le Pen, the future leader of the Front National. With the advent of the Fifth Republic in 1958 the party disappeared.
12. Jonathan Rothwell and Pablo Diego-Rosell, "Explaining Nationalist Political Views: The Case of Donald Trump," Draft Working Paper, Gallup, 2 November 2016.

13 This argument is also developed by Frank Mols and Jolanda Jetten in "Populism and the Wealth Paradox – Why the Economically Well-Off Vote for Populist Parties," *Cicero Foundation Great Debate Paper*, No. 17/04, June 2017. www.cicerofoundation.org/lectures/Mols_and_Jetten_Populism_and_the_Wealth_Paradox.pdf (accessed 5 July 2017).

14 Gwynn Guilford, "Trump supporters worry more about money than other Americans, no matter how rich they are," *Quartz Media*, 12 September 2016. https://qz.com/778089/poll-donald-trump-supporters-worry-about-money-more-than-other-voters-whether-theyre-rich-or-poor/ (accessed 23 March 2017).

15 This project tracked 235 low- and moderate-income households over the course of a year to collect data on how families manage their finances on a day-to-day basis. http://www.usfinancialdiaries.org/ (accessed 4 September 2017).

16 Patricia Cohen, "Anxiety over volatile wages," *New York Times International Edition*, 3–4 June 2017.

17 Revelli, *Populismo*, p. 134.

18 In another study this increased mortality of white non-Hispanic people (male and female) in midlife since the turn of the twenty-first century is predicted to "continue unabated to 2015." It was related to "additional increases in drug overdoses, suicides, and alcohol-related liver mortality, particularly among those with [only] a high-school degree or less." This was true for all age groups from 25–29 through 60–64. Interestingly, in the same period mortality rates were *falling* for blacks and Hispanics, as well as for whites with a college degree (Anne Case and Angus Deaton, "Mortality and Morbidity in the 21st Century," *Brookings Papers on Economic Activity*, BPEA Conference Drafts, 23–24 March 2017).

19 The PNTR eliminated the threat of tariff increases on US imports from China without actually changing the tariff rates. Before 2000 NTR rates were decided on a year-by-year basis by the president and subject to annual approval by Congress. The PNTR, removing the uncertainty for US importers, effectively liberalized the trade between the two countries.

20 Justin R. Pierce and Peter K. Schott, "Trade Liberalization and Mortality: Evidence from U.S. Counties," *Finance and Economics Discussion Series* 2016–094 (Washington: Board of Governors of the Federal Reserve System, 2016). www.federalreserve.gov/econresdata/feds/2016/files/2016094pap.pdf (accessed 27 March 2017).

21 Cf. Pascale Santi, "Santé: Portrait de la France des oubliés," *Le Monde*, 12 May 2017; and "L'état de santé de la population en France. Rapport 2015," *Direction de la Recherche, des Études, de l'Évaluation et des Statistiques* (Paris: Health Ministry, 2017). http://drees.social-sante.gouv.fr/IMG/pdf/rappeds_v11_16032015.pdf (accessed 4 September 2017).

22 Against the background of this "bad health" profile of the typical Trump voter, it seems therefore illogical for Trump to dismantle Obamacare.

23 Max Ehrenfreund and Jeff Guo, "A massive new study debunks a widespread theory for Donald Trump's success," *Washington Post*, 12 August 2016.

24 Albert O. Hirschman, "The Changing Tolerance for Income Inequality in the Course of Economic Development," in Albert O. Hirschman, *Essays in Trespassing – Economics to Politics and Beyond* (Cambridge, London, and New York: Cambridge University Press, 1984), pp. 42–43.

25 Norimitsu Onishi, "The man behind a toxic slogan promoting white supremacy," *New York Times*, 20 September 2019. www.nytimes.com/2019/09/20/world/europe/renaud-camus-great-replacement.html (accessed 14 September 2020).

26 Pim Fortuyn, *De islamisering van onze cultuur – Nederlandse identiteit als fundament* (Uithoorn: Karakter Uitgevers B.V., 2002), p. 70. The title of Fortuyn's book: "The Islamization of our Culture – Dutch Identity as a Foundation" – is telling, explicitly mentioning Dutch identity.
27 Ibid., p. 77.
28 Ibid., p. 101.
29 Matthew Yglesias, "The case for taking Trump's black outreach seriously," *Vox*, 13 November 2019. www.vox.com/policy-and-politics/2019/11/13/20960203/black-voices-for-trump-african-american-polling (accessed 20 November 2019).
30 Ibid.
31 Frank Mols and Jolanda Jetten, "Why Trump and Brexit are Not Working-Class Revolts," *ABC Religion & Ethics*, 15 November 2016. www.abc.net.au/religion/articles/2016/11/15/4575585.htm (accessed 28 March 2017).
32 Ibid.
33 Ian Buruma, "Populism for the Rich," *Project Syndicate*, 4 November 2016. www.project-syndicate.org/commentary/populist-leaders-social-resentment-by-ian-buruma-2016–11 (accessed 28 March 2017).
34 Ibid.
35 Jean-Pierre Stroobrants, "Geert Wilders, itinéraire d'un populiste," *Le Monde*, 10 March 2017.
36 Roberto Stefan Foa and Yascha Mounk, "The Danger of Deconsolidation: The Democratic Disconnect," *Journal of Democracy*, Vol. 27, No. 3, July 2016. http://pscourses.ucsd.edu/ps200b/Foa%20Mounk%20Democratic%20Disconnect.pdf (accessed 27 March 2017).
37 Ibid.
38 Ibid.
39 "An examination of the 2016 electorate based on validated voters," Pew Research Center, 9 August 2018. www.people-press.org/2018/08/09/an-examination-of-the-2016-electorate-based-on-validated-voters/ (accessed 8 September 2018).
40 Ibid.
41 Cf. Kelsy Kretschmer, Gosia Mikolajczak, Leah Ruppanner, and Christopher Stout, "Why white married women are more likely to vote for conservative parties," *The Conversation*, 17 October 2019. https://theconversation.com/why-white-married-women-are-more-likely-to-vote-for-conservative-parties-124783 (accessed 13 November 2019).
42 Quoted in Lucia Graves, "Why Hillary Clinton was right about white women – and their husbands," *Guardian*, 25 September 2017. www.theguardian.com/us-news/2017/sep/25/white-women-husbands-voting (accessed 28 September 2019).
43 Ibid.
44 "Share of votes in the Brexit referendum of 2016 in the United Kingdom, by gender," *Statista*, September 2016. www.statista.com/statistics/567922/brexit-votes-by-gender/ (accessed 29 March 2017).
45 Inigo Alexander, "Three-quarters of newly eligible voters would back remain in second poll," *Guardian*, 10 March 2019. www.theguardian.com/politics/2019/mar/09/new-young-voters-want-peoples-vote-strongly-remain-survey (accessed 4 April 2019).
46 "Share of votes in the Brexit referendum of 2016," *Statista*.
47 "AfD als Partei von Männern für Männer: nur die härtesten Frauen kommen durch," *Merkur*, 3 April 2019. www.merkur.de/politik/afd-als-partei-von-maennern-fuer-maenner-nur-haertesten-frauen-kommen-durch-zr-9635568.html (accessed 3 May 2019).
48 Ibid.

49 Joonas Saloranta, "The Finns, a right-wing political party, has gained popularity among educated business people in Finland," *Sulonorth*, 14 November 2019. https://sulonorth.com/finns-popularity-increases-educated-voters/ (accessed 21 November 2019).
50 "De kiezers van Forum voor Democratie: Veel mannen, weinig jongeren, en tegen het kabinet," WNL.TV, 21 March 2019. https://wnl.tv/2019/03/21/de-kiezers-van-forum-voor-democratie-veel-mannen-weinig-jongeren-en-tegen-het-kabinet/ (accessed 8 September 2019).
51 David Goodhart, *The Road to Somewhere – The Populist Revolt and the Future of Politics* (London: C. Hurst & Co., 2017), p. 3.
52 Susan E. Howell and Christine L. Day, "Complexities of the Gender Gap," *Journal of Politics*, Vol. 62, August 2000.
53 "L'électorat F.N.," *Notes de la Fondation Jean-Jaurès*, no date, p. 10. https://jean-jaures.org/sites/default/files/notes5.pdf (accessed 8 September 2019).
54 Grégoire Normand, "Qui a voté pour Le Pen, qui a voté pour Macron?" *La Tribune*, 24 April 2017. www.latribune.fr/economie/presidentielle-2017/qui-a-vote-pour-le-pen-qui-a-vote-pour-macron-695604.html (accessed 9 May 2017).
55 Thomas Leroy, "Présidentielle: La sociologie du vote," *Public Senat*, 23 April 2017. www.publicsenat.fr/article/politique/presidentielle-la-sociologie-du-vote-59189 (accessed 9 May 2017).

3
Populism and the role of disgust

Populism is very often associated with emotions, and particularly with negative emotions. We have already mentioned the *anxiety* of the populist voter. This anxiety is often multifaceted and can reflect a fear of economic breakdown of oneself or of one's children, the fear of immigrants, the fear of losing one's identity, or a fear of the future in general.[1] These negative emotions, which are multiple, are often shared equally by followers and leaders. A Dutch sociologist, for instance, describes the majority of the voters of the Freedom Party of Geert Wilders as *verongelijkt*. This Dutch word indicates a double sentiment: first, a feeling of having been treated unjustly, and, secondly, a feeling of resentment based on the first feeling.[2] A French author has no hesitation in giving his book the title *Populisme: le grand ressentiment* (Populism: The Great Resentment).[3] Feelings of having been treated unjustly, feelings of anxiety and resentment, can lead to other negative feelings: to feelings of anger, rage, and hatred, which seek an outlet. A survey conducted in France in April and May 2017 during the presidential election, revealed that "the chance that people will vote for the candidate of the FN [Front National] increases proportionately with growing anger, expressed by the French."[4]

Emotions – negative emotions – therefore play an important role in the populist phenomenon. "What we can tell is something inherent in populism," wrote John Lukacs, "which is that within its innate contempt for its opponents and outsiders there is that ever-present compound of hatreds and fears."[5] The populist voter, far from being the emotionally balanced, rational voter of democratic theory, seems not to be emotionally balanced and rational, but rather a complex bundle of negative emotions. Already in the nineteenth century conservative thinkers such as Joseph de Maistre, Edmund Burke, and G. W. F. Hegel had expressed their fears concerning the incompetence of the average voter and had deep-seated reservations about universal suffrage. They were not alone. Even a progressive liberal, such as John Stuart

Mill, thought it necessary to educate the population before granting it the right to vote for the government of the country.[6]

In the nineteenth century criticisms had focused mainly on the *intellectual* deficiency of the masses. Although the emotional instability of the popular classes was mentioned occasionally, it remained a minor argument, as in the case of Tocqueville, who mentioned their feelings of jealousy toward the elites. This changed at the end of the century with the advent of a new science: psychology. An important role was played by the book *Psychologie des foules* (The Psychology of Crowds),[7] written by the French psychologist Gustave Le Bon (1841–1931). The book, first published in 1895, immediately became an international bestseller. Le Bon's argument was that people in a crowd react differently from individuals. While the individual was rational, calculating, and thinking about the consequences of his or her behavior, this changed when he or she was part of a crowd. A crowd had a life of its own and changed not only the behavior and feelings of the individuals of which it was composed, but also its morality. "Taking the word morality to mean a constant respect for certain social conventions and the permanent repression of selfish impulses," wrote Le Bon, "it is evident that crowds are too impulsive and too changing to be susceptible to morality."[8] Why was this the case? Le Bon's explanation was that "our savage, destructive instincts are residues of a primitive age, dormant within each of us. For the isolated individual it would be dangerous to satisfy them, yet once absorbed within an irresponsible crowd, in which his impunity is assured, he has complete freedom to follow them."[9]

According to Le Bon his theory also had implications for democracy. He spoke about "electoral crowds," which would be characterized by "little inclination to discuss, the absence of a critical mind, irritability, gullibility and simplicity."[10] Le Bon's book was written in the 1890s, in the wake of the populist movement in France led by General Boulanger,[11] and this experience will certainly have played its part. He based his criticism on the loud and turbulent mass meetings which accompanied the election campaigns. However, one could counter his theory with the fact that the actual voting took place not among these irrational crowds, but in the solitude of the voting booth. The individual voter, therefore, had in principle still the possibility of reflecting on his choice in a calm environment before casting his ballot.

Feelings of disgust: the case of Donald Trump

Emotions, such as anxiety, fear, resentment, and sometimes even fury and hate, are said to play a major role in the populist vote. There is, however, yet another emotion which is worth analyzing: disgust. This may come as a surprise, because disgust

The populist wave: why did it happen?

is not often mentioned as an emotion which has a political impact. In the case of Donald Trump, however, it is revealing, as it is revealing in the case of other populist leaders. The *New York Times* reported an incident that took place in 2011, when Trump gave testimony under oath in court. During the deposition a female lawyer asked for a break. She wanted to pump breast milk for her baby. When Trump refused and she took out her breast pump, Trump was incensed, telling her: "You're disgusting."[12]

This is not the only occasion on which Trump has vented his feelings of disgust. In December 2015, for instance, during the last debate among the Democratic presidential candidates, when Hillary Clinton asked for a bathroom break, Trump commented: "I know where she went, it's disgusting, I don't want to talk about it. No, it's too disgusting. Don't say it, it's disgusting, let's not talk."[13] Trump repeated three times that it was disgusting, stating that he did not want to talk about it, while he *was* talking about it. This happened some months after another incident, similarly revealing his obsession with disgust. In a Fox News debate anchorwoman Megyn Kelly confronted him with his misogynist expressions, saying: "You call women you don't like 'fat pigs,' 'dogs,' 'slobs,' and 'disgusting animals.'" She asked him if he was waging a "war on women." Later Trump remarked: "You could see there was blood coming out of her eyes, blood coming out of her wherever."[14]

But it is not only blood, urine, and breast milk which elicits Trump's disgust. In November 2015 Politico's Daniel Lippman wrote that in the space of seven weeks Trump had commented at least *eight* times on Marco Rubio's perspiration. "I always say," Trump was quoted as saying, "I have never seen a young person sweat like Marco Rubio ... He drinks more water – he's like a machine. Water, water, water. Sweats, gives a speech. Think of Putin. Pretty tough cookie, right? I think [of] Rubio and I'm saying, you have to be cool. You have to be really cool. And Rubio's going to meet him and walk in, and he's sweating – sweat is pouring down. And Putin's going to look at him and say, 'What the hell is wrong with this guy?'"[15] Trump is described as "a germaphobe," someone who once labeled himself "a clean hands freak," for whom shaking hands is "barbaric." "Shaking hands," he said, "you catch colds, you catch the flu, you catch all sorts of things. Who knows what you don't catch?"[16] In his book *How to Get Rich* (2004) Trump dedicated a whole chapter to his aversion to shaking hands. Under the heading "Avoid the Handshake Whenever Possible" he writes: "Some business executives believe in a firm handshake. I believe in *no* handshake. It is a terrible practice. So often, I see someone who is obviously sick, with a bad cold or the flu, who approaches me and says: 'Mr. Trump, I would like to shake your hand.' It's a medical fact that this is how germs are spread. I wish we could follow the Japanese custom of bowing instead."[17] We see here a preoccupation with health and purity and an obsession with "impure" body fluids, in particular women's, which is characteristic of someone extremely susceptible to feelings of disgust.[18]

Disgust and the quest for purity

But weren't we talking about ideal types of populism? Why are we suddenly paying attention to the idiosyncrasies of one man, even if he happens to be president of the United States? Because disgust is an emotion which features frequently in populist movements and is present in leaders as well as followers. Pierre Rosanvallon writes that the Boulangist movement in France at the end of the nineteenth century was called "*le parti des dégoûtés,*" the party of the disgusted.[19] We will see that extreme feelings of disgust, felt not only by the leader but also by the followers, have a *political* impact. But first something more about the emotion itself. Disgust is an emotion shared by all humans. It is a basic emotion which finds its origin in our need to feed ourselves, but, at the same time, the urge of our physical body to protect itself against health threats. "Eating is an act laden with affect," writes Paul Rozin:

> It involves an extremely intimate exchange between the environment and the self, two entities that are ordinarily quite separate (except in the act of breathing, as well as eating). The insulated, safe self, protected by skin from the rest of the world, experiences a material breach of this boundary a few times every day in the act of eating. The world enters the self. This is an act that [can] be exquisitely pleasurable, but also frightening; an act that nourishes, at the same time as it increases the chances of death or illness by toxins and micro-organisms.[20]

If we eat rotten food our body reacts by vomiting, which means that the impure, health-threatening substance is removed. Often we do not even have to swallow the food, because we are already experiencing the vile smell as "disgusting." Disgust is focused on things that are impure, things which can contaminate our physical body. Therefore, disgust is related to the "nearby", tactile senses: taste, touch, and smell, and less with the "distance" senses: hearing and sight. If we feel something slimy or sticky, if we smell a foul odor, or taste something rotten, we are immediately repulsed.

"Disgust," writes Martha Nussbaum, "concerns the borders of the body: it focuses on the prospect that a problematic substance may be incorporated into the self. For many items and many people, the mouth is an especially charged border. The disgusting has to be seen as alien: one's own bodily products are not viewed as disgusting so long as they are inside one's own body, although they become disgusting after they leave it."[21] "Disgust," she continues, "pertains to our problematic relationship with our own animality. Its core idea is the belief that if we take in the animalness of animal secretions we will ourselves be reduced to the status of animals. Similarly, if we absorb or are mingled with the decaying, we will ourselves be mortal and decaying. Disgust thus wards off both animality in general and the mortality that is so prominent in our loathing of our animality."[22]

Hitler's disgust

However, disgust should not be reduced to a purely physical reaction: the urge to vomit. It is a fully fledged human emotion like anger, shame, fear, and hate. Feelings of disgust can be transferred from food to other objects that are – rightly or not – perceived as contaminating and dangerous. According to three American experts, "For North Americans, elicitors of disgust come from nine domains: food, body products, animals, sexual behaviors, contact with death or corpses, violations of the exterior envelope of the body (including gore and deformity), poor hygiene, interpersonal contamination (contact with unsavory human beings), and certain moral offenses."[23] Disgust resembles fear most: both are mechanisms that defend our physical and moral self.[24]

Because disgust not only protects our physical body from noxious substances, but also our moral person, it is an emotion which can be transferred to people. "Humans," writes William Miller, "are most likely the only species that experiences disgust, and we seem to be the only one that is capable of loathing its own species. We also seem driven to aspire to purity and perfection."[25] The human race is susceptible to being repulsed by other people, who are experienced as different and deviant, just as beggars, people with a handicap, migrants, and homosexuals have been found disgusting by some people at some time.

Adolf Hitler, for instance, is a clear example: he was obsessed by a pathological disgust vis-à-vis the Jews, whom he considered to be *unrein* (impure). In *Mein Kampf* he wrote that for him,

> The moral and other purity of this people was a case in point. One could immediately see from their outward appearance that they didn't like water, unfortunately very often the case, even with your eyes closed. Later the smell of these people in their caftans often made me feel sick. Add to this the unclean clothing and the ignoble appearance. All this already made it difficult for them to be in any way attractive; but one was really repelled, when, looking beyond the physical impurity, one suddenly discovered the moral stains of the chosen people ... If one cautiously probed with a knife into such an abscess, one found a little Jew, like a maggot in a rotting body, often completely dazzled by the sudden light.[26]

In this long litany of disgust Hitler speaks about "purity," "the smell of these people," which made him "feel sick," "unclean clothing," "repelled," "physical impurity," "moral stains," "a maggot in a rotting body." And he goes on, calling the Jews a "spiritual pestilence, worse than the former black death, which once infected the people,"[27] "leech,"[28] "parasite in the body of other peoples," "harmful bacillus,"[29] and "swarm of rats."[30] In 1940 Joseph Goebbels, the German minister of propaganda, produced a film titled *Der ewige Jude* (The Eternal Jew), a film in which Jews were likened to hordes of rats creeping out of filthy sewers, contaminating the "pure" citizens with their diseases. It would take only a few years before this disgust led to the Holocaust and the murder of millions of innocent men, women, and children.

The problem with disgust is that it is not only a gut reaction, inciting people to avoid contact with a contaminated object or person, but it also incites people to destroy the thing perceived as contaminating: "In disgust no less than everything seems to be at stake. It is an exceptional state of alert, an acute crisis of the self, put against something different which cannot be assimilated, a convulsion and a struggle, which is literally a matter of to be or not to be."[31] This dangerous side of disgust, the obsession with the "pure" and the urge to destroy the "impure," is also emphasized by Paul Ekman. "Most people think anger is the most dangerous emotion," he writes, "but I believe disgust is the emotion of the Holocaust. If you look at Joseph Goebbels' writings about the Jews, he talks about them as if they're vermin. He dehumanizes them."[32]

Disgust and the Trump voter

The election of Donald Trump has cast new light on the role of disgust in politics, and particularly in populist politics. According to Jonathan Haidt,

> The role of disgust in politics is especially important in 2016 as Donald Trump talks more about disgust than any major political figure, since, well, some 20th century figures that were concerned about guarding the purity of their nation and ethnic stock. Studying disgust can help you understand Donald Trump and some portion of his political appeal. I haven't studied European right-wing movements, but I've seen hints that disgust plays a role in many of them as well. Anyone interested in the psychology of authoritarianism should learn a bit about disgust.[33]

This is true. Because disgust does not only play a role on the *supply side* of populist politics: the side of the populist leader, but also on the *receiving side*: the side of the populist voter, for whom disgust gets a moral connotation. According to Jesse Prinz, who compared groups in different societies, "Brazilians and low-income Americans tend to think disgusting things are immoral even when they are harmless."[34] Research conducted in the United States in 2008 led to the conclusion that people who describe themselves as conservative have a heightened proclivity to feel disgust.

The populist wave: why did it happen?

This relationship was strongest for purity-related issues, particularly abortion and gay marriage.[35] These results were confirmed by Marco Liuzza and his colleagues, who equally found a link between a person's sensitivity to malodorousness and right-wing authoritarian views. They developed a Body Odor Sensitivity Scale (BODS) and found a positive association between BODS scores and support for Donald Trump.[36] However, the question was whether these results could be generalized and were also valid outside the United States. Therefore more research was conducted – this time in the Netherlands. Interestingly, in the Netherlands also people who were more disgust-sensitive were more xenophobic and shared anti-migrant attitudes. Greater disgust-sensitivity was, according to the authors, "associated with greater likelihood of voting for the PVV [Geert Wilders's populist Party for Freedom], both retrospectively (i.e. past voting) and prospectively (i.e. voting intentions). The PVV's platform emphasizes Dutch cultural traditions, restrictions on immigration, skepticism toward Islamic immigrants, and resistance to EU integration … and as such is likely to hold more appeal for the disgust-sensitive."[37]

Disgust-sensitivity and its link with authoritarianism

The key to understanding these more disgust-prone conservatives, who vote for Trump or Wilders, is their shared authoritarianism. In her book *The Authoritarian Dynamic*,[38] Karen Stenner describes three psychological portraits of people who have voted Republican since the 1980s: the economic liberal "laissez-faire" conservatives, the "status quo" conservatives, and a third group: the "authoritarians." According to Jonathan Haidt, these authoritarians

> Are the most malleable or changeable depending on the political environment (Trump). In times of low moral threat … they are not particularly intolerant … But, when they perceive that the moral order is falling apart, the country is losing its coherence and cohesiveness, diversity is rising, and our leadership seems (to them) to be suspect or not up to the needs of the hour, it's as though a button is pushed on their forehead that says "in case of moral threat, lock down the borders, kick out those who are different, and punish those who are morally deviant." So it is not just rising immigration and diversity that has activated American authoritarians – it may be our rising political polarization itself, which has activated and energized a subset of the electorate that is now lionizing Trump as the first major candidate in a long time who has spoken to their fears and desires.[39]

"Given Hitler's obsessive focus on disgust and vermin in Mein Kampf," continues Haidt, "and the general absence of such talk in classical conservative writings, I would guess that it is most characteristic of authoritarian psychology."[40]

A more than average disgust-sensitivity is a sign of an authoritarian personality. Even in the early stages of the American presidential campaign observers were surprised by the high levels of ethnocentrism, xenophobia, and outright racism which characterized the voters in the primaries of the Republican Party. Exit polls from the South Carolina primary, for instance, revealed that nearly half of the voters wanted undocumented immigrants to be deported immediately and 74 percent favored temporarily barring foreign Muslims from entering the United States.[41] Other polls revealed that a third of Trump's backers in South Carolina supported barring gays and lesbians from entering the country, 38 percent wished the South had won the Civil War, and 20 percent wished Lincoln had not freed the slaves. "It's worth noting that he [Trump] isn't persuading voters to hold these beliefs. The beliefs were there – and have been for some time."[42] Matthew MacWilliams, who conducted a research on the profile of the Trump voter, wrote: "If I asked you what most defines Donald Trump supporters, what would you say? They're white? They're poor? They're uneducated? You'd be wrong. In fact I found a single statistically significant variable predicts whether a voter supports Trump – and it's not race, income or education: it's authoritarianism."[43]

Authoritarians feel insecure. They follow strong leaders, whom they expect to solve the problems with an iron fist. Ready to obey the leader, they react aggressively to "disgusting" and threatening outsiders.[44] Authoritarians, writes Karen Stenner, are "those inclined to discriminate against members of other racial and ethnic groups [and] also rush to protect the 'common good' by 'stamping out' offensive ideas and 'cracking down' on misbehavior, and show unusual interest in making public policy about what other people might be up to in private."[45] In her book she shows convincingly that this personality syndrome does not always lead people to react in the same, predictable way. "It appears to ebb and flow with the changing environment ... sometimes authoritarians behave like authoritarians but at other times are indistinguishable from the pack."[46] Why? Because for an authoritarian to react in an authoritarian way, his or her predisposition must be activated and this happens when he or she is confronted with a threat. Feelings of threat are activated when the authoritarian individual has the impression that his or her moral order is under attack. Authoritarianism, argues Stenner, should therefore not be reduced to merely a static property of the individual psyche, as earlier researchers such as Theodor Adorno and his colleagues did in their study *The Authoritarian Personality* (1950): authoritarianism is "a living, breathing social phenomenon: a dynamical *political* process."[47]

The problem is that authoritarians live in a liberal democratic society, where the media are obsessed with political and sex scandals and endless stories about corrupt politicians. This can only activate the authoritarian's fear of chaos and moral decay and make him or her react in an authoritarian way. In March 2016 Amanda Taub wrote: "Authoritarians may be a slight majority within the GOP, and thus able to force their will within the party, but they are too few and their views too unpopular to win a national election on their own."[48] She was wrong. Disgust-sensitive authoritarians were able to win the presidential election and to send a disgust-sensitive authoritarian president to the White House. Disgust-sensitivity is clearly one of the elements of the populist ideal type. Does this mean that all populists – leaders and followers – share this characteristic? Not necessarily. It will be more present in right-wing populism, focused on identity issues and migration, than in left-wing populism, which is more focused on economic issues and socio-economic inequality.

Notes

1. Taguieff speaks of "the hypothesis that these mobilizations express a fear of the future, which has become totally opaque" (Taguieff, *Nouveau national-populisme*, p. 91).
2. Koen Damhuis, *Wegen naar Wilders – PVV-stemmers in hun eigen woorden* (Amsterdam and Antwerp: De Arbeiderspers, 2017), p. 19.
3. Éric Fassin, *Populisme: Le grand ressentiment* (Paris: Éditions Textuel, 2017).
4. Martial Foucault, George E. Marcus, Nicholas Valentino, and Pavlos Vasilopoulos, "Le rôle majeur des émotions dans le vote," *Le Monde*, 7–8 May 2017. The authors emphasize that this anger is a mobilizing force. Voters who would normally abstain are "more inclined to vote Front National when they are motivated by intense anger."
5. Lukacs, *Democracy and Populism*, p. 229. Note the subtitle of Lukacs's book: *Fear and Hatred*!
6. "I regard it as wholly inadmissible," wrote Mill, "that any person should participate in the suffrage, without being able to read, write, and, I will add, perform the common operations of arithmetic. Justice demands, even when the suffrage does not depend on it, that the means of attaining these elementary acquirements should be within the reach of every person, either gratuitously, or at an expense not exceeding what the poorest, who can earn their own living, can afford" (John Stuart Mill, *Autobiography of John Stuart Mill*, with a preface by John Jacob Coss (New York: Columbia University Press, 1960), p. 170). Mill's remedy, therefore, is clear: "Universal teaching must precede universal enfranchisement" (p. 171).
7. Gustave Le Bon, *Psychologie des foules* (Paris: Félix Alcan, 1930).
8. Ibid., p. 41.
9. Ibid., p. 42.
10. Ibid., p. 151. Although critical of universal suffrage, Le Bon was not a proponent of its restriction: "If the electorate consisted only of people whose heads were filled with science, their votes would not be better than those expressed today. They would follow, above all, their feelings and the party line" (p. 159).
11. Le Bon mentions General Boulanger on page 157 of his book.
12. Cf. Michael Barbaro and Steve Eder, "'You're disgusting': A Trump revelation hiding in plain sight," *New York Times*, 29 July 2015. www.nytimes.com/times-insider/author/michael-barbaro-and-steve-eder/ (accessed 4 April 2017).

13 Alexander Hurst, "Donald Trump and the politics of disgust," *The New Republic*, 31 December 2015. https://newrepublic.com/article/126837/donald-trump-politics-disgust (accessed 4 April 2017).
14 Cf. Thomas B. Edsall, "Purity, disgust and Donald Trump," *New York Times*, 6 January 2016. www.nytimes.com/2016/01/06/opinion/campaign-stops/purity-disgust-and-donald-trump.html (accessed 5 April 2017).
15 Daniel Lippman, "The 8 ways Trump has attacked Rubio's sweating," *Politico*, 3 November 2015. www.politico.com/story/2015/11/donald-trump-marco-rubio-sweat-215471 (accessed 5 April 2017).
16 Hurst, "Trump and the politics of disgust."
17 Donald J. Trump, *How to Get Rich*, with Meredith McIver (New York: Ballantine Books, 2004), p. 69.
18 The incident which made headlines, when Trump mocked a disabled reporter from *New York Times* during a press conference, was also very revealing of his disgust-sensitivity. Disgust-sensitive people, writes Rachel Herz, "are also less likely to be friends with people who have physical disabilities" (Rachel Herz, *That's Disgusting – Unraveling the Mysteries of Repulsion* (New York and London: W. W. Norton & Company, 2012), p. 120).
19 Pierre Rosanvallon, *Le peuple introuvable* (Paris: Gallimard, 1998), p. 136.
20 Paul Rozin, "Food is Fundamental, Fun, Frightening, and Far-Reaching," *Social Research*, Vol. 66, Spring 1999, pp. 13–14.
21 Martha C. Nussbaum, *Hiding from Humanity – Disgust, Shame, and the Law* (Princeton and Oxford: Princeton University Press, 2004), p. 88.
22 Ibid., p. 89.
23 Paul Rozin, Jonathan Haidt, and Clark R. McCauley, "Disgust," in Michael Lewis and Jeannette M. Haviland-Jones (eds), *Handbook of the Emotions* (New York and London: The Guilford Press, 2004), p. 637.
24 Aurel Kolnai calls disgust and fear "a couple": both being "defensive emotions," based on a bodily reaction (respectively the urge to vomit and trembling), and having "psychological depth" (Aurel Kolnai, *Ekel, Hochmut, Haß – Zur Phänomenologie feindlicher Gefühle*, with a postscript by Axel Honneth (Frankfurt am Main: Suhrkamp, 2007), p. 10). However, Kolnai forgets that disgust can also become a very *aggressive* emotion, leading not only to the urge to destroy a disgusting object or animal, but even people who are considered to be "disgusting."
25 William Ian Miller, *The Anatomy of Disgust* (Cambridge, Mass. and London: Harvard University Press, 1997), p. xiv.
26 Adolf Hitler, *Mein Kampf* (Munich: Verlag Franz Eher Nachfolger, 1933), p. 61.
27 Ibid., p. 62.
28 Ibid., p. 339.
29 Ibid., p. 334.
30 Ibid., p. 331.
31 Winfried Menninghaus, *Ekel – Theorie und Geschichte einer starken Empfindung* (Frankfurt am Main: Suhrkamp, 1999), p. 7.
32 Paul Ekman, "I can tell when you're lying" (interview), *FT Weekend*, 29–30 November 2008. The same dehumanizing mechanism could be observed in the speech delivered by President Trump as he celebrated the hundredth day of his presidency in Harrisburg, Pennsylvania, where he read a poem comparing immigrants to "vicious snakes" (cf. David Badash, "Trump calls immigrants 'vicious snakes' as he celebrates 100th day with 'the most divisive speech ever'," *The Civic Rights Movement*, 30 April 2017).

www.thenewcivilrightsmovement.com/davidbadash/trump_celebrates_his_100th_day_like_he_did_his_first_delivering_the_most_divisive_speech_ever (accessed 5 May 2017).

33. Jonathan Haidt, "The Politics of Disgust Animated for the Age of Trump," *The Righteous Mind*, 12 June 2016. https://righteousmind.com/the-politics-of-disgust-animated/ (accessed 17 April 2017).
34. Jesse J. Prinz, *Gut Reactions – A Perceptual Theory of Emotion* (Oxford and New York: Oxford University Press, 2006), p. 141.
35. Yoel Inbar, David A. Pizarro, and Paul Bloom, "Conservatives are More Easily Disgusted than Liberals," *Cognition and Emotion*, Vol. 23, Issue 4, 13 May 2009. http://yoelinbar.nfshost.com/papers/disgust_conservatism.pdf (accessed 11 April 2017).
36. Cf. Marco Tullio Liuzza, Torun Lindholm, Caitlin B. Hawley, Marie Gustafsson Sendén, Ingrid Ekström, Mats J. Olsson, and Jonas K. Olofsson, "Body odour disgust sensitivity predicts authoritarian attitudes," *Royal Society Open Science*, 28 February 2018. http://rsos.royalsocietypublishing.org/content/5/2/171091 (accessed 11 May 2017).
37. Corinne J. Brenner and Yoel Inbar, "Disgust Sensitivity Predicts Political Ideology and Political Attitudes in the Netherlands," *European Journal of Social Psychology*, Vol. 45, Issue 1, 2015. http://yoelinbar.net/papers/disgust_netherlands.pdf (accessed 11 May 2017).
38. Karen Stenner, *The Authoritarian Dynamic* (Cambridge and New York: Cambridge University Press, 2005).
39. Jonathan Haidt, "The Key to Trump is Stenner's Authoritarianism," *The Righteous Mind*, 6 January 2016. http://righteousmind.com/the-key-to-trump-is-stenners-authoritarianism/ (accessed 14 April 2017).
40. Ibid.
41. Cf. Lynn Vavreck, "Measuring Donald Trump's supporters for intolerance," *New York Times*, 23 February 2016. www.nytimes.com/2016/02/25/upshot/measuring-donald-trumps-supporters-for-intolerance.html (accessed 17 April 2017).
42. Ibid.
43. Matthew MacWilliams, "The one weird trait that predicts whether you're a Trump supporter," *Politico*, 17 January 2016. www.politico.com/magazine/story/2016/01/donald-trump-2016-authoritarian-213533.
44. Disgust-sensitivity is different in different groups and individuals. However, "even if you are a political liberal, feeling disgust can temporarily make you more conservative. An experiment by psychologist David Pizarro found that inducing disgust (in this case, via a foul-smelling spray) caused people to become more hostile towards gay men. He notes that while you cannot turn liberals into raging homophobes simply by grossing them out, disgust can be used to catalyse more conservative behaviour. Disgust triggers near a polling station, for example, might tilt undecided voters towards a more conservative decision" (Arwa Mahdawi, "Disgust – how Donald Trump and Brexit campaigners win votes," *Guardian*, 21 June 2016. www.theguardian.com/politics/commentisfree/2016/jun/21/donald-trump-politics-of-disgust (accessed 17 April 2017)).
45. Stenner, *Authoritarian Dynamic*, p. 1.
46. Ibid., p. 4.
47. Ibid., p. 326.
48. Amanda Taub, "The rise of American authoritarianism," *Vox*, 1 March 2016. www.vox.com/2016/3/1/11127424/trump-authoritarianism.

4

The populist program: what do populists want?

The vague populist program

Let us now turn to the second part of the populist ideal type: its ideological dimension. What can we say about the ideology of the populists? One thing is clear: populists want "change," even radical change. They are dissatisfied with the existing political and economic order. But what kind of change do they propose? As a rule the followers don't have a precise idea, which makes them easy prey for demagogues and spin doctors who define the problem in their own way. They blame "the system," "the swamp" which has to be "drained," globalization, immigrants, the experts, the EU, and so on. What is striking is that the problem is redefined in abstract and global terms. This does not mean that populists in government do not take specific measures: they certainly do. But their appeal in election campaigns does not come from these concrete proposals, it comes rather from their positioning as "anti-system" parties, being "outsiders," and, as such, supposedly neither corrupt, nor incompetent. They surf on the generalized *distrust* of the electorate vis-à-vis the government, the parliament, and established political parties. This does not mean that the citizen who votes for a populist party does not harbor also a residue of distrust against even this party, but he will motivate his choice by saying that "one has to give them a chance," giving them in fact a blank check.

The populist voter's need for protection

The introduction of universal male suffrage in the nineteenth century was championed by liberals, who saw the extension of suffrage as a means of enhancing the autonomy, the dignity, and the sovereignty of the ordinary citizen. It was a means of enhancing individual freedom. Populist movements appeal to the sovereignty of the people, telling them that they have the power "to bring the system down." However, the populist voter is not primarily motivated by a desire to enhance his personal freedom, but rather by a need to be protected. While the liberal reformers of the nineteenth century sought to create autonomous, informed, and free citizens, the populists are supported by people for whom protection by the state has become their prevailing and most powerful need.[1] They are even ready to sacrifice a part of their personal freedoms on the altar of this precious protection.

Actually, what we observe here is a democratic regression: the voter for a populist party is no longer the rational citizen of democratic theory, the "model" citizen, the "subject" of history, who compares and discusses the party programs and policy propositions of the different parties before taking a reflective and thoughtful decision. Maybe this "rational citizen" never existed. Voters never did spell out the party programs, but rather voted for parties on the basis of party identification. However, this is different from an infantile state of dependency on the populist leader, whom one trusts blindly – like a young child who blindly and unconditionally trusts its parents.

The psychologist Erik H. Erikson writes: "Where large numbers of people have been prepared in childhood to expect from life a high degree of personal autonomy, pride, and opportunity, and then in later life find themselves ruled by superhuman organizations and machinery too intricate to understand, the result may be deep chronic disappointment."[2] This disappointment, he continues, arouses fears and contributes "to the easy acceptance of slogans which seem to promise alleviation of conditions."[3] Erikson does not explain the populist vote, based on the "acceptance of slogans which seem to promise alleviation of conditions," by a theory of the intellectual deficiency of the voter, as nineteenth-century liberals might have done, but by "psychoneurotic and psychosomatic disturbances."[4] This might be a too harsh judgment and only true for a part of the populist electorate. However, it is certainly a fact that the populist vote is based less upon a rational choice than upon emotion: the populist voter, living in anxiety and fearing for his future and his children's future, is a destabilized voter.

This anxiety of the populist voter is multidimensional. He is insecure about his economic position, his professional prospects, his declining socio-economic status, about his children's future, or about the future in general. Important in this respect is the retreat of the social welfare state, which used to defend and insure the citizen against misfortunes and blows of fate. In the modern, globalized world job security is no longer the rule: workers are dislocated and many people are employed under limited-term contracts. While the need for social security increases, the state's support decreases: "The contemporary state cannot deliver on the social state's promise and its politicians no longer repeat the promise. Instead, their policies portend a yet more precarious, risk-ridden life calling for a lot of brinkmanship while making life projects all but impossible; they call on the electors to be 'more flexible' (that is, to brace themselves for yet more insecurity to come) and to seek individually their own individual solutions to the socially produced troubles."[5]

Growing concerns about identity

But the anxiety of citizens is not only rooted in increasingly precarious working and living conditions. In the preceding chapter we have already mentioned that this anxiety is also fed by growing concerns about identity. This identity, which was self-evident and taken for granted in the past, has become more problematic after the arrival of immigrants and other newcomers with different cultural and religious backgrounds. Walter Russell Mead has described the increasing insecurity of the white American population about their identity as follows:

> Whites who organize around their specific European ethnic roots can do so with little pushback; Italian Americans and Irish Americans, for example, have long and storied traditions in the parade of American identity groups. But increasingly, those older ethnic identities have faded, and there are taboos against claiming a generic European American or white identity. Many white Americans thus find themselves in a society that talks constantly about the importance of identity, that values ethnic authenticity, that offers economic benefits and social advantages based on identity – for everybody but them.[6]

One can imagine the resentment which the words "for everybody but them" arouse in the white population – and not only in the poorest and most disadvantaged sections of this group. They have the impression of "no longer living in the same country in which they used to live," and blame the government for this situation. The government has been too liberal, letting the situation deteriorate. "We suffer already today from a deficiency of the state," writes Marcel Gauchet, "entrenched in its pretensions from another age and in its routines, responding too late to the expectations of the citizen whom it protects badly and for whom it does not provide the assurance of his identity."[7]

Governments cannot always plead their innocence. They have often disregarded the fact that some groups of the population – mostly the poorest and the most vulnerable among them – suffer most from societal changes, such as massive immigration and foreign economic competition. It is not the rich, living in their isolated "gated communities," nor the middle classes in their quiet suburbs, who are directly affected by these problems. And governments and parliaments, most of whose members are recruited from these classes, will not always be aware of the fact that they tend to underestimate the problems. "By the second half of the twentieth century," writes John Lukacs, "the power and authority of the state, and respect for

The populist wave: why did it happen?

it, began to decline ... Popular resentment against 'government' merely masks the essence of this phenomenon from which the United States is not at all exempt ... Successive administrations of the United States have been both unable and unwilling to protect the very frontiers of the American state, through which millions of illegal migrants are pouring in."[8] Lukacs wrote these words in 2002, fourteen years before Donald Trump was elected president of the United States with the promise of building a wall on the Mexican border. Lukacs here already points to the growing disaffection of the American voter with the fact that "successive administrations of the United States have been both unable and unwilling to protect the very frontiers of the American state."

Protection: against what and whom?

Rather than being driven by the need to enhance his or her personal freedom, the populist voter is motivated by a need for protection. The question is: protection by whom and against whom and what? The answer on the question: "by whom?" is clear. It is the national government that has to provide the protection. In a Gallup report we find that "Trump supporters may be more dependent on the government."[9] Trump supporters are more dependent than average on Social Security, or on programs for the elderly and disabled. Populist voters seek protection. But against whom and what? This is less clear, because the resentment and fear which motivate the populist voter are multifaceted. There are two main sources, which are different. The first source is socio-economic, the second is identity-related. As concerns the first: the fear of economic breakdown will lead to demands for protectionist measures against foreign competition. It will also lead to demands for redistribution of income and wealth, demands which are traditionally put forward by the "political left." Demands to curb immigration also have a socio-economic background: immigration is accused of having a negative influence on wages. However, immigration is not only perceived as the source of socio-economic problems, but it is also perceived as the source of identity-related problems. Immigrants with a different cultural and religious background are perceived as a threat to the existing "national identity." Even in the United States, a nation composed of immigrants and built by immigrants, this phenomenon can be observed. And it is not recent. "As the flow of immigrants increased," writes Arthur M. Schlesinger,

> so did resentment among the old-timers. By the 1850s immigrants made up half the population of New York and outnumbered native-born Americans in Chicago. Nativist organizations sprang up, like the Supreme Order of the Star-Spangled Banner and its political front, the American Party, calling for a lengthened naturalization process and

curtailment of the political rights of the foreign-born. They were referred to as Know-Nothings because members of the Supreme Order, when asked about their secret oaths and rituals, would reply, "I know nothing."[10]

In the United States curbs on immigration were introduced on several occasions. The Immigration Act of 1924 was intended to "freeze" the ethnic composition of the American population. Quotas were established with the objective of maintaining the ethnic composition of the US population as it was in 1890, which led to a drastic reduction of immigrants from Southern and Eastern Europe.[11] The Act led also to the total prohibition of Asian immigration. After the Second World War these regulations were eased, which led to increased immigration, particularly of Asians and Hispanics. Problems were compounded by the rise of illegal immigration. "California, whose population rose by 30 percent in the 1980s alone, is still the favored destination of millions south of the border," wrote Paul Kennedy. "In consequence of higher birth rates and continued immigration, half of all children in the state are forecast to be Hispanic by 2030, when whites will compose 60 percent of the elderly population – a troublesome mismatch."[12] Kennedy added: "Demographers predict that perhaps as many as 15 million immigrants will arrive each decade for the next thirty years, and calls are now being made to 'bar the door' … Demographic change can … stimulate the racial worries of poor whites."[13] Paul Kennedy wrote these words in 1994, twenty-two years before Donald Trump reaped the benefits of the populist rage which was slowly building up. A similar warning was given by Samuel Huntington, who predicted the Trump-led "white man's revolt" in 2004 as follows:

> The various forces challenging the core American culture and Creed could generate a move by native white Americans to revive the discarded and discredited racial and ethnic concepts of American identity and to create an America that would exclude, expel, or suppress people of other racial, ethnic, and cultural groups. Historical and contemporary experience suggest that this is a highly probable reaction from a once dominant ethnic-racial group that feels threatened by the rise of other groups. It could produce a racially intolerant country with high levels of intergroup conflict.[14]

Migration is a central issue for populist movements because it combines two basic concerns: economic anxiety and status anxiety on the one hand and identity-related anxiety on the other. But how realistic are these anxieties? Richard Sennett distinguishes realistic and unrealistic elements:

> Europe and North America for centuries have branded the Foreigner as a large, frightening presence, and today, as in the past, the Foreigner has become a symbolic site on which people can project all sorts of anxieties. The difference lies in what these anxieties are … In the labor realm, the Foreigner focuses anxieties about job loss or uselessness.

The populist wave: why did it happen?

> Those anxieties make sense, as we've seen, when the Foreigner is actually abroad, in an Indian call center or software firm; they make no sense projected onto an immigrant streetsweeper. Or rather, they make imaginative sense: the fear of loss of control now has a target close at hand. And in that perverse work of the imagination, it does not register that persecuting these close-by weak outsiders does little to make one's own job secure.[15]

It is, in particular, the identity-related anxiety which feeds the populist vote. And it is here that scapegoating, racism, and xenophobia, which characterize the extreme right, enter the picture. Socio-economic anxiety and identity-related anxiety lead both to different claims and to solutions which come from different ideological backgrounds. This is also the reason why populist movements are so difficult to locate on a traditional left–right scale and why parties, such as the French Rassemblement National, pretend that they are "neither right, nor left." This pretension, to transcend the left–right cleavage of the traditional parties, is presented as "new" and "refreshing." However, in reality this contradiction is a major birth defect of most populist movements.[16] Demands for redistribution and support for fragile groups are traditionally put forward by left-wing socialist and social democratic parties. Promoting equality is a basic characteristic of leftist parties. Identity-related politics, which lead to the discrimination of minorities, to scapegoating, and even to violence, are traditionally championed by extreme right parties. Instead of promoting equality, these parties exclude outsiders and emphasize the inequality between insiders and outsiders.

The populist program: "drawbridge politics"?

The programs of populist parties provide answers to people's need to feel protected. But do the projects they put forward really offer protection? Some analysts consider that they offer at best some short-term protection. In a recently published paper one can read: "We define as populist a party that champions short-term protection without regards for its long-term costs."[17] Offering short-term protection without regards for its long-term costs is certainly one of the characteristics of a populist party. However, to make this the *defining* characteristic seems to me untenable. In the first place, established parties also can offer short-term protection without regards for long-term costs. The growing government debts which are a burden on future generations are a case in point.[18] Secondly, other characteristics seem more appropriate to define the populist phenomenon, particularly its bipolar stance, putting the "people" against the "elite." But even if it is not its defining characteristic, the populist offer of protection is important for its political attractiveness and its ultimate electoral success. The solutions it offers are, most of the time, simple: raise import duties, end free trade, give "sovereignty back to the people" by diminishing the influence of international organizations, and curb or stop migration. Geert Wilders promised his voters "Fewer Moroccans." Donald Trump promised to build a wall on the Mexican border. I would characterize these measures as "drawbridge politics." Drawbridge politics are the reverse side of and a reaction against the wave of neoliberal globalization which started in the 1990s. Drawbridge politics are at the core of almost all populist programs.

Drawbridge politics borrow their ideas from the left, as well as from the (extreme) right. They are, therefore, ideologically difficult to locate. This is one of the reasons that some analysts no longer seek the essence of populism in its ideology, but rather in its *political style*. Rather than focusing on its program and ideological content, they argue, populism should be defined by the way the leader and his or her followers behave: their language and rhetoric, their performance, and the way they present themselves. From this angle, it is no longer a question of *what* is said, but *how* it is said. A representative of this school is Pierre Ostiguy, who added to the classical right–left axis a "high–low axis."[19] While populist movements cannot unequivocally be placed on the right–left axis, they can be on the high–low axis. On the "high" side one can find conventional politics with its impersonal authority, its proceduralism and legalism, which is corroborated by the behavior of conventional politicians, who are well bred, well educated, polished, and often even "stiff". On the "low" side we find populist politics, which is coarse, uninhibited, and culturally popular. It is corroborated by the (bad) behavior of the populist leader, who is authoritarian, charismatic, and strong. According to Ostiguy, "personal versus impersonal authority is perhaps a good synthesis of this polarity."[20]

The problem with this approach is that it reduces the essence of populism to a question of leadership style. Leadership style is certainly important – that is why I made it a part of the ideal type. But it is not enough. The populist ideology, with all its contradictions – even *because* of these contradictions – has its own importance and deserves a place in the ideal type. One can also question Ostiguy's remarks about political style, such as his assumption that conventional politicians necessarily have an "impersonal authority." The authority of "conventional" leaders such as Barack Obama or Angela Merkel is far from "impersonal" and certainly not lacking in charisma. What remains in Ostiguy's "high–low axis" is, therefore, rather the coarse and uninhibited way in which the popular leader expresses himself, in which he differentiates himself from the traditional political elite. "The low generally does not worry overly much about appearing improper in the eyes of the international community," writes Ostiguy, "and also at times apparently seems to enjoy it."[21] This may be true. However, it is not enough to characterize the populist phenomenon. Ideas and policy proposals do count and must be taken into consideration – even if they are mutually contradictory.

Kaltwasser and Mudde seem to grasp the problem better. They define populism as "a thin-centered ideology," which makes it possible "to understand why populism is so malleable in the real world. Due to its restricted ideological core and concepts, populism necessarily appears attached to other concepts or ideological families, which are normally at least as relevant to the populist actors as populism itself. Most notably, political actors have combined populism with a variety of other thin- and thick-centered ideologies, including agrarianism, nationalism, neoliberalism, and socialism."[22] The internal contradictions of populist ideology, rather than obfuscating the ideology of populism, are, therefore, rather an expression of it.

Notes

1. An exception has here to be made for the new rich. They support populist parties to defend themselves *against* the state, which is blamed for taxing them too much: a clear sign of the often contradictory expectations of populist voters.
2. Erik H. Erikson, "Growth and Crises of the Healthy Personality," in Erik H. Erikson, *Identity and the Life Cycle* (New York and London: W. W. Norton & Company, 1994), p. 77.
3. Ibid., p. 77.
4. Ibid., p. 77.
5. Zygmunt Bauman, *Wasted Lives – Modernity and Its Outcasts* (Cambridge: Polity Press, 2004), p. 90.
6. Walter Russell Mead, "The Jacksonian Revolt – American Populism and the Liberal Order," *Foreign Affairs*, Vol. 96, No. 2, March/April 2017, p. 5.
7. Marcel Gauchet, *La démocratie contre elle-même* (Paris: Gallimard, 2002), p. 184.
8. John Lukacs, *At the End of an Age* (New Haven and London: Yale University Press, 2002), pp. 16–17. In an editorial of the *New York Times* of 21 July 1985, one could read the following statement, which sounds prophetic today: "The question ... is not whether this country will control the borders. We will. The question is how harshly. If we don't do so now with calm, humane concern, we will later with xenophobic venom" (quoted by Joseph H. Carens, "Immigration and the Welfare State," in Amy Gutmann (ed.), *Democracy and the Welfare State* (Princeton: Princeton University Press, 1988), p. 229). However, for some authors the coming wave of immigration took on apocalyptic dimensions. In 1995 Immanuel Wallerstein wrote, for instance, that "by 2025 or so, in North America, the EC, and (even) Japan, the population socially defined as being of 'Southern' origin may well range from twenty-five to fifty percent, and much higher in certain subregions and within large urban centers" (Immanuel Wallerstein, *After Liberalism* (New York: The New Press, 1995), pp. 34–35).
9. Rothwell and Diego-Rosell, "Explaining Nationalist Political Views," p. 15.
10. Arthur M. Schlesinger, Jr., *The Disuniting of America – Reflections on a Multicultural Society* (New York and London: Norton, 1992), p. 29.

11 These restrictive policies were also inspired by the October Revolution in Russia, which led to a fear that communist agitators could enter the United States (cf. Sophie Body-Gendrot, *Les États-Unis et leurs immigrants – Des modes d'insertion variés* (Paris: La Documentation Française, 1991), p. 18).
12 Paul Kennedy, *Preparing for the Twenty-first Century* (London: Fontana Press, 1994), p. 313.
13 Ibid., p. 313.
14 Samuel P. Huntington, *Who Are We? The Challenges to America's National Identity* (New York: Simon & Schuster, 2005), p. 20 (first edition 2004).
15 Richard Sennett, *The Culture of the New Capitalism* (New Haven and London: Yale University Press, 2006), p. 167. Employment is not only threatened by delocalization of industries. Robotization is also taking its toll. According to a paper written by two economists of the Massachusetts Institute of Technology, each industrial robot added per thousand workers in the period 1990–2007 reduced employment in the United States by almost six workers (Daron Acemoglu and Pascual Restrepo, "The Race Between Machine and Man: Implications of Technology for Growth, Factor Shares and Employment," The National Bureau of Economic Research, *NBER Working Paper* No. 22252, May 2016. www.nber.org/papers/w22252).
16 Left-wing populist movements, such as Syriza in Greece and Podemos in Spain, seem to lack this contradiction, being more focused on socio-economic problems than on identity-related problems. However, even in Greece there were some xenophobic upheavals, when Germans were vilified for Greece's problems.
17 Luigi Guiso, Helios Herrera, Massimo Morelli, and Tommaso Sonno, "Demand and Supply of Populism," Centre for Economic Policy Research, *Discussion Paper Series DP11871*, 22 February 2017, p. 1.
18 Niall Ferguson mentions that in 2013 private and public debts taken together reached 512 percent of GDP in Japan, 507 percent in Britain, 346 percent in France, 314 percent in Italy, 279 percent in the United States, and 278 percent in Germany. These burdens, he writes, "have no precedent in history" (Niall Ferguson, *The Great Degeneration – How Institutions Decay and Economies Die* (London and New York: Penguin Books, 2013), p. 40). Ferguson adds: "These mind-boggling numbers represent nothing less than a vast claim by the generation currently retired or about to retire on their children and grandchildren, who are obliged by current law to find the money in the future, by submitting either to substantial increases in taxation or to drastic cuts in other forms of public expenditure" (p. 42).
19 Pierre Ostiguy, "The High and the Low in Politics: A Two-Dimensional Political Space for Comparative Analysis and Electoral Studies," The Helen Kellogg Institute for International Studies, *Working Paper* #360, July 2009.
20 Ibid., p. 8.
21 Ibid., p. 9.
22 Cas Mudde and Cristóbal Rovira Kaltwasser, *Populism – A Very Short Introduction* (Oxford: Oxford University Press, 2017), p. 19.

5
Populists in power

Taking quick and simple measures

Until now we have only spoken of populist movements and populist parties. But populist leaders can be successful and enter the governments of their countries. There are many examples: Hugo Chávez in Venezuela, the FPÖ in Austria, the Lega and Five Star Movement in Italy, Syriza in Greece, Viktor Orbán in Hungary, Bolsonaro in Brazil, and Donald Trump in the United States. But how do they put their ideas into effect once in government? Having criticized the preceding "conventional" governments (and "conventional" can equally mean governments of the right or the left), it is clear that they purport to do things completely differently. But can they live up to their promises? These promises concern, first, their government style, and, secondly, the execution of their election platform.

As concerns their government style, populists boast two differences from "conventional" politics. The first is that the populist leader is able to implement his policies *quickly*. The second supposition is that implementing these policies is *quite simple*. Both suppositions support each other.

The assumption that the populist leader will be able to implement his policies quickly has to do with his image of "strongman." Being a "real leader" one expects him to show his "toughness," being able to overcome legal hurdles or eventual obstruction by parliament or civil servants. In fact, this is to misjudge the democratic process, because "only a few laws support too great haste if they have to fulfil their vocation. These laws need time for their proper incubation ... Laws need time to ripen."[1] Populists don't like the slow procedures of parliament and prefer, therefore, quick measures, such as "executive orders" issued by governments. Donald Trump, for instance, signed thirty-two executive orders, actions, and memoranda in the first nine weeks of his presidency.[2]

In his book *The Road to Serfdom*, which was first published in 1944, Friedrich Hayek warned against the urge to disregard established democratic procedure which "precedes the suppression of democratic institutions and the creation of a totalitarian regime."[3] Hayek added:

> In this stage it is the general demand for quick and determined government action that is the dominating element in the situation, dissatisfaction with the slow and cumbersome course of democratic procedure which makes action for action's sake the goal. It is then the man or the party who seems strong and resolute enough "to get things done" who exercises the greatest appeal. "Strong" in this sense means not merely a numerical majority – it is the ineffectiveness of parliamentary majorities with which people are dissatisfied. What they will seek is somebody with such solid support as to inspire confidence that he can carry out whatever he wants.[4]

The first speech of Boris Johnson as British prime minister on 24 July 2019 was a clear example of this. "No ifs or buts," said Johnson, "the time has come to act, to take decisions, to give strong leadership and to change the country for the better."[5] However, despite these strong and powerful words he could not deliver on his promise, made in the same speech, that Britain would leave the EU by 31 October 2019 …

Populist governments as emanation of "the people"

The populist preoccupation with quick and effective measures is fed by the illusion that the implementation of populist policies is a simple affair. It *would* be simple if the populist leader could unilaterally impose his views. However, in a liberal democracy the decision-making process is one of give-and-take, of seeking common ground and reaching compromise. This is not appreciated by the populist voter. "Voters want 'a real leader, not a politician,' by which they generally mean that their own ideas should be adopted and other people's opinions disregarded, because views different from their own are obviously self-interested and erroneous."[6]

The belief that the populist leader will be able to implement his policies quickly and in a simple way, without being hindered by institutional restrictions, is based on the supposition that the populist leader is the representative of "the people" and not of a random group of voters. The populist leader considers himself to be anointed by "the people," not unlike former kings considered themselves to be anointed by god.[7] This is supposed to give him a more powerful mandate than conventional politicians, who, as an estranged "elite," don't represent the people but only themselves and their petty interests. This pretension to represent *the* people denies the fact that society consists of a plurality of groups with different needs and different interests, which, in a liberal democratic state, should be mediated and reconciled. The populist leader, on the contrary, tends to consider the interests of other groups as not legitimate. These are not the interests of "the people," but the interests of the elite or a group connected with the elite, and, therefore, opposed to the interests of "the people."

Jan-Werner Müller has expressed this populist anti-pluralism in a catchy formula: "Populists don't say: 'We are the 99 percent.' They say that they represent nothing less than the full 100 percent."[8] This means that political opponents are no longer considered as fellow citizens, who have the same right to promote their interests as every citizen, but as enemies of "the people." Donald Trump's repeated attacks on the media, calling them "an enemy of the people," are a case in point. This is a dangerous reinterpretation of the *res publica*. In this view the essence of a liberal democracy is no longer the realization of the common good for all citizens, but, on the contrary, a concept which comes close to the theory of the Nazi ideologue Carl Schmitt, who considered the essence of politics the "friend–foe" opposition.[9] Populists in power tend to put the maxim "who is not with us, is against us" into practice.

Attacking the pillars of liberal democracy

Populists in government want to maximize their power. They do this in the name of "democracy." Critics are rebuked with the argument that they received their mandate directly from "the people." And isn't it their vocation and holy duty to execute "the will of the people"? This means that all institutions and groups which act as countervailing powers must be neutralized. Geert Wilders called the Dutch parliament (of which he himself was a member) a *nepparlement*, a fake parliament.[10] He called judges and journalists "messengers of evil": "They represented the system which soon had to be destroyed. In other words: democracy in its present form had to disappear or, at least, had to be 'reconquered'."[11]

Populists find themselves at odds with one of the basic pillars of liberal democracy: the separation of powers. The necessity of this separation was already put forward by Montesquieu, who wrote: "It is an eternal experience that a man who has power is likely to abuse it; he goes so far until he finds the limits … In order to avoid one being able to abuse one's power … power must stop power."[12] In a liberal democracy parliament and the judiciary are the natural countervailing powers of the executive, together with the free press. This was a basic insight of the Founding Fathers of the American Constitution. James Madison, for instance, who was to become the fourth American president, wrote in *Federalist Paper* No. 48:

> All the powers of government, legislative, executive, and judiciary, result to the legislative body. The concentrating these in the same hands is precisely the definition of despotic government. It will be no alleviation that these powers will be exercised by a plurality of hands, and not by a single one. One hundred and seventy-three despots

would surely be as oppressive as one ... As little will it avail us that they are chosen by ourselves. An *elective despotism* was not the government we fought for; but one which should not only be founded on free principles, but in which the powers of government should be so divided and balanced among several bodies of magistracy as that no one could transcend their legal limits without being effectually checked and restrained by the others. For this reason ... the legislative, executive, and judiciary departments should be separate and distinct, so that no person should exercise the powers of more than one of them at the same time.[13]

In his *Farewell Address*, the first American president, George Washington, also emphasized the importance of the division of powers, writing: "The necessity of reciprocal checks in the exercise of political power, by dividing and distributing it into different depositories, and constituting each the Guardian of the Public Weal against invasions by the others, has been evinced by experiments ancient and modern; some of them in our country and under our own eyes. To preserve them must be as necessary as to institute them."[14]

Of course, populists are not the only ones who do not respect the independence of the different branches of government. "Regular" politicians too sometimes try to influence the other branches. However, regular politicians do not question the legitimacy of the division of powers as such. Populists, on the contrary, often do. Therefore, as Cas Mudde rightly argues: "Populism tends to get ugly when it gets into power."[15] Examples of populist regimes which infringe upon the rights of the judiciary and threaten the freedom of the media are legion. The Hungarian prime minister Viktor Orbán is a case in point. In a speech in the summer of 2014 he openly distanced himself from liberal democracy. "We have to state," he said, "that democracy does not necessarily have to be liberal. Just because a state is not liberal, it can still be a democracy."[16] Orbán continued: "We must break with liberal principles and methods of social organization, and in general with the liberal understanding of society," concluding: "And so, in this sense the new state that we are constructing in Hungary is an illiberal state, a non-liberal state."[17]

Orbán's remarks did not come as a complete surprise. In May 2014 the European Court of Human Rights (ECHR) had ruled that the Hungarian government had committed irregularities by firing András Baka, president of the Hungarian Supreme Court. Baka was fired three years before the end of his mandate for his criticism of a new law on the retirement age of judges, changing the retirement age from seventy to sixty-two. This was considered a purge, enabling Orbán's Fidesz government to sack critical judges and appoint more pliable judges in their place. In the ECHR's ruling one could read that "the fear of sanction has a 'chilling effect' on the exercise of freedom of expression and in particular risks discouraging judges from making critical remarks about public institutions or policies, for fear of losing their judicial office."[18] The ruling was confirmed on 23 June 2016.

Similar attacks on the independence of the judiciary could also be observed in Poland after the populist PiS (Law and Justice Party) was returned to government in October 2015. The election victory was followed by a 'coup' by President Andrzej Duda, who refused to accept the legally elected judges and swore in new judges immediately after their nomination by the new PiS-dominated parliament. In February 2017 Małgorzata Gersdorf, president of Poland's Supreme Court, urged the country's judges "to fight for every inch of justice," because, she said, "the courts are easily turned into a plaything in the hands of politicians."[19] At stake was the independence of the courts, after the government proposed "democratizing" the way Polish judges were appointed. Until then, appointments were made by an autonomous judicial council, whose members were chosen by their peers. In the government proposal the incumbent members would be replaced within ninety days of the draft law's enactment. The new members would be selected by parliament, dominated by the PiS party. Despite the protests the law was adopted by the Sejm on 8 December 2017.

Referendums: the populists' magical tool

Populists tout their claim of "giving power back to the people." They are skeptical about representative democracy and consider direct democracy a better alternative. Therefore, referendums are their instruments of choice. Referendums, they argue, offer each individual citizen the opportunity to express his or her opinion on specific issues. Instead of giving a mandate to an elected representative to take a decision, the decision is taken by the citizen him- or herself. At first sight this seems to be true. And our computer age could, indeed, make things a lot easier, enabling citizens, while staying at home, to cast their votes online. In a book first published in 1984, the Italian political scientist Norberto Bobbio considered this option still to be "science-fiction," writing: "As concerns the referendum, which, in the end, is the only device of direct democracy which can be concretely applied and effectively processed in most developed democratic states, it is an extraordinary means for extraordinary events. No one can imagine a state which can be governed by a continuous appeal to the people ... except in the hypothesis, which at the moment is still science-fiction, that each citizen can vote on a computer which stands comfortably at home, just pushing a button."[20]

We are now in the computer age and Bobbio's "science-fiction" has become reality. We do not even need computers to vote, because everyone has a smartphone which could eventually be used for this purpose. However, apart from new problems which have emerged, such as hacking by hostile foreign powers, on closer inspection referendums are far from the silver bullets their protagonists suggest them to be. According to C. B. Macpherson, "The idea that recent and expected advances in computer technology and telecommunications will make it possible to achieve direct democracy ... does not pay enough attention to an inescapable requirement of any decision-making process: somebody must formulate the questions."[21] Indeed, it is a well-known fact that the way in which a question is framed can influence the way in which it is answered. There is, therefore, ample opportunity for manipulation. This will particularly be the case when governments organize referendums. But the problem does not disappear in the case of a popular initiative, where it is groups from civil society rather than governments who formulate the question, as it is often passionate populist minorities who organize these initiatives.

There is also a question concerning the *frequency* of referendums. A populist government will be tempted to organize referendums on a regular basis. At first sight this gives more influence to the people. However, is this really so? Bobbio calls a direct democracy in which the citizens decide constantly on everything "insane."[22] Macpherson argues that "such a system of continual referendums would not really be democratic: worse, by giving the appearance of being democratic, the system would conceal the real location of power and would thus enable 'democratic' governments to be more autocratic than they are now. We cannot do without elected politicians. We must rely, though we need not rely exclusively, on indirect democracy."[23]

Macpherson speaks about democratic governments becoming more autocratic. But what about populist governments? Most of these governments are, as such, already characterized by an authoritarian government style and the centralizing power of a charismatic leader, who considers himself to be the incarnation of the "will of the people." This kind of leader is not likely to feel the need to consult the people. Referendums, in this case, rather than being bottom-up initiatives expressing the will of the people, will be top-down instruments, used by the leader "to show that the people stand behind him." Does this mean that referendums should be categorically rejected as "populist manipulation"? This would certainly go too far and would be to throw the baby out with the bathwater. According to David Held, "the merits of direct participatory democracy have to be re-examined now its technical feasibility is closer at hand ... It is unacceptable to dismiss all types of direct democracy as if they could be realized only through 'unmediated popular voting on a take it or leave it basis'; for direct democracy can take several different forms, just as liberal democracy does."[24] However, the problem with referendums is that, as a rule, they formulate proposals "on a take it or leave it basis." You can vote "yes" or you can vote "no", there are no alternatives. Therefore, referendums should be reserved for "macro-level" and "micro-level" decisions, and not used for "medium-level" decisions. Macro decisions would be those that involve major, historical choices, such as the introduction of a new constitution, which has far-reaching consequences for the future of a country. Micro decisions are decisions on a local or regional level,[25] which concern transport systems, city planning, and so on. Medium-level decisions concern the normal lawgiving process and should normally be reserved for elected national parliaments.

Notes

1. Günther Winkler, *Zeit und Recht* (Vienna and New York: Springer Verlag, 1995), p. 237.
2. "List of Trump's executive orders," Fox News, 28 March 2017. www.foxnews.com/politics/2017/03/28/list-trumps-executive-orders.html (accessed 15 May 2017).
3. F. A. Hayek, *The Road to Serfdom* (London and Henley: Routledge & Kegan Paul, 1979), p. 101.
4. Ibid., pp. 101–102.
5. "Boris Johnson's first speech as Prime Minister: 24 July 2019," Gov.uk, 24 July 2019. www.gov.uk/government/speeches/boris-johnsons-first-speech-as-prime-minister-24-july-2019 (accessed 28 July 2019).
6. Christopher H. Achen and Larry M. Bartels, *Democracy for Realists – Why Elections Do Not Produce Responsive Government* (Princeton and Oxford: Princeton University Press, 2016), p. 318.
7. Even before his election some followers of Donald Trump considered Trump to be "a prophesied president," who was literally "anointed by God." Cf. Chris Enloe, "Was Donald Trump anointed by God to be the next president of America?" *The Blaze*, 20 October 2016. www.theblaze.com/news/2016/10/20/was-donald-trump-anointed-by-god-to-be-the-next-president-of-america/ (accessed 15 May 2017).
8. Jan-Werner Müller, *Was ist Populismus?* (Berlin: Suhrkamp Verlag, 2016), p. 44.
9. Cf. Carl Schmitt, *Der Begriff des Politischen* (Berlin: Duncker & Humblot, 2002), p. 26: "The specific political difference, to which political acts and motives can be reduced, is the difference between friend and foe."
10. Cf. Armen Hakhverdian and Wouter Schakel, *Nepparlement – Een pleidooi voor politiek hokjesdenken* (Amsterdam: Amsterdam University Press, 2017).
11. H. M. van den Brink, *Koning Wilders – Een wintersprookje* (Amsterdam and Antwerp: Atlas Contact, 2017), p. 44.
12. Montesquieu, "De l'esprit des lois," in Montesquieu, *Œuvres Complètes* (Paris: Éditions du Seuil, 1964), p. 586.
13. James Madison, "Federalist Paper," No. 48. In Alexander Hamilton, James Madison, and John Jay, *The Federalist Papers*, with an introduction by Clinton Rossiter (New York and Scarborough, Ontario: New American Library, 1961), pp. 310–311.
14. George Washington, "Farewell Address to the People of the United States," 17 September 1796, in Russel B. Nye and Norman S. Grabo (eds), *American Thought and Writing, Volume Two: The Revolution and the Early Republic* (Boston: Houghton Mifflin Company, 1965), p. 174.

15 Cas Mudde, "The problem with populism," *Guardian*, 17 February 2015.
16 "Prime Minister Viktor Orbán's speech at the 25th Bálványos Summer Free University and Student Camp," 26 July 2014. www.kormany.hu/en/the-prime-minister/the-prime-minister-s-speeches/prime-minister-viktor-orban-s-speech-at-the-25th-balvanyos-summer-free-university-and-student-camp (accessed 16 May 2017).
17 Ibid.
18 Gilbert Reilhac, "European court says Hungary fired judge for criticizing government," Reuters, 27 May 2014. www.reuters.com/article/us-echr-hungary-idUSKBN0E71VI20140527 (accessed 16 May 2017).
19 Christian Davies, "Polish judges urged to 'fight every inch' for their independence," *Guardian*, 26 February 2017. www.theguardian.com/world/2017/feb/26/polish-judges-urged-fight-independence-supreme-court (accessed 16 May 2017).
20 Norberto Bobbio, *Il futuro della democrazia* (Turin: Einaudi, 1995), pp. 48–49.
21 C. B. Macpherson, *The Life and Times of Liberal Democracy* (Oxford: Oxford University Press, 1979), p. 95.
22 Bobbio, *Futuro della democrazia*, p. 34.
23 Macpherson, *Life and Times*, p. 97.
24 David Held, *Democracy and the Global Order – From the Modern State to Cosmopolitan Governance* (Stanford: Stanford University Press, 1995), p. 280.
25 It is interesting that at the end of the nineteenth century the French socialists had already introduced the idea of local referendums: "In the 1890s," writes Pierre Rosanvallon, "the [French] socialists become the apostles of direct democracy and the referendum, wanting to express in this way the sovereignty of the people … On their instigation municipal referendums are organized. In 1888 the municipality of Cluny introduces an innovation, asking voters for the first time to approve a loan for the construction of a fire station and the installation of a waterworks" (Pierre Rosanvallon, *Le sacre du citoyen – Histoire du suffrage universel en France* (Paris: Gallimard, 1992), pp. 508–509). Interestingly, the French socialists considered these local referendums not only an additional tool of democratic governance, but also as a means of democratic *education*: "Instead of waiting for the education of the masses to be fully realized before extending democracy, they want to make of political participation as such a means of apprenticeship" (p. 509). In this way they replaced John Stuart Mill's maxim "preparing for democracy by learning" by a more pragmatic "learning by doing."

Part II

Do we have too much democracy or not enough?

Part 2

How we view the world:
Similarity or not enough?

6
Is democracy a question of supply or demand?

Populists seem to rely on an eighteenth-century theory of direct democracy, inspired by Jean-Jacques Rousseau. This theory presupposes that there exists a "common good" which can be known to each rational individual. Citizens – as rational individuals – not only know this "common good" but they also want its realization. It is, therefore, sufficient that all citizens vote and express their rational "common will" (*volonté générale*) to realize the "common good" or, at least, to take measures which promote the common good. I will label this theory a "theory of democratic demand." According to this theory, a democratic polity realizes the demand of the people for the common good. This demand is directly expressed by their common will. In this theory there is no need for a supply of ideas about the "common good" by political leaders and political parties. The presupposition of this theory is that there is a pre-existing idea of the common good, known intuitively by the citizens, who do not need the support or mediation of other political actors or experts to know what they want.

Joseph Schumpeter's attack on classical democratic theory

One of the first to attack this theory was Joseph Schumpeter in his book *Capitalism, Socialism, and Democracy*, which was first published in 1942.[1] Let me quote Schumpeter at length to see how he develops his argument. "The eighteenth-century philosophy of democracy," writes Schumpeter,

> may be couched in the following definition: the democratic method is that institutional arrangement for arriving at political decisions which realizes the common good by making the people itself decide issues through the election of individuals who are to assemble in order to carry out its will. Let us develop the implication of this. It is held, then, that there exists a Common Good, the obvious beacon light of policy, which is always simple to define and which every normal person can be made to see by means of rational argument. There is hence no excuse for not seeing it and in fact no explanation

for the presence of people who do not see it except ignorance – which can be removed – stupidity and anti-social interest. Moreover, this common good implies definite answers to all questions so that every social fact and every measure taken or to be taken can unequivocally be classed as "good" or "bad." All people having therefore to agree, in principle at least, there is also a Common Will of the people (= will of all reasonable individuals) that is exactly coterminous with the common good or interest or welfare or happiness. The only thing, barring stupidity and sinister interests, that can possibly bring in disagreement and account for the presence of an opposition is a difference of opinion as to the speed with which the goal, itself common to nearly all, is to be approached.[2]

Does this mean that no experts or representatives are needed? Not quite. But their role is reduced. "It is true," writes Schumpeter, "that the management of some of these affairs requires special aptitudes and techniques and will therefore have to be entrusted to specialists who have them. This does not affect the principle, however, because these specialists simply act in order to carry out the will of the people exactly as a doctor acts in order to carry out the will of the patient to get well."[3] Schumpeter criticizes the basic assumptions of this theory. "There is, first," he writes, "no such thing as a uniquely determined common good that all people could agree on or be made to agree on by the force of rational argument," something, he says, which is due to the fact that "to different individuals and groups the common good is bound to mean different things."[4] Not all these differences can be bridged by compromise, because there are "questions of principle which cannot be reconciled by rational argument because ultimate values – our conceptions of what life and what society should be – are beyond the range of mere logic."[5] Clear examples of this are opposing opinions on abortion or euthanasia. But even if we assume a clear answer as concerns the contents of the common good, this will not lead to unanimity, because there will emerge "problems centering in the evaluation of present versus future satisfactions."[6] As a consequence of this, concludes Schumpeter, "the particular concept of the will of the people or the *volonté générale* … vanishes into thin air. For that concept presupposes the existence of a uniquely determined common good discernable to all."[7]

If democratic politics is not the execution of the will of the people who have a perfect knowledge of the common good, what is it? Let us listen to what Schumpeter is telling us. "Though a common will or public opinion of some sort may still be said to emerge from the infinitely complex jumble of individual and group-wise situations, volitions, influences, actions and reactions of the 'democratic process,' the result lacks not only rational unity but also rational sanction."[8] The "common will" which expresses itself in elections will not, therefore, automatically express the "common good." "If we are to argue that the will of the citizens *per se* is a political factor entitled to respect," writes Schumpeter, it must first exist. That is to say, it must be something more than an indeterminate bundle of vague impulses loosely playing about given slogans and mistaken impressions. Everyone would have to know definitely what he wants to stand for. This definite will would have to be implemented by the ability to observe and interpret correctly the facts that are directly accessible to everyone and to sift critically the information about the facts that are not … all this the modal citizen would have to perform for himself and independently of pressure groups and propaganda, for volitions and inferences that are imposed upon the electorate obviously do not qualify for ultimate data of the democratic process."[9]

According to Schumpeter it is a myth that the common will would express the "common good," because "it is not only conceivable but, whenever individual wills are much divided, very likely that the political decisions produced will not conform to 'what people really want.'"[10] This will particularly be the case "with qualitative issues, such as the question whether to persecute heretics or to enter upon a war, the result attained may well, though for different reasons, be equally distasteful to all the people."[11]

Democratic decision-making, such is Schumpeter's conclusion, is no guarantee of the realization of the "common good." Both assumptions of classical, eighteenth-century democracy theory – that the citizens intuitively know the common good and that their "common will" expresses this common good – are pure myths which do not stand up to a reality test. At this point Schumpeter comes up with an alternative theory: the theory of the "manufactured will."

The people's "manufactured will"

In Schumpeter's alternative theory a much greater place is reserved for political leadership. Politicians and parliamentarians are not the humble servants of the people who slavishly execute the wishes of the electorate. On the contrary, they are active actors who mold the political ideas of their followers. Schumpeter inverts the political process. The power of deciding political issues is no longer vested in the electorate, which selects representatives to carry out these decisions, but the voters elect men or women who are to do the deciding.

"The democratic method," writes Schumpeter, "is that institutional arrangement for arriving at political decisions in which individuals acquire the power to decide by means of a competitive struggle for the people's vote."[12] Politicians are competing for the votes of the people, offering them different programs. These programs have a *supply-side character*.[13] They can contain proposals or projects which, before their presentation, were not imagined by the people, but suddenly arouse their enthusiasm. Because voters can have volitions, which "do not as a rule assert themselves directly. Even if strong and definite they remain latent, often for decades, until they are called to life by some political leader who turns them into political factors. This he does, or else his agents do it for him, by organizing these volitions, by working them up and by including eventually appropriate items in his competitive offering."[14] The "common will," as Schumpeter rightly emphasizes, is therefore not so much the will of the voters which, in a natural way, expresses the common good, as a "manufactured will": the product of the supply of ideas by political leaders and parties, competing for power.

It is clear that Schumpeter's concept of democracy: a competition between political elites for the votes of the electorate in order to constitute a government which executes the government's conception of the common good, is a far cry from the populist concept of democracy, which attributes to the people a sound common sense – considered to be absent in the elites – of what has to be done. The irony is, however, that populist policies work exactly in the way as described by Schumpeter. The programs of these parties are not formulated by "the people," but by a select party leadership. Populist parties with charismatic leaders are even more elitist than the traditional parties, because the charismatic leader is able to set the agenda alone.

Retrospective accountability

Schumpeter's critical, but realistic, account of the workings of modern democracy has further been elaborated by two American researchers, Christopher Achen and Larry Bartels, in their book *Democracy for Realists*. "Numerous studies have demonstrated," they write, "that most residents of democratic countries have little interest in politics and do not follow news of public affairs beyond browsing the headlines. They do not know the details of even salient policy debates, they do not have a firm understanding of what the political parties stand for, and they often vote for parties whose long-standing issue positions are at odds with their own."[15] Achen and Bartels argue that the classical "folk" theory of democracy, which is based on the assumption of the informed citizen who knows what he or she wants and what is best for society, is more a pious wish than a reality. They observe that "evidence demonstrates that the great majority of citizens pay little attention to politics. At election time, they are swayed by how they feel about 'the nature of times,' especially the current state of the economy, and by political loyalties typically acquired in childhood. Those loyalties, not the facts of political life and government policy, are the primary drivers of political behavior."[16] For this reason, they write, "the ideal of popular sovereignty plays much the same role in contemporary democratic ideology that the divine right of kings played in the monarchical era. It is 'a quasi-religious commitment' ... a fiction providing legitimacy and stability to political systems whose actual workings are manifestly – and inevitably – rather less than divine."[17]

Does this mean that voters are completely rudderless, voting in a random way, easily swayed by the last opinion they hear? Not really. Because there is a way to assess policies without being more than globally informed. This is voting on the basis of "retrospective accountability." This means that voters do not have to study party programs in detail, nor do they need to follow government policies on a day-to-day basis to form an opinion. Rather they *look back*, assessing the policies of the incumbent government. In this assessment the economic performance of the government is high on the agenda. As Bill Clinton said: "It's the economy, stupid." It is, therefore, often less the future-oriented party programs which determine the choice of the voters, than the economic situation in which the country finds itself on election day. This "retrospective accountability" is the "fall-back position" of the average, uninformed voter. It seems to be rational, but is it? Not really, write the authors, because it can lead to the punishing of governments which conducted the right policies but were not lucky enough to see the end of an economic downturn. It can also lead to the rewarding of weak and mediocre governments which profit from an economic upswing. Achen and Bartels speak therefore about a "blind retrospection," writing that "governments are punished willy-nilly for bad times, including bad times clearly due to events beyond the government's control."[18] Voters have "great difficulty making sensible attributions of responsibility for hard times. However, it is still more troubling to find that voters have great difficulty simply assessing whether times have been good or bad over the course of an incumbent's term in office."[19] This is the reason that the authors express a "profound doubt on retrospective voting as a reliable basis for good government."[20]

The partisan voter: party loyalty instead of a critical mind?

But if retrospective voting does not produce a guarantee of good government, what choice is left for uninformed voters? It is not so much a question of a deliberate choice, as of an ingrained habit. Voters tend to make their choice on the basis of their feelings of belonging to ethnic, religious, and social groups, because "the most important factor in voters' judgments [is] their social and psychological attachments to groups."[21] These "partisan loyalties often carry across generations ... children tend to adopt the partisanship of their parents, and those attachments tend to persist in adulthood. Even when the children of left-wing, working-class parents become middle-class business people, their inherited party loyalties often persist.

Partisanship, like religious identification, tends to be inherited, durable, and not about ideology or theology."[22] Rather than party platforms, it is inherited family positions that often determine someone's choice of party. This can lead to strange situations. Because the details of a party's policy positions do not matter much, "the policies espoused by political parties are often at odds with what the people who are voting for them favor."[23]

Worse, because they often do not know what they want and have no clear ideas on certain items, "citizens are sometimes willing to believe the opposite [to what they originally thought] if it makes them feel better about their partisanship and vote choices."[24] Voters want to minimize the "cognitive dissonance" with positions taken by the party, because such a discrepancy can be the cause of unpleasant feelings. Instead of political parties following the ideas of voters, as is assumed in the classical theory of democracy, voters rather are ready to adapt their views to the prevailing view in their party. This is even the case if the party's position on an item is wrong.[25]

It is clearly in the interest of the party leadership that the voters, in a partisan mood of "my party, right or wrong," express their party loyalty and confirm the role of the leadership as the ideological vanguard. Paradoxically, despite their attacks on the "elite" and their pretension to express "the will of the people," this tendency is even more exacerbated in populist parties with charismatic leaders. Schumpeter spoke about a "manufactured will." The raw material of this "manufactured will" consists of the votes of the electorate. The "manufacturing," however, is mostly done by politicians.

"In every society," write Achen and Bartels, "policy-making is a job for specialists. Policies are made by political elites of one kind or another, including elected officials, government bureaucrats, interest groups, and judges ... politics has been, is, and always will be carried on by politicians, just as art is carried on by artists, engineering by engineers, business by businessmen."[26] The same idea that the common good is something *to be created* by politicians is expressed by Kenneth Minogue, who wrote: "The harmony – the common good or the national interests – must constantly be created by politicians. And where it cannot be created, it must be forced. If soldiers will not volunteer in sufficient numbers, they must be conscripted. If people will not pay their taxes, governments will force them to."[27] For populists, who are touting to represent "the people" and profess to know exactly "the people's will," which, for them, is equivalent to the common good, this may sound like a heresy. However, ironically the populist parties are an extreme example of a top-down policy, not seeking a harmony among a plurality of interests, but imposing their own view as the view of "the people."

Is democracy a question of supply or demand?

The "focus groups" of New Labour

Are policies and policy proposals made by "the people" or by politicians? The tension between the two approaches can be exemplified by the development of "New Labour" in Britain and its leader Tony Blair. In September 1985, when Margaret Thatcher led a Conservative government and Labour was in opposition, the communications expert Philip Gould was appointed Labour's director of communications. Gould wrote a sixty-four-page report, delivered in December 1985. It was damning. Gould concluded that "Labour had too many committees, spent too much of its time speaking to its diminishing number of activists … and spurned new communication methods."[28] Gould's report led to the establishment of a Shadow Communications Agency (SCA), assembling the media specialists of the party, who gave their services to the party gratis. The first result was the introduction of the new red rose emblem.

In 1987, when Thatcher won the elections for the third time, Philip Gould and the SCA intensified their work. Gould

> undertook extensive opinion polling and began an intensive programme of "focus groups", a technique common in advertising and public relations where the views of small groups were carefully probed and their reaction to ideas, words and phrases closely monitored. Using these techniques, Gould was able to build up a clear picture of what current Labour voters, and, very significantly, potential Labour voters, liked and did not like about the party. Properly used, it was a potentially transforming tool for a party in need of reconnecting itself with voters, after years of the hard left dictating what Labour voters wanted, or rather, should be wanting.[29]

At first sight focus groups have a "democratic" image: firms seem "to listen" to the public and adapt their products and marketing methods to the wishes and tastes of potential buyers. However, we should not be fooled. Focus groups are part of a supply-side economy: the seller of goods wants to know how the public feels about a product in order to maximize his or her sales. Labour's innovation was to use focus groups for improving its position in the "political market" by changing its image and attuning its political message more closely to the wishes and expectations of the electorate. One could argue that this gives the electorate a voice in the formulation of the party program, but this is true only in a very restricted sense. It is not the electorate at large giving its opinion, but only some selected individuals. These individuals do not come up with spontaneous proposals, but give their opinions on items and policies that are formulated by the party.

When Tony Blair became party leader in June 1994 he relied heavily on focus groups and he continued to rely on them after he became prime minister in 1997. The results of some of these focus groups were published. The reaction was mixed:

these "publicized focus groups were seen by some as heralding a new responsiveness, but to others they appeared indecisive and indicating a government 'in a permanent election campaign'."[30]

Tony Blair on political leadership

In his memoirs Blair is very positive about the role played by Philip Gould. "He was the one," he writes,

> with the divining rod. His job was precisely to tell us what it was like in the instant. In that he was typical of a very good pollster. But over time, I noticed something else: he was actually a great synthesizer of the public mood. He would analyse it, explain it and predict its consequences with an insight that rose above the mundane expression of "they like this" or "they hate that." It would get to where the public might be brought, as well as to where they presently felt comfortable. In this, he became a strategist not a pollster.[31]

Interestingly, Blair speaks here about "where the public might be brought," which clearly indicates that it is not the politician's vocation to follow the whims of the public mood, but to formulate a project and try to get a majority of the population behind it. But in other passages he expressed his doubts also about Gould's "magical tool," writing,

> Then there was Philip Gould and his focus groups. Philip was a fantastic support, at times as crucial as a morale enthuser as a political strategist, but I used to laugh at how extraordinary the confluence was between his own thoughts and what the groups seemed to say. Also, so much depended on the individual people. Though pollsters always swore blind these groups were selected on a very "scientific" basis, the truth about any group of people chosen like this is that they are utterly in thrall to their own mood on the day, any recent experience, what they think they should think, and above all to the voice in the group which speaks most definitively and so influences the dynamics that will occur within any collection of strangers sitting in a room together for the first time … But so frenzied is the political desire to sniff the prevailing winds accurately that huge emphasis and sanctity is placed upon polls. You begin to realise how the ancient temple priests must have felt in pagan days, trying to read the entrails. I bet they were much like Philip and one of his groups, and the conclusion they arrived at was not greatly different from where they thought things were moving anyway. So they, and polls, should be treated with the utmost caution. But they never are.[32]

Here Blair is expressing his doubts about opinion polls[33] and focus groups. At the end of his memoirs he goes even further, explaining that politics is not a question of following the people's mood, but of taking the lead. During his long experience as a prime minister, ten years at the helm of the British government, he had learned in his day-to-day practice that the reality of politics is not demand-side politics but supply-side politics. "I had started," he writes,

> by buying the notion, and then selling the notion, that to be in touch with opinion was the definition of good leadership. I was ending by counting such a notion of little value and defining leadership not as knowing what people wanted and trying to satisfy them, but knowing what I thought was in their best interests and trying to do so. Pleasing all of the people all of the time was not possible; but even if it had been, it was a worthless ambition. In the name of leadership, it devalued leadership. None of this meant or means that the leader should not seek to persuade, and in doing so use all the powers of charm, argument and persuasion at their command. That's tactics, and they should be deployed effectively and competently. The strategy should be to point to where the best future lies and get people to move in that direction.[34]

Blair's "confession of faith" is one of the strongest and best formulated statements in favor of supply-side democracy: the conviction that politicians should not slavishly follow "public opinion" and should not be afraid to take the lead.[35] "A *leader*," writes Robert Nozick, "is able to weld people's diverse aspirations and activities into a coordinated pattern directed toward particular goals. There are many worthwhile things people can do together. A nation can concentrate upon reducing poverty or advancing serious culture or developing new technology or maximizing individual liberty ... A leader functions to resolve this competition of goals; he provides a vision of a desirable goal, articulates a feasible plan for reaching it, and inspires enough people to move along that path, following him."[36] This does not, however, mean that a leader can "sell" anything. He or she must take into account the aspirations, needs, and demands of the people: the "supply-side" has to take into account the "demand-side," however amorphous and contradictory these demands may be.

Deliberative democracy: an attractive model?

But do we have to acquiesce in this situation? Is it not a perversion of the meaning of democracy that people expect leadership and, rather than demand of politicians that they implement their wishes and demands, tend to vote for parties out of habit without even reading their programs? This is a question raised by James Fishkin, an American political scientist. Fishkin admits that "the public has fewer 'opinions' deserving of the name than are routinely reported in polls. Respondents to polls do not like to admit that they 'don't know' so they will choose an option, virtually at random, rather than respond that they have never thought about the issue."[37] "The public," he continues, "is usually not very informed, engaged, or attentive."[38] Fishkin believes that people have a lack of knowledge about politics. The problem is that they don't really feel this to be a handicap, which is the reason why "it is difficult to effectively motivate citizens in mass society to become informed."[39] Fishkin considers this situation unacceptable. "A democracy of elites or opinion leaders," he writes, "would at best be a democracy *for the people*, but not one in any significant sense *by the people*."[40]

What can be done? Fishkin distinguishes between "raw public opinion," which "is routinely voiced by all the established institutions of mass democracy – initiatives, referenda, public opinion polls, focus groups,"[41] and "refined public opinion," which is the product of deliberation and debate in representative bodies. Fishkin compares both and finds limitations in each. "Raw public opinion" is uninformed and therefore debilitated. "Refined public opinion" is the result of informed deliberation and debate in parliaments. However, the latter creates a "filter," because "at their best, such institutions are sensitive not just to what constituents actually think, but also to what they would think if they were better informed."[42] The decisions taken by representatives are, therefore, only *interpretations* of what the people would have decided had they been better informed.

Fishkin wants to "repair" the deficiencies of both "raw public opinion" and the existing "refined public opinion" of the representative bodies. It is clear that he is not a supporter of initiatives and referendums and other tools of direct democracy, because these only produce "raw," uninformed public opinion. On the other hand, neither is he satisfied with the existing representative democracy, because this puts a "filter" between the interpretation of the wishes of the public and the real wishes of the public had they the chance to deliberate. What must be done, therefore, is to create an informed public, and this can only be done by debate and deliberation. Fishkin gives examples of "deliberative polls," a method which would overcome the existing deficiencies. The first was organized in Great Britain in May 1994, when three hundred randomly selected voters participated in the world's first nationally televised deliberative poll. "The idea is simple," writes Fishkin:

> Take a national random sample of the electorate and transport those people from all over the country to a single place. Immerse the sample in the issues, with carefully balanced briefing materials, with intensive discussions in small groups, and with the chance to question competing experts and politicians. At the end of several days of working through the issues face to face, poll the participants in detail. The resulting survey offers a representation of the considered judgments of the public – the views the entire country would come to if it had the same experience of behaving more like ideal citizens immersed in the issues for an extended period.[43]

One of the projects supervised by Fishkin was *What's Next California*. A selected group of 412 voters was gathered during the weekend of 24–26 June 2011 to discuss the system of direct democracy in California. The randomly selected group stayed together for some days to discuss specific political items. The participants got background information and encountered supporters and opponents of proposals, as well as the intervention of experts and specialists. This process of deliberation caused a section of the public to revise its earlier held opinions. Such an informed debate should be the basis of a deliberative democracy, argues the author: "It allows a microcosm of the country to make recommendations to us all after it has had the chance to think through the issues. If such a poll were broadcast before an election or a referendum, it could dramatically affect the outcome."[44]

The question, however, is: Would it? There is the problem that the participants of such groups, despite the claim that they are "representative samples" of the population, are often not wholly representative and that some categories are overrepresented (for instance those people who are interested enough to participate).[45] But let us assume for a moment that the participants of the sample are completely representative – what then? What does it matter for the rest of the population if this small sample has changed its "raw opinion" into an informed "refined opinion"? Should they follow this informed vanguard which has no legal status and does not represent anything other than their own opinion, which is suddenly presented as "informed"? There is, of course, the possibility that the outcome of such a small-group deliberative process could be followed by a popular vote. However, neither can there be any guarantee that the "refined opinion" will prevail against the "raw opinion" of the rest of the population. Achen and Bartels give an example of such a process in Canada, which is not encouraging. "The practical impact of deliberative theory," they write,

> has been quite modest. The most cited and studied attempts to "scale up" these idealized models of democratic decision-making were large-scale, government-sponsored "citizens' assemblies" intended to consider changes in the election laws of the Canadian provinces of British Columbia and Ontario. In each case, a body of ordinary citizens engaged in an elaborately funded year-long process of education, consultation, and deliberation aimed at recommending a new voting rule to be employed in provincial elections. And in each case, their nearly unanimous recommendation was decisively rejected by their fellow citizens in a subsequent referendum.[46]

In order to overcome these limitations the only solution that would give these deliberations clout and legitimacy is to organize them for the electorate *as a whole*. Therefore, Fishkin came up with a bold proposal, which he called "simple but ambitious." This proposal is to organize a national "Deliberation Day." "Our idea," he writes,

> is simply to have a national holiday in which all voters would be invited and incentivized to participate in local, randomly assigned discussion groups as a preparation to the voting process a week later. Candidates for the major parties would make presentations

transmitted by national media and local small group discussions would identify key questions that would be directed to local party representatives in relatively small-scale town meetings held simultaneously all over the country. A key point is that incentives would be paid for each citizen to participate in this full day's work of citizenship.[47]

Fishkin proposes paying each participant $150. He is very optimistic about the eventual results, writing that "even one day's serious discussion can have a dramatic effect on ordinary citizens becoming more informed and changing their preferences in significant ways."[48]

This proposal is at first sight more realistic. It no longer proposes the formation of a deliberating sample which acts as an "informed vanguard" for the rest of the population, but the whole population is invited and the results are not binding but only a support for making better-informed choices in the election one week later. But is one day really enough to change a "raw" public opinion into a "refined" public opinion? And how many citizens would participate in this "Deliberation Day"? Would they not prefer to spend their new holiday doing other activities: picnicking, jogging, or watching baseball on TV? Is a payment of $150 enough to attract ordinary citizens who are scarcely interested in politics? Won't the items to be discussed be exactly those items which are formulated by politicians and written down in party programs, instead of proposals made by citizens in a bottom-up process? Would not a passionate minority, which would be eager to come, dominate the discussions? With the result that those voters, who are already among the best informed, will further "refine" their choice, while the broad mass of people will stay behind, satisfied with what social scientists contemptuously call "raw" public opinion? Or, worse, would it not in an extremely polarized country such as the United States, which is divided along political, racial, and cultural lines, exacerbate this polarization instead of easing it? These are pertinent questions. Promoting a "deliberative democracy" could certainly make a positive contribution to the formation of an informed citizenry, and seems, therefore, to be a sympathetic initiative – but in practice it would not fundamentally change supply-side politics.

Notes

1. Joseph. A. Schumpeter, *Capitalism, Socialism, and Democracy* (New York and London: Harper and Brothers Publishers, 1947).
2. Ibid., p. 250.
3. Ibid., p. 250.
4. Ibid., p. 251.
5. Ibid., p. 252.
6. Ibid., p. 252.

7   Ibid., p. 253.
8   Ibid., p. 253.
9   Ibid., pp. 253-254.
10 Ibid., p. 254.
11 Ibid., p. 255.
12 Ibid., p. 269.
13 A similar vision had already been developed by Max Weber in 1918. "The politically passive 'mass' does not generate the leader," he wrote, "rather the political leader seeks followers and wins the mass with "demagoguery" (Max Weber, "Parlament und Regierung im neugeordneten Deutschland. Zur politischen Kritik des Beamtentums und Parteiwesens," in Max Weber, *Schriften 1894-1922* (Stuttgart: Alfred Kröner Verlag, 2002), p. 423.
14 Schumpeter, *Capitalism*, p. 270. An example of the appeal of a new political offer is the proposal to introduce a "basic income" in France, made by the socialist presidential candidate Benoît Hamon during the presidential campaign of 2016-2017. This proposal was possibly a determining factor in him winning the primaries of the Socialist Party. However, it was not enough to win the presidency.
15 Achen and Bartels, *Democracy for Realists*, p. 306.
16 Ibid., p. 1.
17 Ibid., p. 19.
18 Ibid., p. 304.
19 Ibid., pp. 304-305.
20 Ibid., p. 299. A similar assessment is made by Gabriel Almond and Bingham Powell, Jr., who write: "Popular control over political leaders is the sustaining myth of democracy." However, "without accurate knowledge of the actions of officeholders and without an understanding of the relationship between those actions and popular goals, a meaningful articulation of interests and exercise of political checks is impossible" (Gabriel A. Almond and G. Bingham Powell, Jr., *Comparative Politics – A Developmental Approach* (Boston: Little, Brown and Company, 1966), p. 186). The authors conclude that "the issues involved in many public activities may well be so complex and specialized that the public is in no position to judge whether what was done was better or worse than any alternatives" (p. 187).
21 Achen and Bartels, *Democracy for Realists*, p. 232.
22 Ibid., pp. 233-234.
23 Ibid., p. 233.
24 Ibid., p. 17.
25 The authors cite the example of the federal budget deficit: "The deficit had decreased by more than half during Bill Clinton's first term as president; yet most Republicans in a 1996 survey managed to convince themselves that it had increased" (ibid., p. 17).
26 Ibid., p. 320.
27 Kenneth R. Minogue, *The Liberal Mind – A Critical Analysis of the Philosophy of Liberalism and its Political Effects* (New York: Vintage Books, 1968), p. 97.
28 Anthony Seldon, *Blair* (London: The Free Press, 2005), p. 130.
29 Ibid., pp. 130-131.
30 Ibid., p. 283.
31 Tony Blair, *A Journey – My Political Life* (New York and Toronto: Alfred A. Knopf, 2010), pp. 24-25.
32 Ibid., p. 298.
33 Pierre Rosanvallon writes that opinion polls tend to present society as a person: "'The French no longer believe in their elites', 'the French reject the parties', 'the French

want to preserve social security' ... in the comments a figure is depicted whose morale, moods, expectations, demands are discovered." Rosanvallon calls it "a certain return to a vision of a nation understood as an entity, with its own, clearly recognizable character" (Rosanvallon, *Peuple introuvable*, p. 444).

34 Blair, *A Journey*, p. 652. Samuel Beer points to the fact that the British constitutional practice favored such a more leadership-oriented stance, because it "had already endowed a Prime Minister with certain well-understood elements of authority and these, in turn, strengthened the position of a party Leader who, although in Opposition, was a potential Prime Minister. When, for instance, a party Leader was summoned by the monarch to accept the commission to form a Government, the Leader made his own decision whether to accept and, if he accepted, what persons to select for his Cabinet. In Cabinet meetings, while he might 'take the voices' on a controverted question, he was not bound to accept the majority view: after all, he had the authority to secure the dismissal of any minister. Similarly, the decision on the resignation of the Government or a request for the dissolution of Parliament was his sole decision" (Samuel Beer, *Modern British Politics – A Study of Parties and Pressure Groups* (London: Faber and Faber, 1969), p. 156).

35 Harry Johnson, referring to the 1946 study "Public Opinion and the Legislative Process" by Cantwell, writes that the study "shows how timid most legislators are in declaring their opinion before finding out what 'the public' thinks. Their fear of not *following* the public correctly amounts to cowardice" (Harry M. Johnson, *Sociology – A Systematic Introduction* (London: Routledge & Kegan Paul Ltd., 1964), p. 351). In the same vein H. L. A. Hart writes: "Even the most high-minded politician may want to stay in office, and a pliant or passive attitude to what the majority thinks right makes this easier than a stern adherence to the theory that his duty is to do what he thinks right, and then to accept his dismissal if he cannot persuade the majority to retain him" (H. L. A. Hart, *Law, Liberty, and Morality* (Stanford: Stanford University Press, 1963), p. 81).

36 Robert Nozick, *Examined Life – Philosophical Meditations* (New York and London: Simon & Schuster Inc., 1989), p. 175.

37 James S. Fishkin, *When the People Speak – Deliberative Democracy and Public Consultation* (Oxford and New York: Oxford University Press, 2011), p. 2.

38 Ibid., p. 13.
39 Ibid., p. 2.
40 Ibid., p. 7.
41 Ibid., p. 14.
42 Ibid., p. 14.
43 James S. Fishkin, *The Voice of the People – Public Opinion and Democracy* (New Haven and London: Yale University Press, 1997), p. 162.
44 Ibid., p. 162.
45 Fishkin himself gives the example of *CaliforniaSpeaks*, a health care deliberation in California, for which 120,000 people were initially solicited. Of the 3,500 people who finally participated, only 60 percent came from this group. About 40 percent were "indirectly recruited" (21 percent friends or family who came along to the event and 19 percent persons recruited by interest groups or grass-roots organizations). Fishkin, *When the People Speak*, p. 219, footnote 14.
46 Achen and Bartels, *Democracy for Realists*, p. 302.
47 Fishkin, *When the People Speak*, pp. 29–30.
48 Ibid., p. 30.

7

Referendums and popular initiatives: can one have too much democracy?

Some analysts suggest that the present crisis of liberal democracy is a sign that our democratic system has become obsolete and no longer represents the will of the people. Their conclusion is that we urgently need *more* democracy and, in particular, more *direct* democracy. According to the proponents of this view, plebiscites, referendums, and popular initiatives would provide, if not a complete and sufficient solution, at least an indispensable means for the popular will to express itself more directly. These analysts do not normally pay attention to the fact that in the past plebiscites, rather than being instruments of democratic governments, were the instruments of choice of autocratic regimes. The word "bonapartism," for instance, is intimately linked with the use of this instrument. Plebiscites were used by Napoleon Bonaparte, as well as by his nephew Louis Napoleon (Napoleon III), to legitimate an autocratic regime after a *coup d'état*.[1] In 1934, after the death of President Von Hindenburg, Adolf Hitler similarly organized a plebiscite on merging the functions of president and chancellor in order to consolidate his absolute power. There exist, therefore, sufficient reasons to be circumspect about the introduction of this instrument, and in particular, if one wants referendums to take place regularly.

The British Brexit drama

On 23 June 2016, British prime minister David Cameron organized a referendum on the question of whether the UK should leave or remain in the European Union. One of the reasons for his initiative was the rise of the United Kingdom Independence Party (UKIP), a populist Eurosceptic party led by Nigel Farage. In the 2014 election for the European Parliament this party, founded in 1993, won 27.5 percent of the vote and surpassed not only the ruling Conservative Party but also Labour, the official party of opposition. For Cameron this was writing on the wall. The referendum was intended to silence once and for all those who wanted Britain to leave the European Union – including the eurosceptics in his own party.

It was not only UKIP which supported the Leave vote. Prominent Conservatives were also involved. One of them was Boris Johnson, the former mayor of London, who toured the country with a "battle bus" with on its side the text: "We send the EU £350 million a week." This was a blatantly false claim, as was also the promise: "Let's fund the NHS [National Health Service] instead."[2]

Against all expectations – not least Cameron's – the referendum was won by the Leave vote by 51.9 percent to 48.1 percent. The total turnout was high: 71.8 percent. However, there were major regional disparities. In England and Wales majorities voted for Brexit, but this was not the case in Scotland and Northern Ireland. In Scotland a majority of 62 percent backed the Remain vote; in Northern Ireland this was 55.8 percent. Although Theresa May, who succeeded David Cameron as prime minister, was in favor of Remain she committed herself to delivering Brexit and "executing the people's will." The UK was expected to leave the EU on 29 March 2019 – two years after the government invoked Article 50 of the Lisbon Treaty. However, the withdrawal agreement, negotiated by Theresa May with the EU, was rejected three times by the parliament in Westminster, creating a legal impasse and obliging Theresa May to ask Brussels for a seven-month extension until 31 October 2019.

The Brexit vote had a number of unintended consequences. One of these was that it bolstered the Scottish independence movement. In 2014 a majority of 55.3 percent of the Scottish population had rejected independence in a referendum. However, the fact that a majority of Scottish voters were in favor of Remain could lead to a quite different result in a new referendum. Another unintended consequence of the Brexit referendum was a return of the "Northern Irish Question." The British divorce from the EU would imply a return of the 210-mile border between Ireland and Northern Ireland. The return of a hard border with checkpoints and customs posts was a nightmare, because it could jeopardize the still fragile peace in this part of the UK and reignite the Troubles, which ended with the Good Friday Agreement in April 1998. For this reason Theresa May negotiated a "backstop" with Brussels, which meant that there wouldn't be a hard border between the two countries and that Northern Ireland would remain aligned to a series of EU regulations, especially on food and goods standards. However, such a "soft" Brexit was unacceptable for Leavers who were in favor of a "hard Brexit" and even a "no deal" Brexit if no common ground with the EU could be found. Theresa May succeeded neither in convincing parliament, nor in convincing her own colleagues: several cabinet ministers left the government. The deadlock meant that Britain participated in 2019 once more in elections for the

European Parliament. The election led to a resounding victory of the Brexit Party, founded only some months before by Nigel Farage, who had left UKIP. The party got 31.6 percent of the vote, while the Conservative Party got only 9.1 percent, the worst result since the party was founded almost 200 years previously.

On 7 June 2019, Theresa May stepped down as leader of the Conservative Party, making place for a new prime minister to be elected in July 2019. She had failed to complete her major task: delivering Brexit. The new prime minister would be chosen by party members from two candidates selected by the parliamentary group, a new procedure intended to give the rank and file of the party more power. On 23 July 2019, "Brexiteer" Boris Johnson, the maverick who helped orchestrate the Leave campaign, was elected party leader. One day later he became the new prime minister. A poll conducted by YouGov had already revealed a radicalization of the Conservative membership. In its report one could read that "a majority (54%) would be willing to countenance the destruction of their own party if necessary."[3] This was not all. "Asked whether they would rather avert Brexit if it would lead to Scotland or Northern Ireland breaking away from the UK, respectively 63% and 59% of party members would be willing to pay for Brexit with the breakup of the United Kingdom."[4] In recent years the Conservative Party has recruited many new members. Membership has leapt to 160,000 from 124,000 in 2018. More than three-quarters of members who joined after the 2017 general election back a "no deal," while this is 60 percent for pre-2015 members. This has led to presumptions of massive entryism by former UKIP supporters, known as "Blukips."[5]

British politics increasingly resembled a battlefield on which a religious war was being fought, in which there seemed no place left for rational arguments. It is ironic that a hard Brexit (not to speak of a "no deal" Brexit) would possibly not only lead to a break-up of the country, but also to harsh external tariffs which would hit in particular those parts of the country that voted to leave. Three years after the Brexit referendum the UK resembled a rudderless ship. And one may ask oneself how it was possible that a parliament that in 1865 was praised by John Bright as "the mother of parliaments" had changed into a collection of warring factions, unable to take a decision on one of the most important questions of its existence. This self-effacement of the British parliament is even more astonishing when one takes into account that in June 2016, at the time of the referendum, a majority of Cameron's cabinet (twenty-four of thirty ministers), as well as a vast majority of 73.6 percent of British MPs, were in favor of EU membership. These included 185 Conservative MPs, 218 Labour MPs, 54 SNP MPs, and 8 Liberal Democrat MPs.[6] Representative government, for centuries the cornerstone of British politics, seemed to have fallen prey to one of the most polarizing forms of populism.

Do we have too much democracy or not enough?

After May's resignation the Brexit drama was far from over. The new prime minister, Boris Johnson, was forced by parliament to ask the EU for a new delay – this time until 31 January 2020. The parliamentary election, organized on 12 December 2019, was won by Johnson with the catchy campaign slogan "Get Brexit done." According to Simon Usherwood, a politics professor at the University of Surrey, "Get Brexit done" was successful because it was "clear, memorable" and "taps into that sense of frustration that others feel that this is dragging on and on." He noted that the phrase is "not inviting people to think about how it is done, or where it might lead, but really just to say: Let's get this out of the way, and then we can think of all the other things."[7]

How populists manipulated the Dutch Ukraine referendum

Britain is not the only case of a referendum that was hijacked by populists. In the last decade pressure from civil society has led in different countries to the introduction of referendums or people's initiatives. An example is a law that came into force on 1 July 2015 in the Netherlands, which gave Dutch citizens the right to take the initiative for an advisory referendum on laws and treaties which were adopted by parliament. The legislative proposal was made by three left-leaning parties: the Labour Party (PvdA), the Green Left party, and D66.[8] It was in particular the center-left D66, a party which has been a fervent promotor of more direct citizen participation in the democratic decision-making process, which was in favor of this new law. After its adoption the general feeling was that it would take some time before the population would make use of this new right. This was because of two inbuilt hurdles: in order to organize a referendum one needed to collect a minimum of 300,000 signatures, and for the result to be valid at least 30 percent of the electorate had to participate in the vote (about 4 million people).

However, it took only a few months before an organization called GeenPeil, a platform of three cooperating populist, Eurosceptic groups, jumped at the opportunity.[9] Its target was a law passed in 2015 by the two chambers of the Dutch parliament which had given the green light for the ratification of the Ukraine–European Union Association Agreement. By September 2015 the organizers of the initiative had gathered 427,939 valid signatures, and on 6 April 2016 the referendum took place. According to the Dutch journalist Laura Starink, a former correspondent in Moscow for the Dutch paper *NRC Handelsblad*, "a quick glance at the website [of GeenPeil] makes clear that the followers have developed ... a pure hatred of Ukraine."[10] This hatred was incomprehensible, because the referendum was organized just a year and nine months after the downing of the Malaysian civilian plane MH17 by a Russian BUK missile above eastern Ukraine. In this criminal act the crew and all passengers died. Of the 298 victims 196 were Dutch citizens, many of them children. One would have expected, therefore, rather sympathy for Ukraine and hate for the aggressor, Russia. This was not the case. On the contrary, the strangest arguments were used, such as the agreement would be a "provocation" of the aggressor, Russia.

The main target of the No campaign, however, was not Ukraine but the EU, and its supposedly undemocratic character. One can certainly criticize the democratic governance of the EU and argue that it could be improved. But this is obviously not a reason to reject an agreement which is in the interest of both the EU and Ukraine, an agreement which brings not only economic benefits, but also has important geopolitical implications for the future of Europe. The referendum led to a heated debate between advocates and opponents of the agreement. On 6 April 2016, the "no" vote won with 61 percent of the vote. Because 32 percent of the population had voted, the vote was declared valid. This meant that – due to the high numbers abstaining – only a small minority of the electorate, in fact a mere 19.7 percent, had been able to go against a law that had been passed by majorities in both chambers of parliament. It put the Dutch government in an awkward position. Although the referendum was only advisory and had no binding character, the government had promised to take the result of the referendum "seriously" and, eventually, renegotiate some aspects of the agreement in Brussels. However, it was clear that the Dutch government could not (and did not want to) block an agreement which had already been ratified by the parliaments of all other EU member states.

This first experience with the new law, therefore, was a wet blanket. The feeling was that a law which was considered to enhance the influence of the ordinary citizen had been hijacked by Eurosceptic populists. The disappointment was felt in particular by D66, a pro-European party, which was the national champion of demanding "more democracy" and was intending to take the next step by introducing also *binding* referendums in the Netherlands. However, in a poll of D66 voters almost one year after the vote, half of the respondents wanted to abolish all referendums, while only 25 percent wanted to keep the advisory referendum. It was telling that only a small minority of 17 percent was still in favor of both advisory and binding referendums.[11] In the Dutch press also there were many negative comments. One analyst warned against "Californian situations."[12] The Raad van State (State Council), the highest court of the Netherlands which also advises the government, wrote a critical comment in its 2016 Annual Report.[13] It emphasized that

> The democratic rule of law, as it has developed [in the Netherlands] in the past two centuries, is based on the concept of representative democracy … However, in everyday language the concept "representation" has changed its meaning. It is scarcely still considered as "representation", but rather as a "principal–agent relationship." In this schedule

the representative acts as the *agent* for his followers, the *principal*. The authority of parliament is conceived as an authority which is derived from the people. According to this vision models of popular democracy are more democratic, because the *principal* decides himself instead of the *agent* ... In addition the representatives themselves are increasingly regarding and behaving themselves as an *agent* for their followers, rather than as a member of a collective. The latest variant considers the parliamentarian as a mouthpiece of opinion polls or as a voice of the silent majority.[14]

The Dutch State Council continued:

> Governance in modern society is a non-stop "business", in which lawgiving and government policy are not the addition of isolated decisions. They are a coherent totality of decisions and measures, which are continuously focused to serve concrete common interests. In this process one has to weigh continuously rights and obligations, advantages and disadvantages, diverging interests and contradictions in society, which have to be coordinated and reconciled. Representative democracy is meant to put this responsibility for a global consideration also in an assembly which is permanently concerned about and responsible to the population for the way in which it serves the common interest. This is in conflict with the ad-hoc character of decision-making through referenda, incidental involvement of citizens and other forms of involvement without responsibility for the consequences.[15]

On 27 September 2017, the parliamentary bill to introduce a binding referendum in the Netherlands came to parliament for a second reading. This was necessary because the bill, which had already been adopted by both houses of parliament, required a change in the Constitution. Therefore a second reading was necessary after the 2017 election in which a majority of two-thirds in both houses was required. It was telling that even the three parties which had taken the initiative for the law – the Labour Party, the Green Left Party, and D66 – no longer upheld the proposal.[16] On 22 February 2018, a majority of the Dutch parliament went further still and abolished the advisory referendum.

Direct democracy in California: a blocked system?

In the Dutch debate described above some analysts referred to the situation in California. California is, indeed, often mentioned as an example of derailed direct democracy. Californians adopted the initiative more than a century ago, on 10 October 1911. It was a product of the "Progressive Era," the period at the beginning of the twentieth century in which there was a popular upheaval against moneyed interests and local party bosses.[17] It led to a movement in favor of strengthening direct democracy at state level, consisting of four measures: the initiative, the popular referendum, constitutional amendments, and the recall of elected officials. The "initiative" meant a new proposal formulated by a citizen or a group of citizens, and the "popular referendum" made it possible to reject a measure which had already been adopted by the state legislature. The constitutional amendments were proposals to change the state constitution, while the "recall" meant that office-holders who had lost the confidence of the voters could be ousted before the legal conclusion of their term.

Direct democracy in California is, therefore, a long-established practice. From 1911 through November 2014, 364 initiatives qualified for the statewide ballot. Voters have approved 123, which is an approval rate of about 34 percent.[18] This system worked reasonably well for the first sixty-seven years, due to the fact that most of the time the instrument was used sparingly. However, things changed fundamentally when a man named Howard Jarvis, who headed an association of property owners, started a tax revolt in the 1970s. The reason was that the property tax paid by house owners more than doubled between 1972 and 1977, due to rising house prices. Jarvis started an initiative, which would become known as Proposition 13, which cut the property-tax rate from about 2.6 percent to 1 percent. It also limited the increase in assessed property values to a maximum of 2 percent a year. In order to prevent other taxes being imposed to compensate for the financial loss, Proposition 13 also required two-thirds majorities in the state legislature for future tax increases. On 6 June 1978, Californians voted on Proposition 13, which was accepted by a great majority.

The immediate consequence was that for local governments the revenue from property taxes fell by more than half. Cities and counties sounded the alarm and threatened to lay off teachers and to cut medical and welfare services. The state jumped in and decided to bail them out, paying a sum which was roughly equivalent to their loss in tax revenues. One year later this emergency measure was made permanent. In exchange the state also became responsible for collecting the (reduced) property tax. It meant that school districts, cities, and counties lost their budget independence and became dependent on the central state government.

With hindsight Proposition 13 was a watershed event: since then the state government has had to operate in the financial straitjacket imposed by Proposition 13. This has led to major budget crises and a massive deterioration of public services. In 1999, twenty years after the adoption of Proposition 13, Peter Schrag wrote in a book with the telling title *Paradise Lost* the following:

> Some twenty years have passed since the passage of California's proposition 13, which set in motion not merely the holy crusade against taxes in which much of the country now seems irretrievably stuck, but a condition of permanent neopopulism in California, and to some extent elsewhere, for which there is no real precedent, even in the Progressive Era of the early years of the twentieth century. During the two decades since the passage of 13, California has been in nearly constant revolt against representative government.[19]

Do we have too much democracy or not enough?

Schrag gave a devastating account of the dire consequences of this populist tax revolt:

> California's schools, which, thirty years ago, had been among the most generously funded in the nation, are now in the bottom quarter among the states in virtually every major indicator – in their physical condition, in public funding, in test scores ... The state, which has almost doubled in population since the early 1960s, has built some twenty new prisons in the past two decades. But it has not opened one new campus of the University of California for nearly three decades. Its once-celebrated freeway system is now rated as among the most dilapidated road networks in the country. Many of its public libraries operate on reduced hours, and some have closed altogether. The state and county parks charge hefty admission fees. The state's social benefits, once among the nation's most generous, have been cut, and cut again, and then cut again. And what had once been a tuition-free college and university system, while still among the world's great public educational institutions, struggles for funds and charges as much as every other state university system, and in some cases more.[20]

Schrag wrote these words in 1999. Ten years on, apparently nothing had changed. On the contrary, a huge budget deficit led to a recall petition against Democratic governor Gray Davis, who was replaced mid-term. Even in California this was a unique event.[21] The recall process was heavily criticized. James Fishkin spoke about a "near-circus atmosphere of the California gubernatorial recall election," which would provide "a disquieting counterpart to the serious democratic expectations of ... the Progressive reformers who designed it."[22] The new governor, who replaced Gray Davis, was the Republican candidate and Hollywood movie star Arnold Schwarzenegger. Unfortunately, during his governorship (2003–2011) no improvement could be observed either: the budget deficit deepened further and by the end of his term his popularity had reached the same low level as his predecessor's.

In a special report the magazine *The Economist* expressed its concern, writing that in the mid-1970s "California had an AAA credit rating, the best there is. Today its rating is A–, the worst among all 50 states and not much better than 'junk.'"[23] The report averred that "the state has, at least for the time being, ceased to be the world's dream factory. Instead California is now called a 'dysfunctional', 'ungovernable' and even 'failed' state."[24] Schwarzenegger blamed the popular initiatives. "All of those propositions tell us how we must spend our money," he said. "This is no way, of course, to run a state."[25] Jack Citrin, a professor of political science at the University of California, Berkeley, wrote: "In a sense, the bargaining and coalition-building that used to be a feature of the legislative process now has moved into the arena of direct democracy, stage managed by lobbyists and campaign consultants. Incredibly complex policy matters are being decided by voters with limited knowledge and it is easy to point to unintended consequences that pose serious adjustment problems. And while the academic and political establishment rail against the excesses of the initiative process, no serious reform seems likely. The mistrust of elected officials that helped fuel Proposition 13 remains intact."[26]

Direct democracy as a business

The excesses to which Citrin referred were many. Proposition 13 led to a surge in initiatives, changing the very character of the initiatives in the process. Gathering the necessary signatures became a business, in which idealistic volunteers were replaced by paid "circulators." "The circulators are independent contractors who work for several petition-management firms at the same time and often have four or more petitions simultaneously on their folding tables ... A hard-working and determined circulator can earn up to $50 an hour. Since paid circulators, unlike volunteers, are interested only in volume, not the underlying cause, the quality of the signatures is low."[27]

The paid circulators have driven up the cost of getting a proposition on the ballot. If a proposition gets the necessary number of signatures, the costs further explode, due to expensive TV campaigns and state-wide direct mailing actions. Before Proposition 13, spending on initiatives was about $9m per election; ten years later it was $127m.[28] The consequence is that a process which was originally meant as a "safety valve" for citizens to correct the legislature, has become an instrument of corporate interests which possess the necessary financial means to start an initiative or attack an initiative with a counter-initiative. Measures to protect the environment or improve the health of citizens, for instance, are attacked by companies which fear that these measures will negatively impact their sales. Plastic bag makers wanted to stop California from banning plastic bags that litter the state. The cigarette industry, too, was active: "Altria, R. J. Reynolds ... knowing that price increases will cost them customers, have spent $66.3 million to defeat Proposition 56, the $2-per-pack tobacco tax hike. Philip Morris USA and its related entities alone have given almost $41 million to the opposition campaign."[29]

Against the spirit in which they were intended, popular initiatives became increasingly dominated by big moneyed interests. But this was not all. In the fall of 2016 California's Legislative Analyst's Office authored a report that Proposition 13, which Jack Citrin had declared "was opposed by the elite, supported by the masses,"[30] had been in particular a boon to wealthier Californians. "Because higher-income households own more higher-value homes and Proposition 13 tax relief is proportionate to home wealth," wrote the authors, "the majority of Proposition 13 tax relief (in dollar terms) goes to higher-income households."[31] Additionally, local communities, being deprived of the property tax instrument, had increased sales and utility taxes, which impose a relatively higher burden on lower-income citizens. The authors of the report concluded: "Proposition 13 didn't necessarily relieve Californians of paying for the services they demand from local government; but it did produce a change in who pays the price. In many respects, the burden has been shifted down the income scale, so that the poorer taxpayers are shouldering more of these costs."[32] It is telling that it took almost four decades to find this out.

The commercialization of Californian direct democracy has led to much criticism. According to James Fishkin,

> direct democracy in California was born in the hopes of bringing the people into the governance process, but it has led to a kind of audience democracy. Voters have become consumers of television sound-bite campaigns and new-media messaging, not authors of the laws they give to themselves. It was supposed to take the role of money out of politics but it has, instead, created a vast appetite for advertising. Getting on the ballot costs millions of dollars to pay for professional signature gatherers because the threshold of signatures required is so high (5 percent of the number of voters who turned out in the last election for statutes, and 8 percent for constitutional amendments). So instead of the process being open to everyone, it is open mostly to those organized interests that can pay the entrance fee.[33]

The commercialization also led to a *spamming effect*, due to the overload of ballot propositions. In 2016 another analyst called the California ballot for this reason "an epic joke."[34] "I'm talking about the California November voter guide," he wrote, "which this year clocks in at 224 pages, thanks to 17 statewide ballot propositions – the longest ballot in a quarter-century ... In 2016, the Golden State's experiment with direct democracy has imploded, producing little more than outsized salaries for a handful of political consultants. Somebody needs to tranquilize this beast and end our misery."[35] The author concluded: "Plenty of Californians carp about state government, but I can't find one who truly believes it's a good idea to become a state legislator once every two years. We hire people to do the job through elections, and we have plenty of ways to hold them accountable ... To fix the excesses of direct democracy, it will take representative democracy."[36]

Representative democracy has a unique, important quality, which distinguishes it from direct democracy. In the words of the British political scientist Bernard Crick: "MPs do have a valuable and specific kind of knowledge rarely possessed by outside experts, civil servants or even, one should dangerously add, by Ministers who have been in office too long: political knowledge. They know that politics is the art and skill of conciliating, in some creative manner, differing interests."[37]

James Madison's warning against "factions"

In the *Federalist Papers* James Madison warned against the formation of "factions." A faction was, for Madison, "a number of citizens, whether amounting to a majority or minority of the whole, who are united and actuated by some common impulse of passion, or of interest, adverse to the rights of other citizens, or to the permanent and aggregate interests of the community."[38] According to Madison, "the most common and durable source of factions has been the various and unequal distribution of property. Those who hold and those who are without property have ever formed distinct interests in society."[39] What Madison feared was that democracy could threaten the property interests of the rich. However, in twenty-first-century California rather the contrary is the case: it is the rich who threaten the interests of the poor.

With all these problems one would expect that in recent years the appetite of the Californian population for direct democracy would have diminished. However, this seems not to be the case. James Fishkin and colleagues conducted a project called "What's Next California?"[40] This project was, according to the organizers, the first statewide "deliberative poll." In this project, which took place in Torrance, California, over the weekend of 24–26 June 2011, a scientific sample of 412 registered voters was gathered, to discuss thirty proposals in four basic areas: the initiative process, the legislature, state/local relations, and tax/fiscal issues.[41] The participants were asked to answer questions before and after they had a chance to intensively discuss the different arguments. "Despite the evident problems," wrote Fishkin, "California voters have more confidence in the ballot initiative than they do in other elements of their state government. After spending a weekend immersing themselves in the issues and questioning competing experts about possible reforms, 65 percent of the sample expressed disappointment with California's state government in general and 70 percent expressed disappointment in the Legislature, but only 37 percent were disappointed in the ballot initiative."[42] The voters' disappointment in the government and in the legislature is an expression of a lack of trust in the chosen representatives. Since the 1980s this lack of trust seems to have become a general feature of electorates in Western countries.

The erosion of social solidarity

However, Peter Schrag points to another possible explanation of the explosion of popular initiatives in California: demographics. "The state's latter-day populism," he writes, "and the squeeze on taxes and public services it brought, occurred precisely during the period when the state was undergoing those demographic changes: from a society that thought of itself (and in many ways was) overwhelmingly white and middle class to one in which whites will soon be just another minority and where Hispanics, Asians, and blacks already constitute a sizeable majority in school enrollment and in the use of many other public services."[43] The question for this white middle class is whether it is prepared to pay "for them," the others. What is at stake here is a question of social solidarity and the feeling of belonging together, of being members of one nation. In essence it is the same problem as in Italy, where the Northern League (Lega Nord, now called Lega) was unwilling to pay for the poorer parts of Italy, and the same problem as in Belgium, where the far-right Flemish (Dutch-speaking) populist party Vlaams Belang (Flemish Interest) was unwilling to pay for the poorer and French-speaking Walloons.

In California this problem is not only a question of massive (and often illegal) immigration. The problem is compounded by the "rootlessness" of many new inhabitants. Schrag speaks about "a place inhabited by ... 'resident expatriates' ... These global citizens, regardless of race and ethnicity, have only a tentative loyalty to the place where they live or to anything – other than perhaps their own ethnic group, or native village, or gated development, or elite school – that would resemble a nation or community."[44] California, this shining example of "the global village," seems to have become an example of a state where demographic changes have led to a lack of social cohesion and a loss of "social capital," such as has been described by Robert D. Putnam in his book *Bowling Alone*. "In the 1990s roughly three in four Americans *didn't* trust the [federal] government to do what is right most of the time," wrote Putnam.[45] If you have a system of direct democracy in a state where the citizens have an ingrained mistrust of both the federal and the state government and their chosen representatives, you get a miserable result. California is the proof.

The title of this chapter is: Can one have too much democracy? The answer is: Yes, you can. California is a clear example. According to Karen Stenner,

> It is well known that the American political system was purposely designed as a system of checks and balances, which multiplied the arms of government, assigned them distinct functions, and set them forever at odds with one another. It is also a system designed to shift power downward, with multiple levels of government, frequent elections at every level, and as many decisions as possible, as often as possible, left in the hands of the electorate. The benefits of these arrangements are the stuff of American folklore. But the costs of such a system are the amplification of conflict, the propagation of adversaries, and the constant airing of disagreement: conditions we now know are guaranteed to activate the authoritarian dynamic, starkly polarize the electorate, and increase the manifest expression of intolerance. Little wonder, then, that the "home of the brave" seems perpetually prone to fear-driven politics and irrational public policy.[46]

The American historian Richard Hofstadter wrote that "American politics has often been an arena for angry minds." He observes a *paranoid style*, which would be characterized by "heated exaggeration, suspiciousness, and conspirational fantasy."[47] The deep distrust of political elites in large swathes of the American electorate seems to have deep historical roots.

Another critical voice is Sabino Cassese, a judge in the Italian Constitutional Court, who writes:

> An ultimate menace to democracy comes from the ever increasing demand for democracy, in particular for direct [democracy]. The temptation of unlimited democracy runs the risk of corrupting democracy itself. "Democratic fundamentalism" and unlimited democratic ambitions risk promoting the tyranny of small groups, or promoting popular, but harmful decisions. If you just think of the referendums in California, where elected representatives have been recalled, taxes cut, laws rejected and new laws written. This has provoked periodic budget crises in a state which, moreover, is rich. More democracy, observed some German analysts, can mean promoting short-term interests or [the interests] of more active, single groups and undermine representative democracy, or the *Gemeinwohl*, which we can call the long-term common interest.[48]

It is telling that Cassese here speaks of "democratic fundamentalism." The fact is that "democratic fundamentalists" have no, or not enough, consideration for the liberal aspects of the modern democratic state, of its arrangements and institutions which defend the unalienable rights of the individual and minorities against the majority. However, despite the many negative consequences democratic fundamentalism is on the rise – even in countries where representative democracy seemed to be sacrosanct, such as the Netherlands or the United Kingdom, with its venerable parliament in Westminster, which claims to be the oldest parliament in the world. In 1964 (a year which seems today light-years away) Anthony Birch could still express the sense of superiority the British felt vis-à-vis other countries, proud of their parliament, when he wrote confidently:

> Some doctrines about political representation which are current in other countries have never been seriously canvassed in Britain. Thus, there has been no support in this country for the Populist doctrine that representation is an inferior alternative to direct democracy which is made necessary only by the fact that the population is too large for all citizens to meet in person … It has occasionally been proposed that a referendum might be held on a particular issue, but the proposals do not ever appear to have been taken seriously. And there has been no support at all for the idea that the initiative and the referendum should be adopted as permanent institutions of government, as in Switzerland, so that the representatives could be by-passed.[49]

After the Brexit referendum and the pro-Brexit vote in 2016 these words seem to have been written in another age. It *was* indeed another age. And the question is whether the populist assault on representative democracy is only a temporary storm or an enduring phenomenon which, while not completely replacing representative democracy, will change its workings fundamentally.

Direct democracy in Switzerland: an instrument of far-right populists?

The Californian system of direct democracy has many vices. However, it doesn't have only vices. It was introduced in 1911 as a reaction against the growing political influence of corporate interests and the activities of corrupt local party bosses, giving the last word to the electorate. Defenders of the system point to important citizens' initiatives, such as Proposition 20 in 1972, which created the Coastal Zone Conservation Act, leading to the protection of California's coast from massive housing development and environmental risks, or to Proposition 9, the Political Reform Act of 1974, which led to the creation of the Fair Political Practices Commission, tasked to regulate campaign finance and lobbying.[50] However, after the adoption of Proposition 13 the disadvantages have clearly outweighed the benefits, resulting in a dysfunctioning system.

Another example of direct democracy in action is Switzerland. The Swiss system of direct democracy resembles in many respects the Californian system, and, as with California, it has a long history. The Swiss Constitution of 1848, which was modeled after the Constitution of the United States, had a provision for state-organized mandatory referendums, to be held only when the government wanted to change the Constitution. However, from 1874 optional legislative referendums also became possible: laws adopted by parliament could be vetoed by the population. In 1891 a new step was taken, when citizens' initiatives were introduced for a direct partial amendment of the Constitution. Finally, in 1921, referendums on international treaties also could be organized, giving citizens a direct influence on foreign policy.[51]

These instruments of direct democracy at the federal level were an extension of an old Swiss tradition of direct democracy, the so-called *Landsgemeinde*: local, regional, and even cantonal assemblies of voters, coming together in the open air to deliberate and take majority decisions. This Swiss system of direct democracy resembled the practice in ancient Athens, where citizens gathered in the *agora*, the marketplace. The difference with neighboring Germany could not be greater. From the time of the Prussian king Frederick the Great at the end of the eighteenth century, German liberal reformers were more interested in the development of a *Rechtsstaat*, a state where the rule of law was guaranteed, than in a democratic polity. Both approaches had their negative sides. In Germany the weak democratic tradition was one of the factors which facilitated the Nazi dictatorship. On the other hand, the weak liberal tradition in Switzerland has an inbuilt tendency to lead to direct-democratic majority rule which rides roughshod over the interests of minorities.

This tendency is not new. As early as August 1893 – only shortly after the adoption of the law on citizens' initiatives – 60.1 percent of the electorate voted for an initiative banning the ritual slaughter of animals. Although it was defended on the grounds of animal welfare, it was supported by anti-Semites. The initiative was clearly directed against the Jewish community, the only group in the country which used this practice.[52] Another issue concerns female suffrage. In most European countries women got the right to vote after the First World War. However, Swiss men were extremely reluctant to extend this right to the other sex. In fact Switzerland became the *last* European country to adopt universal suffrage. At the federal level women got the right to vote only in 1971. At the cantonal level even later. Still in 1990 (!) the assembly of – male – voters of the canton Appenzell Innerrhoden refused to grant women the right to vote. Women achieved this right only after a decision of the Constitutional Court.[53]

Swiss direct democracy and xenophobia

In the last twenty years the Swiss system of direct democracy has regularly featured negatively in the news because of the adoption of discriminatory measures against minorities, and in particular against foreigners and Muslims. This wave of xenophobia is fanned by populist right-wing parties, which use initiatives and referendums for promoting their political agenda. Direct democracy has become the instrument of choice for spreading their xenophobic message.

This situation is compounded by the fact that Switzerland belongs to the European vanguard as concerns the development of extreme right parties. "Apart from the Poujade movement in France in the 1950s," writes Damir Skenderovic, "after the Second World War in no country were there parties to the right of the political spectrum with deliberate reference to fascist models. Since then seven different parties of the popular right have succeeded in Switzerland in entering parliament, more than in any other West European country."[54]

The Swiss right-wing parties were different from likeminded movements elsewhere, because "they were more than merely rudimentary organized political activists. They built relatively stable, party-like organization structures and could occupy a constant place in the Swiss party landscape."[55] Right-wing populist parties were, above all, early phenomena in Switzerland. Some were founded in the 1960s, a full decade before they appeared elsewhere in Europe.[56] In particular the SVP, the Swiss People's Party (Schweizerischer Volkspartei) plays an important role. In 2003 this party got 26.7 percent in the parliamentary election and became the country's largest party. Because in Switzerland there exists a *Konkordanzsystem*, a system in which all parties participate permanently in a great government coalition, this gave the SVP two members in the eight-member government.[57] The party leader, Christoph Blocher, a billionaire who finances the party, became minister of justice. On 8 February 2004, an initiative was adopted, supported by Blocher, on "the lifelong detention of incurable, extremely dangerous sexual and violent delinquents." The text became thereby a part of the Swiss Constitution. However, lifelong detention, which lacks provision for any review procedure, was incompatible with the European Convention on Human Rights, ratified by Switzerland. Because Blocher refused to propose a supporting law which met the requirements of the European Convention, the penal law was changed only four years later, in August 2008 – after Blocher had quit the government – to accomodate prevailing human rights standards.[58]

The "minaret initiative"

A much more controversial event, however, was the adoption of a new initiative, launched in 2009 by the SVP and the EDU,[59] another right-wing party, to impose a national ban on the construction of new minarets. The campaign posters, pasted on walls all over the country, were of an unknown hostility: they featured black, missile-shaped minarets alongside a woman covered head-to-toe in a niqab. Fear of terrorism was mixed with fear of *Überfremdung* – the odd German word coined by the extreme right to indicate the fear of "being drowned by a flood of foreigners." The initiative was put to the ballot on 29 November 2009. It was passed with a majority of 57.5 percent of the votes and had majorities in twenty-two of the twenty-six cantons. The ban was written directly into the Constitution. The SVP had, indeed, skillfully addressed the fears of the population.

This fear of minarets and *Überfremdung* seems exaggerated if one keeps in mind that only 4 of the roughly 150 Swiss mosques and prayer rooms have minarets and only two more were planned at the time. None of the existing minarets is used for the call to prayer.[60] Muslims account for only 5 percent of the total population. Most of them come from Kosovo and Turkey and don't share the fundamentalist Salafist traditions of countries such as Saudi Arabia, nor their dress codes. "Jewish groups," commented Martha Nussbaum on the Swiss initiative, "reminded the public that Jews for centuries were not allowed to construct synagogues or cupola roofs."[61] The government was obliged to draft a supporting law on the ban and, as was the case with the initiative on the lifelong detention of certain categories of delinquents, Switzerland again ran the risk of violating international conventions.

The deportation of criminal foreigners

Emboldened by these successes, in 2010 the SVP launched a new initiative, this time on the deportation of criminal foreigners. On 28 October 2010, the initiative was adopted with a majority of 52.9 percent of votes against a more moderate proposal by the government. In the supporting law, drafted later by parliament and the government, a role was still reserved for the courts instead of automatic deportation, demanded by the SVP, because it would violate the European Convention on Human Rights and the UN Convention on the Rights of the Child.[62]

The SVP, however, wanted a complete and full implementation of the deportation initiative and therefore introduced a new initiative, the *Durchsetzungsinitiative*, an "initiative for full implementation." If accepted, it would not only mean that the list of crimes which would lead to deportation would be longer, but also that deportation would take place automatically, without regard for individual circumstances.[63] Moreover, it would put Switzerland at odds with international human rights conventions. This time the SVP had less success: on 3 March 2016, the initiative was rejected by a majority of 58.9 percent of votes. Had this initiative been accepted, it would have been a total assault on Switzerland's representative order. "What we are experiencing now with the implementation initiative," said the social democratic senator Hans Stöckli, "is the suspension of the lawgiver, of parliament."[64]

However, in the meantime the SVP had launched another initiative, titled "against massive immigration." This initiative was put to the ballot on 9 February 2014. The initiative was passed with 50.3 percent of the votes. It was striking that the initiative was rejected in places where immigrants lived, such as the urban areas in and around Zürich and Geneva, while the conservative, rural regions were mostly in favor. The German weekly *Die Zeit* asked what could be the cause, because, wrote the paper, "Switzerland is doing as well as almost any other country in Europe. The unemployment rate is historically low, the economy is booming, the demographic aging process has slowed down – all this thanks to immigration. However, on this Sunday not the head, but the underbelly decided what the Swiss wrote on their ballot."[65]

The problems with international conventions were this time even greater than in the preceding cases. The text of the initiative imposed quotas. This was against bilateral treaties with the European Union, within which since 1999 there has existed a regime of free movement of persons. The EU was not willing to accept any exceptions and immediately halted a research cooperation agreement. This meant that the government had to draft a supporting law, which would circumvent these problems and meet the demands of the EU. It took the Swiss government almost three years before, in December 2016, it found a compromise.

Do we have too much democracy or not enough?

Critics of the Swiss system

The Swiss system of direct democracy has increasingly been criticized. One of the most prominent critics was the German president Joachim Gauck, who, during a visit to Switzerland in 2014, said that "direct democracy can contain dangers, when citizens vote on highly complex subjects."[66] Gauck added that he was a convinced supporter of representative democracy, with which Germany "fares well."[67] The German paper *Die Welt* wrote: "The number of popular initiatives is increasing and the wishes of the people are becoming ever more extreme."[68] In the period 1891–2015 in Switzerland a total of twenty-two initiatives were adopted. Over a period of 125 years this seems a rather moderate number. However, the picture changes if one takes into account that ten of these initiatives – almost half – were adopted after 2002.[69] And four of these adopted initiatives were launched by the extreme right.

"Switzerland's direct democracy," wrote Brian Daigle, "has highlighted one glaring (and unfortunately not-uncommon globally) problem with such a system: the negative effects on minority groups. One of the persistent criticisms of democracy as a system, especially in places unchecked by institutional mechanisms or an overarching legal construct to restrain the scope of voting, has been what is often referred to as the 'tyranny of the majority.' This concept emphasizes that the will of the majority, unchecked, could infringe upon the rights or abilities of minority groups (whether they be political, religious or ethnic) to live their lives as their fellow countrymen would."[70]

François Cherix, a Swiss essayist, remarks that direct democracy "isn't in itself a driver of populism … Unfortunately, the way it works in Switzerland, which is to say without any safeguards, it serves as its catalyst. It has an enormous proficiency in assembling the dissatisfied behind a simple idea."[71] The conditions for organizing referendums and initiatives seem, indeed, to be far too easy. To organize a referendum against a law proposal one needs 50,000 signatures within a hundred days and to organize an initiative one needs 100,000 signatures within eighteen months.[72] The barrier is, therefore, rather low,[73] certainly if one takes into account that the collection of signatures has become a paid business, as in California. According to insiders "a popular initiative costs between 2 and 5 francs per signature,"[74] which comes close to the sum paid in California. There are in Switzerland neither precise regulations concerning the financing, nor detailed prescriptions on the transparency concerning the supporters, of the proposals.

It is clear that the Swiss model is attractive to other populists. In December 2017, for instance, the Austrian extreme right Freedom Party (FPÖ) demanded the introduction of Swiss-style initiatives in its coalition negotiations with the conservative party ÖVP. The party even made it a condition for its participation in government. It proposed organizing a referendum as soon as 250,000 citizens had asked for one. Thomas Angerer, a historian of the University of Vienna, commented: "The FPÖ knows that its chances of remaining for a long period in government are rather restricted. It wants, therefore, to put pressure on the conservatives to prepare for a more comfortable future in opposition. In Switzerland Christoph Blocher [the former leader of the Swiss People's Party SVP] has proven that one can change the general political climate on subjects which are advantageous for populisms by imposing certain key issues."[75] The FPÖ's conservative coalition partner did not refuse the demand of the FPÖ, but raised the number of signatures for an initiative to 900,000, which is more than 14 percent of the electorate, and added some constitutional hurdles, which could postpone its full introduction until 2022.

Notes

1 Napoleon I organized a plebiscite in December 1799, after the *coup d'état* which installed the Consulate. He used a second plebiscite in May 1802 to legitimate his position as "Consul for Life." In May 1804 a plebiscite was organized to found the empire. Following in his uncle's footsteps, Louis Napoleon, who was a democratically elected president of the Second French Republic, organized a plebiscite in December 1851 after a *coup d'état*. In November 1852 he organized another plebiscite, this time to restore the empire.
2 Jonathon Read, "Boris Johnson appears to finally admit his '£350m a week' claim was wrong," *New European*, 11 September 2019 (updated 18 September 2020). www.theneweuropean.co.uk/brexit-news/boris-johnson-350-million-a-week-nhs-claim-55554 (accessed 23 September 2020).
3 Matthew Smith, "Most Conservative members would see party destroyed to achieve Brexit," YouGov, 18 June 2019. https://yougov.co.uk/topics/politics/articles-reports/2019/06/18/most-conservative-members-would-see-party-destroyed (accessed 5 July 2019).
4 Ibid.
5 Cf. Rob Merrick and Benjamin Kentish, "No-deal Brexit support and 'blatant entryism' surges among grassroots Conservatives and former Ukip voters," *Independent*, 30 June 2019. www.independent.co.uk/news/uk/politics/conservative-leadership-news-latest-no-deal-brexit-boris-johnson-ukip-jeremy-hunt-a8978206.html (accessed 6 July 2019).
6 "EU vote: Where the cabinet and other MPs stand," BBC News, 22 June 2016. www.bbc.com/news/uk-politics-eu-referendum-35616946 (accessed 6 July 2019). In this number is not included Jo Cox, a Labour MP and Remainer, who was killed on 16 June 2016.
7 Karla Adam, "'Get Brexit done': Boris Johnson's effective but misleading slogan in the British election," *Washington Post*, 12 December 2019. www.washingtonpost.com/world/europe/get-brexit-done-boris-johnsons-effective-but-misleading-slogan-in-the-uk-election/2019/12/12/ec926baa-1c62-11ea-977a-15a6710ed6da_story.html (accessed 28 December 2019).
8 D66 stands for Democraten 1966 (Democrats 1966). 1966 is the year the party was founded.
9 The three groups were the populist weblog GeenStijl, Burgercomité EU, and the Eurosceptic Forum voor Democratie.

10 Laura Starink, *Slag om Oekraïne – Referendum over een land in opstand* (Amsterdam and Antwerp: Uitgeverij Augustus, 2016), p. 8.
11 "Peiling: Helft D66-kiezers wil geen referenda meer," *EenVandaag*, Opiniepanel, 6 March 2017. http://opiniepanel.eenvandaag.nl/uitslagen/72539/peiling_helft_d66_kiezers_wil_geen_referenda_meer (accessed 7 July 2019).
12 Dr. A. J. Kruiter, "Voorkom Californische toestanden na dit referendum," *NRC Handelsblad*, 7 April 2016.
13 "Jaarverslag 2016," Raad van State, The Hague. https://jaarverslag.raadvanstate.nl/ (accessed 4 September 2017).
14 Ibid.
15 Ibid.
16 Remco Meijer, "Bindend referendum verder weg dan ooit: Zelfs initiatiefnemers trekken handen ervan af," *De Volkskrant*, 27 September 2017.
17 Cf. Kurt Lenk and Franz Neumann, "Einleitung," in Kurt Lenk and Franz Neumann, *Theorie und Soziologie der politischen Parteien* (Neuwied am Rhein and Berlin: Luchterhand, 1968), p. lxi: "In 1832 Jackson (1767–1845) proclaimed 'To the victor belong the spoils', and since then at the inauguration of a new president in a perfect system of patronage all civil servants of the federal administration were changed – even including the mail carrier. The offices were given by the local cliques to those supporters who had helped the 'boss' to finance the election campaign."
18 "History of initiative and referendum in California," *Ballotpedia*, 12 November 2016. https://ballotpedia.org/History_of_Initiative_and_Referendum_in_California (accessed 4 September 2017). In 2016 135 ballot initiatives were filed and 15 were put on the ballot. In 2018 66 ballot initiatives were filed and 8 were put on the ballot ("California 2020 ballot propositions," *Ballotpedia*, no date. https://ballotpedia.org/California_2020_ballot_propositions (accessed 23 September 2020)).
19 Peter Schrag, *Paradise Lost – California's Experience, America's Future* (Berkeley and Los Angeles: University of California Press, 2004), pp. 9–10 (first edition 1999).
20 Ibid., p. 8.
21 Shikha Dalmia, Adrian Moore, and Adam B. Summers, "Don't blame voters for California's budget woes," *Wall Street Journal*, 3 October 2009.
22 Fishkin, *When the People Speak*, p. 213, footnote 26.
23 Andreas Kluth, "The people's will," Special report: Democracy in California, *The Economist*, 20 April 2011.
24 Ibid.
25 The populist recall and the subsequent election campaign were compared by other observers to "a yard full of headless chickens." Cf. Charlie Leduff, "California Recall is part vote, part entertainment spectacle," *New York Times*, 28 July 2003. www.nytimes.com/2003/07/28/us/california-recall-is-part-vote-part-entertainment-spectacle.html (accessed 4 September 2017).
26 Jack Citrin, "Proposition 13 and the Transformation of California Government," *The California Journal of Politics & Policy*, Volume 1, Issue 1, 2009. http://escholarship.org/uc/item/7mt1q84g (accessed 4 September 2017).
27 "War by initiative – A case study in unintended consequences," *The Economist*, 20 April 2011.
28 Ibid.
29 "The sad state of California's direct democracy," *Sacbee*, 15 October 2016.
30 Citrin, "Proposition 13."

31 Michael Hiltzik, "Four decades later, California experts find that Proposition 13 is a boon for the rich," *Los Angeles Times*, 30 September 2016.
32 Ibid.
33 James S. Fishkin, "How to fix California's democracy crisis," *New York Times*, 10 October 2011. Even the conservative Heritage Foundation concluded that "if it had been a Progressive goal to reduce the influence of money in politics, that certainly has not happened through the initiative process, as the sums spent on initiatives in recent decades have come to dwarf spending on races for state political office" (Ronald Pestritto and Taylor Kempema, "The Birth of Direct Democracy: What Progressivism Did to the States," The Heritage Foundation, Report Political Process, 25 February 2014, p. 23).
34 David Dayen, "The California Ballot Is an Epic Joke," *The New Republic*, 23 September 2016.
35 Ibid.
36 Ibid.
37 Bernard Crick, *The Reform of Parliament* (London: Weidenfeld and Nicolson, 1970), p. 182.
38 James Madison, *The Federalist Papers*, No. 10, in Hamilton, Madison, and Jay, *Federalist Papers*, p. 78.
39 Ibid., p. 79.
40 The three organizers were James S. Fishkin of the Center for Deliberative Democracy at Stanford University, Zabrae Valentin of California Forward, and Lenny Mendonca of McKinsey & Company.
41 Cf. James S. Fishkin, "How to fix California's democracy crisis." The PBS NewsHour-produced documentary about the project can be watched at www.youtube.com/watch?v=k5cpYoMuMDU (accessed 5 September 2017).
42 Ibid.
43 Schrag, *Paradise Lost*, pp. 10–11.
44 Ibid., p. xxvi.
45 Putnam, *Bowling*, p. 47 (emphasis added, MHVH).
46 Stenner, *Authoritarian Dynamic*, pp. 332–333.
47 Richard Hofstadter, "The paranoid style in American politics," *Harper's Magazine*, November 1964. https://harpers.org/archive/1964/11/the-paranoid-style-in-american-politics/.
48 Sabino Cassese, *La democrazia e i suoi limiti* (Milan: Mondadori, 2017), p. 55.
49 A. H. Birch, *Representative and Responsible Government – An Essay on the British Constitution* (Toronto: University of Toronto Press, 1964), pp. 227–228.
50 Zev Yaroslavsky, "Can Californians handle direct democracy?" *Los Angeles Times*, 6 November 2016. www.latimes.com/opinion/op-ed/la-oe-yaroslavsky-ballot-initiative-20161106-story.html (accessed 5 September 2017).
51 An initiative does not automatically lead to a referendum. It needs the support of the parliament. If this support is not achieved within one year, a referendum can go forward, but only after the Supreme Court has decided that the question of the initiative is not unconstitutional or incompatible with international or European law. Additionally, the parliament has the right to make a counter-proposal, and referendums on EU membership (an FPÖ election promise!) are excluded (see Nina Weissensteiner, "Direkte Demokratie: Hohe Hürden für Referenden bis nach 2022 garantiert," *Der Standard*, 16 December 2017. https://derstandard.at/2000070508180/regierungsprogramm-oevp-fpoe-kurz-strache-direkte-demokratie (accessed 15 January 2018)).

52 Cf. "Eidgenössische Volksinitiative 'für ein Verbot des Schlachtens ohne vorherige Betäubung.'" www.admin.ch/ch/d/pore/vi/vis1.html (accessed 7 September 2017).
53 Cf. Gebhard Kirchgässner, "Direkte Demokratie und Menschenrechte," Center for Research in Economics, Management and the Arts (CREMA), *Working Paper* No. 2009-18, p. 8.
54 Damir Skenderovic, "Das rechtspopulistische Parteienlager in der Schweiz: Von den Splitterparteien zur Volkspartei," *Traverse: Zeitschrift für Geschichte – Revue d'histoire*, Vol. 14, No. 1, 2007, p. 45.
55 Damir Skenderovic, "Die Schweiz als Avantgarde des europäischen Rechtspopulismus," *Geschichte der Gegenwart*, 14 December 2016. https://geschichtedergegenwart.ch/die-schweiz-als-avantgarde-des-europaeischen-rechtspopulismus/ (accessed 23 September 2020).
56 The Nationale Aktion was founded in 1961, Vigilance (Geneva) in 1965, and the Republikanische Bewegung in 1970. This was early in comparison with the French Front National (founded in 1972) and the Belgian Vlaams Blok (1979), while Jörg Haider's takeover of the Austrian FPÖ and its subsequent transformation into an extreme right populist party took place in 1986.
57 "The *Konkordanzsystem*, this proportional 'magical formula' for the composition of the Swiss Federal Council, was not adopted until 1959," writes Arend Lijphart, "but the cantons adopted similar practices at a much earlier date" (Arend Lijphart, *Democracy in Plural Societies – A Comparative Exploration* (New Haven and London: Yale University Press, 1977), pp. 100–101). The formula consisted of a permanent 2-2-2-1 representation of the main parties in the Federal Council (the national government). In the original make-up this meant two seats for the Liberal Party (FdP), two seats for the Christian Democratic Party (CVP), two seats for the Social Democratic Party (SPS), and one seat for the SVP. Because of the electoral gains of the SVP in the elections of 19 October 2003, the formula was changed, attributing two seats to the SVP and one seat to the CVP.
58 Cf. Kirchgässner, "Direkte Demokratie," p. 1.
59 The full name of this party is "Eidgenössisch-Demokratische Union."
60 Cf. Nick Cumming-Bruce and Steven Erlanger, "Swiss ban building of minarets on mosques," *New York Times*, 29 November 2009.
61 Martha C. Nussbaum, *The New Religious Intolerance – Overcoming the Politics of Fear in an Anxious Age* (Cambridge, Mass., and London: The Belknap Press of Harvard University Press, 2012), p. 45.
62 Cf. Johannes Ritter, "Wir ausschaffen das," *Frankfurter Allgemeine Zeitung*, 28 February 2016.
63 Johannes Ritter mentions that the Swiss paper *Neue Zürcher Zeitung* had applied the initative to past criminal offenses of Swiss politicians: "The result: several parliamentarians, some of whom were from the SVP, would have been deported if they were a foreigner and if, at that time, one had applied to them the rules of the implementation initiative."
64 Florence Vuichard, "In der Schweiz herrscht zu viel Demokratie," *Die Welt*, 3 February 2015.
65 Mathias Daum, "Die Schweiz sagt 'Fuck the EU'," *Die Zeit*, 9 February 2014.
66 "Gauck: Direkte Demokratie birgt Gefahren," *Handelszeitung*, 1 April 2014.
67 Ibid.
68 Vuichard, "In der Schweiz."
69 "Von Volk und Ständen angenommene Volksinitiativen," *Bundeskanzlei*, no date. www.admin.ch/ch/d/pore/vi/vis_2_2_5_8.html (accessed 9 September 2017).

70 Brian Daigle, "Switzerland: The ultimate democracy?" *The National Interest*, 7 September 2014.
71 Quoted in Romain Rosso, "Suisse: Les limites de la démocratie directe," *L'Express*, 6 April 2017.
72 The required number of signatories for initiatives was 50,000 until this was changed in 1977. The change was made because of the introduction of the women's vote in 1971, which doubled the number of voters.
73 In 1891, when the popular initiative was introduced, one still needed the signatures of 7.65 percent of the (male) citizens entitled to vote. After the introduction of the female vote and the doubling of the signatures in the 1970s the quorum became 2.6 percent. Because of demographic growth, the actual quorum is under 2 percent (Florence Vuichard, "In der Schweiz").
74 Rosso, "Suisse."
75 Quoted in Blaise Gauquelin, "En Autriche, le FPÖ veut imposer le 'modèle suisse' du référendum," *Le Monde*, 16 December 2017.

8

Open primaries: do they "give the power back" to the people?

In the last chapter we argued that referendums and popular initiatives should be used only sparingly and not become regular tools of political decision-making. One reason for this is that referendums and initiatives are used by populist demagogues, as has been the case in Switzerland, the UK, and the Netherlands. Another reason is that politics is essentially a supply-side affair, in which politicians formulate proposals and seek to convince a majority, as we argued in chapter 6. In this chapter we will turn our attention to another political device, used in a number of liberal democracies: open primaries. These are also presented as "giving the power back" to the people. But do they?

"Giving the people a voice": primaries in the United States

One of the basic institutions of a modern democracy is the political party: a political organization, led by professionals, competing for the votes of the electorate. Political parties are in most countries fairly modern phenomena. For most of the nineteenth century politics was not yet a profession but the activity of "honorable citizens," for whom "representing the people" was something they did in their spare time. These "honorable citizens" were, as a rule, people with high social status. They were lawyers, large landowners, or businessmen, who were rich enough to do political work without being paid. This changed, however, in the last decades of the nineteenth century, when new mass political parties emerged and, from an unpaid activity, politics became a paid profession. Max Weber analyzed this transformation from the "honorable citizen" to the professional politician in his famous essay "Politics as a Vocation," published in 1919. He distinguished between two kinds of politician: "Either: one lives 'for' politics, or 'from' politics."[1] "The one who lives 'from' politics as a profession," he wrote, "is the one who tries to turn it into a permanent source of income, the one who lives 'for' politics is the one for whom this is not the case."[2] Weber added however, "the opposition is not exclusive,"[3] emphasizing that the professional politician could also be an idealist.

The professionalization of politics led to an increase in the power of the "party machines," the elected representatives and the local and national party functionaries. The first was paid by the state, the functionaries were working for the party and paid by the party. It was these two categories that had a predominant influence on the election of the candidates for political functions and on the content of the party platforms. "As electorates increased in size, party organizations became more important and party discipline stronger. Hence the responsiveness of elected representatives to their constituencies diminished, as did the responsiveness of governments to elected representatives."[4]

In the United States the power of the local party bosses and "party machines," which were accused of corrupt alliances with special interests and the mafia,[5] led to a popular reaction in the Progressive Era of the early decades of the twentieth century. "What the majority of the Progressives hoped to do in the political field," writes Hofstadter, "was to restore popular government as they imagined it to have existed in an earlier and purer age."[6] This led to "a series of changes in the mechanics of political life – direct primaries, popular election of Senators, initiative, referendum, recall, the short ballot, commission government and the like."[7]

In particular the direct primary to nominate candidates was a revolutionary innovation. It replaced the party convention, considered to be too "elitist." The direct primary intended "to give the power back to the people" by giving a vote to each registered voter who self-identified with the party. However, this innovation was already being criticized in 1909 by Henry Jones Ford, who wrote that

> One continually hears the declaration that the direct primary will take power from the politicians and give it to the people. This is pure nonsense ... All that the direct primary, or any other political reform, can do is to affect the character of the politicians by altering the conditions that govern political activity, thus determining its extent and quality. The direct primary may take advantage and opportunity from one set of politicians and confer them upon another set, but politicians there will always be so long as there is politics.[8]

Hofstadter, forty-six years later, knowing how the system worked, doubted even whether another kind of politician had emerged, writing: "The direct primary, for instance, for all its wide adoption throughout the country, did not noticeably change the type of men nominated for office. It was expensive both to the government and to the candidates – for it introduced two campaigns in the place of one. It put a new premium on publicity and promotion in nominating campaigns, and thus introduced into the political process another entering wedge for the power of money. Without seriously impairing the machines, it weakened party government and party responsibility."[9]

Do we have too much democracy or not enough?

Open primaries: who are the real winners?

The populist expectation was that direct primaries would "give the power back to the people." However, in practice it opened up new opportunities for passionate minorities and rich private interest groups to influence the nomination process. In the 1970s direct primaries got a new boost in the United States, when the Democratic Party, after the Chicago convention of 1968,[10] reformed its nomination process. This led to an increase in state primaries selecting the delegates to the national convention. From 23 in 1972, Democratic primaries rose to 28 in 1976 and 31 in 1980, while Republican primaries rose from 28 in 1976 to 36 in 1980. The result was that in 1980 70 percent of the delegates were chosen in primaries.[11] In recent years the number has further increased. In 2016 the Democrats organized a record number of forty-one state and territorial primaries, while the Republicans organized a total of thirty-nine.[12] "The resulting proliferation of direct primaries ultimately made both major parties' presidential nominations 'more democratic' in crude populist terms," wrote Achen and Bartels, "while diluting the influence of political professionals, whose firsthand knowledge of the competing candidates' strengths and weaknesses had helped to weed out amateurs and demagogues."[13]

Recently there have also been proposals to extend the primaries from the rank and file of party membership to the public as a whole. These "open primaries" were a real revolution, allowing nonmembers to choose the party's nominees.[14] This was the case with a proposal put on the ballot in California in June 2010, to introduce a "Top Two-Vote Getter" (TTVG) system. This system "would allow voters in *all* primaries (US House, US Senate, state) to cast ballots for any candidate, regardless of their own or the candidate's party identification. The two candidates receiving the most votes – again, regardless of party – would proceed to a runoff election."[15] The rationale behind the proposition was that party members (of both the Democratic and Republican parties) were more radical and polarized than non-party members. Giving the vote to non-party members was expected to produce more moderate candidates. However, as Eric McGhee explained:

> One of the most common objections to TTVG is that it will encroach upon each party's right to control its own fate. Open primaries give voters who have not taken an interest in the success of the party – and may even have actively opposed its goals – as much say in deciding nominees as those who have been dedicated followers. Opponents express particular concerns about *raiders*: voters who seek to clear the way for their own party's nominee by voting for the weakest candidate in the opposing party. Since this weak candidate may also be more extreme, substantial raiding could undermine TTVG's moderating effect.[16]

This led some opponents to "argue that weakening party influence in elections will create a vacuum that will be filled by organized interests with agendas that are less transparent and public-spirited."[17] This assessment is shared by Larry Bartels, who writes: "The proliferation of primaries has increased the power of the active segment of the voting public that participates in primaries, at the expense of professional party elites. But there have been other winners and losers as well. Convention delegates, their deliberative role having largely disappeared with the advent of mass public choice, have become increasingly subservient to the candidate organizations they are elected to support."[18] The open primaries, which suppress deliberation among party delegates at conventions, not only "disown" the party members, but, additionally, tend to kill the basic ingredients of a sound and healthy democracy: deliberation, discussion, and debate – which are the oxygen for a democratic process.

The loss of influence of political parties

Why are we paying attention to these direct primaries in the United States? Because in Europe they have recently become models to emulate against the background of a massive loss of membership of the political parties. In the last few decades of the twentieth century, parties – from the left as well as from the right – lost their mass following and their membership numbers decreased dramatically. To give some examples: in the UK membership of both the Labour Party and the Conservative Party peaked in the early 1950s. In 1953 the Conservatives had 2.8 million members and Labour claimed over a million. From this period on we can observe a steady decline. While in the mid-1990s the Conservatives still had 400,000 members, by December 2013 this had fallen to a mere 149,800. In March 2017 Labour claimed 517,000 members.[19] In 2016 in the UK only 1.6 percent of the electorate was a member of a political party.

In Germany the situation was no better, although the development was different from that in the UK. The Christian Democratic Union, which had 360,000 members in 1948, was confronted with a steady decline until the 1960s, but from 1968 to 1983 it grew to 734,555 members. This was followed by a new decline from the 1990s. At the end of 2016 the CDU had 431,920 members. The Social Democratic Party didn't fare any better. After its membership peaked in 1976 with 1,022,191 members, it steadily decreased to 432,706 in 2015.[20]

In France there was a similar situation. From 2007 a steady decline in the membership of the two main parties, Les Républicains (former UMP) and the Socialist Party (PS) can be observed. In 2007 Les Républicains (at the time still called UMP) had 370,000 members, the PS 256,000. In 2015 these numbers were respectively 178,920 and 131,000, which means that in eight years both parties had lost almost half of their membership.[21]

Party membership as a percentage of national electorates varies strongly in Europe. Austria and Cyprus rank highest with both about 17 percent of the electorate. In Latvia and Poland, however, it is not even 1 percent, while in old, established democracies, such as the UK and France, it does not reach 2 percent.[22] Apparently, political parties in Europe are no longer capable of attracting citizens in the way they did before. Moreover, the composition of the membership has changed. The remaining party members are more likely to come from the public sector than from other sectors of society. This has important consequences. Can one still regard them as part of civil society? Or perhaps they "rather … constitute[e] the outer ring of an extended political class. In terms of background, education and employment, they may have more in common with the party central office or even the representatives of the party in public office than with the traditional party on the ground. This would suggest that the real social roots of political parties … are now to be found outside the boundaries of the formal party and are made up of a loosely and horizontally organized myriad of supporters, adherents and sympathisers."[23]

One cause of the popular revolt against "the elites" can certainly be found here: not only are the representatives in parliament experienced as a caste which is not concerned about the daily worries of the "common man," but also the parties have become elitist organizations – including the traditional parties of the left. In the United States, where party membership is more fluid and depends in most cases on self-declaration, the same tendency can be observed in the growing number of people who declare themselves to be independent.[24] Hans Magnus Enzensberger, a German author, wrote: "The politicians are insulted that people are less and less interested in them, but they ought to ask themselves what is the cause of this? I suspect that the politicians have fallen victim to a self-deception, that they have an incorrect definition of politics."[25] The first reaction of the politicians, confronted with this loss of party membership, was to try to organize the electorate in a new way. Their new magical tool? Primaries.

Open primaries in the UK and France

In Europe the loss of membership has led some political parties to rethink the way in which they select candidates. An example is the UK, where the Labour Party in a Special Conference, organized in March 2014 in London, changed the leadership selection procedure. The initiative was launched by Ed Miliband, who wanted to introduce the OMOV (one member one vote) system. The selection of the party leader – and implicitly the party's candidate for the future prime minister – would be made by full members, affiliated members, and registered supporters of the party. The new selection procedure was in place when, on 8 May 2015, after the party's defeat at the 2015 general election, Ed Miliband resigned as leader. There were four candidates and the new leader would be chosen by "instant-runoff voting," also called "alternative vote," a procedure in which the voters rank the candidates. The vote started on 14 August 2015, and was closed on 10 September. To the great surprise of all the contest was won by Jeremy Corbyn, a sixty-six-year-old, left-wing backbencher, who won 59.5 percent of the first-preference votes.

Corbyn had the reputation of being a maverick. He had, for instance, suggested that Tony Blair should be tried for the war in Iraq, while at the same time turning a blind eye to the Russian aggression in Ukraine, accusing NATO rather than Putin of the ongoing war. Corbyn's sympathies are clearly situated on the extreme left. He is a columnist of the *Morning Star*, a daily newspaper which is connected with the Communist Party of Britain.[26] Corbyn called this paper "the most precious and only voice we have in the daily media."[27] How was it possible that this "dark horse" candidate, who had served as a little-known and inconspicuous backbencher for thirty-two years (he became an MP in 1983!), suddenly became the favorite? The great majority of his colleagues in the Labour faction were upset. They considered Corbyn a relic of the past, a remnant of the "old left," which was destined to fade away. Was the new voting system to blame?

The completely open system certainly offered unexpected opportunities for well-organized outsiders to influence the vote. "Labour has been severely criticized for its chaotic handling of the contest," wrote the *Guardian*, "after Miliband introduced the new system whereby new supporters could pay £3 to take part in the vote. It meant the party had to scramble to weed out infiltrators from other parties."[28] The specter of Trotskyist infiltration was raised when a year later information emerged that in 1988 Corbyn had signed a petition asking for the rehabilitation of Leon Trotsky.[29] Tom Watson, Corbyn's deputy, sent him a four-page document, detailing "evidence that Trotskyists had been attending meetings of grass-roots pro-Corbyn Momentum pressure group and seeking to influence the Labour leadership election."[30] Watson added: "It's not a conspiracy theory … It's a fact."[31]

The fear of raiders, expressed in the United States by critics of open primaries, seemed to be supported by these events. Open primaries could offer well-organized groups of outsiders a unique chance to influence the choice of the party's candidates. Trotskyist entryism into the Labour Party was not new. In the 1980s Labour had already risked being taken over by hard-left activists. They were finally expelled. Ed

Miliband's OMOV system, "to bring the party closer to the voter," generously granting the right to vote to an unknown multitude, risked opening the door to passionate minorities who did not share the party's platform, to infiltrate and influence the party.

In France, in 2011, the Socialist Party (together with the small Radical Left Party) introduced for the first time an "open primary" to select its candidate for the presidential election in 2012. The Socialist Party had organized primaries before: in 1995 and 2006. However, the participation in these primaries had been restricted exclusively to party members. In 2011, on the contrary, the primary was open to all registered voters who claimed to support "the values of the left and of the Republic" – a rather vague "profession of faith" – and who were willing to pay one euro. In the first round of the primary, organized on 9 October 2011, a total of 2,661,231 people voted. In the second round, on 16 October 2011, the number of voters was 2,860,157. François Hollande was chosen as the official candidate. The success of these "open primaries" was vindicated when, in May 2012, Hollande won the presidential election against the incumbent president Nicolas Sarkozy.

The "open primary" seemed, therefore, to be a promising procedure. Not only was the whole process closely followed by the media, capturing people's attention for months, but it also seemed a good method of testing the popularity of the candidates. By nominating the most popular candidate, the party enhanced its chances of winning the presidential election. This was the reason why the Socialist Party repeated the same procedure in 2016 and the Républicains followed in their footsteps, equally organizing "open primaries."

However, this time things did not work out so smoothly. In the primaries of the Républicains former prime minister François Fillon was chosen – against the party's favorite, former president Nicolas Sarkozy. The socialist president François Hollande, deeply unpopular, did not even participate in the primaries of his own party. To everyone's surprise Benoît Hamon was selected, a leftist who belonged to the internal opposition against the socialist government. Neither Fillon, nor Hamon, was successful. Fillon was soon accused of fraud, allegedly allowing his wife to be paid for many years for a fake job. The socialist candidate Hamon, a party rebel, did not succeed in convincing the rank and file of his own party and got only 6.36 percent of the vote in the first round of the presidential election. Both candidates were eliminated in the first round. In the end it was Emmanuel Macron, a political outsider with his brand new "En Marche" movement, who won the second round against Marine Le Pen, the candidate of the extreme right Front National.

In France also, the problem of entryism by "raiders" was mentioned. An MP of Les Républicains observed that "voters of the Front National and the left came to vote in the right's primary, hoping to distort the result. This phenomenon of 'strategic' voters existed also in the left's primary, with sympathizers of the Greens and communists coming to promote Benoît Hamon against Manuel Valls."[32] In the summer of 2017 the leadership of the Républicains sent a questionnaire to its members, asking them if the party should continue with the system of open primaries. Of the 40,912 members who answered 70 percent were against.[33] Daniel Fasquelle, a candidate for the party leadership contest in December 2017, said: "The role of the party is to appoint its candidate, if not what is the point of becoming a member?" He too expressed his fear of raiders: "sympathizers of the left who could have voted."[34]

Apparently, open primaries suffer from the same deficiency as another instrument which was once touted as a "magical tool": the opinion poll, developed by George Gallup in the 1930s. When the first opinion polls were organized, they were considered a supporting technique for the elections, because they represented "the voice of the people." This was also Gallup's original idea. "The polls should permit him [Gallup] to answer the question, formulated earlier by Abraham Lincoln: 'What I want, is to realize what the people want to realize and the question for me is how precisely to discover this.'"[35] At that time even the French communist trade union CGT welcomed the opinion poll as "a new instrument available for democracy."[36] We know now that opinion polls are capable of accurately predicting election results, as well as completely missing the point. Because what the polls measure is not a well-defined and stable public opinion, but rather a changing public mood, which can easily be influenced. Fluid and volatile, it is capable of changing overnight. And it is these volatile polls which are still the lode stars of many politicians. "Washington today," writes Fareed Zakaria,

> is organized around the pursuit of public opinion. It employs armies of people to continually check the pulse of the American people on every conceivable matter. It hires others to determine the intensity of their feelings on these issues. It pays still others to guess what people might think tomorrow. Lobbyists, consultants, and politicians all use this information as the basis for their actions. And through this whole process everyone keeps praising the wisdom, courage, rectitude, and all-round greatness of the American people. The only reassuring aspect of this sorry spectacle is that, as the pandering has gone up, the public's attitude toward politicians has gone down.[37]

Zakaria concludes that "what has changed in Washington is not that politicians have closed themselves off from the American people and are unwilling to hear their pleas. It is that *they do scarcely anything but listen to the American people.*"[38]

While primaries did give power to the rank-and-file members of political parties, open primaries in fact gave this power away to non-party members with the in itself noble intention of "listening to the people" and "to solve the problems of democracy by introducing more democracy." However, in practice they have not been the imagined "magical tool," capable of compensating the diminished attraction of the political parties. By introducing open primaries the political parties have outsourced the decision on who will be the party's candidate to an unknown mass of voters, to potential outsiders, and sometimes to hostile raiders.

Notes

1 Max Weber, "Politik als Beruf," in Weber, *Schriften 1894–1922*, p. 521.
2 Ibid., p. 522.
3 Ibid., p. 521.
4 C. B. Macpherson, *Democratic Theory – Essays in Retrieval* (Oxford: Oxford University Press, 1979), p. 180.
5 Robert Merton links the influence of the mafia on American local politics in the 1930s to the fact that Italian immigrants, having arrived after the Irish and East European Jews, found their social ascent blocked. It was with their "new, and often illegally earned, Italian wealth" that they found an entrée "into the ruling circles … and came to achieve a substantial degree of political influence" (Robert K. Merton, *Social Theory and Social Structure* (New York: The Free Press, 1965), p. 193).
6 Hofstadter, *Age of Reform*, p. 257.
7 Ibid., p. 257.
8 Henry Jones Ford, "The Direct Primary," *North American Review*, Vol. 190, No. 644, 1909, p. 2. Quoted in Achen and Bartels, *Democracy for Realists*, p. 62.
9 Hofstadter, *Age of Reform*, pp. 267–268.
10 The National Convention of the Democratic Party, organized in Chicago on 26–29 August 1968, presented the spectacle of great divisions against the background of the war in Vietnam and the assassinations, shortly before, of Martin Luther King and Democratic presidential candidate Robert Kennedy. The nomination of Hubert Humphrey, Johnson's vice-president, led to bloody protests outside the building. After the convention the McGovern–Fraser commission proposed changing the nomination process by introducing primaries for registered Democratic voters. The Democratic Party's reform was followed by the Republican Party.
11 Drew DeSilver, "Near-record number of primaries this year, but not quite as early," Pew Research Center, 17 February 2016. www.pewresearch.org/fact-tank/2016/02/17/near-record-number-of-primaries-this-year-but-not-quite-as-early/ (accessed 11 September 2017).
12 Ibid.
13 Achen and Bartels, *Democracy for Realists*, p. 15.
14 Ibid., p. 78.
15 Eric McGhee (with contributions from Daniel Krimm), *At Issue – Open Primaries* (San Francisco: Public Policy Institute of California, February 2010), p. 4.
16 Ibid., p. 4.
17 Ibid., p. 4.
18 Larry M. Bartels, *Presidential Primaries and the Dynamics of Public Choice* (Princeton: Princeton University Press, 1988), p. 6.

19 Cf. "Membership of UK Political Parties," House of Commons, Briefing Paper No. SN05125, 15 March 2017. http://researchbriefings.parliament.uk/ResearchBriefing/Summary/SN05125 (accessed 11 September 2017).
20 Cf. "Parteien in Deutschland – Zahlen und Fakten," Bundeszentrale für politische Bildung. www.bpb.de/politik/grundfragen/parteien-in-deutschland/zahlen-und-fakten/ (accessed 12 September 2017).
21 Cf. Samuel Laurent, "Des Républicains au PS, la désertion des militants," *Le Monde*, 22 September 2015. www.lemonde.fr/les-decodeurs/article/2015/09/22/des-republicains-au-ps-la-desertion-des-militants_4766932_4355770.html (accessed 13 September 2017).
22 Cf. Ingrid van Biezen, "The decline in party membership across Europe means that political parties need to reconsider how they engage with the electorate," London School of Economics and Political Science, Europp Blog. http://blogs.lse.ac.uk/europpblog/2013/05/06/decline-in-party-membership-europe-ingrid-van-biezen/ (accessed 13 September 2017).
23 Ibid.
24 Cf. Samantha Smith, "5 facts about America's political independents," Pew Research Center, 5 July 2016: "In 2014, 39% of the public identified as independents, which was larger than the shares calling themselves Democrats (32%) or Republicans (23%). In 2004, roughly equal shares identified as Democrats (33%), independents (30%) and Republicans (29%)." www.pewresearch.org/fact-tank/2016/07/05/5-facts-about-americas-political-independents/ (accessed 15 September 2017).
25 Quoted in Ulrich Beck, *Democracy without Enemies* (Cambridge: Polity Press, 1998), p. 37.
26 The paper was founded in 1930 by the Communist Party of Great Britain (CPGB) with the title "The Daily Worker." Since 1945 it has been owned by a cooperative. In 1966 it was renamed the "Morning Star." The paper survived through Soviet patronage and subvention. When the CPGB disappeared in the early 1990s, its successor became the Communist Party of Britain. The paper's editorial line remains anchored in the program of the Communist Party of Britain. The party has a Management Committee on which nine trade unions have a seat. One of these, Unite, actively supported Corbyn's candidacy. Cf. also Edward Platt, "Inside the Morning Star, Britain's last communist newspaper," *New Statesman*, 4 August 2015. www.theguardian.com/politics/2016/aug/10/tom-watson-sends-corbyn-proof-of-trotskyist-labour-infiltration (accessed 18 September 2017).
27 Rowena Mason, "Labour leadership: Jeremy Corbyn elected with huge mandate," *Guardian*, 12 September 2015. www.theguardian.com/politics/2015/sep/12/jeremy-corbyn-wins-labour-party-leadership-election (accessed 18 September 2017).
28 Ibid.
29 Ben Riley-Smith, "In 1988 Corbyn called for the 'complete rehabilitation' of Leon Trotsky," *Telegraph*, 15 August 2016.
30 Heather Stewart, "Tom Watson sends Corbyn 'proof of Trotskyist Labour infiltration'," *Guardian*, 10 August 2016. www.theguardian.com/politics/2016/aug/10/tom-watson-sends-corbyn-proof-of-trotskyist-labour-infiltration (accessed 19 September 2017).
31 Ibid.
32 Bastien Bonnefous and Alexandre Lemarié, "Si on en finissait avec les primaires …," *Le Monde*, 19 April 2017.
33 Matthieu Goar, "La primaire déjà passée de mode à droite," *Le Monde*, 29 September 2017.
34 Ibid.
35 Quoted in Pierre Rosanvallon, *Bon gouvernement*, p. 296.
36 Ibid.

37 Fareed Zakaria, *The Future of Freedom – Illiberal Democracy at Home and Abroad* (New York and London: W. W. Norton & Company, 2004), pp. 166–167 (emphasis added, MHVH).
38 Ibid., p. 166.

9
Reinforcing the independent agencies

Populists want "to give the power back to the people." They want to make the distance between the representatives and the represented as short as possible. They abhor not only "elitist parliaments" but equally "elitist governments." However, even populists must admit that the citizen still has influence on these democratic institutions through his or her vote. Therefore, populists consider those bodies and agencies which are invested with real power, but are *not* elected, as far greater enemies. These agencies are, as a rule, staffed by experts and technocrats, people whom populists consider to be enemies of "the common man."

Why do we have independent central banks?

An example is the European Central Bank, which is a favorite target of Eurosceptic populists from the left and from the right. The bank has exclusive authority over European monetary policy. Neither the European Parliament, nor the European Commission or national governments, have direct influence on its policies. The bank is a collegial body that makes decisions with complete independence. However, this is not acceptable to the Spanish leftist populist movement Podemos, which, in a program proposal of 2014, demanded the "democratization of the BCE [European Central Bank], making it accountable to the European Parliament, which should appoint its members."[1]

The independence of the European Central Bank is not, however, without reason written into European treaties. According to the official founding protocol "neither the ECB, nor a national central bank, nor any member of their decision-making bodies shall seek or take instructions from Community institutions or bodies, from any government of a Member State or from any other body."[2] This independence is modeled after the statute of the Bundesbank, the German central bank. The Germans had their reasons for insisting on this independence, having bad memories of the massive inflation of the 1920s which was one of the factors which undermined the political system of the Weimar Republic, leading to the rise of Hitler.[3] But more contemporary events have also led to this choice. Until 1993, for instance, the French central bank was not independent. It was the government which decided, and governments – from the left as well as from the right – were inclined to print banknotes to solve their short-term budget problems. It led to unsustainable inflation, which undermined the long-term development of the French economy. Between 1973 and 1982 inflation was never under 9.1 percent per year.[4] This changed radically when, in 1993, the French government decided to follow the German example and to make the central bank independent. Since that time inflation in France has never exceeded 2.8 percent, reached in 2008.[5]

"Illiberal democracies"

Independent bodies fulfill important functions in contemporary democracies. Already in 1925 John Maynard Keynes was pleading for their creation, writing: "Our task must be to decentralise and devolve wherever we can, and in particular to establish semi-independent corporations and organs of administration to which duties of government, new and old, will be entrusted; – without, however, impairing the democratic principle or the ultimate sovereignty of Parliament."[6] Keynes emphasized that they should respect the "ultimate sovereignty of Parliament." However, in order that these bodies could properly function parliaments and governments could interfere only indirectly. "Most western nations have developed a variety of safeguards against the abuse of democracy," writes Samuel Brittan. "They include written constitutions, second chambers, Human Rights legislation, judicial review of laws, international courts and much else. They need to be strengthened rather than pushed aside."[7]

However, populist governments, pretending to represent "the sovereign people," have an innate tendency to undermine these safeguards in the name of the people and "democracy." An example is Poland, where the Law and Justice Party (PiS), led by Jarosław Kaczyński, after winning the elections in 2015 started to reform the judicial system. The previous parliamentary majority had – legally – elected new judges for the Constitutional Tribunal. They were to replace judges whose term was to end in 2015 – including a date after the installation of the new government. The new PiS government refused to accept these judges and appointed its own judges. It led to a profound constitutional conflict which paralyzed the Polish constitutional system. The Venice Commission of the Council of Europe, asked for an opinion, wrote that "the effects of the [government] Amendments ... endanger not only the rule of law, but also the functioning of the democratic system, because they could render an important factor of checks and balances ineffective. Human rights would be endangered since the right to a fair trial before an independent court – the Constitutional Tribunal – is compromised."[8]

The Polish government did not give in, however, but continued to undermine the liberal foundations of the Polish state. On 12 July 2017, a new law was voted on by parliament, which gave the parliament (which means: the PiS majority) the power to dismiss members of the National Council of the Judiciary and appoint twenty-two of its twenty-five members.[9] It thereby abolished the independence of this council, which appoints all judges, including the judges of the Supreme Court. The latter, together with the Constitutional Tribunal, forms the apex of the Polish judicial system.[10] The vice-president of the European Commission, Frans Timmermans, announced on 20 December 2017 that the European Commission was proposing to the European Council to start a procedure, based on Article 7 of the EU Treaty,[11] which could suspend Poland's voting rights in the European Council. However, the problem was that the other EU members must take a unanimous decision. The Hungarian prime minister Viktor Orbán, who prides himself on being an "illiberal democrat" and who is introducing similar policies in his own country, forcibly retiring judges and weakening the Constitutional Court, announced that he would vote against.[12]

The necessity of checks and balances

Populist governments, claiming to execute "the will of the people," tend to attack the system of checks and balances which is the foundation of liberal democracy. This tendency is compounded by the authoritarian character of populist leaders, who do not like to be hemmed in by other government agencies. This does not mean that these kinds of conflict cannot emerge in long-established democracies, as becomes clear from the following example from the US. "The great prestige of the Supreme Court was shown in 1937," writes Harry Johnson,

> when President Franklin D. Roosevelt, exasperated by the fact that the Court had declared several New Deal measures unconstitutional, proposed a measure to increase the number of justices from nine to fifteen. Most people ... were against this so-called Court-packing plan. Many people were shocked, or professed to be.[13]

Franklin D. Roosevelt, the champion of the New Deal and the defender of the free world in the Second World War, a populist "court-packer"? Legally, he had the law on his side, but morally and psychologically his proposal was badly received: "The Court-packing plan was perfectly constitutional, for the Constitution leaves it to Congress to decide how many members the Supreme Court should have. Yet President Roosevelt probably never proposed a more distasteful measure."[14]

The role the American Supreme Court has played has been different in different historical periods, sometimes active, other times more restrained. The question is, according to Archibald Cox, who served in 1973 as Special Watergate Prosecutor in the Department of Justice: "What role should the judicial branch play in the government of the American people? Should the Court play an active, creative role in shaping our destiny, equally with the executive and legislative branches? Or should it be characterized by self-restraint, deferring to the legislative branch whenever there is room for policy judgment and leaving new departures to the initiative of others?"[15] The choice depended on the historical circumstances and on the personality of the acting chief justice of the Court. Under Chief Justice Earl Warren in the 1950s and early 1960s, "the Court has spearheaded the progress in civil rights, administration of criminal justice, protection of individual liberty, and the strengthening and extension of political democracy."[16] "Although the gains of decisions advancing social justice are evident,"[17] Cox argues that "the dilemma is insoluble. There is no rule by which a judge may know where to place the emphasis, nor any scale by which the contemporary critic can measure the balance struck."[18]

With the advent of the populist president Donald Trump the US system of checks and balances was again at risk. Confronted with bureaucratic opposition by the federal bureaucracy, the president claimed to be the victim of the "deep state," a conspiracy of powerful groups of unelected bureaucrats who were secretly pursuing their own agendas.[19] Jon Michaels admits that the federal agencies

> Function somewhat autonomously from their political masters, drawing on their own sources of legal authority, expertise, and professionalism ... Officials inside these agencies can defend environmental and workplace safety standards, international alliances, and the rule of law. They can investigate, document, and publicize instances of high-level government malfeasance. And they can do so, in no small part, because a good number of them are insulated by law from political pressure, enjoy de facto tenure, and have strong guild codes of professional behavior.[20]

Michaels emphasizes that the purpose of these agencies is "not to pursue a private agenda contrary to the public will but to execute that will – to deliver to the people the goods and services that their elected representatives have decreed, and to do so fairly and effectively."[21] Even the personnel of the agencies should be reassuring to the average citizen: "In fact, one could make a good case that the bureaucrats ... are closer to and more in tune with median voters than the mostly rich, elite politicians who control them."[22] For the populist leader and his voters, this is no reason to trust these professionals. On the contrary, they harbor a deep suspicion vis-à-vis these unelected agencies. In a survey conducted in the US in which the respondents were asked to indicate their trust in political institutions, Trump voters claimed to be "more trusting of Congress and the American voter," while Clinton voters claimed to be "more trusting of government regulators and agencies."[23]

When independent agencies become the object of turf wars, their legitimacy is in danger. In 2013 the Democratic Party changed the rule that candidates for federal judgeship needed sixty Senate votes to be confirmed, thereby undermining the bipartisan basis of nominations. The Democrats, holding a Senate majority at that time, decided that fifty-one votes would be enough for all federal judges – those of the Supreme Court excepted. When the Republicans gained a Senate majority in 2014 they blocked Obama's last nomination for the Supreme Court, extending the new voting system to include Supreme Court nominations. When Democrats filibustered President Trump's first nominee for the Supreme Court, the Republicans abolished the filibuster rule and appointed on 10 April 2017 Justice Neil M. Gorsuch, giving the Supreme Court a majority of conservative, Republican-leaning justices (five against four). This conservative majority was further strengthened after the appointment of Justice Brett Kavanaugh in July 2018, a fact which should comfort Trump. However, even with a "friendly" Supreme Court a conflict cannot be ruled out as long as it fulfills its task: to limit the power of the political majority when it infringes upon basic individual rights that are protected by the Constitution.[24] "The conventional wisdom about the court – that justices vote with their party – was too often wrong."[25]

In the American political system even the filibuster has been introduced with the intention of making majorities more moderate. The filibuster is a method of obstructing the lawgiving process by speaking for an unlimited amount of time. The filibuster allows a minority of forty-one senators to block a Senate majority of fifty-nine, by refusing to vote. It was introduced in 1806, but used only for the first time in 1837, when the inconveniences for minorities of decisions taken by simple majorities became clearer. It was a time in which majoritarian democracy risked endangering the liberal principles of the American Constitution. "By Tocqueville's time," writes Robert Dahl, "it was necessary to sound a new liberal warning. By concentrating all power in the people or rather in majorities, democracy also posed grave risks to liberty."[26] The filibuster is frequently attacked by Senate majorities, calling the procedure "undemocratic." However, both Republicans and Democrats have used the filibuster when in a minority position. According to the constitutional law scholar Bruce Ackerman, "The filibuster permits the Senate to play a moderating role within the constitutional system of checks and balances. Except when there is a decisive landslide, it requires the majority party to moderate its initiatives to gain the support of at least a few minority Senators."[27]

Majoritarian democracy or partnership democracy?

The underlying question is: What conception of democracy does one have? The American philosopher Ronald Dworkin identifies two different views. On the one hand the "majoritarian view," which holds that democracy is government by strict majority rule. However, he writes, "there is no guarantee that a majority will decide fairly; its decisions may be unfair to minorities whose interests the majority systematically ignores."[28] On the other hand he identifies the "partnership view" of democracy, which "means that the people govern themselves each as a full partner in a collective political enterprise so that a majority's decisions are democratic only when certain further conditions are met that protect the status and interests of each citizen as a full partner in that enterprise."[29] This means that one treats the political opponent with respect. Dworkin regrets that "we do not treat someone with whom we disagree as a partner – we treat him as an enemy or at best as an obstacle – when we make no effort either to understand the force of his contrary views, or to develop our own opinions in a way that makes them responsive to his. The partnership model so described seems unattainable now because it is difficult to see how Americans on rival sides of the supposed culture wars could come to treat each other with that mutual respect and attention."[30] The independence of the Supreme Court is a valuable asset. Even admitting that the Supreme Court's "record is stained with serious error at almost every period of its jurisprudence,"[31] Dworkin emphasizes that he has retained his "enthusiasm for trusting important matters of political morality to constitutional judges."[32]

The system of checks and balances built into the American Constitution by the Founding Fathers is not only the backbone of the American political system, it is also the backbone of *every* liberal democracy. In his book *Le bon gouvernement* (The Good Government) Pierre Rosanvallon praises these independent agencies as "new forms of impersonality," which, he writes, "have a corrective function vis-à-vis the tendency toward illiberalism. The increasing constitutionalization of democracies is one of its major expressions."[33] "And it is their autonomy," he continues, "which constitutes from now on one of the surest safeguards to ward off a drifting toward authoritarianism by the governments."[34]

> The independent surveillance and regulation authorities … are for their part responsible for a steadily increasing number of sectors of economic, social, and even political life (for instance as concerns the organization of elections) … It is institutions … organized in a collegial way, characterized by the duty to fulfill an expectation of impartiality. They are in charge of exceptional cases, overseeing the functioning of particular markets, defending rights in order to avoid the effects of favoritism, domination, discrimination,

monopoly, which destroy the equality of rights, the autonomy of persons, or the public character of certain resources or activities.[35]

Independent agencies as stabilizers of liberal democracy

Independent agencies have become important stabilizers of modern liberal democracies. "In our view," write Marshall Breger and Gary Edles, "structural and organization elements and statutory constraints, along with agency traditions and practices, have evolved together to permit independent agencies to conduct their business fairly and effectively while keeping them somewhat above the political fray."[36] "Keeping them somewhat above the political fray" is, indeed, their main contribution in a polarized environment: "Independent agencies reflect the resolution of a tug-of-war between agency factions and the political branches and allow policy warfare to be waged subtly, away from 'center court,' where affected interests can jockey for dominance."[37]

Independent agencies play a role in many domains. One of these is, for instance, the fight against corruption. "A strong anti-corruption agency is a huge strength in the fight against corruption – when they are independent of the government and empowered to investigate allegations, they have the potential to hold even the most powerful people in society to account."[38] The supposed or real corruption of the "elite" is a favorite theme of populists. "Consequently," write Mudde and Kaltwasser, "fighting and preventing corruption are crucial strategies for diminishing the demand side of populist politics … An important part of the legitimacy of *liberal* democracy comes precisely from the existence of autonomous institutions, which are able to hold state officials and elected politicians accountable to the citizens."[39]

Instead of being instruments in the hands of "technocrats" and "experts," which diminish the power of "the people," as populists claim, these impartial agencies defend rather the interests of the individual citizen against arbitrariness and the power of vested interests. This does not mean that they always and everywhere defend the interests of the individual citizen, because in the real world nothing is perfect.[40] However, the likelihood that in most cases they do is an established fact.

Notes

1 Vicenç Navarro and Juan Torres López, "Un Proyecto económico para la gente – Democratizar la economía para salir de la crisis mejorando la equidad, el bienestar y la calidad de vida, una propuesta de debate para solucionar los problemas de la economía española," Podemos, November 2014, paragraph 5.1.3., p. 11. http://s01.s3c.es/imag/doc/2014-11-28/DocumentoEconomicoPodemos.pdf (accessed 28 September 2017).

Do we have too much democracy or not enough?

2. "Consolidated Version of the Treaty on European Union and of the Treaty Establishing the European Community," Protocol (No. 18) on the Statute of the European System of Central Banks and of the European Central Bank (1992), Chapter III, article 7, *Official Journal of the European Union*, 29 December 2006. www.ecb.europa.eu/ecb/legal/pdf/ce32120061229en00010331.pdf (accessed 28 September 2017).
3. The hyperinflation was a national catastrophe. "By the end of November 1923, a single U.S. dollar bought 4.2 trillion marks, a barely comprehensible exchange rate ... Germans carried suitcases and pushed wheelbarrows full of money – to buy a loaf of bread or a pair of shoes. They swarmed over the countryside and railroad yards like biblical gleaners or latter-day thieves, gathering potatoes that had been left behind in the field or coal that had fallen off train cars, or they dismantled fences and took the wood for heating. Prices changed two and three times a day" (Eric D. Weitz, *Weimar Germany – Promise and Tragedy* (Princeton and Oxford: Princeton University Press, 2007), p. 102).
4. In 1973 it was 9.2 percent, in 1974 13.7 percent, in 1975 11.8 percent, in 1976 9.6 percent, in 1977 9.4 percent, in 1978 9.1 percent, in 1979 10.8 percent, in 1980 13.6 percent, in 1981 13.4 percent, and in 1982 11.8 percent. Cf. "France-Inflation.com." http://france-inflation.com/inflation-depuis-1901.php (accessed 2 October 2017).
5. Ibid.
6. John Maynard Keynes, "Am I a Liberal?" in John Maynard Keynes, *Essays in Persuasion* (London: Macmillan and Co., 1931), p. 331. The text was an address to the Liberal Summer School at Cambridge in 1925.
7. Samuel Brittan, "The devil in democracy – Majorities and pluralities can often be very misleading," *Financial Times Magazine*, 28–29 July 2007.
8. "Opinion on Amendment to the Act of 25 June 2015 on the Constitutional Tribunal of Poland," adopted by the Venice Commission at its 106th Plenary Session, Venice, 11–12 March 2016. www.venice.coe.int/webforms/documents/default.aspx?pdffile=CDL-AD(2016)001-e (accessed 3 October 2017).
9. "Polish ruling PiS lawmakers submit bill to replace judges, opposition protests," Reuters, 12 July 2017. www.reuters.com/article/us-poland-politics-court/polish-ruling-pis-lawmakers-submit-bill-to-replace-judges-opposition-protests-idUSKBN19X2F6 (accessed 3 October 2017).
10. "Poland: Draft law threatens Supreme Court," Human Rights Watch, 20 July 2017. www.hrw.org/news/2017/07/20/poland-draft-law-threatens-supreme-court (accessed 4 October 2017).
11. Cf. European Commission, Press Release "Rule of Law: European Commission acts to defend judicial independence in Poland," 20 December 2017. http://europa.eu/rapid/press-release_IP-17-5367_en.htm (accessed 5 January 2018).
12. Interestingly, Bruce Ackerman had already expressed, in 1992, his doubts about the acceptance of independent courts in the countries of Central Europe. "The American example of judicial review," he wrote, "has undoubtedly inspired judges elsewhere. But its slow and painful development in its native land does not encourage hopes for a quick transplant, especially in such uncongenial soil as Eastern Europe. Communism gravely weakened the uncertain tradition of judicial independence that Eastern Europe had inherited from the Austro-Hungarian and Russian empires ... the high prestige of the judiciary in America contrasts painfully with the low estate of the judges of Eastern Europe. To put the point gently, being a judge was not a high-status occupation under Communism ... Given the low status of the judiciary, why should the new generation of politicians and police follow

13 Johnson, *Sociology*, p. 351.
14 Ibid., p. 351. "One lesson to be drawn from the events of 1937," wrote Allen Potter, "is that a direct challenge to the independence of the Supreme Court is politically dangerous." However, he added: "A more subtle lesson is that it is part of the art of judicial statesmanship not to obstruct the elected branches of the government too much" (Allen M. Potter, *American Government and Politics*, London: Faber and Faber Limited, 1969), p. 262. It was a question, therefore, of finding a delicate balance.
15 Archibald Cox, *The Warren Court – Constitutional Decision as an Instrument of Reform* (Cambridge, Mass.: Harvard University Press, 1968), p. 2.
16 Ibid., p. 4.
17 Ibid., p. 23.
18 Ibid., pp. 22–23.
19 Juliet Eilperin, Lisa Rein, and Marc Fisher, "Resistance from within: Federal workers push back against Trump," *Washington Post*, 31 January 2017. www.washingtonpost.com/politics/resistance-from-within-federal-workers-push-back-against-trump/2017/01/31/c65b110e-e7cb-11e6-b82f-687d6e6a3e7c_story.html?utm_term=.23d17fd8b0eb (accessed 3 October 2017).
20 Jon D. Michaels, "Trump and the 'Deep State' – The Government Strikes Back," *Foreign Affairs*, Vol. 96, No. 5, September/October 2017, p. 53.
21 Ibid., p. 53.
22 Ibid., p. 54.
23 Cf. "2017 Edelman trust barometer." www.edelman.com/trust2017/trust-and-us-presidential-election/ (accessed 6 January 2018).
24 Cf. website of the US Supreme Court. www.supremecourt.gov/about/biographies.aspx (accessed 4 October 2017).
25 Patti Waldmeir, "Party politics provides a poor guide to positions of the Supreme Court," *Financial Times*, 2 July 2004. This does not mean, however, that in increasingly polarized situations the judges are "ideology-free." As Robert Dahl rightly remarks, "Inevitably, in interpreting the constitution judges bring their own ideology, biases, and preferences to bear" (Robert A. Dahl, *How Democratic Is the American Constitution?* (New Haven and London: Yale University Press, 2003), p. 55). He adds, "The Supreme Court has often used its power to impose policies that were little more than reflections of the political ideologies of a majority of members of the Court" (p. 167). Individual judges of the Court differ in the way they assume an attitude of self-restraint or activism. "The doctrine of judicial self-restraint," writes Edward McWhinney, "takes note of the fact that the court is an appointive, non-elective body that can make no valid claims of having a popular 'mandate,' and that its members' prestige and public standing depend, in certain measure, on their political non-involvement and the extent to which they in fact stay aloof from the exigent here-and-now" (Edward McWhinney, *Comparative Federalism – States' Rights and National Power* (Toronto: Toronto University Press, 1965), p. 32). "The argument in favour of the other – activist – view of the judicial role," he writes, "is that the judges are an elitist group of high talents, aspirations, and ideals; that, though they may not be omniscient or for that matter philosopher-kings, they are normally far better equipped intellectually than most people in government; and that, so long as they are aware of their own limitations, there is no grave risk of abuse of their great powers" (p. 33). In the polarized situation of the Trump era, however, nominations for the Supreme Court have become part of an

ideological culture war. After Neil Gorsuch (forty-nine years old), Donald Trump nominated Brett Kavanaugh (fifty-three years) and Amy Coney Barrett (forty-eight years). Because Trump's strategy of nominating young justices would create for many decades a conservative-leaning Supreme Court, proposals have been put forward to appoint justices for single eighteen-year terms, rather than for life (cf. "Weak is strong – America's highest court needs term limits," *The Economist*, 15 September 2018).

26 Dahl, *Dilemmas of Pluralist Democracy*, p. 105.
27 Bruce Ackerman, "A threat to impartiality in the American Senate," *Financial Times*, 16 May 2005.
28 Ronald Dworkin, *Is Democracy Possible Here? Principles for a New Political Debate* (Princeton and Oxford: Princeton University Press, 2008), p. 131.
29 Ibid., p. 131. Dworkin's "partnership democracy" resembles the "idea of an overlapping consensus," developed by John Rawls in his book *Political Liberalism* (New York: Columbia University Press, 1993), pp. 133–172. According to Rawls this idea of an "overlapping consensus" makes it possible "that there can be a stable and just society whose free and equal citizens are deeply divided by conflicting and even incommensurable religious, philosophical, and moral doctrines" (p. 133).
30 Dworkin, *Is Democracy Possible Here?*, pp. 132–133.
31 Ibid., p. 156.
32 Ibid., p. 157. Dworkin proposes term limits of a maximum fifteen years instead of the present lifelong tenure, because he is worried about "an ideological administration appointing young ideological justices whose tenure on the Court will last for generations, long after the nation has steered itself back to the middle as, so far, it always has" (p. 158). Dworkin's fear seems to be confirmed by President Trump's practice of appointing relatively young justices.
33 Rosanvallon, *Bon gouvernement*, p. 179.
34 Ibid., p. 180.
35 Ibid., p. 180.
36 Marshall J. Breger and Gary J. Edles, *Independent Agencies in the United States: Law, Structure, and Politics* (Oxford and New York: Oxford University Press, 2015), p. 16.
37 Ibid., p. 16.
38 "What's At Stake?" Anti-Corruption Agency Strengthening Initiative, Transparency International. www.transparency.org/whatwedo/activity/anti_corruption_agency_strengthening_initiative (accessed 6 January 2018).
39 Mudde and Kaltwasser, *Populism*, p. 110.
40 Famous is the Lochner v. New York case of 1905, in which the US Supreme Court overturned the New York "Bakeshop Act," a labor law which restricted the working hours of bakery employees to ten hours a day and sixty hours a week. The majority of the US Supreme Court considered the law to be an "interference with the right and liberty of the individual to contract." This decision is seen as a landmark case in which the Court overstepped the boundaries of its judicial powers.

Part III

Twenty proposals to defend liberal democracy: reforming politics and education

Part III

10
Not more, but less direct democracy is needed

The recent wave of populism resembles a ferocious worldwide tsunami, ravaging the foundations of liberal democracy – a rogue, giant wave against which, apparently, we cannot defend ourselves. But can't we defend ourselves? Can't we defend our liberal democracies? Are we just lame ducks, waiting passively for things to happen, hoping that the storm will pass and the worst will soon be over? Certainly not: there is a lot we can do. And we can act on different levels: on the level of the democratic institutions, on the level of political parties, on the level of education of citizens, and – last, but not least – on the level of society at large.

In 1984 Norberto Bobbio wrote: "I don't think that I am too reckless when I say that our time could be called *L'ère des démocraties*."[1] This "era of democracies," which started with the end of the Portuguese dictatorship in 1974, got into a higher gear after the fall of the Berlin Wall and the end of communism, leading to an increasing number of countries embracing liberal democracy. Samuel Huntington called it "The third wave of democratization."[2] However, some voices were already warning against the "end of history" euphoria[3] which dominated in the West, criticizing Fukuyama's idea that the end of communism was the "Cunning of Reason" by which a Hegelian "World Spirit" had shown that the realization of a capitalist market economy and a liberal democracy were the *nec plus ultra* – the ultimate goals – of world history. Robert Dahl wrote: "Looking back on the rise and decline of democracy, it is clear that we cannot count on historical forces to insure that democracy will always advance – or even survive, as the long intervals in which popular governments vanished from the earth remind us."[4] And he added: "Democracy, it appears, is a bit chancy. But its chances also depend on what we do ourselves. Even if we cannot count on benign historical forces to favor democracy, we are not mere victims of blind forces over which we have no control. With an adequate understanding of what democracy requires and the will to meet its requirements, we can act to preserve and, what is more, to advance democratic ideas and practices."[5]

Twenty proposals: reforming politics and education

Dahl is right. History is not preordained, it is an open process and we cannot foresee where it will take us. No one had foreseen the sudden end of communism and the demise of the Soviet Union. No one, likewise, had foreseen the populist wave which since 2010 has swelled to dramatic dimensions, submerging even the US, which touted itself as the "torchbearer for the free world" and "the vanguard of liberal democracy."

From the third wave of democratization to its reverse wave

However, Samuel Huntington was realistic enough not to present the advance of liberal democracy as a linear progressive process. After each wave of democratization he observed the development of a counter-current, which he called a "reverse wave."

The first reverse wave began in 1922 with Mussolini's March on Rome. Of the seventeen countries which adopted democratic institutions between 1910 and 1931, only four maintained them throughout the 1920s and 1930s.[6] The second reverse wave began in the early 1960s, when particularly in Latin America a shift toward authoritarianism took place.[7]

It is clear that after the "third wave of democratization" we have entered today the third reverse wave. However, the force of this third wave, which is striking not only Latin America, but also Europe and the US, seems to be much stronger than that of the second and resembles more and more the first reverse wave of the interbellum. What can we do?

In this and the following chapters I will present a number of recommendations which could help us to get out of the crisis. Of course, these recommendations are not a cure-all for all our problems, but, taken together, they could invert the present trend, in which authorities – confronted with the populist challenge – often react in the wrong way by giving in to demands to introduce forms of direct democracy, thereby exacerbating the problem they want to solve.

Proposal #1: ban the populist toolkit: not more but less direct democracy is needed

In recent years it has become something resembling a Pavlov dog reaction: when governments or political parties are confronted with the disaffection of the electorate, they tend to accept at face value the opinion of critics, who blame the existing system of parliamentary democracy for not being "democratic" enough. This leads to proposals and measures which make it possible to "better listen to the man in the street." As a rule, this means introducing new methods of direct democracy, in particular initiatives and referendums, considered to be adequate instruments for bringing politicians "closer to the people."

An American scholar called these forms of direct democracy, not without reason, "the right of the people to make fools of themselves."[8] We have seen how these new tools, meant to enhance and improve our democracies, have been hijacked by populist demagogues and agitators to promote their own illiberal agendas. In some cases the results have been catastrophic. The decision taken by the British prime minister David Cameron to organize on 23 June 2016 a referendum on British membership of the European Union is a case in point. An uninformed public was bombarded with fake arguments, half-truths, and blatant lies. One of these was that the money which would be saved by leaving the EU would be used to improve the National Health Service.[9] What made the situation even worse was Cameron's promise that he would respect and implement the outcome of the referendum, notwithstanding the fact that legally it had only an advisory character. "There is no binding legal process to force Cameron to invoke article 50 [of the Lisbon Treaty – the article about leaving the Union]," wrote the *Guardian* on the day of the referendum. "In theory he could ignore the public and disregard a Brexit vote. In practice he has repeatedly promised that the result will stick – and there may be no going back on that line now."[10] It was, indeed, a promise made by the prime minister which was decisive and not the letter of the law. Cameron put his personal credibility above the sovereignty of parliament, the foundation and cornerstone of the British constitutional order. The bitter irony is that a majority of the parliament would have voted to remain in the European Union.

Another example of a recently introduced form of direct democracy that was hijacked by populists is the Ukraine initiative in the Netherlands. The referendum on the association agreement between Ukraine and the EU was held on 6 April 2016, and won by its opponents. Although the referendum had only an advisory character, Dutch prime minister Mark Rutte promised to "at least acknowledge the result."[11] During the EU summit of December 2016, Rutte succeeded in convincing the European Council of Heads of State and Governments to adopt a declaration explaining that the treaty did not guarantee EU membership to Ukraine, nor was the EU obliged to provide military assistance to this country (two arguments that were used by opponents of the treaty). On 30 May 2017, after receiving this declaration, the Dutch Senate ratified the treaty with a two-thirds majority.[12]

Neither are the existing practices of direct democracy in California and Switzerland encouraging. In California not only are the initiatives blocking government action by causing permanent budget problems, but they are, additionally, increasingly hijacked by private interests. In Switzerland, where the system until recently seemed to work reasonably well, the initiatives have been hijacked by the populist far right to advance its xenophobic agenda.

Max Weber had already criticized the referendum in 1918, because, he wrote, "it answers only with 'Yes' or 'No'."[13] For this reason "it would also ... obstruct in a negative way the adoption of those laws which depend on a compromise between opposing interests."[14] Referendums and initiatives promote polarization and stand in the way of seeking and formulating compromises, which is the work of parliaments. Ralf Dahrendorf called the referendum "a resignation of politics before its obligation to [organize] a democratic debate, in the place of which one takes a snapshot of public opinion."[15] And Karl Mannheim considered that "the plebiscitary element in democracy" had "made the largest contribution to the destruction of the system. The plebiscitary principle drives people towards ... crowd psychology. This crowd psychology is one of the chief evils to be feared, a precipice before which democracy stands."[16]

Does this mean that referendums and initiatives have to be avoided in all circumstances? No, sometimes clear choices have to be made. However, these instruments should be used sparsely and be reserved only for extraordinary situations, such as, for instance, the adoption of a new constitution or a fundamental change in the character of the state. An example is the referendum organized in Greece on 8 December 1974, after the collapse of the military junta. Greek voters were asked whether they wanted to retain the republic, introduced by the junta, or preferred the return of the monarchy. Another example is the referendum organized in France by De Gaulle on 28 September 1958, on the introduction of the Constitution of the Fifth Republic.

Proposal #2: defend the independent agencies

In chapter 9 we saw the important role played by independent agencies in liberal democracies. This is particularly true for independent judiciaries, independent Supreme Courts, independent central banks, and independent anti-corruption watchdogs. We have seen how illiberal regimes, such as the PiS government in Poland and Viktor Orbán's Fidesz government in Hungary, are attacking the independence of the courts, paving the way for the introduction of an authoritarian regime.

Independent Supreme Courts are necessary countervailing powers in liberal democracies. Together with the mass media and other independent agencies, they are among the first targets attacked by populist governments. Trump's attacks on the "fake media" are a case in point.

In the United States nominations for the Supreme Court have always been part of ideological culture wars and political struggles – with the risk of an increasing politicization. To counter this politicization and make the Supreme Court more bipartisan three measures should be considered. In the first place the practice of appointing young justices for life which makes it possible for a president to "govern beyond the grave," should be changed by introducing term limits, for instance eighteen-year terms.[17] In the second place presidents should not be able to appoint more than two justices during their presidency. In the third place the (new) rule that justices are confirmed by a simple Senate majority – or, eventually, only by fifty senators plus the vice-president – should be abolished and the former rule of a three-fifths vote (60–40) reinstated.

Proposal #3: abolish open primaries

In chapter 8 we analyzed how political parties in Europe, confronted with a loss of membership, have increasingly "outsourced" the selection of candidates by organizing open primaries, which offer non-members the opportunity to have a decisive influence on the selection process. Touted as a procedure which helps to select the "most popular candidate," thereby apparently increasing the possibility of winning an election, this system has many biases.

In the first place it takes the decision away from the party leadership and the party members, who are the people most able and qualified to judge the character, leadership potential, and convictions of a candidate. Instead, the selection is made by outsiders, who lack this detailed knowledge. These outsiders make their choice rather on the basis of superficial criteria, such as the candidate's "good looks," his or her "sympathetic personality," or the fact that the candidate is known as a "media personality." Further, the open primary makes it possible for the selection process to be influenced by passionate minorities – and even by members of other political parties, who have an interest in selecting the weakest candidate in order to promote the chances of their own candidate in the election. According to Michael Walzer,

> Once primaries are established, and especially once open primaries are established, state and local organizations lose their hold. The candidate makes his appeal not through an articulated structure but through the mass media. He does not negotiate with local leaders, speak to caucuses, form alliances with established interest groups. Instead, he solicits votes, as it were, one by one, among all registered voters without regard to their attachment to the party, loyalty to its programs, or willingness to work for its success. In turn, the voters encounter the candidate only on the television screen, without political mediation. Voting is lifted out of the context of parties and platforms; it is more like impulse buying than political decision making.[18]

It is telling that populist parties, which claim to represent "the people," do not extend this power to outsiders, or even to sympathizers. Decisions on candidates are often made in the backrooms of the party leadership and most of the time the position of the leader is not even open to discussion for insiders. This is not, of course, the model to follow. A democratically organized political party should give its members, and not outsiders, the last word in the selection process.

Notes

1. Bobbio, *Futuro della democrazia*, p. XIII.
2. Samuel P. Huntington, *The Third Wave – Democratization in the Late Twentieth Century* (Norman: University of Oklahoma Press, 1993), p. 21.
3. Cf. Francis Fukuyama, "The End of History?" *The National Interest*, No. 16, Summer 1989, pp. 3–18.
4. Robert A. Dahl, *On Democracy* (New Haven and London: Yale University Press, 1998), p. 25.
5. Ibid., p. 25.
6. Huntington, *Third Wave*, p. 17.
7. Ibid., p. 19.
8. Daniel M. Warner, "Direct democracy: The Right of the People to Make Fools of Themselves; The Use and Abuse of Initiative and Referendum, A Local Government Perspective," *Seattle University Law Review*, Volume 19, No. 1 (1995). http://digitalcommons.law.seattleu.edu/sulr/vol19/iss1/2/ (accessed 9 October 2017).
9. Cf. "EU referendum: Brexit 'could boost NHS by £100m a week'," BBC, 4 June 2016. www.bbc.com/news/uk-politics-eu-referendum-36450749 (accessed 9 October 2017).
10. "Is the EU referendum legally binding?" *Guardian*, 23 June 2016. www.theguardian.com/politics/2016/jun/23/eu-referendum-legally-binding-brexit-lisbon-cameron-sovereign-parliament (accessed 10 October 2017).
11. "Netherlands rejects EU–Ukraine partnership deal," BBC, 7 April 2016. www.bbc.com/news/world-europe-35976086 (accessed 14 October 2020).
12. "Netherlands ratifies EU–Ukraine treaty," *EU Observer*, 30 May 2017. https://euobserver.com/foreign/138060 (accessed 11 October 2017).
13. Weber, "Parlament und Regierung," p. 420.
14. Ibid., p. 420.
15. Ralf Dahrendorf, *Die Krisen der Demokratie* (Munich: C. H. Beck, 2002), p. 76.
16. Karl Mannheim, *Man and Society in an Age of Reconstruction* (London and Henley: Routledge & Kegan Paul, 1980), p. 356.
17. Supreme Court appointees are becoming younger: "In the 1930s the average age of the 10 most recent confirmed justices was about 58. Gorsuch's swearing in [on 10 April 2017, MHVH] ... put that figure at 51.7 years." Cf. Gwyn Guilford, "117 years of data show why today's Supreme Court nominees have more influence than ever," *Quartz*, 10 July 2018. https://qz.com/1324841/brett-kavanaughs-age-at-53-means-that-he-may-wield-influence-on-the-supreme-court-for-a-very-long-time/ (accessed 4 September 2018).
18. Michael Walzer, *Spheres of Justice – A Defense of Pluralism and Equality* (New York: Basic Books Inc., 1983), p. 307.

11

A plea for a *cordon sanitaire*

Proposal #4: keep populist parties out of governments: a plea for a *cordon sanitaire*

Should populist parties be invited to participate in coalition governments? This is, indeed, a burning question, and different answers are possible, depending on the expectation one has of the result. Would the participation of a populist party influence the other parties in the coalition and lead to a radicalization of a country's policies? Or, on the contrary, would the participation of a populist party in a broader coalition with mainstream parties have a moderating effect on this party and, eventually, change the party? The latter approach was recommended by Pierre-André Taguieff, who wrote: "Today it's about defining the best way … to promote their integration into the 'normal' political game … In politics even the 'devils' can be tamed and integrated into common mankind."[1]

Different strategies have been adopted in different countries. An important factor is the character of the populist party. A far-left populist party is different from a far-right populist party. The former lacks the nationalism and xenophobia of the latter. It is the far-right populist parties which cause most problems. They are openly racist or denounce other cultures as "incompatible" with (superior) Western culture; they often glorify violence, and do not hide their fascist or neo-Nazi roots. Examples are the Belgian Vlaams Belang, Jobbik in Hungary, the Swedish Democrats (Sverige Demokraterna, SD), Golden Dawn in Greece, and, to a certain extent, the Austrian Freedom Party (FPÖ). As a rule, mainstream parties exclude these parties from entering coalition governments. Their value systems are too different. In Belgium, for instance, the mainstream parties have installed a *"cordon sanitaire"* – an agreement not to cooperate with Vlaams Belang. In France such a *cordon sanitaire* exists for the Rassemblement National, despite a process of *dédiabolisation* conducted by its leader Marine Le Pen, who distanced herself from her father Jean-Marie Le Pen and changed the name of the party.

Twenty proposals: reforming politics and education

Since 2000 there has been an increasing number of national governments in which far-right populist parties have participated, as well as governments that have been supported by them. A case in point is Austria, where in 2000 the conservative party ÖVP formed a coalition government with the FPÖ of Jörg Haider. At that time it caused a shockwave in Europe.[2] The member states of the EU introduced sanctions. However, these sanctions did not change Austria's course and even worked to Haider's advantage. "With hindsight … the EU intervention in the internal affairs and sovereignty of a member state had been proven over-hasty and contra-productive. The 'EU Quarantaine' had only increased Haider's popularity and led to an anti-EU mood in broad sections of the Austrian population."[3] The EU ended its sanctions after a committee of 'Three Wise Men' had presented a report in September 2000, which was rather positive. The conservative prime minister Wolfgang Schüssel promised that he would 'tame the dragon' and the Austrian example was considered a testing ground for the theory that by participating in governments the populists would 'become more moderate.' The Austrian example was important, because the Freedom Party was a party with Nazi roots.[4]

"Taming the dragon": the Austrian experience

The "taming" seemed to work. In order to enter government the Freedom Party had to accept Austria's EU membership and to distance itself from its Nazi past. The controversial party leader, Jörg Haider, did not get a ministerial portfolio and abdicated as party leader.

Participation in government soon led to severe tensions within the party, in particular when the FPÖ suffered great electoral losses. The party, which had got 26.9 percent of the vote in the parliamentary elections of 1999, shrunk to 16.9 percent in 2002. Its coalition partner, the ÖVP, on the contrary, got 42.3 percent and won by 15.4 percent. It led to euphoria in the European press. Even former critics of Schüssel congratulated him on his success. The German magazine *Der Spiegel* published an article titled "The hour of the dragon killer."[5] The tensions within the Freedom Party, caused by its electoral defeat, led in 2005 to a scission. The Freedom Party left government, but a rump of the old party, led by Jörg Haider, remained in government under the new party label "Alliance for the Future of Austria" (Bündnis Zukunft Österreich, BZÖ).

Not only the press, but also social scientists shared the opinion that cooptation of populists was a silver bullet. In a book chapter titled "Populist Parties in Government: Damned to Fail?" the authors wrote: "When in 2000 Haider's FPÖ entered government, the expectations of its functionaries and voters were high, because the demands made to 'the elite' for so many years, could finally be realized. However, the perception created by political communication, that, once in government, in politics everything is possible, encountered institutional obstacles."[6]

Was Schüssel's strategy: "to tame the dragon," so successful in effect? In the short term this seemed to be the case. However, what about the long term? Although the scission of the Freedom Party was good news, it was as if Schüssel had chopped off one head of the dragon, only for it to immediately grow another.

The original Freedom Party, liberated from the constraints of its participation in government, re-radicalized under its new leader Heinz-Christian Strache, attacking the EU and making migration the main topic of the party's campaign during the parliamentary election of 2008. The radical Freedom Party and not its moderate offshoot BZÖ became the third party, winning 17.54 percent of the vote, against 10.7 percent for the latter. In 2013 the Freedom Party further improved its score, winning 20.51 percent of the vote, while the BZÖ fell back to a miserable 3.53 percent. A sign that the FPÖ had become a respectable member of the Austrian political landscape was the presidential election of 4 December 2016, in which the candidate of the FPÖ, Norbert Hofer, won 46.2 percent of the vote against Alexander Van der Bellen, an independent candidate, who was a member of the Green Party.[7] In the parliamentary election of 15 October 2017, the Freedom Party won 27.4 percent of the vote, its best result since its foundation.

Taking advantage of the tensions between the two "traditional" coalition partners, the conservative ÖVP and the social democratic SPÖ, the Freedom Party was ready to enter a new coalition with the conservatives. This time, however, not as a tolerated "poor member of the family," but as a party taking its rightful place at the government table. In December 2017 the new ÖVP–FPÖ government was in place. Its leader, Heinz-Christian Strache, became vice-chancellor. In the coalition deal both parties had agreed to share power almost equally.[8] It was not politics but a scandal which brought this government down on 18 May 2019.[9]

The Austrian example shows that a strategy of accepting far-right populist parties as coalition partners, rather than "taming the dragon," can backfire. When the parties are in government they can temporarily moderate their radical stances but – back in opposition – they quickly re-radicalize. Populist parties in government normally also use a double strategy: they behave as a government party (particularly when they can claim the achievement of demands that are important for their electorate) and, at the same time, act as an opposition party. According to Albertazzi and McDonnell, "As mainstream parties across Europe are increasingly accepting the idea of having to form coalitions with populists, the latter's presence in power is bound to become more common in the foreseeable future."[10] But is the presence of populist parties really "bound to become more common," as these authors maintain? This is not self-evident, because it depends to a great extent on the political strategy of the democratic mainstream parties.

"Taming populists": the Scandinavian and Italian experience

We have to debunk the increasingly accepted theory that radical right populist parties are "tamed" by participation in coalition governments. Let us give another example, this time from Denmark. Here we have a far-right populist party that was founded as a tax protest party in 1972 under the name Progress Party (Fremskridtspartiet). When, in 1984, the party's founder, Mogens Glistrup, was jailed for tax fraud, he was succeeded by Pia Kjærsgaard, who changed the party into an anti-immigration party. In 1995 she split off and continued with an offshoot of the Progress Party, called the Danish People's Party (Dansk Folkeparti). In the parliamentary elections of 2001 this party got 12 percent of the vote and became the country's third party. The party did not enter the government coalition but supported the liberal–conservative minority government in parliament.

This *de facto* government responsibility did not harm the party. In the parliamentary elections of 2005 it got 13.2 percent of the vote, and in 2007 13.9 percent. The party continued to support the government from 2001 through 2011. This support enabled it to further its anti-immigration agenda. "The bourgeois government," wrote Jorgen Andersen, "has tightened the rules on immigration more than the Danish People's Party could have dreamed of in the mid-1990s."[11] This was not only the effect of a supposed moderation of the populists, but rather of a hardening of attitudes among the governing coalition: "In 2006, the vice-chairman of the Liberal Party declared that his party and the Danish People's Party to a large extent had shared values."[12] When, in the parliamentary election of 2011, the party fell back to 12.3 percent of the vote, it ended its support of the government and joined the opposition. This strategy worked out very well: in 2015 the party won 21.1 percent of the vote and became the country's second largest party. From 2015 it is again supporting the government.[13]

Killing the dragon? Let us have a look at another example. This time from Norway. We have here a populist party, the Progress Party (Fremskrittspartiet, FrP), whose history is somewhat similar to that of the Danish People's Party. The Progress Party was founded in 1973 also as an anti-tax protest party, which radicalized after 2000 into an anti-immigration and anti-Islam party. Over the last twenty years, in parliamentary elections, the party has won almost always between 15 and 20 percent of the vote.[14] In 2013 the party entered government for the first time, in a coalition with the Conservative Party. This cooptation of the populists by the mainstream did not kill

A plea for a cordon sanitaire

the party. In the parliamentary election on 11 September 2017, the party got an honorable 15.3 percent. Compared with the results of 2013 (16.3 percent) it had lost only 1 percent since it entered government. Both the Conservative Party and the Progress Party have announced that they want to continue their coalition.

Another country where populists entered government is Finland, where, in 2015, the populist Finns Party (formerly True Finns) entered a coalition government with the Conservative Party and the Center Party. The Finns Party made an electoral breakthrough in 2011, when it became the country's third largest party with 19.1 percent of the vote. In 2015 it even became the second largest with 17.7 percent. Did the party become more moderate during its time in government? On 10 June 2017, the party chose a new leader. His name was Jussi Halla-Aho, the most radical of the candidates, a man who had been convicted by the Finnish Supreme Court for incitement to racial hatred. The choice of this new leader led to the centrists and conservatives ending the coalition, evoking "diverging values."[15] More than half of the Finns Party MPs left the parliamentary group and were thereafter expelled from the party. They formed a new group, called New Alliance, which continues to support the government.

We see here a repeat of the FPÖ scenario in Austria, where, after participation in government the party split into two parts, one of which continues to support the government while the other joins the opposition. However, it is too early to call the Finnish case a victory for the "dragon killers." We have seen in the Austrian case that not the moderates, but rather the extremists have a chance of gaining in the next elections. In France the *cordon sanitaire* which keeps the Rassemblement National outside the national government seems to work. However, it has not prevented the party from increasing its share of the vote over the years. In May 2017 Marine Le Pen got 33.94 percent of the vote in the second round of the presidential election against Macron, who won with 66.06 percent. It was a huge disappointment to Le Pen. The defeat caused internal strife in the party, leading to the departure of its vice-president, Florian Philippot. Philippot, a former partisan of Chévènement's radical left, warned of a *rediabolisation*, a re-radicalization of the party.[16] Such a development would confirm the tendency that radical right parties, even if they have temporarily taken a more moderate stance when in government (or, in the case of the Front National/Rassemblement National, when they hoped to win the presidency), easily re-radicalize when in opposition, respectively when they have no longer the immediate hope of winning a presidential election.

Killing the dragon? A last example is Italy, where we can observe a new "populist phenomenon," namely a coalition government of a left-wing and a right-wing populist party governing together. The first to introduce this model was Greece, but here the coalition was completely dominated by the left-wing Syriza party.[17] This was not the case in Italy. In the parliamentary election of 4 March 2018 the left-wing populist Five Star Movement got 227 seats (32 percent of the vote) and the far-right populist Lega got 125 seats (17 percent of the vote). Did the far-right Lega suffer from its participation in government? Lega leader Matteo Salvini, who was interior minister, conducted an aggressive anti-immigrant policy which got a wide media coverage. The strategy worked. The balance of power between the two coalition partners was soon completely inverted. In the European elections of May 2019 the Lega party obtained 34.4 percent of the vote, the Five Star Movement only 17.1 percent. In opinion polls conducted in July 2019, 40 percent of the respondents expressed their support for Lega.[18] It became therefore tempting for Salvini to end the coalition government in order to organize new elections which would enable him to govern alone. On 20 August 2019, the government fell. Although Salvini's bid to govern alone after organizing a snap election was blocked by the Five Star Movement, which formed a new coalition with the left-wing Democratic Party, the Italian case seems to confirm the fact that rather than killing far-right populist parties, their participation in coalition governments contributes to strengthening their legitimacy. This is confirmed by recent research. Sarah de Lange writes:

> It is evident that parties are "neither amnesiac nor myopic" and that previous coalition experience inspires new ones. Coalition formation theorists have identified at least two ways in which previous coalition experiences impact on coalition outcomes, namely through familiarity and inertia. Familiarity refers to the fact that "in any coalition-forming situation a coalition will form containing that set of partners most familiar with working together" … In other words, parties with government experience have an advantage in the coalition formation process and parties that have governed together are especially likely to govern together again.[19]

The familiarity effect is based on the mutual trust of politicians who have already worked together in government. When far-right populist parties have proven to be trustworthy partners, they can expect to be chosen again as a coalition partner when the coalition is able to maintain its majority in the elections.

The necessity of building a cordon sanitaire

The same analysts who adhere to "killing the dragon" theories also warn against setting up a *cordon sanitaire*. While the participation of the populists in government might kill them, a *cordon sanitaire* is supposed to make them prosper. But is this really the case? Let us have a look at Belgium, a country where the mainstream parties have installed such a *cordon*, refusing to cooperate with the radical right party

Vlaams Belang (former Vlaams Blok) after this party began to make rapid electoral gains. Critics said that this strategy would only promote the further advance of the party, which would complain of being a victim and claim to be ostracized by the country's "political elite."

The critics seemed to have been right. The Vlaams Blok/Vlaams Belang got 10.4 percent in the parliamentary elections of 1991, 12.3 percent in 1995, 15.4 percent in 1999, 17.9 percent in 2003, and 18.9 percent in 2007.[20] Its advance seemed unstoppable and the point at which it might become a kingmaker, choosing which coalition it would support, seemed to be fast approaching. However, after 2007 the tables turned. In the parliamentary election of 2010 the party got 12.4 percent. The worst, however, had yet to come. On 25 May 2014 the party got 3.69 percent. In a commentary Corinne Deloy of the Fondation Robert Schuman wrote that Vlaams Belang "is clearly on the decline and even threatened with extinction."[21] However, this downward trend was not permanent. In the May 2019 parliamentary election Vlaams Belang bounced back and got 18.8 percent of the vote – almost the same score it had in 2007. It was a reason for party leader Tom Van Grieken to demand the end of the *cordon sanitaire*. However, the mainstream Belgian parties should maintain their policy and keep the radical right Vlaams Belang out of a government coalition, even when this leads to an increasingly complicated coalition-forming.[22]

Another example of a *cordon sanitaire* is the case of the Dutch Centrum Partij, a racist party which emerged in the 1980s and launched the slogan "The Netherlands for the Dutch." "The other Dutch political parties ignored the Centrum Partij," wrote Sniderman and Hagendoorn, "believing that paying no public attention to the issue of immigration was the best way to contain prejudice. The strategy was not without merit. The Centrum Partij soon collapsed due to internal struggle."[23]

A *cordon sanitaire* implies not only the exclusion of the populist parties from the centers of power. It equally means upholding the law, banning the denial or justification of the Holocaust, and enforcing laws regarding racist hate speech. Public funding should be restricted if there are indications that a party is openly hostile to the rights and freedoms guaranteed by the European Convention on Human Rights. In Germany the concept of *streitbare Demokratie*, "militant democracy," is written into the Constitution.[24] It means that a liberal democracy should not be too tolerant toward its enemies. It is the old question: should one tolerate the intolerant? Germany paid a heavy price for the belief that by letting Hitler enter government it would "tame" him. Of course, modern populist parties are no copies of the NSDAP, but there are examples of right-wing nationalist populist parties that are governing alone, without being restricted by moderate coalition partners, which are clearly undermining the liberal foundations of the state. This is the case, for instance, with

Orbán's Fidesz government in Hungary and the Law and Justice (PiS) government in Poland. In Turkey and Venezuela this process has degenerated even further: in these countries the populist governments of Erdogan and Maduro have installed outright authoritarian regimes.

"Cartel parties"?

Building a *cordon sanitaire* means that mainstream parties, which previously would have been less inclined to form coalition governments, are obliged to govern together. This has led to "great coalitions" of conservatives and social democrats in countries such as Germany, Belgium, and the Netherlands. Ideological differences between government parties have been downplayed. This has led to the criticism that the mainstream parties have become "cartel parties", a term coined by political scientists Richard Katz and Peter Mair.[25]

Katz and Mair identified four stages in the development of political parties: these are respectively the stage of the elite party, the mass party, the catch-all party, and the cartel party. The elite party was the census model, prevalent in the nineteenth century. The mass party (1880–1960) represented organized interests of civil society. The catch-all party (from 1945) emerged with the decline of the mass party, when voters lost their former identities and became volatile. Finally, the cartel party (from 1970) is a recent phenomenon. It is characterized by a loss of membership, which for the authors was a sign that the parties had moved away from civil society, leading to an "interpenetration of party and state."[26] This process was accompanied by increased state funding and a de-ideologization: the left–right divide became less pertinent and parties tended to resemble one another. There was collusion among the old parties to keep new parties out. In the same way that firms collude and form a cartel to defend their group interests, so, went the argument, political parties tend to form a "cartel party."

It is no surprise that this theory was warmly welcomed by populists, who saw in it a confirmation of their thesis that the mainstream political parties formed "a system" and that only they themselves formed the democratic opposition. Soon the word "cartel party" became instrumental in the populist's vocabulary to denounce "the system." Dutch far-right populists, for instance, on Twitter use the hashtag #kartelpartij (cartel party) to attack the mainstream parties in the Netherlands. Sympathizers of the extreme right populist AfD party in Germany use the same hashtag in German: #Kartellpartei, while Swedish populists use the hashtag #kartellpartiet.

However, the "cartel party" theory was rightly criticized by Ruud Koole, a Dutch political scientist. "What is new about a cartel of parties?" he asked. "That established parties try to prevent the entry of newcomers into the party system is a phenomenon as old as the parties themselves."[27] He denied the claim that new parties were blocked from entering the political system. On the contrary, he argued, due to increased voter volatility "more new parties than ever had a chance to win a seat in parliament."[28] The emergence of the populists rather confirms this thesis.

Notes

1. Taguieff, *Nouveau national-populisme*, p. 103.
2. This was not the first time that the FPÖ had been part of a coalition government. In the period 1983–1987 it formed a coalition with the social democratic party SPÖ. At that time the FPÖ was still considered a more or less mainstream liberal party. After the election of Jörg Haider as party leader in 1986, and his transformation of the FPÖ into a far-right populist party, the coalition government came to an end.
3. Günter Bischof, "'Watschenmann der europäischen Einigung'? Internationales Image und Vergangenheitspolitik der Schüssel/Riess-Passer-ÖVP/FPÖ-Koalitionsregierung," in Michael Gehler, Anton Pelinka, and Günter Bischof (eds), *Österreich in der Europäischen Union – Bilanz seiner Mitgliedschaft, Austria in the European Union – Assessment of Her Membership* (Vienna, Cologne, and Weimar: Bohlau Verlag, 2003), p. 453.
4. The FPÖ was the successor organization of the Verband der Unabhängigen (Federation of Independents), founded in 1949, which was considered a haven for former Nazis. The FPÖ's founder in 1956 was Anton Reinthaller, a former prominent member of Hitler's NSDAP and an SS officer. He was succeeded in 1958 by Friedrich Peter, who equally was a former SS officer. Later the party would gain – temporary – respectability, until Jörg Haider was to transform it into a far-right populist party.
5. Walter Mayr, "Die Stunde des Drachentöters," *Der Spiegel*, No. 49, 2 December 2002. www.spiegel.de/spiegel/print/d-25832002.html (accessed 5 September 2017).
6. Günther Pallaver and Reinhold Gärtner, "Populistische Parteien an der Regierung – Zum Scheitern Verdammt? Italien und Österreich im Vergleich," in Frank Decker (ed.), *Populismus: Gefahr für die Demokratie oder nützliches Korrektiv?* (Wiesbaden: Verlag für Sozialwissenschaft, 2006), p. 104.
7. The presidential elections were on 24 April 2016, with a second round on 22 May 2016. On 22 July 2016, the results of the second round were annulled after the Constitutional Court of Austria had decided that the electoral law had been disregarded in 20 of the 117 districts and 77,900 votes had been counted too early. A new election was organized for 4 December 2016.
8. Cf. Kirsti Knolle, Shadia Nasralla, and Alexandra Schwarz-Goerlich, "Austrian conservatives bring far right into government," Reuters, 16 December 2017. www.reuters.com/article/us-austria-politics/austrian-conservatives-bring-far-right-into-government-idUSKBN1E928K (accessed 10 January 2018).
9. The scandal was the so-called "Ibizagate" – the publication on 17 May 2019 of a secretly recorded video of a meeting in Ibiza between Strache and a woman posing as the niece of Igor Makarov, a Russian oligarch. They discussed the possibility that the oligarch would buy the Austrian tabloid *Kronen Zeitung*, which then would support the FPÖ in the 2017 parliamentary election in exchange for government contracts should the FPÖ enter government.

10 Daniele Albertazzi and Duncan McDonnell, *Populists in Power* (Oxford and New York: Routledge, 2015), pp. 172–173.
11 Jorgen Goul Andersen, "Nationalism, New Right, and New Cleavages in Danish Politics: Foreign and Security Policy of the Danish People's Party," in Christina Schori Liang (ed.), *Europe for the Europeans: The Foreign and Security Policy of the Populist Radical Right* (Aldershot: Ashgate, 2007), p. 112.
12 Ibid., p. 112.
13 In 2002 William Downs wrote on the Danish situation: "Like Le Pen's Front National, Mogens Glistrup's Progress Party now faces the possibility of its own collapse with the emergence of the splinter Dansk Folkeparti. If dividing the far right is one step toward conquering it, then anti-extremist forces in Denmark can derive some measure of satisfaction from the splintering process that has already taken place" (William M. Downs, "How Effective is the Cordon Sanitaire? Lessons from Efforts to Contain the Far Right in Belgium, France, Denmark, and Norway," *Journal of Conflict and Violence Research*, Vol. 4, No. 1, 2002, p. 43). However, with hindsight this splintering process did not bring much satisfaction, as the "splinter," the Dansk Folkeparti, got 21.1 percent of the vote in 2015!
14 In the 1997 parliamentary election the party got 15.3 percent, in 2001 14.6 percent, in 2005 22.1 percent, in 2009 22.9 percent, and in 2013 16.3 percent. In 1997, 2005, and 2009 the party was the second largest in the country, in 2013 the third largest.
15 Cf. Anne-Françoise Hivert, "La coalition au pouvoir en Finlande se sépare de l'extrême droite," *Le Monde*, 14 June 2017.
16 Olivier Faye, "Pour Le Pen, le risque de la rediabolisation," *Le Monde*, 30 September 2017.
17 The first coalition government of far-left and far-right populists was formed in Greece after the parliamentary elections of January 2015. The far-left Syriza party of Alexis Tsipras got 149 of 300 seats in parliament, the far-right ANEL party 13 seats. ANEL obtained only one ministry – the ministry of defense – for its leader Panos Kammenos. After a split in Syriza new elections took place in September 2015 in which Syriza got 145 seats and ANEL 10 seats. Both parties continued their cooperation in the coalition. Kammenos left the government in January 2019, being opposed to a deal with Macedonia to change its name. However, some ANEL parliamentarians continued to support the government.
18 "La Lega al 40 per cento? È una grande bolla (e si sgonfierà molto presto)," *Linkiesta*, 8 July 2019.
19 Sarah L. de Lange, *From Pariah to Power: The Government Participation of Radical Right-Wing Populist Parties in West European Democracies* (Antwerp: Universiteit van Antwerpen Faculteit Politieke en Sociale Wetenschappen, 2008), p. 158.
20 "Verkiezingsuitslagen Vlaams Blok/Vlaams Belang," *De Redactie.Be*, 22 November 2011. http://deredactie.be/cm/vrtnieuws/politiek/1.1160001# (accessed 7 September 2017).
21 Corinne Deloy, "The Nationalists of the New Flemish Alliance wins the General Elections in Belgium," Fondation Robert Schuman, 25 May 2014. www.robert-schuman.eu/en/doc/oee/oee-1516-en.pdf (accessed 7 September 2017).
22 This does not mean that implementing a *cordon sanitaire* does not have its negative aspects. As a rule it leads to a grand coalition, and as Jones and Matthijs rightly remark: "Grand coalitions may also create the impression of depriving the electorate of a meaningful voice, as there is no longer any element of real choice between policies. As a result, the electorate is driven away from the centre and towards the extremes of both right and left" (Erik Jones and Matthias Matthijs, "Democracy without Solidarity: Political Dysfunction in Hard Times – Introduction to Special Issue," *Government and Opposition*, Vol. 52, No. 2, 29 December 2016, p. 203). www.sais-jhu.edu/sites/default/files/Jones%20

%26%20Matthijs%20G%26O%202017.pdf (accessed 8 September 2017). Cas Mudde warns that "so-called *cordons sanitaires* – coalition governments, such as that in Belgium, that explicitly seek to exclude populist parties – will become increasingly difficult to sustain. In the many countries where populists now represent the third- or second-biggest party, a *cordon sanitaire* would force all the other parties to govern together, which would have the unintentional effect of re-creating the very conditions that led to the rise of European populism in the first place" (Cas Mudde, "Europe's Populist Surge – A Long Time in the Making," *Foreign Affairs*, Vol. 95, No. 6, November/December 2016, p. 30). The dilemma described by Mudde is real, and either choice, for or against a *cordon sanitaire*, has its negative side. I believe, however, that the risks of allowing populists to enter government outweigh the risks of maintaining a *cordon sanitaire*.

23 Paul M. Sniderman and Louk Hagendoorn, *When Ways of Life Collide – Multiculturalism and Its Discontents in The Netherlands* (Princeton and Oxford: Princeton University Press, 2009), p. 61.

24 In order to defend the liberal democratic order the German Constitution contains the so-called *Ewigkeitsklausel*: "paragraphs for eternity" that cannot be changed, even by a parliamentary majority. These immutable paragraphs are the first twenty articles of the Constitution which concern basic aspects of the liberal democratic order, such as respecting human rights, the division of powers, the multi-party system, and the independence of the judiciary. Article 21, paragraph 2 of the Constitution provides the opportunity of declaring a party *verfassungswidrig*, "in conflict with the Constitution," and to ban a party. This article has been implemented twice by the German Supreme Court: in 1952 with the Sozialistische Reichspartei, a neo-Nazi party, and in 1956, with the KPD, the communist party (cf. Prof. Dr. Hans-Gerd Jaschke, "Streitbare Demokratie," *Bundeszentrale für politische Bildung*, 19 September 2006. www.bpb.de/themen/9GO863,0,Streitbare_Demokratie.html) (accessed 8 September 2017).

25 Cf. Richard S. Katz and Peter Mair, "Changing Models of Party Organization and Party Democracy: The Emergence of the Cartel Party," *Party Politics*, Vol. 1, No. 1, 1995; Richard S. Katz and Peter Mair, "The Cartel Party Thesis: A Restatement," *Perspectives on Politics*, Vol. 7, No. 4, December 2009.

26 Katz and Mair, "Cartel Party Thesis," p. 755.

27 Ruud Koole, "Cadre, Catch-All or Cartel? A Comment on the Notion of the Cartel Party," *Party Politics*, Vol. 2, No. 4, 1996, p. 515.

28 Ibid., p. 516.

12

Fight corruption, restore trust, and change party financing

Proposal #5: fight corruption

In the preceding chapters I made four recommendations to defend our liberal democracies against the populist wave. These four measures resemble building dykes to contain the rising flood. However, building dykes is not enough. We should at the same time look at the root causes of populist disaffection with representative democracy and ask ourselves whether this disaffection is justified.

One of these root causes is a loss of citizens' trust in their representatives and governments. According to Charles Tilly a certain distrust on the part of citizens vis-à-vis politicians is not calamitous and may even be a sign of normality. "Surprisingly," he writes, "a kind of *distrust* ... becomes a necessary condition of democracy. Contingent consent entails unwillingness to offer rulers, however well elected, blank checks. It implies the threat that if they do not perform in accordance with citizens' expressed collective will, citizens will not only turn them out but also withdraw compliance from such risky government-run activities as military service, jury duty, and tax collection."[1]

A "certain distrust" is here depicted as the default attitude of the critical citizen, who is not easily fooled and does not take the promises made during election campaigns at face value. However, this "standard distrust" must not exceed certain limits. Because trust is the foundation of a well-organized society. "Trust acts like a lubricant," writes Francis Fukuyama, "that makes any group or organization run more efficiently."[2] And Adam Seligman defines trust as "a form of belief that carries within it something unconditional and irreducible to the fulfillment of systematically mandated role expectations."[3] Trust is the unconditional belief that the other person will fulfill his or her role. It is an expectation that is particularly important when it concerns the person or persons one has elected to represent one in parliament or in government.

However, the present mood in Europe and the United States does not express trust, not even the moderate "certain distrust," which Tilly considers a sound attitude of the electorate. Today, in vast parts of the Western world there reigns a deep distrust.[4] Parliamentarians and politicians are not only criticized for being disconnected from the "real life" of citizens and considered to form a separate "caste" with their own, specific group interests. It is worse than that: they are viewed as inherently corrupt.

The depletion of trust

A report of a survey conducted by the Pew Research Center states that "public trust in government remains near historic lows. Only 20% of Americans today say they can trust the government in Washington to do what is right 'just about always' (4%) or 'most of the time' (16%)."[5] Compare this with the year 1958, when three-quarters of the American population trusted the federal government to do the right thing almost always or most of the time.[6]

Not only in the United States is the trust of citizens in politicians eroding. In a global survey of citizens' opinions about the prevalence of corruption, organized by Transparency International, respondents expressed a high level of distrust: "When asked: 'Do you regard political parties as corrupt or very corrupt?', nine out of ten Italians, three-quarters of Americans, and almost the same percentage of Czechs replied 'yes'. Parliaments did not fare much better: two-thirds of Canadians and more than half of British citizens found their parliaments or legislatures to be 'corrupt'."[7]

Of course, these are opinions and not hard facts, but citizens' opinions are not totally unfounded. Let us take, for example, Denmark, a country which for many years has led the Corruption Perceptions Index of Transparency International as the least corrupt country. In 2015 20 members of parliament, which is 11 percent of the 179 members, did not declare their outside activities or financial interests in their asset declaration.[8] Danish MPs are only small offenders. In recent years there have been much more flagrant transgressions. In the late 1990s in Germany, for instance, there was the "Kohl scandal." This concerned the East German Leuna oil refinery, which, in 1992, together with a chain of petrol stations, was sold to the French Elf Aquitaine group. For its help Chancellor Kohl's CDU party received a secret commission of £10 million. The illegal deal would have been made with the support of French president François Mitterrand.[9] The CDU received another commission from the Thyssen company which sold forty-six tanks to Saudi Arabia. For this transaction Thyssen needed a suspension of export control limitations. Thyssen paid DM 1 million in cash into CDU secret accounts.

Illegal party financing is at the heart of many corruption scandals in which politicians are involved. This includes cases of employing civil servants who, although paid from public funds, in fact work for the party – as was the case with Jacques Chirac when he was mayor of Paris. In a verdict passed in 2011 Chirac was declared guilty of having employed twenty-eight party activists who were paid by the municipality. He got a two-year suspended prison sentence.[10] Chirac's successor as French president, Nicolas Sarkozy, promised to do better. "This France will be an example of a modern and responsible democracy," he wrote in his election manifesto.[11] Sarkozy promised to restore political morality. However, apparently he was not an example of more virtuous behavior. On the contrary. In 2012 he was accused of having accepted a €50 million donation from Libya's Gaddafi to finance his election campaign. Foreign donations are illegal in France.[12] He was also accused of seeking cash payments from the super-rich L'Oréal heiress Liliane Bettencourt. In October 2017 the National Financial Public Prosecutor (PNF) had gathered enough evidence to start a criminal procedure. According to the paper *Le Monde* it would be "the first time that a former president of the Republic would be accused of 'corruption' in a public trial."[13]

However, corruption is not always a question of demand. It can equally be a question of supply. This is, for instance, the case when a firm or a foreign power offers money to a politician or a political party in the hope of gaining influence. In France there is the example of the centrist politician François Bayrou, who was a presidential candidate in 2002. "At that time via a French personality above suspicion, who acted as intermediary, unknown Russians had offered to pay for the complete campaign expenditure. The message was explicit: 'We have been following your career for a long time, we believe in your political future. And we are ready to finance you.'"[14] Bayrou did not accept the generous offer but alerted the French authorities. In Britain in 2008 the Russian oligarch Oleg Deripaska made a similar offer, proposing to donate £50,000 to the Conservative Party.[15]

Corruption is not restricted to illegal ways of party financing. Politicians are also eager to line their own pockets. "In Croatia former Prime Minister Ivo Sandar was found guilty in 2012 of taking large scale bribes of more than 12 million Euros from a Hungarian energy company and an Austrian bank. In Romania former Prime Minister Adna Nastase attempted to commit suicide after being found guilty of taking a 1.5 million Euro bribe in 2004."[16] French presidential candidate François Fillon allegedly allowed his wife and children to be paid for fake jobs as parliamentary assistants.[17] The total sum implied was about €1 million.[18]

According to Colin Crouch, "corruption is a powerful indicator of the poor health of a democracy, as it signals a political class which has become cynical, amoral and cut off from scrutiny and from the public."[19] If the population begins to believe that corruption is not the problem of a few individual politicians, but of politicians as a class, one can expect a populist backlash. However, instead of solving the problem in most cases populism will only compound and exacerbate it.

Populist parties and corruption

Fighting corruption is very difficult because, as one author wrote: "anticorruption policies are not just like other policies: they target the government itself (or at least the bureaucracy that supports it), contrary to most other policies that target in one way or another civil society … To give an analogy, it is equivalent to expecting a thief to arrest himself."[20] Corruption, as a rule, is lowest in open, democratic societies, where there is a free press and an independent judiciary, and where there are independent agencies, such as anti-corruption watchdogs and courts of auditors, whose activities not only expose corrupt practices but also lead to prosecutions – even of persons at the highest levels. This is why these institutions, if they work properly, are so important. They are based on *confidence*, which is the institutional equivalent of *trust* accorded to individuals.[21]

Ironically, it is the populist parties, attracting the votes of disaffected voters, which, as a rule, undermine the independent judiciary, the free press, and independent agencies in the name of "democracy." Moreover, these parties are not examples of impeccable behavior. In 2017 Front National leader Marine Le Pen was accused of fraud, allegedly letting her assistants in the European Parliament work for the party. The fraud was estimated at €5 million.[22] In Italy the populist leader Silvio Berlusconi came to power after the *mani polite* ("clean hands") campaign, promising that he would fight the endemic corruption of the Italian political system. In fact he only made the problem worse. In Transparency International's Corruption Perception Index Italy was in 31st place in 2002, in 41st place in 2007, in 55th place in 2008, and in 63rd place in 2009.[23] "From this point on it has been overtaken by countries, such as Turkey, Cuba, Namibia, Samoa, Jordan and Bahrain, to mention only a few," wrote Paul Ginsborg.[24] And he continued: "The governments of Silvio Berlusconi, which were in power for the greatest part of the last decennium (2001–6, 2008–10), have never given the impression of being concerned about this dramatic deterioration of public morals. On the contrary … [they have] worked against transparency, competition and control, in favor of a rampant, clientelist capitalism."[25] The problem was not only public morals but also Berlusconi's private morals. Berlusconi was accused of secret deals with his personal friend Vladimir Putin. These deals concerned huge energy contracts with Russia from which Berlusconi, according to WikiLeaks, was "profiting personally and handsomely."[26] According to Antonio Gibelli, "one estimates that Berlusconi's property has been multiplied tenfold since his entrance on the political scene."[27]

Twenty proposals: reforming politics and education

Similarly, during the years that the Austrian radical right FPÖ party and its successor BZÖ participated in government (2000–2007) it became tainted by corruption scandals. In the beginning FPÖ leader Haider and the FPÖ finance minister Karl-Heinz Grasser declared themselves to be against Austria's acquisition of eighteen Eurofighter jets, a €1.7 billion contract. "Haider even advertised his opposition to the deal in a nationwide billboard campaign," wrote *Der Spiegel*. "But then they both suddenly threw their weight behind the deal. This soon gave rise to speculation that right-wing populist Haider's expensive election campaign could have been bankrolled by German sources."[28] This speculation was not unfounded. It was later revealed that EADS, the manufacturer of the Eurofighter, had paid €113.5 million into dubious accounts of offshore postbox companies. It was proven that EADS had paid €878,500 to former FPÖ staff for consultation with the aim of bringing about a *Stimmungsverbesserung* ("improvement in sentiment"). Curiously, this sum was paid *after* the contract for the acquisition of the jets had already been signed and the sentiment was no longer in need of "being improved."[29]

Proposal #6: change party financing

Not only is corruption undermining the foundations of democracy. Another problem is the growing direct and indirect influence of rich individuals and business lobbies on the political process. For this reason Colin Crouch went so far as to label the system we live in a "post-democracy." In this post-democracy, he writes, "the mass of citizens plays a passive, quiescent, even apathetic part, responding only to signals given them. Behind this spectacle of the electoral game, politics is really shaped in private by interaction between elected governments and elites that overwhelmingly represent business interests."[30] And, he continues: "Under the conditions of a post-democracy that increasingly cedes power to business lobbies, there is little hope for an agenda of strong egalitarian policies for the redistribution of power and wealth, or for the restraint of powerful interests."[31]

The growing influence of business lobbies is, indeed, a matter of great concern. Of course firms and companies have the right to contact governments and parliamentarians to explain their point of view about policies and legislation. However, this should not lead to secret "deals" in which there is an exchange of material benefits for political influence. For this reason the mandatory registration of lobbyists and transparency on "who contacted whom and when" is of importance.

Although in many countries stricter codes of conduct have been introduced, this still leaves much to be desired, in particular as concerns the implementation of these measures. "In France, a joint report by *Transparency-France* and *Regards*

Citoyens showed that between 2007 and 2011 there were 9300 meetings between Ministers and lobbyists involving 5000 organisations represented by 16000 people – but there were only 127 lobbyists registered in 2011 by the National Assembly," writes Laurence Cockcroft, a co-founder of Transparency International.[32] This opaque situation was a reason for the socialist government of President Hollande adopting in December 2016 a new law, called Sapin 2, which created a new agency, the High Authority for the Transparency of Public Life (Haute Autorité pour la Transparence de la Vie Publique). Lobbyists were required to register before 1 January 2018, on the Authority's website, indicating their identity, the number of employees, their expenditure, field of activity, the organizations they represent, and the contacts they had with office-holders. Lobbyists were, apparently, not pleased: by 16 November 2017, only 226 names had been registered out of an estimated total of 800 to 1,000 lobbyists.[33] More would follow, however, because the new law has teeth: lobbyists who fail to register risk a year's imprisonment and a fine of €15,000.

Even if the secret collusion between lobbyists and politicians could be constrained by increased transparency and control, there still remains a major problem: the financing of political parties. Legal contributions by firms and companies to political parties offer the opportunity to influence the policies of these parties. Often this will not take the form of a clear *quid pro quo*; rather, it will create the necessary goodwill toward the generous donor, which he or she could need in the future.[34]

The history of party financing in the United States is a case in point. After accusations of having accepted corporate donations for his 1904 presidential campaign, President Theodore (Teddy) Roosevelt declared himself in favor of changing the law. This led to the Tillman Act of 26 January 1907, which was the first legislation in the US to prohibit monetary donations by corporations in national election campaigns. Henceforth donations could only be made by individuals. On 25 June 1910, another regulation, the Federal Corrupt Practices Act was introduced, which laid down campaign spending limits for US House election campaigns and demanded the disclosure of all money received and spent during federal campaigns. In 1911 this Act was amended: henceforth it applied also to the Senate. Until 1971 all contributions of $50 and more per calendar year had to be reported. Candidates for the Senate could spend 3 cents per vote obtained in the last election, up to a $25,000 maximum. Corporate contributions were banned.

However, the law had some flaws: it had neither disclosure requirements for individual candidates, nor an effective enforcement regime. Corporations could also circumvent the law by letting their staff donate (and reimbursing them). The most significant problem, however, was the increasing role of so-called *soft money*. This concerned money that was not given directly to a party or a candidate, but that indirectly supported them by "issue advocacy," that is, by paying for TV ads, posters, billboards, and so on, which expressed support for the ideas of a certain candidate. This situation led the senators McCain (R) and Feingold (D) to propose a Bipartisan Campaign Reform Act (BCRA), which was adopted on 6 November 2002, and became effective on 1 January 2003. The law prohibited national Political Action Committees (PACs) from raising or spending any funds which were not subject to federal limits. It also constrained "issue advocacy" by prohibiting ads paid for by corporations or non-governmental organizations, as well as ads which named a federal candidate within thirty days of a primary or caucus or sixty days of a general election.

However, these attempts to restrict the influence of "big money" on the elections were jeopardized in 2008 after the Federal Electoral Commission banned a film about Hillary Clinton, financed by Citizens United, an initiative supported by the energy magnates Charles and David Koch, on the grounds that it violated the provision of the BCRA that no political ads were allowed within thirty days of a primary. When, in 2010, Citizens United challenged this decision, the US Supreme Court took a historic decision. It ended all limits on corporate expenditure with the argument that these limits were an infringement of the First Amendment, which guaranteed free speech.

This decision was highly controversial. The constitutional guarantee of free speech was a guarantee given to citizens of the United States. But was it logical to grant free speech to impersonal mammoth organizations, such as corporations? The Supreme Court decided that corporations could contribute directly to political parties, but not to the campaigns of individual candidates. However, they could do so indirectly by forming PACs. The results of this decision were immediately visible. "The Citizens United judgement opened the way for a big increase in campaign spending. Total expenditure on Congressional and Presidential campaigns rose from $2.3 bn. in 2008 to $3.7 bn. in 2012 – to nearly $7 bn. in 2015/16 (with two thirds of this being generated by Congressional campaigns)."[35] One week after the decision of the Supreme Court President Obama gave the following warning in his State of the Union Address:

> It's time to require lobbyists to disclose each contact they make on behalf of a client with my administration or with Congress. It's time to put strict limits on the contributions that lobbyists give to candidates for federal office. With all due deference to separation of powers, last week the Supreme Court reversed a century of law that I believe will open the floodgates for special interests – including foreign corporations – to spend without limit in our elections. I don't think American elections should be bankrolled by America's most powerful interests, or worse, by foreign entities. They should be decided by the American people. And I'd urge Democrats and Republicans to pass a bill that helps to correct some of these problems.[36]

Obama's warning evokes reminiscences of Eisenhower's famous Farewell Address of 1961, in which he warned of the influence of the military-industrial complex on the American democratic system. "In the councils of government, we must guard against the acquisition of unwarranted influence," said Eisenhower, "whether sought or unsought, by the military-industrial complex. The potential for the disastrous rise of misplaced power exists and will persist."[37] Today it is not only the military-industrial complex, but the totality of the country's mighty corporations, as well as the class of the super-rich, who threaten to destabilize the American democratic system, changing it into a "plutocracy with a democratic face." Obama's warning against influence by foreign entities also has to be taken seriously after it became known that Donald Trump and other prominent Republican politicians had received $7.35 million from an oligarch linked to Russia[38] and after the Trump campaign was accused of collusion with the Kremlin.

To get an idea of the impact of the Supreme Court's decision one should compare the money spent by PACs in 2012 with the year 2008. In 2012 PACs were called *super PACs* because of the sheer amount of money raised.

> Three of the largest super PACs – American Crossroads, Restore Our Future, and Priorities USA Action – spent more than $305 million combined in the 2012 election cycle alone … PACs spent more than $151 million on the presidential election (not including primaries) in 2008, or approximately $0.50 per U.S. citizen. In 2012, PACs and super PACs spent more than $560 million, or approximately $1.78 per U.S. citizen. With this 350% increase in spending, *the fear is that a small group of extremely wealthy individuals or corporations can buy a president.*[39]

The phenomenon of a "plutocratization" of the American political system can be observed not only on the federal level, but also on the state level. "More and more very wealthy men are running for and winning office as state governors," writes *The Economist*.[40] "America has had wealthy governors before – think of Nelson Rockefeller and Franklin Roosevelt, both of whom governed New York. But their proliferation is new."[41] Less well off candidates drop out of the race because they cannot compete with their rich rivals. "The 0.1% are pushing aside other gubernatorial hopefuls," concludes the paper.[42] It is telling that the administration of the populist president Donald Trump "seems today effectively to be the richest in the country's history. According to *Forbes* the accumulated fortunes of its members reach 4.4 billion dollars (3.7 billion euros), which is fifteen times the amount of the administration of George W. Bush."[43] We are witnessing the emergence of a new "gilded age" in which the super-rich are ruling the world and writing the laws. The absence of limits on campaign funding has distorted a level playing field and favored those billionaire and multimillionaire contenders who are able to self-fund their campaigns. Donald Trump is its most visible – and controversial – example. Already in 1999 the British historian Eric Hobsbawm was warning about this situation. "The degree of wealth that is today available to individuals," he wrote,

> is absolutely incredible. Speaking in global terms, the wealth in the hands of 1 percent of the world population is immense. How will this affect politics? It is not clear. We have signs from the United States that private individuals can now manage to conduct presidential campaigns, or considerably influence them, with their private financial means. Today, the rich are able to do what once could only be done by large collective organizations. I am not sure whether we fully understand the profound implications of this phenomenon.[44]

It is clear that the American system of party financing is not sustainable if one doesn't want to endanger the democratic foundations of its institutions. Charles Tilly has warned that processes of de-democratization occur more rapidly than surges of democratization, because, as he explains: "In [its] simplest terms, de-democratization occurs chiefly as a consequence of withdrawal by privileged, powerful political actors from whatever binding consultation exists, whereas democratization depends on integrating large numbers of ordinary people into consultation ... Privileged, powerful elites ... have much greater means and incentives than ordinary people to escape or subvert democratic compacts when those compacts turn to their disadvantage."[45] Sarah Chayes has formulated some proposals to cure what ails American politics. "A policy program to achieve that kind of change," she writes, "would begin with placing sharp curbs on campaign contributions and ending the anonymity that many significant political donors enjoy. Shifting to public-only financing for campaigns may seem radical, but that would be the best solution. Lobbying regulations must be tightened and fiercely enforced. Conflicts of interest must be defined more broadly. Ethical breaches must be swiftly sanctioned in a rigidly nonpartisan fashion."[46] It is clear that curbing the influence of corporate interests on the political process is urgent.[47] Could the US in this respect learn something from Germany?

Government funding of parties: the German example

This is, of course, a somewhat prickly question. Because in matters of democratic institutions post-war Germany has been a dedicated pupil of the United States. Its Constitution, its federalism, its separation of powers, the role of the Supreme Court, all this has been faithfully copied from the United States. This time, could Germany teach its former teacher a lesson?

Costa Rica (1954) and Argentina (1955) were the first to introduce direct government funding for political parties.[48] Germany followed in 1959 and was the first

European country to introduce this system. Until then Germany had, like other countries, only a system of indirect government support through tax benefits for donations by natural and juridical persons. However, this system clearly favored parties with rich donors. Therefore, in 1958 the *Bundesverfassungsgericht* (Supreme Court) took the decision that political parties would receive a state subvention based on the number of seats in parliament. When some years later this arrangement was challenged in court by the Land Hessen, it led, on 19 July 1966, to a different decision by the Supreme Court, prohibiting direct party financing by the state, although still allowing the subvention of political campaigns.

However, these new rules did not work because in practice it was difficult to differentiate between party expenditures and campaign expenditures. Therefore, in 1992 the Supreme Court returned to its initial position of 1958 and parties could – again – receive direct state subvention. This decision was taken against the background of declining party membership, which had a negative impact on the financial position of the parties. But this was not the only reason. The German system intended to create a level playing field: "It should be guaranteed that parties dispose of the financial means, necessary for the fulfilment of their tasks. If they were dependent exclusively on financial sources from civil society, such as contributions from members or donations, it would risk favoring those parties which represent pro-business or employer-friendly positions. Their competitors, who represent rather the interests of underprivileged groups of the population would suffer from great disadvantages in the competition."[49] German state subsidies apply when a party gets 0.5 percent of the vote for elections to the national or European parliament. This also gives new, small parties a chance to receive state funding.

In 2017 German political parties received one euro per vote for the first 4 million votes, and thereafter €0.83 per vote. The state paid an additional €0.45 for each euro received by a party in membership contributions, with a maximum of €3,300 per person per year.[50] The political foundations associated with the parties also received subsidies, based on the election results of the last four parliamentary elections. We should not forget that Germany learned its own lesson the hard way after the experience of the illegal party funding scandal (Kohl scandal) of the 1990s. Therefore the system of direct state funding is accompanied by strict regulations concerning transparency. How much money is raised and spent by the parties is published in yearly financial reports, together with the names of all persons and firms donating more than €10,000. Sanctions for illegal party financing have been strengthened. Party functionaries who are involved in illegal funding activities risk a prison sentence of up to three years.

The German system has been copied by most European countries. However, an exclusive or too one-sided reliance on state subvention of political parties must be avoided. Parties should not lose "their character of social organizations which have their roots in the people and should not morph into organs of the state."[51] This is exactly the reproach put forward against state-subsidized parties by Richard Katz and Peter Mair in their famous "cartel party thesis,"[52] accusing parties of having changed into a "cartel" by employing the resources of the state to limit political competition.

In general, this criticism is unfounded. However, in some countries the pendulum swings too far to one side. Spain, Italy, and Belgium are examples of countries where state funding has become more important than private funding. In 2012 in Spain 79.8 percent of parties' revenues were state subsidies. In Italy this was 74.3 percent, and in Belgium 76.8 percent.[53] In 2015 political parties in Belgium received €70 million in subsidies. This is seven euros per inhabitant and seven times more than in neighboring Netherlands, where parties only received one euro per inhabitant. The Belgian sociologist Luc Huyse famously remarked that political parties in his country were "hooked up to a morphine drip."[54]

It is clear that a one-sided dependence on the state must be avoided in the same way as a one-sided dependence on private corporate finance. In some countries changes to the system have begun. In Spain, for instance, where in 2011 parties still received €82 million, in 2015 they received only €52 million.[55] Does this mean that the "cartel party thesis" is valid? Not really. As Piccio and Van Biezen argue, the system of state funding "provides a more level playing field for political actors with unequal resources."[56] However, it is necessary to maintain a sound mix of private financial sources and state subsidies. For this reason the German system stands out as a model. In this country state subsidies can never exceed the total amount of other revenues, such as membership fees and commercial sources of income. Additionally, there exists an absolute ceiling of 50 percent. In this way a delicate balance between private and public sources of revenues is maintained.

Notes

1 Charles Tilly, *Democracy* (Cambridge and New York: Cambridge University Press, 2008), p. 94.
2 Francis Fukuyama, "Social Capital," in Lawrence E. Harrison and Samuel P. Huntington (eds), *Culture Matters – How Values Shape Human Progress* (New York: Basic Books, 2000), p. 98.
3 Adam B. Seligman, *The Problem of Trust* (Princeton: Princeton University Press, 2000), p. 44.
4 The level of trust differs for different groups within the same country. According to Marco Revelli the trust in institutions felt by voters for the populist Italian Five Star Movement is, for instance, "close to zero," while the trust felt by voters for the Democratic Party is "at the maximum of the scale" (cf. Revelli, *Populismo*, p. 135).

5 "Public trust in government 1958–2017," Pew Research Center, 3 May 2017. www.people-press.org/2017/05/03/public-trust-in-government-1958-2017/ (accessed 19 September 2017).
6 Ibid.
7 Laurence Cockcroft and Anne-Christine Wegener, *Unmasked – Corruption in the West* (London and New York: I. B. Tauris, 2017), p. 1.
8 "Corruption Perceptions Index 2016," Transparency International. www.transparency.org/news/feature/europe_and_central_asia_an_overall_stagnation (accessed 19 September 2017).
9 Tony Paterson and Paul Webster, "Mitterrand 'gave £10m to Kohl'," *Guardian*, 24 January 2000. www.theguardian.com/world/2000/jan/24/germany.paulwebster (accessed 19 September 2017).
10 "Jacques Chirac found guilty of corruption," *Guardian*, 15 December 2011. www.theguardian.com/world/2011/dec/15/jacques-chirac-guilty-corruption (accessed 20 September 2017).
11 Nicolas Sarkozy, *Témoignage* (Paris: XO Éditions, 2006), p. 278.
12 John Lichfield, "Nicolas Sarkozy DID take $50 million of Muammar Gaddafi's cash, French judge is told," *Independent*, 15 December 2011. www.independent.co.uk/news/world/europe/nicolas-sarkozy-did-take-50-million-of-muammar-gaddafis-cash-french-judge-is-told-8435872.html (accessed 20 September 2017). (In fact the donation was €50 million. It was paid in euros and not in dollars, MHVH.)
13 Gérard Davet and Fabrice Lhomme, "Le parquet assimile Sarkozy à 'un délinquant'," *Le Monde*, 15–16 October 2017. www.lemonde.fr/societe/article/2017/10/14/le-parquet-national-financier-assimile-nicolas-sarkozy-a-un-delinquant-chevronne_5200852_3224.html (accessed 25 October 2017).
14 Hélène Blanc and Renata Lesnik, *Les prédateurs du Kremlin (1917–2009)* (Paris: Seuil, 2009), pp. 330–331.
15 Cf. Marcel H. Van Herpen, *Putin's Propaganda Machine – Soft Power and Russian Foreign Policy* (Lanham and London: Rowman & Littlefield, 2016), pp. 101–106.
16 Laurence Cockcroft, "Corruption in Europe: What Can Be Done?" *Cicero Foundation Great Debate Paper*, No. 13/03, April 2013, p. 5. www.cicerofoundation.org/lectures/Laurence_Cockcroft_Corruption_in_Europe.pdf (accessed 21 September 2017).
17 Cf. Angelique Chrisafis, "François Fillon under formal investigation for 'fake jobs offences'," *Guardian*, 14 March 2017. www.theguardian.com/world/2017/mar/14/francois-fillon-placed-under-formal-investigation-over-fake-jobs (accessed 21 September 2017).
18 Elise Vincent, "Affaire Fillon: un million d'euros de salaires suspects, selon 'Le Canard enchaîné,'" *Le Monde*, 1 February 2017. www.lemonde.fr/affaire-penelope-fillon/article/2017/02/01/affaire-fillon-un-million-d-euros-de-salaires-suspects-selon-le-canard-enchaine_5072634_5070021.html (accessed 21 September 2017).
19 Crouch, *Post-Democracy*, p. 10.
20 Joseph Pozsgai, PhD, "A Systems Model on Corruption and Anticorruption Reform – International, Domestic Pressure, and Government Strategies to Preserve the Status Quo," *Air and Space Power Journal*, Vol. 8, No. 3, 3d Quarter 2017, p. 43.
21 This useful distinction has been made by the sociologist Niklas Luhmann. Cf. Seligman, *Problem of Trust*, pp. 18–19.
22 Saim Saeed and Maïa de la Baume, "National Front jobs case cost Parliament €5M," *Politico*, 28 April 2017. www.politico.eu/article/le-pen-owes-e5m-in-fake-jobs-case-says-parliament/ (accessed 22 September 2017).

23 Cf. Paul Ginsborg, *Salviamo Italia* (Turin: Giulio Einaudi Editore, 2010), p. 17.
24 Ibid., p. 17.
25 Ibid., p. 17.
26 Rob Evans, Luke Harding, and John Hooper, "WikiLeaks cables: Berlusconi 'profited from secret deals' with Putin," *Guardian*, 2 December 2010. www.theguardian.com/world/2010/dec/02/wikileaks-cables-berlusconi-putin (accessed 22 September 2017).
27 Antonio Gibelli, *Berlusconi ou la démocratie autoritaire* (Paris: Éditions Belin, 2011), p. 128.
28 Jürgen Dahlkamp, Dinah Deckstein, Jörg Schmitt, and Gerald Traufetter, "Investigation into Dubious EADS Austria Deal Intensifies," *Spiegel Online*, 12 November 2012. www.spiegel.de/international/business/investigation-into-dubious-eads-austria-deal-intensifies-a-866646-2.html (accessed 22 September 2017).
29 Michael Nikbakhsh, "Eurofighter: EADS zahlte 878.500 Euro an Ex-FPÖ Mitarbeiter," *Profil*, 4 July 2017. www.profil.at/wirtschaft/eurofighter-eads-ex-fpoe-mitarbeiter-honorar-8216728 (accessed 26 September 2017).
30 Crouch, *Post-Democracy*, p. 4.
31 Ibid., p. 4.
32 Cockcroft, "Corruption in Europe," pp. 5–6.
33 Cf. Philippe Blachèr, "Lobbys: Nouvelle année, nouvelles pratiques," *Le Monde*, 18 November 2017. Another measure to avoid collusion between politicians and private interests is a law on "trust in political life," passed on 15 September 2017, which forbids French parliamentarians to exercise, individually or in a corporation, consultancy activities.
34 As concerns this *quid pro quo* it is interesting how it is perceived by Donald Trump, who writes: "For years, I supported the governor of New York Mario Cuomo. I was one of his largest campaign contributors … After he was defeated for reelection … I called Mario to ask for a perfectly legal and appropriate favor involving attention to a detail at the Department of Housing and Development, which at the time was being run by his son Andrew. Mario told me that this would be hard for him to do … Finally, I asked Mario point-blank, 'Well, are you going to help me?' In a very nice way, he essentially told me no. I did the only thing that felt right to me. I began screaming. 'You son of a bitch! For years I've helped you and never asked for a thing, and when I finally need something … you aren't there for me. You're no good. You're one of the most disloyal people I've known' (Trump, *How to Get Rich*, pp. 165–166). Cuomo's "disloyalty" was rather a sign of moral decency, distancing himself from shady "backroom deals."
35 Laurence Cockcroft and Anne-Christine Wegener, "An Enemy to Democracy? Political Party Finance and Corruption in the West," *Cicero Foundation Great Debate Paper*, No. 17/01, January 2017, p. 4. http://www.cicerofoundation.org/lectures/Cockcroft_Wegener_An_Enemy_to_Democracy.pdf (accessed 26 September 2017).
36 "Obama's state of the Union transcript 2010: Full text," *Politico*, 27 January 2010. www.politico.com/story/2010/01/obamas-state-of-the-union-address-032111?o=3 (accessed 26 September 2017).
37 "Military-industrial complex speech, Dwight D. Eisenhower, 1961." http://avalon.law.yale.edu/20th_century/eisenhower001.asp (accessed 26 September 2017).
38 According to Ruth May, "Donald Trump and the political action committees for Mitch McConnell, Marco Rubio, Scott Walker, Lindsey Graham, John Kasich and John McCain accepted $7.35 million in contributions from a Ukrainian-born oligarch who is the business partner of two of Russian president Vladimir Putin's favorite oligarchs and

a Russian government bank." Cf. Ruth May, "GOP campaign took $7.35 million from oligarch linked to Russia," *Dallas News*, 3 August 2017. www.dallasnews.com/opinion/commentary/2017/08/03/tangled-web-connects-russian-oligarch-money-gop-campaigns (accessed 27 September 2017).
39 Andee Kaplan, Eric Hare, Heike Hofmann, and Dianne Cook, "Can you buy a president? Politics after the Tillman Act" (emphasis added, MHVH), *Chance*, no date. http://chance.amstat.org/2014/02/president/ (accessed 27 September 2017).
40 "The yacht primary – The rise of rich governors," *The Economist*, 21 October 2017.
41 Ibid.
42 Ibid.
43 Jérémie Baruch, Nicolas Bourcier, Jean-Baptiste Chastand, Anne Michel, and Maxime Vaudano, "L'obsession de Trump contre l'impôt," *Le Monde*, 7 November 2017.
44 Eric Hobsbawm, *On the Edge of the New Century*, Eric Hobsbawm in conversation with Antonio Polito (New York: The New Press, 2000), p. 89 (first Italian edition in 1999, MHVH).
45 Tilly, *Democracy*, p. 195.
46 Sarah Chayes, "Kleptocracy in America – Corruption is Reshaping Governments Everywhere," *Foreign Affairs*, Vol. 96, No. 5, September/October 2017, p. 150.
47 Other American analysts have proposed government funding for political parties, such as Joshua Cohen, who writes: "in a just society political opportunities and powers must be independent of economic or social position – the political liberties must have a fair value – and the fact that they are independent must be more or less evident to citizens. Ensuring this manifestly fair value might, for example, require public funding of political parties and restrictions on private political spending, as well as progressive tax measures that serve to limit inequalities of wealth and to ensure that the political agenda is not controlled by the interests of economically and socially dominant groups" (Joshua Cohen, "Deliberation and Democratic Legitimacy," in James Bohman and William Rehg (eds), *Deliberative Democracy – Essays on Reason and Politics* (Cambridge, Mass., and London: The MIT Press, 1999), p. 69).
48 Cf. Thomas Drysch, *Parteienfinanzierung: Österreich, Schweiz, Bundesrepublik Deutschland* (Wiesbaden: Springer, 1998), p. 96.
49 Heinrich Pehle, "Die Finanzierung der Parteien in Deutschland," *Bundeszentrale für politische Bildung*, 20 May 2015. www.bpb.de/politik/grundfragen/parteien-in-deutschland/42042/finanzierung (accessed 28 September 2017).
50 Cf. "Die Staatliche Parteienfinanzierung (Stand: 20. Oktober 2017)," *Deutscher Bundestag*. www.bundestag.de/blob/189364/00049e50b907e0dd5145cfaeb1d0631f/staatl_partei_finanz-data.pdf (accessed 10 January 2018).
51 Pehle, "Finanzierung der Parteien."
52 Cf. Katz and Mair, "Cartel Party Thesis."
53 Cf. Daniela R. Piccio and Ingrid van Biezen, "Political Finance and the Cartel Party Thesis," in Jonathan Mendilow and Eric Phélippeau (eds), *Handbook of Political Party Funding* (Cheltenham and Northampton, Mass.: Edward Elgar Publishers, 2018), Table 4.2, p. 72.
54 Quoted in "Politieke partijen krijgen 70 miljoen aan financiering: 'Abnormaal veel, niet gezond,'" *De Redactie*, 30 May 2017.
55 Cf. "Los partidos politicos recibiran 52,7 milliones de euros en subvenciones en el año 2015," *20 Minutos*, 30 January 2015.
56 Piccio and Van Biezen, "Political Finance," p. 68.

13

The Sisyphean task of making public life more moral

In the eighteenth century political thinkers had a very high opinion of democracy and of the moral character of democratic politicians. In "The Spirit of the Laws" Montesquieu considered *virtue* the defining characteristic of a democracy. "It is clear," he wrote, "that one needs less virtue in a monarchy, where the person who executes the law considers himself above the law, than in a popular government, where the one who executes the law is himself subject to it."[1] In the same vein, James Madison had the hope that America's democratic system would "extract from the mass of the society the purest and noblest characters which it contains."[2] Although undoubtedly some of "the purest and noblest characters" have felt the vocation to serve their people in a completely unselfish way, always putting the common good above their personal interests, we have to remember Hegel's famous dictum that "nothing great has been realized in the world without passion."[3] Hegel added that the word "passion" (*Leidenschaft*) meant for him "the activity of man inspired by particular interests, by special objectives or, if one so wishes, selfish purposes."[4]

Politicians are human beings like everyone else, they are no angels. Even the noblest politician, who is not interested in material gain and works for the good of his or her country, is not insensitive to fame and to maintaining a good reputation. The question is how one can rein in the dark side of politicians. This question is not new. However, in our modern, globalized world, in which money interests have exponentially grown, it has become more pressing than ever.

In his essay "On Perpetual Peace" Immanuel Kant was optimistic about the possibilities of reining in and domesticating the dark side of human nature. "As hard as it may sound," he wrote, "the problem of setting up a state can be solved even by a nation of devils (so long as they possess understanding)."[5] He saw the solution in setting up a constitution which was framed in such a way that it contained enough safeguards and counterbalances to create a viable democratic state. This realistic approach should be followed today. The question is: What are the measures that could be taken? Let us list some.

Proposal #7: make politicians sign a "moral charter"

Politicians could be asked to sign a "moral charter" when they enter parliament. In this charter they would pledge to publish their complete tax returns, as well as their affiliations with external commercial and non-commercial entities. Other obligations could be added. Sarah Chayes proposes, for instance, a pledge "to spend a certain minimum amount of time interacting with ordinary constituents, and to work for more stringent campaign finance, conflict-of-interest, and oversight legislation and enforcement."[6]

One could object that, as a rule, elected representatives when they enter parliament are sworn in, which makes the signing of such a moral charter superfluous. However, the formulas used for these ceremonies are rather minimal. In the Netherlands, for instance, new parliamentarians use the following formula: "I swear (or declare) that in order to be appointed member of parliament I didn't directly or indirectly ... give, nor promise any gift or privilege. I swear (or declare) that I, in order to do or not to do something in this office, haven't accepted, neither will accept, directly or indirectly, any gift or any promise."[7] This is a general anti-corruption pledge and indicates rather what the representative promises *not* to do. It does not contain a positive pledge: that the deputy will actively work to campaign for more stringent campaign financing, for better control of conflicts of interest, and for strict enforcement of the existing rules. Deputies who sign the charter show their willingness to take their anti-corruption pledge seriously and will be more motivated to act in accordance with the letter of its text, because they can be called to account by their constituents.

Proposal #8: give independent ethics watchdogs more power

Signing a "moral charter," however, is not enough. Even if a representative enters parliament with the best of intentions, he or she may be tempted by opportunities for personal gain and runs the risk of being bribed.[8] For this reason an appeal to man's moral character is not enough. One needs additional control mechanisms. This may be disappointing from the moral point of view, but it takes into account the reality of human nature. "Coercing people to do the right thing," writes Robert George, "even when it is successful, does not make them morally better; it does nothing more than produce external conformity to moral norms. Morality, however, is above all an internal matter, a matter of rectitude in choosing: one becomes morally good precisely, and only, by doing the right thing *for the right reason*."[9] Unfortunately, this will not always be the case. Therefore parliaments often have their own ethics watchdogs.

In the US both the House and the Senate have ethics committees. The Senate Ethics Committee consists of six members: three Democrats and three Republicans, which means that each party has a power of veto. In practice this watchdog has teeth only if there is bipartisan cooperation and the explicit will of its members to let the exigency of morals prevail over partisan loyalties. It is clear that in a time of growing polarization this is not always the case. The Ethics Committee of the House of Representatives, for instance, was criticized for its lenient behavior after a corruption scandal sent three congressmen to jail. It led in 2008 to a new, independent nonpartisan entity, the Office of Congressional Ethics (OCE) which had the power to monitor the ethical conduct of deputies.

The OCE was rather effective. Although it did not have subpoena power, it had its own staff of investigators and could start an investigation after receiving an anonymous complaint. The OCE was overseen by a six-member board, who voted on whether to refer a case to the full House Ethics Committee. Even if the House Ethics Committee decided to dismiss the case as unfounded, it was required to release the OCE report. This transparency and publicity functioned as a powerful deterrent for members of the House.[10] However, in January 2017 the Republican House majority voted to replace the OCE with a new entity, the Office of Congressional Complaint Review, which would no longer take anonymous complaints and would again be answerable to the House Ethics Committee. The plan led to an outcry. Citizens for Responsibility and Ethics, a Washington-based ethics watchdog, called the OCE "one of the outstanding ethics accomplishments of the House of Representatives, and it has played a critical role in seeing that the congressional ethics process is no longer viewed as merely a means to sweep problems under the rug."[11] The plan was reversed under bipartisan pressure within twenty-four hours after the initial vote.

Ethics watchdogs are unpopular with the group whose behavior they monitor. It is, therefore, no surprise that they are permanently under attack. An example is the US Office of Government Ethics (OGE), which oversees the conduct of federal employees, including those working in the White House. When, in July 2017, its director, Walter M. Shaub Jr., departed, President Trump named David J. Apol as his successor. Shaub, who had had many conflicts with Apol in the past, called Apol's approach to government ethics "loosey-goosey."[12]

The new director immediately developed the habit of contacting the White House before the office sent letters to members of Congress who asked questions about the ethical behavior of White House personnel. Shaub disapproved of this practice and said that "moves like this jeopardize O.G.E.'s independence."[13] He expressed his concern that "with Mr Apol in charge, decades' worth of ethics rulings might be revised in a way that will make it easier for Mr. Trump and members of his administration to bend federal ethics rules."[14] His prediction was soon confirmed by the facts, when the White House set up a legal defense fund for Trump aides who faced questioning in the investigation into Russian meddling in the 2016 presidential election. The OGE scrapped a policy that banned lobbyists from making anonymous donations toward the legal bills of White House staff. Shaub commented: "It's very depressing ... It's unseemly for the ethics office to be doing something sneaky like that."[15] He added: "We are truly in an ethics crisis right now, and something has got to be done about it."[16]

It is no surprise that a populist administration like Donald Trump's tries to undermine the independence of an ethics watchdog. However, not only populist governments are prone to taking such actions. Governments and parliaments, in general, are reluctant to set up ethics watchdogs which scrutinize their behavior. These independent agencies or committees are often set up after flagrant corruption scandals which lead to a public outcry.

In Britain, for instance, a new ethics watchdog was set up in 2009 after a scandal broke out concerning the huge amount of expenses claims made by members of parliament for private expenses. MPs had claimed the reimbursement of expenses made for the purchase of furniture, the redecoration of second homes, and the cost of swimming pools.[17] The new agency, the Independent Parliamentary Standards Authority (IPSA) controls expenses and publishes a regularly reviewed "Scheme of MPs Business Costs and Expenses," which indicates what costs will be reimbursed.[18] However, we should keep in mind that even after a watchdog has been set up, it remains an endangered species, prone to be attacked from different sides by those who feel threatened by its actions. For this reason guarantees have to be built in to safeguard its independence.[19]

Proposal #9: introduce term limits for office-holders

Another proposal is to restrict the number of terms deputies can serve in parliament. One could argue against such a measure on the ground that it would oust experienced politicians from parliament and thereby weaken parliament vis-à-vis the government.[20] On the other hand, restricting the number of terms would lead to a more open system, with more rotation, bringing in newer, fresher, and younger candidates and avoid the formation of a political caste. One could balance both exigencies by restricting parliamentary careers to a total of twelve to fifteen years: long enough to get experienced representatives but avoiding the creation of "life-long backbenchers." Such limits, for example, have been proposed for the US by Republican congressman Mike Gallagher, who wants to introduce a six-term limit (twelve years) in the House and a two-term limit (twelve years) in the US Senate.[21] "Imposition of term limits," writes Bernard Grofman, "will strengthen the party system by enhancing the role of political parties in candidate recruitment and strengthening the importance of party labels as voting cues."[22] Additionally it will reduce influence of special interests, because "retired legislators hired by interest groups as lobbyists will be of lesser value to these groups because there will soon be no legislators remaining in the legislative with whom these lobbyists served."[23]

Proposal #10: forbid the accumulation of political offices

In some countries politicians have the opportunity to combine several public offices. An example is France, where, until recently, politicians were able to combine the function of mayor with the function of parliamentarian or senator. The figure of the *député-maire* (deputy-mayor) or *sénateur-maire* (senator-mayor) was widespread. At the end of 2013 228 members of parliament were mayor, which is 39 percent of the total. On 31 March 2017, a new law came into force, which ended this so-called *cumul*. At that time about one-third of parliamentarians and senators were still mayor. They had to decide which function they wanted to keep.[24] It is clear that a system in which the same small elite is able to combine mandates in local, regional, and national parliaments, and has the option of combining the function of parliamentarian or senator with the function of mayor, is not sound for a democratic polity. It promotes the formation of a political caste and has the additional disadvantage that members of parliament and senators, instead of developing a broad, overall view of the national interest, tend to become myopic, using their function of representative to further the local interests of their municipality.[25]

Proposal #11: forbid deputies to employ family members

In some countries representatives are allowed to employ their family members – spouses, children but also other relatives – as paid parliamentary assistants or paid campaign assistants. It is clear that this practice, although it cannot be called corruption, is part of a grey zone, and in recent years has increasingly been criticized as an improper use of public funds. On 22 April 2008, the European Parliament voted to end this practice under a new assistants' statute, which came into force in July 2009.

Exemptions were allowed for parliamentarians who had already employed family members. They could continue the practice until 2014.[26]

In November 2017 at least eleven members of the US Congress, six Democrats and five Republicans were keeping an immediate family member on the payroll. The daughter of Texan representative Joe Barter, for instance, earned $59,714 for her work as campaign treasurer for her father. In the 2012 election cycle (two years) she made nearly $132,000.[27] The numbers in the US seem small in comparison with Britain, where, in March 2017, MPs were employing a total of 130 relatives. After the MPs' expenses scandal of 2009 there are plans to change the rules and from 2020 to bar children and spouses of MPs from working as assistants, paid with taxpayers' money.[28]

Employing one's family members was, until recently, also a widespread practice used by parliamentarians in France. However, the system came under attack in 2017 after the "Penelopegate" affair, named after Penelope, the spouse of presidential candidate and former prime minister François Fillon. Not only had Fillon employed his wife and children as parliamentary assistants, but allegedly they had not even worked. The total sum paid came close to one million euros.[29] In March 2017 Fillon also had to admit that one month earlier he had accepted a 13,000 euro gift of two suits offered by an expensive Paris tailor. The scandal became the ground for a complete overhaul of the existing system by the new president, Emmanuel Macron, who promised a thorough "moralization" of French politics. Part of this "moralization" was a new law "for trust in political life," passed on 15 September 2017. The new law forbids members of government, parliamentarians, and local office-holders to employ their own family members, their partners, or family members of their partners.[30]

France, which has been hit by many corruption scandals, is slowly adapting its rules, copying the practices of Anglo-Saxon and Nordic countries, where a dominant Protestant culture is less permissive of abuses than in this traditional Catholic country.[31] In majoritarian Protestant Germany the rules are clear. Deputies are granted an allowance of €19,913 per month (in the year 2017) to employ one or more assistants. However, "assistants who are relatives, spouses or persons related by marriage are excluded."[32] The deputy is free to employ relatives but has to pay them from his or her own pocket.

Proposal #12: end revolving-door practices of politicians by making specific jobs off-limits to former office-holders

After leaving parliament or government a cooling-off period of at least four years should be respected, during which former office-holders or parliamentarians cannot accept a role in a company or firm with which they had professional contact during their time in office. Accepting positions in some selected firms must even be declared completely off-limits. The fact, for instance, that Gerhard Schröder, a German chancellor, shortly after leaving office accepted a leading (and well paid) job in the Kremlin's Nord Stream gas pipeline project is a political – and moral – scandal. Even more so if one takes into account that in 2001 he had cancelled a €7.1 billion debt owed by Moscow to the German government for purchases from the former German Democratic Republic.[33] Schröder's appointment had the semblance of a *quid pro quo*. This morally reprehensible behavior underlines once more the necessity of taking measures in order to avoid collusion between office-holders and economic interests. In Schröder's case these economic interests were compounded by the geopolitical interests of a hostile power.

The "revolving door" between international firms and politicians is a well-known phenomenon. This system, in which politicians alternate public functions and well-paid jobs in the private sector, undermines the credibility of politicians and jeopardizes public trust in their integrity. Politicians who move from a regulating or policymaking function to a lobbying function are accused of using their inside information and access to former colleagues in their private interests. A well-known case is that of José Manuel Barroso, president of the European Commission, who, after leaving office, became non-executive chairman of the American investment bank Goldman Sachs. This bank was not only involved in the 2008 subprime crisis but also "edited" Greece's books to get it into the Eurozone. It led to an online petition, organized by Barroso's former staff, who attacked his "morally reprehensible" behavior and called for "strong exemplary sanctions."[34] The petition was signed by 120,000 people. It led to questions by the European ombudsman to Barroso's successor, Jean-Claude Juncker, who answered that Barroso had respected the eighteen-month cooling-off period before taking up the new job.

Barroso's case was not an exception. Many politicians make use of these lucrative "revolving doors," and politicians from the left are no less interested than conservatives:

> Tony Blair (Labour) went for two million pounds per year as "special adviser" to the American superbank JP Morgan, former Prime Minister John Major (Conservatives) to the Swiss bank Crédit Suisse, Alistair Darling (Labour), former Finance Minister during the [2008] crash, to the American bank Morgan Stanley and former leader of the Conservatives William Hague to the American financial giant Citibank.[35]

One could add former chancellor George Osborne, "who has had a one-day-a-week role at the BlackRock Investment Institute, a unit of the world's biggest asset manager, for a salary of £650,000 (in 2017). Mr. Osborne ... brought in pensions deregulation that benefited the firm."[36]

In Britain in 1975 a special Cabinet Office body was founded, the Advisory Committee on Business Appointments (ACOBA), an agency overseen by the parliamentary Public Administration and Constitutional Affairs Committee. *The Economist* wrote in 2019 that "ACOBA is under attack for being toothless ... Ministers increasingly seek employment in areas where they used to run policy. ACOBA's main condition is to require former public servants not to lobby their old department on behalf of their new employer, for two years. But the real worry is that jobs may be rewards for decisions taken while in office."[37] In the Netherlands the situation is no different. Dutch prime minister Wim Kok, a social democrat, became a member of the supervisory board of the bank ING, and former minister of finance Onno Ruding, a Christian democrat, went to Citibank.[38]

It is clear that installing a short cooling-off period is not enough and that jobs in certain clearly defined firms, such as banks and investment firms, should be declared off-limits to office-holders. Holding political office-holders to account might seem a Sisyphean task; it is, however, urgent if one wants to counter the populist argument that politicians have become a self-serving caste. A liberal democracy can only function if its politicians and office-holders work for the public good.

Notes

1 Montesquieu, *De l'esprit*, p. 537.
2 Quoted in Charles A. Kupchan, *The End of the American Era – U.S. Foreign Policy and the Geopolitics of the Twenty-first Century* (New York: Alfred A. Knopf, 2002), p. 324.
3 Georg Wilhelm Friedrich Hegel, "Vorlesungen über die Philosophie der Geschichte," in G. W. F. Hegel, *Werke*, Band 12 (Frankfurt am Main: Suhrkamp Verlag, 1970), p. 38.
4 Ibid., p. 38.
5 Immanuel Kant, *Political Writings*, edited by H. S. Reiss (Cambridge and New York: Cambridge University Press, 1991), p. 112.
6 Chayes, "Kleptocracy in America," p. 150.
7 "Wet beëdiging ministers en leden Staten-Generaal." www.denederlandsegrondwet.nl/9353000/1/j9vvihlf299q0sr/vi32nmel4fzh (accessed 10 October 2017). Swearing is asked from believers, declaring from non-believers.
8 The opportunities and privileges may be completely legal, as in Italy, where deputies and senators pay 40 percent less for their pensions than the average Italian (cf. Tito Boeri, *Populismo e stato sociale* (Bari and Rome: Editori Laterza, 2017), p. 28).
9 Robert P. George, *Making Men Moral – Civil Liberties and Public Morality* (Oxford: Clarendon Press, 1995), p. 25.
10 Eric Lipton, "With no warning, House Republicans vote to gut independent Ethics Office," *New York Times*, 2 January 2017. www.nytimes.com/2017/01/02/us/politics/

with-no-warning-house-republicans-vote-to-hobble-independent-ethics-office.html (accessed 10 October 2017).
11 Ibid.
12 Eric Lipton, "New Ethics chief has fought to roll back restrictions," *New York Times*, 26 July 2017. www.nytimes.com/2017/07/26/us/politics/david-apol-office-of-government-ethics-trump.html (accessed 10 October 2017).
13 Ibid.
14 Ibid.
15 "Trump ethics watchdog 'scraps ban on anonymous donations towards White House staff legal fees,'" *Independent*, 14 September 2017. www.independent.co.uk/news/world/americas/us-politics/trump-ethics-watchdog-anonymous-donations-white-house-staff-legal-fees-lobbyists-scraps-ban-a7946441.html (accessed 10 October 2017).
16 Ibid.
17 Cf. "MPs' expenses: Full list of MPs investigated by The Telegraph," *Telegraph*, 8 May 2009. www.telegraph.co.uk/news/newstopics/mps-expenses/5297606/MPs-expenses-Full-list-of-MPs-investigated-by-the-Telegraph.html (accessed 11 October 2017).
18 Cf. "Scheme of MPs' business costs & expenses," IPSA. www.theipsa.org.uk/publications/scheme-of-mps-business-costs-expenses/ (accessed 15 January 2018).
19 Walter Shaub made thirteen proposals to improve government ethics. See Walter Shaub, "Policy Proposals on Ethics," The Campaign Legal Center, 9 November 2017. www.campaignlegalcenter.org/sites/default/files/W%20Shaub%20Legislative%20Proposal%20-%209%20November%202017_0.pdf (accessed 20 November 2017).
20 This is the argument used by Olivier Faure, leader of the socialists in the French parliament, against a proposal of the French government to restrict the number of parliamentary mandates to three consecutive terms. Deputies, who are "established and experienced," who were able "to take position against the government," would, in his words, be "decapitated" after three mandates, leading to "a weakening of the countervailing power vis-à-vis the president of the republic" (cf. Manon Rescan and Solenn de Royer, "Emmanuel Macron peaufine sa réforme constitutionnelle," *Le Monde*, 21 December 2017).
21 Rep. Mike Gallagher (R-WIS), "A time for congressional term limits," *The Hill*, 3 April 2017. http://thehill.com/blogs/congress-blog/politics/326940-a-time-for-congressional-term-limits (accessed 11 October 2017).
22 Bernard Grofman, "Introduction to the Term Limits Debate: Hypotheses in Search of Data," in Bernard Grofman (ed.), *Legislative Term Limits: Public Choice Perspectives* (Boston, Dordrecht, and London: Kluwer Academic Publishers, 1996), p. 4.
23 Ibid., p. 5.
24 Baptiste Bouthier, "Cumul des mandats: C'est la fin du député-maire," *Libération*, 31 March 2017. www.liberation.fr/france/2017/03/31/cumul-des-mandats-c-est-la-fin-du-depute-maire_1558882 (accessed 11 October 2017).
25 One could object that US senators also defend the interests of their home state. However, there is a major difference between representing a state in a federal republic and defending the interests of a small town in rural France.
26 Cf. Andrew Willis, "Grumbling as some MEPs continue to employ family members," *EU Observer*, 20 January 2011. https://euobserver.com/institutional/31676 (accessed 12 October 2017).
27 Linley Sanders, "It's not just Trump: Congress members hire family members for political jobs," *Newsweek*, 2 November, 2017. www.newsweek.com/democrats-also-pay-family-public-dollars-699548 (accessed 20 November 2017).

28 Ben Riley-Smith, "MPs will be banned from hiring family members at the public's expense, IPSA says as 130 relatives of MPs could lose their jobs," *Telegraph*, 15 March 2017.
29 Cf. Christian Hartmann, "France's scandal-hit François Fillon put under formal fraud investigation," *Newsweek*, 14 March 2017. www.newsweek.com/francois-fillon-investigation-prosecutor-penelopegate-french-election-2017–567795 (accessed 12 October 2017).
30 "Loi organique et loi ordinaire du 15 septembre 2017 pour la confiance dans la vie politique," *Vie publique*, 18 September 2017. www.vie-publique.fr/actualite/panorama/texte-discussion/projet-loi-organique-projet-loi-ordinaire-retablissant-confiance-action-publique.html (accessed 12 October 2017).
31 Max Weber characterized the practice of the Catholic Church as "to punish heretics, but be mild for sinners" (Max Weber, "Die protestantische Ethik und der 'Geist' des Kapitalismus," in Weber, *Schriften 1894–1922*, p. 151).
32 "Der Abgeordnete und seine Mitarbeiter," *Deutscher Bundestag*. www.bundestag.de/dokumente/textarchiv/2015/kw32_finanzierung_buero/384390 (accessed 15 January 2018).
33 Cf. Christian Fuchs, Paul Middelhoff, and Fritz Zimmermann, "Wenn Männer zu sehr lieben – Gerhard Schröder und Russland: Szenen einer Beziehung," *Die Zeit*, 17 August 2017.
34 Cf. Nils Pratley, "Barroso's new job puts Brussels elite in a tight spot," *Guardian*, 6 September 2016. www.theguardian.com/business/nils-pratley-on-finance/2016/sep/06/jose-manuel-barroso-goldman-job-puts-european-commission-in-a-tight-spot (accessed 12 October 2017).
35 Joris Luyendijk, *Kunnen we praten* (Amsterdam and Antwerp: Atlas Contact, 2017), p. 38.
36 "The sweet hereafter – Cheer up, sacked MPs. A big payday awaits," *The Economist*, 14 December 2019. www.economist.com/britain/2019/12/12/cheer-up-sacked-mps-a-big-payday-awaits (accessed 30 December 2019).
37 Ibid.
38 Luyendijk, *Kunnen we praten*, p. 33.

14
How to get rid of political castes

Proposal #13: avoid creating political castes

One of the complaints one often hears – and not only from populists – is that politicians have become a "class" with its own interests. Instead of representing the interests of voters, they are accused of having become a "cozy in-crowd," increasingly defending their own personal and group interests. Christopher Lasch had already warned in 1995 that "the growing insularity of elites means, among other things, that political ideologies lose touch with the concerns of ordinary citizens. Since political debate is restricted, most of the time, to the 'talking classes,' as they have been aptly characterized, it becomes increasingly ingrown and formulaic."[1] The mutual alienation between the political elite and the average voter is not only a question of jargon and language. It is also caused by the increased visibility of the elite's behavior. Self-serving politicians and corruption have always existed, but they tend to get more publicity in the media today. This increased visibility is amplified by social media, whose users can, in a few days, organize a worldwide buzz.

The idea that politicians form a separate caste is not always a question only of perception. We have already mentioned the growing influence of the super-rich in the United States, who not only fund political parties and political campaigns but also increasingly seek office. The danger of a "plutocratization" of the democratic system was already raised a century ago by Max Weber, who wrote that "the leadership of a state or a party by people who (in the economic sense of the word) live exclusively for politics and not from politics, means necessarily a 'plutocratic' recruitment."[2] Therefore, it is necessary to curb the influence of "big money" and to introduce a system of state funding for political parties in countries in which such a system does not yet exist. But this is not enough. Because it is not only money which can lead to the formation of a political caste. It is equally education. Robert Dahl pointed to this problem when he wrote: "From ancient times to the present day … virtually all thoughtful advocates of democratic and republican government have strongly emphasized how democracy is threatened by inequalities in economic resources." He continued: "I am inclined that the long-run prospects for democracy are more seriously endangered by inequalities in resources, strategic positions, and bargaining strength that are derived not from wealth or economic position but from special knowledge."[3]

The National School of Administration: France's elite school

Can a democracy be endangered by special knowledge? There is good reason to take a closer look at the role of experts and specialists in our democratic societies. In some countries there exist exclusive educational institutions tasked with the formation of the political and administrative elites. A well-known example is the École Nationale d'Administration (ENA) in France. This National School of Administration, founded in 1945, is an elite school which was originally set up to broaden access to the civil service. The idea behind the initiative was to fight nepotism by "democratizing" the civil service. According to strict meritocratic rules, the candidates, university graduates with mostly a political science background, take a tough entrance exam to be admitted to a prestigious two-year course. Graduates are referred to as *énarques*. They have become members of a new, respected nobility, whose badge of honor is not a question of family traditions or of an inherited title, but of intellectual excellence. In the seventy-five years of its existence this institute has produced four presidents and six prime ministers.[4] *Énarque* politicians like to surround themselves with other *énarques*, employing them as advisers in their cabinets. President Emmanuel Macron, for instance, who is an *énarque*, started his political career as an adviser to President François Hollande, who is equally an *énarque*.

The problem is that the ENA, originally founded to create an open system of meritocratic recruitment, is increasingly perceived by the French public as a closed bastion, generating a caste of new mandarins whose presumed expert knowledge is miles distant from the preoccupations of the population. They are accused of a lack of creativity. "The énarques are made to obey," wrote Jean-Claude Barreau, "and not to command. The ENA is a school of administration, not a school of government."[5]

When, in 2007, the centrist presidential candidate François Bayrou (not an *énarque*) proposed abolishing the school, he was faced with a storm of criticism.[6] This did not silence critics of the ENA. In 2012 Olivier Saby, himself an *énarque*, published a diary, titled *Promotion Ubu Roi*.[7] In this diary he accused the school of being a "factor in France's decline."[8] The school was creating only docile administrators and managers, who were incapable of invention or innovation: conformists, lacking in imagination and courage, who would be unable to conduct the necessary reforms the French political system so urgently needed. In 2015 Saby got the support of another *énarque*, Adeline Baldacchino, who published a book, titled *La ferme des énarques* (Énarques Farm).[9] The title was an allusion to George Orwell's book *Animal Farm*, in which all animals are equal but some are "more equal" than others. Baldacchino also criticized the privileges and extreme conformism and risk-avoiding behavior of this elite, its tendency "to see nothing, hear nothing, say nothing."[10] The French political scientist Marcel Gauchet spoke about "personnel recruited on an extraordinary small basis, coming from a single institution, [which is] itself the provider of a very questionable education."[11]

In 2016 even the prominent conservative politician Bruno Le Maire, himself an *énarque*, declared that he wanted to abolish the ENA. "The senior civil servants trained by ENA are not satisfied with running [only] the government administration," he said. "As politicians, ministers, CEOs, they run the whole country."[12] Le Maire expressed his determination to fight this "confiscation of power by a small group."[13] One year later *énarque* Le Maire became minister of economy and finance in the government of *énarque* President Macron, whose government style was characterized by some as an *épistocratie*, which means "a government style in which the power is assigned to experts."[14]

When former ENA students take the lead in attacking the very institution which promises them a brilliant career and denounce its "confiscation of power," it is clear that there is a problem. However, the basic idea on which the school is founded, is sound. As Lucian Pye emphasizes: "Equality means that recruitment to political office should reflect achievement standards of performance and not the ascriptive considerations of a traditional social system. The assumption in a developed political system is that people must have displayed appropriate merit to gain public office and that officeholders should have met some competitive test of competence."[15] Meritocratic selection was an advance compared with traditional forms of selection, based on "old boys" clubs, family networks, and the privilege of class and money, leading to quasi-hereditary dynasties. But the meritocratic principle should not be taken to extremes.

According to Michael Walzer, "plutocrats and meritocrats … are tyrants as much as autocrats are, and their personalities are distorted in comparable ways."[16] This may sound exaggerated. However, it is a fact that plutocrats, such as Donald Trump and Silvio Berlusconi, tend to have an overblown self-image, thinking that their business experience automatically translates into extraordinary talents in other domains. Meritocrats may lack this business experience, but they tend to think that their intellectual prowess is a sign of being chosen and predestined as part of an elite, born to rule. According to Otfried Höffe, one of the arguments one might deploy against an "expertocracy" is that "politics is not only a question of facts, but also of interests and decisions based on values."[17] For these questions responsibility still lies with the citizens and not with the experts: "Each attempt to promote the common good against their will, each paternalism or maternalism, is, by its very nature, excluded in a democracy."[18] On 26 April 2019, President Macron announced that he plans to close the ENA "in order to build something that functions better."[19] The reason? "Because it doesn't resemble our society: too many children of the bourgeoisie, not enough with a modest family background."[20]

The "Oxbridge" political elite in Britain

There are other ways to select senior civil servants than take place in France, as is the case, for instance, with the "Fast Stream" in Britain. On the website of Fast Stream, the government's official recruitment website, one can read the following words of welcome:

> Britain needs leaders – people who are prepared to commit themselves to solving big issues. Are you one of them? We need talented people to lead the future Civil Service. Whoever you are, whatever your background, the Fast Stream is the fastest route to real leadership.[21]

This sounds good. Each British citizen is here invited to think about a career in the civil service, whatever his or her background. There is an emphasis not only on intellectual capabilities, but also on social abilities. New jobs are reserved on a fifty–fifty basis for male and female applicants, 9 percent for disabled people, and 10 percent for non-white minorities.

Fast Stream, however, is less a recruiting agency for politicians than is the case with the ENA. And when we look at the background of British politicians we get a completely different picture. A government report reveals that 38 percent of members of the House of Lords and 24 percent of members of the House of Commons have graduated from "Oxbridge" (the elite universities of Oxford and Cambridge), compared with less than 1 percent of the adult population.[22] The difference between the people and the members of both Houses is not only a question of education, but also of wealth: 38 percent of members of the House of Lords and 24 percent of MPs are on the *Sunday Times* Rich List.[23] This list is published annually and includes the 1,000 wealthiest people or families resident in the UK. The "poorest" member on this list still has a net value of over £100 million.[24] According to the report, "a lack of diversity in the people who run the country is a problem in and of itself: the risks are 'group think' and a lack of understanding of those with different backgrounds."[25]

And the authors ask: "Are top jobs about what you know, or who you know? Is some talent locked out?"[26] These are, indeed, pressing questions.

Is meritocracy jeopardized in the United States?

But what about America? In his book *The Closing of the American Mind*, published in 1987, Allan Bloom wrote:

> Thus, Harvard, Yale and Princeton are not what they used to be – the last resorts of aristocratic sentiment within the democracy. The differentiations based on old family or old wealth have vanished. The old wounds that used to be inflicted by the clubbable on the unclubbable, in our muted version of the English class system, have healed because the clubs are not anything to be cared about seriously. All this began after World War II, with the GI Bill. College was for everyone. And the top universities gradually abandoned preference for the children of their alumni and the exclusion of outsiders, especially Jews. Academic records and tests became the criterion for selection ... No longer do any universities have the vocation of producing "gentlemen" as well as scholars. Snobbism of the old sort is dead.[27]

Bloom describes the evolution of the Ivy League universities from bastions of the rich and privileged to more open institutions, increasingly recruiting their students on meritocratic grounds. But that was in 1987, at a time when the amounts paid for undergraduate tuition and fees were still reasonably low. However, this situation has fundamentally changed. According to the National Center for Education Statistics, the average amount for undergraduate tuition and fees, which in 1980–1981 was $4,586, had in 2014–2015 reached $11,487: an increase of 250 percent![28] This has led to an explosion of student loan debt. In 2014 19 percent of student loan borrowers owed more than $50,000. This was 6 percent in 2001.[29] In 2010 the total student loan debt surpassed the total credit card debt held by Americans, and in 2012 it surpassed the $1 trillion mark.[30]

This means that the shift toward meritocracy, welcomed by Allan Bloom, is increasingly jeopardized and that higher education risks becoming (again) the privilege of the rich and the upper middle class. This development was criticized by Bernie Sanders in the 2016 presidential campaign, denouncing the fact that "hundreds of thousands of bright young people cannot afford to go to college, and that millions of others leave school with a mountain of debt that burdens them for decades."[31] Sanders promised to "fight to make sure that every American who studies hard in school can go to college regardless of how much money their parents make without going deeply in debt."[32] He proposed to make tuition free at public colleges and universities.

Should parliaments "mirror" the population?

The situation seems, therefore, rather complex: parliaments and governments whose members came from the plutocratic (or aristocratic) "high society" were criticized for their lack of representativeness. To overcome this problem, meritocratic systems of education were introduced, open to members of all classes of society, including the poorest. But these meritocratic systems, such as the ENA in France and Ivy League universities in the US, have been accused, in turn, of being "elitist." William F. Buckley, Jr., an American conservative author and founder of the *National Review* magazine, "once remarked, that he would rather be governed by the first two thousand people listed in the Boston telephone directory than by the Harvard faculty."[33] This sounds exaggerated? Maybe.

A solution, proposed by two Dutch political scientists, is "mirroring." In their book *Nepparlement* (Fake Parliament)[34] they criticize the Dutch parliament not only because the profile of the average deputy tends to be the "white, well-to-do, middle aged man,"[35] but also because the deputies are more highly educated than the average Dutch citizen. About 90 percent of the deputies have a university or college degree, compared with about one-third of the population.[36] The authors denounce what they call a "diploma democracy" in which opinions of the lower-educated classes are not sufficiently represented. "The political opinions of parliamentarians," they write,

> match almost perfectly the opinions of the higher educated, richer Dutchmen. Citizens with lower and secondary education and lower and middle incomes miss out completely in this respect. We can attribute this lack of ideological mirroring to the almost complete absence of people with primary and secondary education in the most important representative institutions of our country. The ease with which higher educated, better-off citizens appropriate the office of representative should, in our opinion, be corrected.[37]

The solution they offer is that parliament should "mirror" the different groups of the population. In this case it would mean making space for people with only primary and secondary education on the candidate lists of the political parties. And not only for them. "The benefits of mirroring," they write, "are not only restricted to one variable ... Ethnic minorities and young people, for instance, also want to be more fully involved in decision-making processes inside, as well as outside the political arena."[38]

Systems which promote mandatory quotas for certain categories of people already exist. In France, for instance, the first law promoting complete gender equality in parliament dates from the year 2000. When, nevertheless, parties did not do enough to put women on their candidate lists, in 2012 financial penalties were introduced. These penalties were doubled in 2014. It led to a historic record in the June 2017 parliamentary election, when 38.8 percent of the deputies were women.[39] Ironically, this success for gender equality was accompanied by the same social inequality as in the Netherlands: only 3 percent of the deputies came from a worker or employee background, while this group represents about one-half of the active population.[40] Imposing quotas based on gender are relatively uncontroversial. However, this changes when quotas for other categories are introduced. As Daniel Bell remarked on the introduction of quotas for admission to universities:

> Quotas themselves are no simple matter. If "representation" is to be the criterion of position, then what is the logic of extending the principle only to women, blacks, Mexicans, Puerto Ricans, American Indians, Filipinos, Chinese, and Japanese … Why not to Irish, Italians, Poles, and other ethnic groups?[41]

The same objection can be made here. When quotas are introduced to promote the presence of people with primary or secondary education on the candidate lists, why not also introduce quotas for people of color, the LGBT community, the disabled, and so on? There is an additional problem: voters want to elect the best candidates, men or women. A parliament, of which one-half or more of its members would have only primary or secondary education, doesn't seem to have enough intellectual baggage for its complex task – notwithstanding the fact that there are always naturally talented people who are able to overcome a lack of formal education. Making more place for such people would be welcome, but a real "mirroring" of the electorate in a parliament does not seem a good idea.

Another author who proposes some kind of "mirroring" is David Van Reybrouck. In his book *Against Elections* he attacks the system of electoral democracy and proposes a "lottocracy," a system in which representatives of the people are not chosen but appointed by drawing lots, re-establishing an old Athenian custom. "I believe the systemic crisis of democracy can be remedied by giving sortation a fresh chance," he writes,[42] adding: "The risk of corruption reduces, election fever abates and attention to the common good increases."[43] However, he himself seems not to be so sure that this system will be an improvement, because he proposes to organize a Senate chosen by lot alongside an elected parliament. Will a representation organized by "rolling the dice" lead to better government? One may doubt it. People who win this lottery may not be willing to do the job or will at least lack the necessary drive and ambition. Not to speak about their competence. And will they really be less corrupt, as the writer assumes?

How to get rid of political castes

An increasing distrust of experts?

The problem, in fact, may lie elsewhere. One would expect that, logically, citizens would select the best and the brightest to represent them in parliament. It would be illogical and counterintuitive for them to vote for people who have no special knowledge of the political process. However, in the case of the United States, Daniel Bell observed a striking phenomenon:

> Long ago, travelers to these shores noted the extreme egalitarianism of American manners and customs and warned of the "leveling" consequence of the glorification of the common, rather than the uncommon, man: for if one holds that each man is as good as the next, it is easy to say, as has often been the case, that no man can claim to be better than the next. Unfortunately, good and better are never defined. That no man should claim birth alone as the inherent possessor of a status is understandable; in that respect each man is as good as the next. But populism goes further: that some are more qualified than others to assert opinions is vehemently denied.[44]

Here Daniel Bell is putting his finger on a sore point: the lack of recognition, if not outright denial, of the existence of expert knowledge. This may seem strange, because in domains outside politics this skepticism is less present: if one takes a plane one trusts the pilot to be an experienced professional, and if one has to go to hospital for an operation one tries to get the surgeon with the best reputation. In politics, however, everyone tends to consider him- or herself an expert and to downplay the expertise of professionals. "The bigger concern today," writes Tom Nichols, "is that Americans have reached a point where ignorance – at least regarding what is generally considered established knowledge in public policy – is seen as an actual virtue. To reject the advice of experts is to assert autonomy, a way for Americans to demonstrate their independence from nefarious elites – and insulate their increasingly fragile egos from ever being told they're wrong."[45] Nichols points at "the Dunning–Kruger effect," named after two psychologists who observed that "the less skilled or competent you are, the more confident you are that you're actually very good at what you do."[46] This is a danger for democracy, he argues, because "the workings of such a representative democracy … are exponentially more difficult when the electorate is not competent to judge matters at hand. Laypeople complain about the rule of experts and demand greater involvement in complicated national questions, but many of them express their anger and make these demands only after abdicating their own important role in the process: namely, to stay informed and politically literate enough to choose representatives who can act wisely on their behalf."[47] Nichols warns: "Unless some sort of trust and mutual respect can be restored, public discourse will be polluted by unearned respect for unfounded opinions. And in such an environment, anything and everything becomes possible, including the end of democracy and republican government itself."⁴⁸

In the preceding chapter we mentioned the need to rebuild trust. But how can trust and mutual respect be restored? It is not only a question of the public who has the duty "to stay informed and politically literate enough to choose representatives who can act wisely on their behalf." It is also a question of the expert elite fulfilling *their* share of the deal. We have to ask ourselves why the meritocratic principle, instead of promoting the public's trust in politicians, has had an inverse effect, and why politicians are increasingly considered as a separate caste with their own interests, which are not necessarily congruent with those of the population at large.

John Rawls on the flaw in the liberal concept of meritocracy

This is apparently to do with a flaw in the liberal concept of meritocracy. Meritocracy is based on the liberal principle of equality. The fundamental equality of citizens in a liberal democratic system leads to the creation of equal opportunities for all to develop one's natural abilities and talents. The existence of less privileged positions at birth should be compensated by creating a level playing field. Meritocracy is thus based on the creation of equal starting points. However, it does not take into account the end points. A successful French student who has obtained his ENA degree, as well as his American colleague who graduated from an Ivy League university, both have several times the earning power of their less successful former classmates. John Rawls has questioned the liberal principle that those who, due to their natural talents, are more successful, should have a right to be better paid, because this would privilege unduly people with greater natural endowments. John Rawls, therefore, criticizes a meritocratic society, which is exclusively based on the principle of equality of opportunity. "This form of social order," he writes,

> follows the principle of careers open to talents and uses equality of opportunity as a way of releasing men's energies in the pursuit of economic prosperity and political dominion. There exists a marked disparity between the upper and the lower classes in both means of life and the rights and privileges of organizational authority. The culture of the poorer strata is impoverished while that of the governing and technocratic elite is securely based on the service of the national ends of power and wealth. Equality of opportunity means an equal chance to leave the less fortunate behind in the personal quest for influence and social position.⁴⁹

Rawls argues that promoting equality of opportunity is necessary, but not enough, to create a just society. He pleads for the introduction of an extra condition for the legitimation of unequal end results. This condition is the "difference principle," which means that "the advantages of persons with greater natural endowments are to be limited to those that further the good of the poorer sectors of society."[50] "In this way," he writes, "the idea of *noblesse oblige* is carried over to the conception of natural aristocracy."[51] This means that people who have followed more successful intellectual careers may receive better payments only if this benefits the situation of the poorer classes. This principle should *a forteriori* be applied in the case of politicians, whose explicit task it is to promote the common good. However, the problem with Rawls's "difference principle" is that it is difficult to operationalize and can lead to contradictory positions. A politician will answer that in fact all his or her activities serve the common good from which also the poorer classes benefit. It is the basic problem of the well-known "trickle down" theory that says that extra money given to the rich leads to investments, which create employment for the poor – a theory that is both defended and contested by prominent economists. This is not to say that Rawls is not right. He is right that politicians should adopt a spirit of *noblesse oblige* and must be proud to serve the common good and should be concerned that the laws they make and the measures they take benefit the least privileged classes of society, particularly in the fields of welfare and fiscal policy.

Notes

1 Christopher Lasch, *The Revolt of the Elites and the Betrayal of Democracy* (New York and London: W. W. Norton & Company, 1995), p. 80.
2 Weber, "Politik als Beruf," p. 523.
3 Robert Dahl, *Democracy and Its Critics* (New Haven and London: Yale University Press, 1989), p. 333.
4 These were Presidents Valéry Giscard d'Estaing, Jacques Chirac, François Hollande, and Emmanuel Macron, and Prime Ministers Laurent Fabius, Édouard Balladur, Alain Juppé, Lionel Jospin, Dominique de Villepin, and Édouard Philippe.
5 Jean-Claude Barreau, *De l'immigration en général et de la nation française en particulier* (Paris: Le Pré aux Clercs, 1992), p. 114.
6 "Suppression de l'ENA: Bayrou sous le feu des critiques," *Les Échos*, 3 April 2007.
7 Olivier Saby, *Promotion Ubu Roi*, with the collaboration of Christophe Quillien (Paris: Flammarion, 2012).
8 Quoted in Patrick Fauconnier, "L'ENA – Facteur de déclin français?" *Le Nouvel Observateur*, 25 October 2012. http://tempsreel.nouvelobs.com/education/20121025.OBS7128/l-ena-facteur-de-declin-francais.html (accessed 24 October 2017).
9 Adeline Baldacchino, *La ferme des énarques* (Paris: Michalon, 2015).
10 Quoted in Gilles Heuré, "L'ENA est-elle une école dangereuse?" *Télérama*, 23 October 2015. www.telerama.fr/idees/l-ena-est-elle-une-ecole-dangereuse,132669.php (accessed 24 October 2017).
11 Gauchet, *La démocratie*, p. 197.

12 Quoted in Denis Peiron, "L'ENA, prestigieuse et critiquée," *La Croix*, 1 September 2016. www.la-croix.com/France/Politique/LENA-prestigieuse-critiquee-2016-09-01-1200786043 (accessed 26 October 2017).
13 Ibid.
14 Alexandre Viala, "Le macronisme ou le spectre de l'épistocratie," *Le Monde*, 19 October 2017.
15 Lucian W. Pye, *Aspects of Political Development* (Boston and Toronto: Little, Brown and Company, 1966), p. 46.
16 Michael Walzer, *Thick and Thin – Moral Argument at Home and Abroad* (Notre Dame and London: University of Notre Dame Press, 1994), p. 37.
17 Otfried Höffe, *Ist die Demokratie zukunftsfähig?* (Munich: Verlag C. H. Beck, 2009), p. 278.
18 Ibid., p. 278.
19 Benoît Floc'h, "Macron confirme la disparition de l'ENA et des grands corps," *Le Monde*, 26mApril 2019. www.lemonde.fr/politique/article/2019/04/26/macron-confirme-la-disparition-de-l-ena-et-des-grands-corps_5455235_823448.html (accessed 4 May 2019).
20 Ibid.
21 Fast Stream website: https://www.faststream.gov.uk/ (accessed 31 October 2017).
22 "Elitist Britain?" Report from the Social Mobility and Child Poverty Commission and the Social Mobility Commission, 28 August, 2014. www.gov.uk/government/publications/elitist-britain (accessed 31 October 2017).
23 Andrew Sparrow, "Closed shop at the top in deeply elitist Britain, says study," *Guardian*, 28 August 2014.
24 The Sunday Times Rich List 2017. http://nuk-rich-list-ui-2017-uk-prod.eu-west-1.elasticbeanstalk.com/richlist/view/group6/950/rank/#list (accessed 4 May 2019).
25 "Elitist Britain?"
26 Ibid.
27 Allan Bloom, *The Closing of the American Mind – How Higher Education has Failed Democracy and Impoverished the Souls of Today's Students* (New York and London: Simon & Schuster, 1987), p. 89.
28 Digest of Education Statistics, National Center for Education Statistics (sums are in constant dollars to account for inflation). https://nces.ed.gov/programs/digest/d15/tables/dt15_330.10.asp?current=yes (accessed 4 May 2019).
29 Patrick Gillespie, "Student debt over $50K is on the rise," CNN, 12 September 2014. http://money.cnn.com/2014/09/12/news/economy/student-loan-debt-50000-or-more/index.html (accessed 3 November 2017).
30 Cf. Neal McCluskey, "Most college cost fixes miss the root problem," Cato Institute, 13 September 2016. www.cato.org/publications/testimony/most-college-cost-fixes-miss-root-problem (accessed 3 November 2017).
31 "It's time to make college tuition free and debt free," Website Bernie Sanders. https://berniesanders.com/issues/its-time-to-make-college-tuition-free-and-debt-free/ (accessed 3 November 2017).
32 Ibid.
33 Quoted in William A. Galston, *Anti-pluralism – The Populist Threat to Liberal Democracy* (New Haven and London: Yale University Press, 2018), p. 111.
34 Hakhverdian and Schakel, *Nepparlement*. The title of the book refers to the accusation, made by the populist Geert Wilders on 17 September 2015, that the Dutch parliament would be a "nepparlement" (fake parliament).

35 Ibid., p. 75.
36 In 2016 30.4 percent of the Dutch population had only primary-level education, 39.9 had secondary-level education, and 29.7 percent had higher education (cf. "Onderwijs in cijfers," Rijksoverheid). www.onderwijsincijfers.nl/kengetallen/sectoroverstijgend/nederlands-onderwijsstelsel/hoogst-behaalde-onderwijsniveau (accessed 6 November 2017).
37 Hakhverdian and Schakel, *Nepparlement*, p. 8.
38 Ibid., p. 73.
39 "Législatives 2017: 224 femmes élues, un chiffre historique," *Le Monde*, 19 June 2017. www.lemonde.fr/elections-legislatives-2017/article/2017/06/19/legislatives-2017–223-femmes-elues-un-record_5146848_5076653.html (accessed 6 November 2017).
40 Cf. "L'assemblée ne compte quasiment plus de représentants des milieux populaires," *Observatoire des inégalités*, 12 June 2017. www.inegalites.fr/L-Assemblee-ne-compte-quasiment-plus-de-representants-des-milieux-populaires (accessed 6 November 2017). In the first French post-war legislature (1945–1951) this percentage was still 18.8 percent and the highest ever. The decline of deputies with a worker or employee background is a consequence of the decline of the communist party and the gentrification of the socialist party.
41 Daniel Bell, *The Coming of Post-Industrial Society – A Venture in Social Forecasting* (New York: Basic Books, 1976), p. 418.
42 David Van Reybrouck, *Against Elections – The Case for Democracy* (London: The Bodley Head, 2016), p. 151.
43 Ibid., p. 152.
44 Daniel Bell, *The End of Ideology* (Glencoe: The Free Press, 1960), p. 104.
45 Tom Nichols, "How America Lost Faith in Expertise and Why That's a Giant Problem," *Foreign Affairs*, Vol. 96, No. 2, March/April 2017, pp. 60–61.
46 Ibid., p. 65.
47 Ibid., p. 73.
48 Ibid., p. 73.
49 John Rawls, *A Theory of Justice* (London, Oxford, and New York: Oxford University Press, 1973), pp. 106–107. One can find a similar criticism in Daniel Bell, *The Cultural Contradictions of Capitalism* (London: Heinemann, 1979), pp. 263–264: "Equality of opportunity has been the overriding definition of equality in the liberal societies of the West … By and large this principle has been unchallenged … The outcomes of the competition between individuals are disparate degrees of status, income, and authority. These disparate outcomes have been justified on the ground that they are freely gained and earned by effort. This is the basis of the idea of a just 'meritocracy' … But in recent years there has been an outcry that the disparate outcomes are too large and unequal, and that public policy ought to seek greater equality of outcomes – in short to *make* persons more equal in income, status, or authority."
50 Rawls, *Theory of Justice*, p. 74.
51 Ibid., p. 74.

15
The need for democratic education

Proposal #14: introduce "democratic education" in the curriculum of secondary schools

In recent years the common man's distrust of experts and politicians has rapidly increased. Although this distrust is legitimate in specific cases, one has to distance oneself from the simplistic slogan "they're all corrupt," often used by populists of all stripes and colors. Because they're *not* all corrupt. And *if* there is corruption, this is no less present in populist parties, as the examples of the French Rassemblement National and the Austrian Freedom Party show. Corruption can be fought by concrete measures, such as improving transparency and publicity, and by introducing sanctions. But it is not only politicians who should make an effort. Citizens too have a responsibility to fulfill *their* part of the deal. As we saw in the last chapter, according to Tom Nichols "laypeople complain about the rule of experts and demand greater involvement in complicated national questions, but many of them express their anger and make these demands only after abdicating their own important role in the process: namely, to stay informed and politically literate enough to choose representatives who can act wisely on their behalf."[1] This is, indeed, the other side of the coin. If representatives should do their utmost to be transparent and to subject themselves to the piercing eyes of ethics watchdogs, they should expect the voter to put some effort into following and understanding what is going on.

Here we are back at the heart of the problem: the lack of interest of many citizens. Political scientists have proposed different solutions to this problem. James Fishkin proposed organizing a "D-day" – a "deliberation day" – before an election. During this day the public would be informed by experts and actively discuss the issues at stake. However, let us assume for a moment that the public is indeed willing to participate; would one day then be enough to compensate for their lack of understanding and lack of interest throughout the rest of the year? It would be "too little, too late." Not to mention the public's reluctance to participate in such a top-down organized event (for this reason Fishkin proposes paying each participant $150).

We are in fact back at the problem formulated in 1861 by John Stuart Mill in his book *Considerations on Representative Government*. Mill argued that a modern democracy needed educated, informed, and enlightened citizens. Because he considered the working class of his epoch not educated enough he was reluctant to support the introduction of universal male suffrage. Universal male suffrage, he argued, could only be introduced after the general public had acquired enough education to form an informed opinion. We are now more than 150 years on, and the level of education of even the least educated has made enormous progress. Illiteracy, which was still rampant in Mill's days, standing at more than 30 percent of Britain's population,[2] has been all but eradicated and someone leaving school at sixteen today has a basic knowledge of history, mathematics, and geography, of which the same age cohorts in 1861 could only have dreamed. John Stuart Mill would certainly be delighted to see this progress and meet today's great-great-grandchildren of the nineteenth-century proletariat.

Disaffected millennials

So, one could ask: what exactly is the problem? The problem is that although the general level of education has risen, *political* education – the education to become an active citizen of a liberal democratic state – has scarcely improved. There is yet another problem, which has been highlighted by two American political scientists: this is the fact that "younger generations in long-standing democracies are much less likely to consider it 'essential' to live in a democracy than earlier cohorts."[3] This is particularly true of millennials, the birth cohort born after 1980, "who are more likely to express hostile views of democracy. And they vote for anti-establishment parties and candidates that disregard long-standing democratic norms in ever greater numbers."[4]

American millennials come out on top of this disaffected generation. According to the authors, "the country in which skepticism of democracy is most widespread is Russia, where since 1995, an average of 26 percent of respondents have stated that having a democratic political system is a 'bad' way to run the country. In the United States, 23 percent of the millennials now express the same sentiment."[5] That 23 percent of American millennials reject democracy, which is almost the same percentage as that of Russian citizens, who have never lived in a real democracy, is downright scary. This trend of disaffected millennials is also evident in other developed democracies, although to a lesser degree than in the US. It is a sign of the failure of our liberal democratic societies to transfer our basic values to the younger generation. It is a failure of, among other things, our system of civic and democratic education.

One can debate the importance of education for a political system. Heinz Eulau, for instance, writes: "I know of no political order in the real world which, even if we could agree on its being close to perfection, has been created out of or by an educational system. If anything, the relationship between politics and education, it seems to me, is the other way round. If the political order is sound, stable, legitimate ... education and all that is implied by education ... flourishes. If the political order is in trouble, education is in trouble."[6] It is certainly true that the political order influences the educational system. However, this influence is not one way, as this author suggests. An educational system can play an active role in the development of a political system: weakening or conversely strengthening the values on which this system rests. Let us consider how the educational system fulfills this role.

Civic education: my own negative experience

Let me tell you my own experience. At my secondary school in a provincial Dutch town the history course started in the first year with the Greco-Persian Wars. Each year we advanced, adding a few centuries. In the second year the subject was the Roman Empire. In the third year it was the Middle Ages. In the fourth year the Renaissance, and so on. The history course ended in the year 1910. When I did my final exam and left secondary school I didn't know why the First World War broke out, nor what happened after this war. The rise of fascism? A blank spot. The rise of Hitler? No idea. But I knew in detail the workings of medieval feudal society and the history of the struggle between emperor and pope. In the last year at school there was also a special course on politics. It was called *Staatsinrichting*, which means "institutions of the state." The course was taught by a sixty-year-old, humorless, bald civil servant, who taught the course in his spare time to earn some extra money. It was literally a course about institutions – and in particular about numbers. How many people were there in parliament? How many votes did you need to win a seat in parliament? How many members did the provincial parliaments and the Senate have? The course was utterly boring. We were told that the Netherlands was a democracy, but the teacher did not explain in any detail what a democracy was. One thing was sure: neither the history lessons, nor the course "institutions of the state" helped or inspired us to become critical and active citizens. What went wrong? A lot. Let me continue:

The need for democratic education

- The course was a *top-down* event: the teacher had all the relevant knowledge and we were expected to know nothing and just to write down the facts he told us and learn these facts later by heart.
- The course was *fact-oriented* and not problem-oriented: the teacher decided what were the relevant facts. We were not asked what was relevant for us, because we were considered to be *tabulae rasae* (in plain English: clean slates who knew nothing).
- The course was a *passive* event: the pupils sat and listened to the teacher. Nothing happened that might stimulate our imagination. There were no meetings with politicians, no visits to representative bodies. The course remained abstract and, in particular, boring.
- The course *lacked interaction and debate*. The only interaction was the unequal interaction from teacher to pupil. Pupils were not encouraged to ask questions.

I consider this course a missed opportunity. Later, when I myself worked with students, I tried to change the context completely.

- The first thing was to establish the principle on which every democracy is based: equality. All members of the group were equal, myself, the teacher, included. This did not mean that I didn't know more about the subject than my students – I did, but this did not play a role in the process. We were a group of equals and as such we wanted to improve our collective knowledge.
- This approach meant also that I, as a teacher, did not impose my authority, deciding one-sidedly what the group should know. The approach was not fact-oriented but problem-oriented. We discussed in the group the problems in which we, as a group, were interested and chose issues together.
- Most important of all: the course was not a passive event in which pupils listened to the all-knowing teacher, but an active event, full of interaction and debate among participants. Regularly, at the beginning of a session, a poll was conducted, asking each person's opinion on a problem which would be discussed in a "parliamentary session." In role-play students represented different political parties. Sometimes they played "devil's advocate," defending positions they themselves opposed. The debate was filmed on video. After the debate the group watched the video to analyze and discuss the different arguments. Finally, a new poll was undertaken to see whether some participants had changed their opinion. If this was the case, they were asked to explain why they had changed their opinion. The debates focused on societal problems, in particular those on which opinions were polarized because of different value systems. How many refugees should and

could the country accept? Should the state subsidize religious schools? Should the use of soft drugs be decriminalized? Sometimes the "parliamentarians" had the task of forming a coalition government, which meant that they had to come to a compromise between the different positions. These debates and "coalition negotiations" were active learning processes in which "democracy" was not "taught" as a passive subject but was experienced and practised as a "real life event."

- These discussions and debates were alternated with the critical reading of classical texts, which threw a light on a problem the group had discovered during the discussions. It was not the theory which led to the praxis, but the problem which led to the theory.
- Sometimes the group also sought contact with "real politics," and went to the municipal council to attend debates, or representatives of NGOs were invited to talk about their work.

John Dewey and Robert Dahl on democratic education

American readers will recognize in this educational method elements proposed by John Dewey (1859–1952) in his book *Democracy and Education*. Dewey states that "a democracy is more than a form of government; it is primarily a mode of associated living, of conjoint communicated experience."[7] For this reason, he argued, education must not take place in an isolated place, outside society. On the contrary,

> The school must itself be a community life in all which that implies ... In place of a school set apart from life as a place of learning lessons, we have a miniature social group in which study and growth are incidents of present shared experience. Playgrounds, shops, workrooms, laboratories not only direct the natural active tendencies of youth, but they involve intercourse, communication, and cooperation, – all extending the perception of connections.[8]

Dewey formulated these proposals as early as 1916. Similar proposals are put forward by Robert Dahl, who writes in his 1998 book *On Democracy*:

> If citizens are to be competent, won't they need political and social institutions to help make them so? Unquestionably. Opportunities to gain an enlightened understanding of public matters are not just part of the definition of democracy. They are a requirement for democracy.[9]

This doesn't imply, he continues, that

> a majority of citizens may not make mistakes. They can and do. This is precisely why advocates of democracy have always placed a high value on education. And civic education requires not only formal schooling but public discussion, deliberation, debate,

The need for democratic education

controversy, the ready availability of reliable information, and other institutions of a free society.[10]

"If the institutions for civic education are weak," he concludes,

> only one satisfactory solution remains. They must be strengthened ... Perhaps the institutions for civic education that were created in democratic countries during the nineteenth and twentieth centuries are no longer adequate. If this is so, then democratic countries will need to create new institutions to supplement the old ones.[11]

It is telling that eighty-two years after Dewey published *Democracy and Education*, Robert Dahl still felt obliged to emphasize that "civic education requires not only formal schooling but public discussion, deliberation, debate, controversy." Apparently, the experience of the average American high school student was not so very different from mine in the Netherlands.[12]

What exactly does the word "liberal" mean in "liberal democracy"?

The objective of civic education is to let young citizens experience what it means to live in a democracy. Therefore, I prefer to use the term "democratic education" rather than "political education," which might evoke memories of the indoctrination practices of authoritarian regimes. In this democratic education theoretical insights are important too. Everyone thinks they know what a democracy is and can name its basic elements: government by the people, a system of "one man one vote," majority rule, and the alternation of government. However, it is different if one asks them to explain the term "*liberal* democracy." The reason is that not only does the word "liberal" have different connotations in different countries, but these connotations are also often contradictory. In the United States, for instance, a "liberal" is someone who votes for the Democratic Party, who is pro-choice, anti-NRA,[13] and, as a rule, in favor of gay marriage.[14] In the Netherlands, on the contrary, a *liberaal* is someone who votes for the Party for Freedom and Democracy (VVD), a conservative pro-market party which has more affinity with the Republican Party of the United States than with the Democratic Party. In Britain the Liberal Democratic Party has found a place in the middle of the political spectrum between Labour and the Conservative Party. Until Macron's new party La République en Marche (LRM), liberals had in France almost disappeared from the political scene.[15] There reigns, for this reason, complete confusion about where liberals should be placed on the left–right continuum.

But this is not all. There is yet another problem, which is that since the 1990s terms such as "ultra-liberal" and "neoliberal" have enriched the political jargon.

Mostly used by the left, these terms have increasingly become international invectives. The American philosopher Susan Neiman, for instance, writes: "Since the end of the Cold War, neoliberalism – the view that free unregulated markets producing ever-increasing amounts of shoddy goods are the basis of human happiness – has assumed not merely religious but absolutist tones."[16] Neoliberalism here is associated with unregulated markets and the production of "shoddy goods." In France the term *ultra-libéral* has become a derogatory term to denounce pro-business policies. The word "liberal," therefore, has not only become a source of confusion, but has also become a bone of contention. Because how can one expect an American Republican to defend "liberal democracy," when he despises and rejects his liberal fellow countrymen? And how can a French socialist show enthusiasm for liberal democracy when "ultra-liberalism" is for him the source of all evil?

One of the basic conditions for conducting a debate is the use of clear and unambiguous concepts, and it is evident that this is not the case here. The French economist Charles Wyplosz criticized the term "ultra-liberalism" as follows:

> The word is launched. It is not even necessary to explain it. One launches a slogan and one stops thinking. Please let us think. Firstly, why "ultra"? Undoubtedly, because "liberalism" sounds rather good, it is not the knockout blow one wants to deliver. By adding "ultra" one permits a word with a positive connotation to be transformed into something clearly repulsive. However, what is exactly the difference between liberalism and ultra-liberalism? The mystery remains complete, the rejection total, and one passes onto the next emergency.[17]

Liberalism, taken in its original sense, cherishes individual freedom as the most important value, and, as Wyplosz rightly remarks, it has, as such, a positive connotation. Early liberals defended the freedoms of the individual, such as freedom of speech, freedom of the press, and freedom of association, against intrusive absolutist and authoritarian governments. But this early liberalism, while preaching freedom for all, also had its internal contradictions.

The first liberal thinkers, such as John Locke (1632–1704), Adam Smith (1723–1790), and William Robertson (1721–1793), declared "life, liberty, and property" to be unalienable natural rights. The right to private property was considered part of man's natural right of liberty, because "the recognition of property is clearly the first step in the delimitation of the private sphere which protects us against coercion; and it has long been recognized that 'a people averse to the institution of private property is without the first element of freedom'."[18] The positive role of private property for the development of man's freedom, which is in itself an undeniable fact, became, however, hypostasized in the sense that private property became for liberals something sacrosanct and inviolable. This emphasis on the value of private property was accompanied by the view that the creation of riches by a modern market economy worked best when it was kept outside the realm of politics. The idea was that a market would function in an optimal way if it was left to its own devices, according to the precept *laissez faire, laissez aller.*

However, this liberal dogma had two shortcomings. In the first place it underestimated the important role of politics and of the state in delivering and upholding the basic structure in which a market economy could function, such as the role of an independent judiciary in guaranteeing the observance of contracts, or the role of the government in education or the construction of roads, ports, and all kinds of infrastructure. Secondly, it underestimated the way in which the inviolable character assigned to private property, instead of strengthening a basic tenet of the liberal creed: man's equality, could, in the end, undermine it. Because a free and unregulated market led to great economic inequalities between the haves and the have-nots. So long as poor citizens could profit from these inequalities through a Rawlsian "trickle-down" effect, there was no problem. But when the accelerated accumulation of riches on one side was accompanied by a relative deterioration or stagnation of the living conditions of the rest of society, creating a zero-sum situation, the liberal order, as such, was jeopardized. "Without constant efforts to approximate undominated equality," writes Bruce Ackerman, "talk of a free market degenerates into an ideological apologia for the rich and powerful."[19]

A critical discussion of liberal democracy in the classroom should, therefore, include liberalism's positive aspects as well as its negative aspects. It should discuss its emphasis on the liberty of the individual, guaranteed by freedom of expression, freedom of the press, freedom of religion, freedom of association, and the freedom to assemble and to petition. However, it should also discuss liberalism's ideological blind spots: its touting of unregulated "free markets" and its mistaken belief that markets, left to themselves, tend to establish "a natural harmony."

The term "liberal democracy" needs not only a profound discussion of the exact meaning of the word "liberal," but also of the meaning of the second part of the term: the word "democracy." Both terms: "liberal" and "democracy", taken together, seem to form a seamless unity. However, this is less evident than one may assume. Liberalism is a doctrine about the scope and purpose of government. It is a doctrine, in particular, about *limited* government, about protecting the individual against an all-powerful and intrusive state. Liberalism and state power, therefore, are at odds. Democracy, on the other hand, does not have this ambivalent relationship with the power of the state. Democracy is a doctrine on the *method* of government. This method is government by the majority. It does not say anything about the aims of government. A democratic regime can legally adopt laws that are unjust or run counter to common sense. If these measures are supported by the majority they can be labeled "democratic."

It is the word "liberal" in the concept "liberal democracy" which gives direction to a democracy. By emphasizing the inviolability of the individual and by defending the rights of the individual, it limits the actions of the democratic majority and protects the rights of minorities. It defines a "common good" which is inclusive for *all* citizens, and not only for the majority of the moment. This means, as Norberto Bobbio rightly remarks, that "liberalism and democracy are antithetical in the sense that democracy pushed to its furthest limits ends in the destruction of the liberal state."[20]

Teaching the younger generation the benefits of a liberal democracy means making them conscious of the delicate balance which exists between its two constituent parts: "liberal" and "democracy." While unlimited economic liberalism leads to growing inequality, which saps the foundations of a political liberal order, unrestrained democracy, the one which is touted by populists, leads to an authoritarian state which rides roughshod over the freedoms of the individual. The younger generation should be made aware that the existence of a liberal democracy is a recent historical phenomenon and is, therefore, neither self-evident, nor should be taken for granted. One should rather take to heart Robert Kagan's warning. He writes:

> Who is to say that Putinism in Russia or China's particular brand of authoritarianism will not survive as far into the future as European democracy, which, after all, is less than a century old on most of the continent? Autocracy in Russia and China has certainly been around longer than any Western democracy. Indeed, it is autocracy, not democracy, that has been the norm in human history – only in recent decades have the democracies, led by the United States, had the power to shape the world.[21]

According to Norberto Bobbio, "Today non-democratic liberal states would be inconceivable, as would non-liberal democratic states."[22] I think that here Bobbio is wrong. Although a non-democratic liberal state is rare, there are some examples, such as late twentieth century Hong Kong under British rule and Wilhelminian Germany which, although it had universal male suffrage, was not very democratic, but had a developed *Rechtsstaat* with an independent judiciary. Unfortunately, Bobbio's statement that non-liberal democratic states would be "inconceivable" has also been disproved by the facts. In recent years new EU member states, such as Poland and Hungary, which embraced liberal democracy after the fall of communism, have developed into illiberal democracies.[23] They are a warning of what can go wrong. These "illiberal democracies" have forgotten that the essence of liberal politics is not the stubborn defense of one's own "unnegotiable values," against the values of one's opponents, but a conciliatory activity, because, as Bernard Crick writes, "politics can change laws peacefully and find paths of compromise amid differing values so long as there is a broad consensus about procedures."[24] These "procedural values" imply "a minimal respect … for freedom, toleration, respect for truth, as well as empathy and willingness to resolve disputes by discussion."[25] The German sociologist Georg Simmel called compromise "one of the greatest inventions of mankind."[26] He is right. The fact that liberal democracy is based upon this great invention is one of the essential lessons that should be taught to the new generation.

Proposal #15: lower the voting age to sixteen

The boost given to the democratic education of sixteen- and seventeen-year-old adolescents in high schools should be accompanied by a lowering of the voting age to sixteen. This measure would have a strong motivating influence. Democratic education would no longer be experienced as just "an obligatory part of the curriculum," like other subjects, but as direct preparation for students' new role as active citizens. They would feel taken seriously and the new responsibility would motivate them to be even more active in the democracy lessons.

Proposals to lower the voting age to sixteen are not new and in some countries the possibility of voting at sixteen already exists. In 2013 it was introduced in the United States at a local level in Takoma Park, Maryland, an urban suburb of Washington DC with 17,000 inhabitants. It was followed in 2015 by Hyattsville, Maryland, similarly a suburb of Washington, DC. The experience was very positive: sixteen- and seventeen-year-olds voted four times more than older voters.[27] In 2016 an initiative was organized in San Francisco to follow this example, but Proposition F, calling for the lowering of the voting age to sixteen, was rejected by the electorate by a small margin of 52 percent.[28] The grass-roots movement in the US to promote lowering the voting age is coordinated by an NGO, named Vote16USA.[29]

It is clear, however, that in the US the movement to lower the voting age is still in its infancy. Other countries have made more progress. In Brazil sixteen- and seventeen-year olds got the right to vote on 2 March 1988. After more than twenty years of military dictatorship (1964–1985), the new constituent assembly adopted a proposal to broaden the franchise.[30] In Germany the franchise has been extended to sixteen-year-olds at the local level in seven of the sixteen *Länder* (federal states); in two of them at the regional state level also.[31] However, proposals to extend the franchise for national elections has also not yet found a majority.

In Britain the discussion got a boost when the Scottish government let sixteen-year-olds vote in the independence referendum on 18 September 2014. It was interesting that the turnout of the sixteen and seventeen-year-olds was 75 percent, considerably higher than the 54 percent of the eighteen- to twenty-four-year-olds.[32] In an editorial the *Guardian* took up a stance in favor of an enlargement of the franchise to include sixteen- and seventeen-year-olds. "Aged 16," wrote the *Guardian*, "a teenager can get married or enter a civil partnership and consent to a sexual relationship, pay income tax and national insurance, become a company director, join the army or a trade union and give their full consent to life or death medical procedures."[33] There was no reason, concluded the paper, to treat sixteen-year-olds as incapable minors. The Scottish initiative "should now be made one of the most lasting," because it was "an idea whose time has come."[34] Following in the footsteps of the Liberal Democratic Party, which was already in favor of broadening the franchise, the Labour Party vowed in April 2015 to extend the vote to sixteen-year-olds.[35] The question became more urgent with the upcoming Brexit referendum in 2016. On 18 November 2015, a cross-party coalition in the House of Lords endorsed a proposal to let sixteen-year-olds vote in the referendum.[36] The proposal was rejected. A decision with far-reaching consequences. In the referendum there was a small majority for Brexit. It was in particular the older generation which had voted to leave. Seventy-five percent of eighteen- to twenty-four-year-olds had voted to remain. In a poll conducted by Student Room among sixteen- and seventeen-year-olds on the day of the Brexit result, 82 percent of this age group voted to remain. Had sixteen- and seventeen-year-olds had the right to vote, Britain would not have voted to leave the EU.[37]

In France, where there was scarcely a debate on the subject, the National High School Union (Union nationale lycéenne) organized a referendum among 57,000 high school students, the results of which were published on 19 January 2017. Sixty-two percent of the respondents were in favor of a lowering of the voting age to sixteen years.[38]

Voting at sixteen: the encouraging Austrian example

Austria was in 2009 the first EU member state to extend the right to vote in national and European elections to sixteen-year-olds. This country was, therefore, a good testing ground to observe how this new measure would work out. As was the case with earlier increases in the franchise, critics predicted doom. Two political scientists, Chan and Clayton, for instance, concluded that "there is a *prima facie* case against lowering the voting age."[39] According to them, "the absolute level of political competence is the key variable in determining whether the voting age should be reduced."[40] Young voters, they wrote, "are apparently less competent than older voters, but are they competent enough?"[41] Not really, they concluded, although they had to admit that not only sixteen- and seventeen-year-olds, but also eighteen- to twenty-one-year-olds lacked the necessary competence. In fact there existed "a competence gap

The need for democratic education

between young people into their early to mid-20s and older groups, and not just between 16 and 17-year-old and older citizens."[42]

These skeptical remarks were contradicted by Austria's experience. In 2009, when this age group voted for the first time for the European Parliament, there was, first, no difference in turnout between the 16–17 year and the 18–21 year age groups. The younger group was not only more positive about European integration, but, according to Sylvia Kritzinger, a political scientist, it was also clear that "the youngest age cohort was very capable of identifying and voting for the party which fitted best with their ideological position."[43] She concluded that "the negative consequences from lowering the voting age, which critics feared, haven't materialized."[44] The younger voters were not less competent.

What is important is that the lowering of the voting age in Austria has been accompanied by the introduction of a new curriculum, called "History and Political Education," in the eighth grade of secondary school.[45] Kritzinger and Zeglovits emphasized that "a lowering of the voting age, insofar as other countries tend to consider this, should necessarily be accompanied by preparatory measures."[46] They added: "In order to avoid social discrimination, the Austrian results further show that one should crucially also involve young people, like apprentices, who cannot be reached by preparations at school … For this reason one should in addition to the different school projects (as, for instance, discussion forums with politicians, activities in school democracy, internships, research of subjects relevant to the election, travelling exhibitions, workshops, etc.) emphasize extracurricular measures."[47]

Voting at sixteen: making voting a habit

Why is extending the voting age to sixteen- and seventeen-year-olds a good idea? In the first place, because it could reverse the trend that young voters tend to vote less than older age cohorts. This trend can be observed across different nations and is rather permanent. A study, for instance, which "compared the propensity to vote by birth cohort across sixteen Western Europe nations from the 1960s to the early 1990s … confirmed that younger Europeans were consistently less likely to cast a ballot than older cohorts."[48] However, none of these young birth cohorts were younger than eighteen years. And young people of eighteen years and older differ in many respects from their juniors, differences which have a direct impact on their readiness to vote. "Why does age matter for turnout?" ask Zeglovits and Aichholzer. "It has been argued that the age between 18 and the mid-twenties is a critical phase in one's lifecycle and, thus, the 'political biography'. In young adulthood people have to make many important decisions that influence their whole life, such as deciding on an educational career, finding a job, choosing a partner, starting a family or moving to a new town. Therefore young people simply seem to be too preoccupied to worry about politics."[49] However, this is not the case with their juniors. As concerns sixteen-year-olds, one can expect higher turnout, because they are still "embedded in social surroundings of family and school ... young voters would hence 'learn to vote' in a more sheltered environment."[50] This does not mean that members of this age group let themselves be influenced by their parents and family. "Researchers at Edinburgh University found that classroom debates and lessons in politics were more important than parental influence in fostering political interest among 16- and 17-year-olds."[51]

Not only will sixteen- and seventeen-year-olds, after participation in a democracy curriculum, vote more, but this propensity to vote will have an enduring impact. "The first election leaves a footprint in one's voting biography and fosters voting as a habit."[52] A well-prepared sixteen-year-old voter has a chance of becoming a more motivated voter than an eighteen- or nineteen-year-old voter for another reason as well: the direct preparation in school will influence his or her perception of their ability to exert political influence. This perception is important, as Gabriel Almond and Sidney Verba emphasize in their classic study *The Civic Culture*: "The extent to which citizens in a nation perceive themselves as competent to influence the government affects their political behavior."[53] This does not mean that this young birth cohort would be more uncritical than the next cohort and accept the political status quo at face value. On the contrary, they have strong ethical convictions and in this respect share a certain distrust of political institutions, including a distrust of politicians and political parties, with the "older" youth group. This distrust, however, far from being a danger for democracy might rather be a sign of its health, as Ronald Inglehart and Christian Welzel explain:

> Confidence in institutions has been declining for several decades, in almost all advanced Western democracies. Because it is often assumed that high confidence in institutions is crucial to democracy, this sharp decline of confidence has drawn much attention, reviving the thesis of a legitimacy crisis ... But *is* a high level of confidence in institutions actually crucial to the flourishing of democracy? Do lower levels of confidence in institutions produce less effective democracies?[54]

The authors deny that this is the case. "Surprising as it may seem in the light of the literature on this subject," they write, "public confidence in institutions does not seem to affect a society's democratic performance in any systematic way. High or low levels of confidence in institutions can be found in any type of political system, regardless of its democratic performance. Some long-standing authoritarian states, such as China, show high levels of confidence in institutions, whereas some long-established democracies, such as the United States, show low levels of confidence in institutions."[55] They conclude: "It confirms the interpretation … that the decline of confidence does not pose a threat to democracy. On the contrary, it reflects the emergence of less deferential, more elite-challenging publics in modern societies, which we interpret as conducive to democracy."[56]

The broadening of the franchise to sixteen-year-old voters should be undertaken for its own merits and not for electoral or partisan reasons, as was apparently the case with the Scottish referendum, where the government in Edinburgh hoped to win extra support for Scottish independence. The "young vote" has recently become an important issue. Fareed Zakaria, for instance, declared that young people "want to live in a world that is open, that is connected, that is pluralistic, that is diverse."[57] He pointed to Britain's Brexit vote and concluded: "Had the vote been, you know, an under-forty vote, Brexit would have lost dramatically."[58] But young voters do not *per se* function as a bulwark against populists, as Zakaria's discussion partner Niall Ferguson rightly objected. "Macron got almost no support from younger French voters," he said. "They were all behind the communist, Mélenchon."[59] However, one may expect that a young generation, which is well prepared and has had ample opportunity to discuss all arguments of different sides in the classroom (including the arguments of populists), will be more able to make a reasoned choice and become active voters. Their informed and at times elite-challenging behavior will enrich liberal democracy rather than being a liability.

Notes

1 Tom Nichols, "How America Lost Faith," p. 73.
2 David Mitch, "Education and Skill of the British Labour Force," in Roderick Floud and Paul Johnson (eds), *The Cambridge Economic History of Modern Britain, Vol. I: Industrialisation, 1700–1860* (Cambridge: Cambridge University Press, 2004), p. 344.
3 Yascha Mounk and Roberto Stefan Foa, "Yes, people really are turning away from democracy," *Washington Post*, 8 December 2016. www.washingtonpost.com/news/wonk/wp/2016/12/08/yes-millennials-really-are-surprisingly-approving-of-dictators/?utm_term=.e2d0210c3a99 (accessed 14 November 2017).
4 Ibid.
5 Ibid. According to Yascha Mounk, "Civic education in all its forms stood at the core of the American project. Then, amid an era of unprecedented peace and prosperity, the idea that support for self-government had to be won anew with every passing generation started to fade. Today, it is all but extinct" (Yascha Mounk, *The People vs. Democracy – Why Our Freedom Is in Danger and How to Save It* (Cambridge, Mass., and London: Harvard University Press, 2018), p. 246).
6 Heinz Eulau, "Political Science and Education: The Long View and the Short," in Klaus von Beyme (ed.), *Theory and Politics – Theorie und Politik – Festschrift zum 70. Geburtstag für Carl Joachim Friedrich* (The Hague: Martinus Nijhoff, 1971), p. 344.

7   John Dewey, *Democracy and Education*, edited by Jim Manis (Hazleton: Pennsylvania State University, 2001), p. 91.
8   Ibid., pp. 364–365.
9   Dahl, *On Democracy*, p. 79.
10 Ibid., p. 79. Ronald Dworkin makes similar remarks. He writes: "The most daunting but also most urgent requirement is to make a Contemporary Politics course part of every high school curriculum. I do not mean civics lessons in which students are taught the structure of our government or history courses in which America's story is celebrated. I mean courses that take up issues that are among the most contentious political controversies of the day ... The dominant pedagogical aim must be to instill some sense of the complexity of these issues, some understanding of positions different from those the students are likely to find at home or among friends, and some idea of what a conscientious and respectful argument over these issues might be like" (Dworkin, *Is Democracy Possible Here?*, pp. 148–149). Dworkin adds: "The courses might well include a suitably simplified examination of classics of Western political philosophy from both the conservative and liberal traditions: some understanding of the ideas of Aquinas, Locke, Kant, Rawls, and Hayek, for example, mainly through secondary sources if necessary" (p. 149).
11 Dahl, *On Democracy*, p. 80.
12 Fareed Zakaria compares the educational methods of his high school in Mumbai, "in which the premium is placed on memorization and constant testing," with the "different world" he encountered when he went to college in the United States. "While the American system is too lax on rigor and memorization ... it is much better at developing the critical faculties of the mind, which is what you need to succeed in life. Other educational systems teach you to take tests; the American system teaches you to think" (Fareed Zakaria, *The Post-American World* (New York and London: W. W. Norton & Company, 2008), p. 193). We should keep in mind, however, that Zakaria's eulogy of the American educational system refers to college and not high school.
13 The National Rifle Association (NRA) is an American gun rights advocacy group, situated on the right side of the political spectrum.
14 Cf. Friedrich Hayek, who complained about "the deliberate deception practiced by American socialists in their appropriation of the term 'liberalism' ... It has ... become almost impossible for a Gladstonian liberal to describe himself as a liberal without giving the impression that he believes in socialism" (F. A. Hayek, *The Fatal Conceit – The Errors of Socialism*, The Collected Works of Friedrich August Hayek, Vol. I, edited by W. W. Bartley, III (London: Routledge, 1990), p. 110).
15 The reason for this is that after the Second World War the most important parties: the Gaullist party, the socialist party, and the communist party were all in favor of government interference in the economy. A small pro-market liberal party, the Parti Libérale Démocrate, led a marginal existence.
16 Susan Neiman, *Why Grow Up? Subversive Thoughts for an Infantile Age* (London: Penguin Books, 2016), p. 190.
17 Charles Wyplosz, "De quoi l'ultra-libéralisme est-il le nom?" *Le Figaro*, 29 December 2015.
18 F. A. Hayek, *The Constitution of Liberty* (London and Henley: Routledge & Kegan Paul, 1976), p. 140.
19 Ackerman, *Future of Liberal Revolution*, p. 10.
20 Norberto Bobbio, *Liberalism and Democracy* (London and New York: Verso, 2005), pp. 48–49. The difference between liberalism and democracy was explained brilliantly by

Ortega y Gasset, who wrote: "Liberalism and Democracy happen to be two things which begin by having nothing to do with each other, and end by having ... meanings that are mutually antagonistic. Democracy and Liberalism are two answers to two completely different questions. Democracy answers this question – 'Who ought to exercise the public power?' The answer it gives is – the exercise of public power belongs to the citizens as a body. But this question does not touch on what should be the realm of the public power. It is solely concerned with determining to whom such power belongs. Democracy proposes that we all rule; that is, that we are sovereign in all social acts. Liberalism, on the other hand, answers this other question, – 'regardless of who exercises the public power, what should its limits be?' The answer it gives – 'Whether the public power is exercised by an autocrat or by the people, it cannot be absolute: the individual has rights which are over and above any interference by the State'" (J. Ortega y Gasset, *Invertebrate Spain* (New York, 1937), p. 125. Quoted in Hayek, *Constitution of Liberty*, pp. 442–443).

21 Robert Kagan, "Is Democracy in Decline? The Weight of Geopolitics," *Brookings*, 26 January 2015. www.brookings.edu/articles/is-democracy-in-decline-the-weight-of-geopolitics/ (accessed 15 November 2017).

22 Norberto Bobbio, *Liberalism*, p. 38.

23 It is telling that Fareed Zakaria in his book *The Future of Freedom*, first published in 2003, could still write: "Poland, Hungary, and the Czech Republic ... are furthest along in consolidating their democracies" (Zakaria, *The Future of Freedom*, p. 52). The slipping of two of these countries into an authoritarian spiral, while maintaining a democratic façade, has proceeded at a surprisingly fast pace. This development contradicts Zakaria's apodictic statement that "once rich, democracies become immortal" (p. 70). He puts the definition of "rich" at a GDP per capita of $9,000. However, in 2016 GDP per capita in these countries was a multiple of this sum: in the Czech Republic it was $33,200, in Slovakia $31,300, in Poland $27,800, and in Hungary $27,500 (data from CIA "The World Factbook, Country Comparison GDP Per Capita.". www.cia.gov/library/publications/the-world-factbook/rankorder/2004rank.html) (accessed 15 November 2017).

24 Bernard Crick, *In Defence of Politics* (London and New York: Penguin, 1992), p. 247.

25 Ibid., p. 247.

26 Georg Simmel, "Das Ende des Streits," in Georg Simmel, *Aufsätze und Abhandlungen 1901–1908*, Vol. I (Frankfurt am Main: Suhrkamp, 1995), p. 338.

27 Cf. Zachary Crocket, "The case for allowing 16-year-olds to vote," *Vox*, 7 November 2016. www.vox.com/policy-and-politics/2016/11/7/13347080/voting-age-election-16 (accessed 15 November 2017).

28 Cf. Lydia O'Connor, "Lower voting age proposal fails in San Francisco, wins smaller victory in Berkeley," *Huffington Post*, 10 November 2016. www.huffingtonpost.com/entry/votingproposals_us_581919bce4b00f11fc5c859c (accessed 16 November 2017).

29 The website of Vote16USA is http://vote16usa.org/ (accessed 16 November 2017).

30 Cf. Gustavo Villela, "Na Constituinte de 88, jovens de 16 anos conquistam direito de votar no Brasil," *O Globo*, 20 June 2014. http://acervo.oglobo.globo.com/fatos-historicos/na-constituinte-de-88-jovens-de-16-anos-conquistam-direito-de-votar-no-brasil-12938949 (accessed 16 November 2017).

31 These federal states are Lower Saxony, Brandenburg, Bremen, Mecklenburg-Vorpommern, Nord Rhine Westphalia, Saxony Anhalt, and Schleswig Holstein. On the regional level voting rights for sixteen-year-olds exist only in Brandenburg and Bremen. Cf. "Mach's ab 16! in Brandenburg." www.machs-ab-16.de/waehlen-ab-16/wahlrecht-16-deutschland (accessed 17 November 2017).

32 "Ballots for bairns," *The Economist*, 11 June 2015. www.economist.com/news/britain/21654091-scotland-set-lower-voting-ageand-others-may-follow-ballots-bairns (accessed 17 November 2017).
33 "The Guardian view on lowering the voting age to 16," Editorial, *Guardian*, 28 September 2014. www.theguardian.com/commentisfree/2014/sep/28/the-guardian-view-on-lowering-the-voing-age (accessed 20 November 2017).
34 Ibid.
35 "Labour Votes To Lower Voting Age To 16," *Huffington Post*, 7 April 2015. www.huffingtonpost.co.uk/2015/04/07/labour-vow-to-lower-voting-age-to-16_n_7015622.html (accessed 20 November 2017).
36 Michael White, "Should 16-year-olds be allowed to vote?" *Guardian*, 19 November 2015. www.theguardian.com/politics/blog/2015/nov/19/should-16-year-olds-be-allowed-to-vote (accessed 20 November 2017).
37 Aftab Ali, "EU referendum: UK result would have been remain had votes been allowed at 16," *Independent*, 24 June 2016. www.independent.co.uk/student/news/eu-referendum-uk-result-students-votes-at-16-remain-brexit-leave-a7101821.html (accessed 21 November 2017).
38 Cf. Catherine Vincent, "Les citoyens de demain," *Le Monde*, 25 February 2017.
39 Tak Wing Chan and Matthew Clayton, "Should the Voting Age be Lowered to Sixteen? Normative and Empirical Considerations," *Political Studies*, Vol. 54, 2006, p. 555.
40 Ibid., p. 554.
41 Ibid., p. 554.
42 Ibid., p. 554.
43 Sylvia Kritzinger, "Ready to vote? Eine Betrachtung der jüngsten Wähler in Österreich," *Euractiv*, 23 May 2014. www.euractiv.de/section/europawahlen-2014/opinion/ready-to-vote-eine-betrachtung-der-jungsten-wahler-in-osterreich/ (accessed 22 November 2017).
44 Ibid.
45 Cf. Sylvia Kritzinger and Eva Zeglovits, "Wahlen mit 16 – Chance oder Risiko?" in Jörg Tremmel and Markus Rutschke (eds), *Politische Beteiligung junger Menschen – Grundlagen, Perspektiven, Fallstudien* (Wiesbaden: Springer, 2016), p. 196.
46 Ibid., p. 196.
47 Ibid., p. 197.
48 Pippa Norris, *Democratic Phoenix – Reinventing Political Activism* (Cambridge and New York: Cambridge University Press, 2002), p. 89.
49 Eva Zeglovits and Julian Aichholzer, "Are People More Inclined to Vote at 16 than at 18? Evidence for the First-Time Voting Boost among 16- to 25-Year-Olds in Austria," *Journal of Elections, Public Opinion and Parties*, 24(3), 3 July 2014. www.ncbi.nlm.nih.gov/pmc/articles/PMC4864896/ (accessed 22 November 2017). The higher participation rate of the younger age cohort would reverse the low participation rate, which is usually – almost dogmatically – attributed to the young voter. Verba and Nie write thus: "Most studies of political participation have found a distinctive curve of participation associated with age … In the early years after a citizen reaches voting age, participation rates are generally low. Then they rise during the middle years and decline in later years" (Sidney Verba and Norman H. Nie, *Participation in America – Political Democracy and Social Equality* (New York: Harper & Row, 1972), p. 138).
50 Zeglovits and Aichholzer "Are People More Inclined to Vote?"
51 "Ballots for bairns."
52 Zeglovits and Aichholzer, "Are People More Inclined to Vote?"

53 Gabriel A. Almond and Sidney Verba, *The Civic Culture – Political Attitudes and Democracy in Five Nations* (Princeton: Princeton University Press, 1963), p. 183.
54 Ronald Inglehart and Christian Welzel, *Modernization, Cultural Change, and Democracy – The Human Development Sequence* (Cambridge and New York: Cambridge University Press, 2005), p. 250.
55 Ibid., p. 252.
56 Ibid., p. 253.
57 Niall Ferguson and Fareed Zakaria, *The End of the Liberal Order?* (London: Oneworld, 2017), p. 32.
58 Ibid., p. 32.
59 Ibid., p. 33.

Part IV

Twenty proposals to defend liberal democracy: reforming society

16
How to handle "fake news" and "alternative facts"

Proposal #16: defend the truth in a "post-truth" world

The recent wave of populism has enriched the language with several new concepts. One of these is the term *fake news*; another is the word *post-truth*. A search on Google gives for "fake news" 67,600,000 results and for "post-truth" 41,900,000.[1] Oxford Dictionaries chose the word "post-truth" as the Word of the Year 2016, defining it as an adjective "relating to or denoting circumstances in which objective facts are less influential in shaping public opinion than appeals to emotion and personal belief." The authors of Oxford Dictionaries said they chose the word because it "has seen a spike in frequency in the context of the EU referendum in the United Kingdom and the presidential election in the United States."[2] It is clear that "post" in the term "post-truth" does not indicate a time sequence, such as in the term "post-twentieth century," but indicates rather that truth, as such, has become irrelevant. Populists tend not to accept and, especially, they do not *want* to accept the narratives of experts and politicians, even if these are based on established fact.

Of course, relativism and doubts concerning the status of accepted truths are not new. Human history provides plenty of examples of heretic sects and dissident movements which called into question the truth of traditional philosophies and religions. The most radical skeptics and iconoclasts were scientists, who through tireless trial and error and through disciplined logical inference subverted old truths and interpretations, causing "scientific revolutions" which established new paradigms.[3] Copernicus's and Galileo's replacement of the geocentric cosmology by a heliocentric system is one of the best-known examples (even if it took the Vatican more than 350 years to accept this paradigm). New truths did not only replace old truths, but truths could also be different in different countries. Blaise Pascal (1562–1623), for example, wrote famously in his *Pensées*: "Truth lies on this side of the Pyrenees, error on the other."[4] What was true for a Frenchman was not true for a Spaniard, and vice versa.

However, what we are talking about here is of a different nature. Scientists rely on facts. If new facts no longer fit into an established theory, the theory will be changed and a new paradigm will be put in its place. Today's populists, on the contrary, do not rely on facts, they *create* their own "facts." During the Brexit campaign in the UK, for instance, protagonists of the Leave vote promised that Brexit would free up an additional £350 million a week for the cash-strapped National Health Service (NHS). Leave's campaign director, Dominic Cummings, called it "the most effective argument" of the Brexiteers. "Of course, the pledge was utterly unfounded," wrote the *Financial Times*.[5] Not only did the UK not pay £350 million a week to the EU, but only £137 million, but also the suggestion that the money would go to the NHS was an invention. Contrary to Leave's promise one could expect that, due to the sum the UK had to pay to the EU for the divorce and the ensuing economic slowdown after Brexit, no substantial increase to the NHS budget would take place. Brexit could even cause a deterioration of the NHS, because of its negative impact on the recruitment and retention of foreign medical personnel. It was estimated that it could lead to a shortage of 20,000 nurses by 2025/2026.[6] In July 2017 Dominic Cummings described the referendum as a "dumb idea," admitting that leaving the EU could be "an error."[7]

Trump's "alternative facts"

The fact that Cummings admitted that leaving the EU could be a "dumb idea" does credit to him. Because even the slightest sign of self-doubt was lacking in the Trump administration. The world was, for instance, baffled when President Trump's counselor Kellyanne Conway invented the term "alternative facts" when, in a Meet the Press interview on 22 January 2017, she defended the White House press secretary Sean Spicer. Spicer had clearly exaggerated the size of the crowd attending Trump's inauguration, stating that "this was the largest audience ever to witness an inauguration."[8] Photographs showed a quite different reality. Conway's "alternative fact" was just another term for a plain lie. Lying and false claims have been a hallmark of the Trump presidency.[9] In November 2017 fact checkers of the *Washington Post* counted 1,628 false or misleading claims made by the president over 298 days, which is 5.5 per day.[10]

"The hallmark of factual truth," writes Hannah Arendt, "is that its opposite is neither error nor illusion nor opinion, no one of which reflects upon personal truthfulness, but the deliberate falsehood, or lie."[11] Arendt adds: "Since the liar is free to fashion his 'facts' to fit the profit and pleasure, or even the mere expectations, of his audience, the chances are that he will be more persuasive than the truthteller."[12] If "post-truth" statements, fake news, and "alternative facts" become the new normal, democracy is in danger. Because democracies are built on trust and trust is built on the expectation that the other is telling the truth. A cynical regime, which is not trustworthy but invents its own fake "truths," undermines the very foundations on which a democracy is built. In this case, writes Friedrich Hayek, "The word truth itself ceases to have its old meaning. It describes no longer something to be found, with the individual conscience as the sole arbiter of whether in any particular instance the evidence (or the standing of those proclaiming it) warrants a belief; it becomes something to be laid down by authority."[13] It leads to "the spirit of complete cynicism as regards truth … the loss of the sense of even the meaning of truth, the disappearance of the spirit of independent inquiry and of the belief in the power of rational conviction."[14]

The creation of "alternative facts" and the suppression of unwelcome real facts is not a new strategy, invented by populists. It is practiced by all totalitarian regimes. In the Soviet Union, where the official paper of the Communist Party had the title *Pravda* (The Truth), it was an ingrained habit "to rewrite history." When Trotsky fell into disgrace he was removed from Soviet history books. Trotsky's name was no longer mentioned as the organizer of the Red Army. He became non-existent. Facts disappeared. And not only facts. Pictures which could prove unwelcome facts also disappeared. Long before modern photoshopping was invented the Soviets "remade" pictures. They removed Trotsky and other leaders who had fallen from grace from official photographs. There is an example where Stalin was originally photographed with four other leaders at his side. In successive "remakes" of the picture the other leaders disappear one by one, until, in the end, only Stalin remains – alone – in the picture. Hannah Arendt warned: "Before mass leaders seize the power to fit reality to their lies, their propaganda is marked by its extreme contempt for facts as such, for in their opinion fact depends entirely on the power of man who can fabricate it."[15]

Facts are important because they influence opinions. To verify (or falsify) the truth of complex theories is not easy. However, it is different for single events or facts, which can easily be checked. Asked what future historians would think of who was to blame for the outbreak of the First World War, French prime minister Clemenceau answered: "This I don't know. But I know for certain that they will not say Belgium invaded Germany."[16] There are facts which cannot be denied, nor "rewritten." Abraham Lincoln is attributed the quip "You can fool *all* the people *some* of the time, *some* of the people *all* of the time – but *not* all the people all of the time."[17] According to the philosopher Thomas Nagel, "Pursuit of the truth requires more than imagination: it requires the generation and decisive elimination of alternative possibilities until, ideally, only one remains, and it requires a habitual readiness to attack one's own convictions."[18] Attacking one's own convictions in order to find the truth is different from a government or a party which imposes its invented truths on citizens. In the end the truth will prevail. However, this is not an automatic process. It depends on free science, free speech, and a free press, which are the cornerstones of a free society.

The "bubbles" created by social media

Attacking "fake news" and "post-truth" has become difficult, however, in particular through the emergence of social media. A lot has already been written about the *bubbles* which are created by them. Users only communicate with people who share the same ideas and become less and less exposed to diverging opinions or to new information which could challenge their ideas. This gives disseminators of fake news the opportunity to create their own audience which is immune to alternative views.

In itself the existence of bubbles is not a new phenomenon. Self-selection of audiences and reading publics existed previously. In Germany readers of *Die Zeit* and the *Süddeutsche Zeitung* are different from the readers of the tabloid *Bild*. Similarly, in the UK the readership of the *Sun* is different from the readership of the *Guardian* or the *Financial Times*. In fact, the press also created bubbles, exposing the public less to divergent voices than, for instance, radio and TV. Buying your ideological opponent's paper is not obvious: you have to go to the newsstand, pay for it, and then return home to read it. With the advent of radio this changed. You had only to turn the knob a bit to the right or to the left to hear a quite different opinion. The impact of TV was even greater. Just by zapping from one channel to the other you could see people airing opinions which, in normal circumstances, you didn't hear. Maybe, therefore, radio and TV can with more reason be called "social" than today's "social media": not only could you unexpectedly come into contact with unknown, new opinions, but often you listened to the radio and watched TV in the company of family or friends and could discuss with them what you had just heard or watched. In the Netherlands sociological studies have confirmed that pillarized Dutch society, in which different ideological and religious groups led an isolated existence, was "opened up" by the introduction of television.[19]

Social media clearly have had an inverse effect, reinforcing existing bubbles rather than opening them up. The use of Twitter and Facebook during the American presidential campaign of 2016 confirms this trend. A study shows that the formation of bubbles was not a symmetric process, taking place on both sides of the ideological divide, but was rather an *asymmetric* process which characterized the followers of

How to handle "fake news" and "alternative facts"

Donald Trump. While @HillaryClinton retweeters linked to a mix of traditional professional media, such as the *Washington Post*, the *New York Times*, CNN, ABC, and NBC, as well as to more partisan sites, like The Huffington Post, MSNBC, or The Daily Beast, this was different for @realDonaldTrump retweeters: "Breitbart became the center of a distinct right-wing media ecosystem, surrounded by Fox News, the Daily Caller, the Gateway Pundit, the Washington Examiner, Infowars, Conservative Treehouse, and Truthfeed."[20] While attention to more partisan outlets on the left was more tightly interwoven with attention to the traditional media, this was not the case for the Breitbart-centered group of Trump followers, which was further from the mainstream. According to the authors, this "insulation of the partisan right-wing media from traditional journalistic media sources, and the vehemence of its attacks on journalism in common cause with a similarly outspoken president, is new and distinctive."[21]

This is an alarming trend. David Roberts, an analyst, spoke in this context of the emergence of a "tribal epistemology": "Information is evaluated based not on conformity to common standards of evidence or correspondence to a common understanding of the world, but on whether it supports the tribe's values and goals and is vouchsafed by tribal leaders. 'Good for our side' and 'true' begin to blur into one."[22] This process is reinforced by the relative decline of the press media and the explosive growth of social media. On 1 July 2016, there were in the US almost 287 million users of the Internet, which is 85 percent of the population. In the same year there were in the US 232 million users of Facebook and about 67 million users of Twitter.[23] Compare this with the fact that only three papers in the US sell more than one million copies per day: *USA Today* (2,280,000), the *Wall Street Journal* (two million), and the *New York Times* (about one million). The decline of traditional media can also be measured by the fact that in 2010 in the US the same number of papers was sold as in 1950, when the population was only half its present size.[24]

How to fight "post-truth" and "alternative facts"?

The question is how one can fight fake news and defend the truth in an environment in which the influence of social media can only be expected to increase and in which the consumers of populist "alternative facts" and propaganda tend to live in their own information universe – apart and isolated from the rest of society.

- A first recommendation is to be extremely vigilant and to defend free speech and the freedom of the media. The only – few – restrictions that can be justified, are hate speech: speech that incites violence, or that discriminates on grounds of gender, sexual orientation, race, or disability. "The reason for protecting free speech," writes A. C. Grayling, "is that it keeps bad views out in the open where they can be challenged, giving the arguments against them a full chance to be heard."[25]

- A second recommendation is defending the truth by debunking "alternative truths." This can be done by rigorous fact-checking. We have to take into account, however, that these fact-checking agencies – mostly organized by think-tanks and quality papers – often do not reach the public they are intended to reach, because of the very existence of bubbles which function as self-reinforcing echo chambers which do not absorb outside information.
- To open up these bubbles a third recommendation, put forward by Cass Sunstein, former administrator of the White House Office of Information and Regulatory Affairs of the Obama administration, is interesting. He proposed adding a button "opposing point of view" to Facebook pages.[26] A worthwhile suggestion because it could incite the curiosity of the user to look once in a while outside his or her own "epistemological tribe."
- A fourth recommendation would be to add the item "propaganda" to the curriculum "democratic education" of secondary schools because it is important to reach the younger generation while one still has access to them. According to the slogan "Forewarned is forearmed" high school students should be made familiar with how propaganda works and they should be shown examples of Soviet and Nazi propaganda, as well as discussing the most glaring examples of "alternative facts" presented by populist, as well as mainstream, politicians. A successful program, launched in 2014 in Finland to boost the population's resilience to post-truth and fake news, could serve as a model. According to the chief communications specialist of the Prime Minister's Office, "the first line of defense is the kindergarten teacher."[27]

Proposal #17: beware of populists acting as agents of hostile foreign powers

Populism is not a new phenomenon. Populist movements have emerged at different moments in the history of modern mass democracy. However, the present wave of populism is different from earlier waves due to the presence of two factors which create a completely different environment. The first factor is the emergence of social media, which have considerably amplified the populist phenomenon. The second factor is the activity of hostile foreign powers, which try to use populist movements in other countries for their own geopolitical interests.

Russia has become the main actor in this field. It has succeeded in becoming, if not a coordination center, at least an active sponsor of these movements. In its contacts with populists abroad the Kremlin has profited from the fact that it possesses a double "soft power." On one hand it can present itself as an authoritarian state, defending religious and "traditional values," such as the family and "straight sexuality," against "Western decadence." As such, it can earn the goodwill of far-right populist parties and movements. On the other hand, it can present itself as the legitimate heir of the defunct Soviet Union, the center of world communism, which makes it attractive to far-left populists.

By assembling both far-right and far-left populist parties under its wings the Kremlin has copied its old strategy of having its own "boots on the ground" in Western countries. Before the demise of the Soviet Union these "boots on the ground" were the communist parties. Today they are the populist parties. The innovation is that the Kremlin has succeeded in attracting *both* the extreme right and the extreme left.

The Kremlin's four foreign policy objectives

While the ideological drive of the Soviet Union was to create other communist states in its periphery, this ideological drive is absent today. The creation of populist regimes abroad *per se* is not an objective of the Kremlin. There are two reasons for this. In the first place, Russia itself does not qualify as a populist regime. Although Russia shares the illiberalism of populist movements, it lacks their democratic fervor. Populism is a product of liberal democratic societies. Populists claim that "the people" are the basis of sovereignty, and they extol direct democracy and referendums and respect the alternation of power. Russia is neither a liberal, nor a democratic state. It is an authoritarian regime with a fake "democracy," in which pluralism is absent and the alternation of power is excluded.

The second reason that the creation of populist regimes abroad as such is not an objective of the Kremlin is the fact that populist regimes tend to be more nationalist, which is not always in Moscow's interest. The populist Law and Justice government in Poland, for instance, is not less, but rather more anti-Russian than previous Polish governments.

The only reason, therefore, for Moscow to support populist movements and parties abroad is that these can promote the Kremlin's foreign policy objectives. These are four. The Kremlin's major objective is a roll-back of American power and influence in the world and particularly in Europe. This can be done by undermining NATO, which is regarded by Moscow as a direct threat. A second objective is a weakening of the EU, because, as a united bloc, it is capable of withstanding Russian pressure.

A third objective is to help establish friendly governments in Paris and Berlin with the aim of forming a Moscow–Paris–Berlin axis (eventually extended to Rome).[28] This new constellation, in which the US is expelled from Europe and Russia is surrounded by friends, would create favorable conditions for the realization of the Kremlin's fourth foreign policy objective, which is to create a "sphere of privileged interest" in its Near Abroad. This was one of the hidden objectives of President Medvedev's proposal for a Pan-European Security Pact of 5 June 2008.[29] Medvedev reformulated this foreign policy aim more clearly on 31 August 2008, in an interview with the Russian TV Channel One, when he laid down the "Five Principles" of Russian foreign policy. One of these principles was "the right to protect the life and dignity of our citizens wherever they are," another was the claim that Russia "has regions where it has its privileged interests."[30] To claim the right to protect the life and dignity of Russian citizens *wherever they are* is contrary to international law, as is the claim to have "privileged interests" in neighboring countries. The aggressive implications of Russia's foreign policy principles were shown in August 2008, when the Russian army invaded Georgia to "rescue" Georgian citizens who, shortly before, had received Russian passports. Joe Biden, the US vice-president, criticized the Russian behavior during the 2009 Munich Conference on Security Policy, declaring "We will not recognize any nation having a sphere of interest. It will remain our view that sovereign states have the right to make their own decisions and choose their own alliances."[31]

The Russian foreign policy principles are in fact a return to the theory of the *Großraumordnung*, the "Order of the Great Area," of the Nazi ideologue Carl Schmitt, a doctrine that attributes great powers the right to claim an exclusive influence and *droit de regard* vis-à-vis the smaller surrounding countries.[32] According to Schmitt, "in the big world every real Reich has claimed for itself such an area of its 'spatial sovereignty' (*Raumhoheit*) that exceeds its national frontiers."[33] This doctrine also implies that any intervention in this "privileged" space by foreign powers (*raumfremde Mächte*) was forbidden. This doctrine fits very well with the foreign policy of a revisionist, neo-imperialist power as is today's Russia, which, after Georgia, attacked Ukraine and annexed the Crimea. It is no coincidence that the "Five Principles" of the Russian foreign policy doctrine is a seamless copy of the "Brezhnev doctrine" of the Soviet Union, which accorded only "restricted sovereignty" to the countries in the sphere of influence of Soviet Russia.[34]

Populist parties as the Kremlin's foreign policy tools

It seems counter-intuitive that populist parties which claim to "give sovereignty back to the people" and pretend to "take back control" collaborate with a hostile foreign power which wants to weaken the West and undermine liberal democracy. However, in almost the same way in which the communist parties in Western Europe followed without question the directives from the Kremlin, today's populists follow faithfully and loyally the "Moscow line."

Their support of the Kremlin is unwavering. They are, therefore, an invaluable trump card for the Kremlin masters, supporting all or most of the Kremlin's foreign policy objectives. They are, as a rule, anti-American, anti-NATO, and eurosceptic, and do not condemn Russia's aggressive policies in the former Soviet space. On the contrary, in recent years many members of populist parties have been recruited to function as "election monitors" in the Crimea and in the occupied regions of Georgia and Ukraine, providing a fake "international legitimacy" to the Russian aggressor. The list of 135 supposed "monitors" in the Crimea included representatives of the far-right Front National (France), Jobbik (Hungary), Ataka (Bulgaria), Vlaams Belang (Belgium), and the Freedom Party FPÖ (Austria), while the extreme left was also represented by Die Linke from Germany.[35]

The populists condemn Western sanctions against Russia, imposed after Russia's annexation of the Crimea and its interference in the American presidential election of 2016. One could, therefore, consider populist parties as the Kremlin's "forward defense," in the same way as was the case with the former communist parties. However, while in the Soviet era the Kremlin had an iron grip on the communist parties, this is different today: the populists are rather drawn to the Kremlin, attracted by what Goethe called a *Wahlverwandtschaft*: an elective affinity, a spontaneous attraction based on a similarity of political preferences: a mix of authoritarianism, illiberalism, anti-Americanism, and euroscepticism.

In chapter 11 we recommended keeping populist parties out of government by building *cordon sanitaires*. It is clear that the geopolitical risks caused by Kremlin-friendly ideologies and activities of populist parties are an additional reason to keep populist parties out of government.[36] Combatting populism is not only necessary to defend liberal democracy against its enemies within the Western democracies, but it may be even more urgent in order to defend our free societies against external enemies whose aim it is to undermine the Western democratic order.[37]

Notes

1. Accessed 4 December 2017.
2. https://en.oxforddictionaries.com/word-of-the-year/word-of-the-year-2016 (accessed 5 December 2017).
3. Cf. Thomas S. Kuhn, *The Structure of Scientific Revolutions* (Chicago and London: University of Chicago Press, 2012).
4. Blaise Pascal, *Pensées and Other Writings* (Oxford and New York: Oxford University Press, 1999), p. 23.
5. Cf. James Blitz, "The Brexit risks for the NHS," *Financial Times*, 1 June 2017. www.ft.com/content/7658ec98-202f-11e7-b7d3-163f5a7f229c (accessed 5 December 2017).
6. Ibid.
7. Rob Menick, "Brexit: Vote Leave chief who created £350m NHS claim on bus admits leaving EU could be "an error"," *Independent*, 4 July 2017. www.independent.co.uk/news/uk/politics/brexit-latest-news-vote-leave-director-dominic-cummings-leave-eu-error-nhs-350-million-lie-bus-a7822386.html (accessed 5 December 2017).
8. Cf. Jon Swaine, "Donald Trump's team defends 'alternative facts' after widespread protests," *Guardian*, 23 January 2017. www.theguardian.com/us-news/2017/jan/22/donald-trump-kellyanne-conway-inauguration-alternative-facts (accessed 5 December 2017).
9. Compare the explosion of fake news and "post-truth" in Trump's America with the experience of the French sociologist Michel Crozier who studied in America in the 1950s: "One thought to live in the time of the French Revolution, under the famous inscription 'Here begins the land of truth,'" he writes. "Race, color, religion, ideology, nothing like that had the least importance. The great army of scientists was open to anyone who came to serve the cause of Truth, on the only condition to respect the norms of science and the rule of evidence: nothing would be taken for granted if one didn't have a proof. No other condition, no ulterior motive: a cat is a cat ... All chairs of Harvard University, rigid and all in the same black color, have the same model and carry the emblem of the University: a gilded emblem in three parts in gothic letters: VE-RI-TAS ... How wonderful ... having to sit on chairs *Veritas*!" (Michel Crozier, *Le mal américain* (Paris: Fayard, 1980), pp. 44–45).
10. Glenn Kessler, Meg Kelly, and Nicole Lewis, "President Trump has made 1,628 false or misleading claims over 298 days," *Washington Post*, 14 November 2017. www.washingtonpost.com/news/fact-checker/wp/2017/11/14/president-trump-has-made-1628-false-or-misleading-claims-over-298-days/?utm_term=.be055a903b39 (accessed 6 December 2017). Simon Serfaty writes – ironically – that Trump "maintains a distant relationship with facts, which he replaces with what he himself has called 'truthful hyperbole,' and 'an innocent form of exaggeration'" (Simon Serfaty, "Trump's Moment in History," *The National Interest*, No. 152, November/December 2017, p. 38).
11. Hannah Arendt, "Truth and Politics," in Hannah Arendt, *The Portable Hannah Arendt*, edited by Peter Baehr (New York and London: Penguin Books, 2000), p. 562.
12. Ibid., p. 564.
13. Hayek, *The Road to Serfdom*, p. 121.
14. Ibid., p. 121.
15. Hannah Arendt, *The Origins of Totalitarianism* (New York and London: Harcourt Brace Jovanovich, 1973), p. 350.
16. Quoted in Arendt, "Truth and Politics," p. 554.

17 Quoted by Bertram M. Gross in "Some Questions for Presidents," in Gross (ed.), *A Great Society?* (New York and London: Basic Books, 1968), p. 311.
18 Thomas Nagel, *The View from Nowhere* (Oxford and New York: Oxford University Press, 1989), p. 9.
19 In the Netherlands the advent of TV is attributed a role in the so-called *ontzuiling* of Dutch society: the phenomenon that Dutch society, which previously was divided into strictly separated Catholic, Protestant, and neutral "pillars" with their own organizations and political parties "opened up." According to a sociological study, the new medium offered "a window on the world." "Something which before was not possible or at least not evident or obvious, namely information from other parts of society, became possible from 1951" (cf. C. J. M. Schuyt and Ed Taverne, *1950. Welvaart in zwart-wit* (The Hague: SDU Uitgevers, 2000), p. 364).
20 Yochai Benkler, Robert Faris, Hal Roberts, and Ethan Zuckerman, "Study: Breitbart-Led Right-Wing Media Ecosystem Altered Broader Media Agenda," *Columbia Journalism Review*, 3 March 2017. www.cjr.org/analysis/breitbart-media-trump-harvard-study.php (accessed 6 December 2017).
21 Ibid.
22 David Roberts, "Donald Trump and the rise of tribal epistemology," *Vox*, 22 March 2017. www.vox.com/policy-and-politics/2017/3/22/14762030/donald-trump-tribal-epistemology (accessed 6 December 2017).
23 Alessandro Dal Lago, *Populismo digitale – La crisi, la rete e la nuova destra* (Milan: Raffaello Cortina Editore, 2017), p. 12.
24 Ibid., p. 13.
25 A. C. Grayling, *Liberty in the Age of Terror – A Defence of Civil Liberties and Enlightenment Values* (London, Berlin, and New York: Bloomsbury, 2009), p. 73.
26 Marc-Olivier Bherer, "Heureuses trouvailles," interview with Cass Sunstein, *Le Monde*, 5 August 2017.
27 Cf. Eliza Mackintosh, "Finland is winning the war on fake news. What it's learned may be crucial to western democracy," CNN, May 2019. https://edition.cnn.com/interactive/2019/05/europe/finland-fake-news-intl/?fbclid=IwAR3Nrz1sf1qszsnIEvQjlyc0_BELMtcvaDhKzrYE38E_wIdgc6IgjVws-v4 (accessed 8 May 2019).
28 On the Moscow–Berlin–Paris triangle as one of the Kremlin's foreign policy objectives see Van Herpen, *Putin's Propaganda Machine*, p. 257.
29 For a critique of this proposal see Marcel H. Van Herpen, "Medvedev's Proposal for a Pan-European Security Pact – Its Six Hidden Objectives and How the West Should React," The Cicero Foundation, *Cicero Working Paper*, WP 08–03, October 2008. www.cicerofoundation.org/lectures/Marcel_H_Van_Herpen_Medvedevs_Proposal_for_a_Pan-European_Security_Pact.pdf (accessed 7 December 2017).
30 Cf. Paul Reynolds, "New Russian world order: the five principles," BBC, 1 September 2008. http://news.bbc.co.uk/2/hi/europe/7591610.stm (accessed 7 December 2017).
31 "Remarks by the Vice President at the 45th Munich Conference on Security Policy," 7 February 2009. www.presidency.ucsb.edu/ws/index.php?pid=123108 (accessed 7 December 2017).
32 Cf. Carl Schmitt, *Völkerrechtliche Großraumordnung mit Interventionsverbot für raumfremde Mächte – Ein Beitrag zum Reichsbegriff im Völkerrecht* (Berlin: Duncker & Humblot, 1991).
33 Carl Schmitt, *Der Nomos der Erde im Völkerrecht des Jus Publicum Europaeum* (Berlin: Duncker & Humblot, 1997), p. 256.

34 Leonid Brezhnev, general secretary of the Communist Party of the Soviet Union, wrote an article in the *Pravda* of 15 July 1968 in which he defended the doctrine of restricted national sovereignty for members of the Warsaw Pact. This "Brezhnev doctrine" was used as a legitimation for the military intervention of five members of the Warsaw Pact in Czechoslovakia on 21 August 1968.

35 Cf. Halya Coynash, "Piskorski & Moscow's other far-right 'observers' in Crimea, Donbas & beyond," *Human Rights in Ukraine*, 18 March 2015. http://khpg.org/en/index.php?id=1426594552 (accessed 7 December 2017). On 16 March 2014, Aymeric Chauprade, Marine Le Pen's foreign policy adviser, was an observer in Crimea at the fake referendum on joining Russia (cf. Van Herpen, *Putin's Propaganda Machine*, p. 257). The German weekly *Die Zeit* reports that the extreme right AfD was also active in the monitoring business: "Since, three years ago, the party entered the first German [regional] parliaments, at least eleven AfD deputies of regional assemblies … have travelled as election monitors … to Donbas, to the occupied territories around Donetsk and Luhansk and to Nagorno-Karabakh" (cf. Christian Fuchs, Paul Middelhoff, and Fritz Zimmermann, "Putin's AfD-Truppe," *Die Zeit*, 17 August 2017).

36 Unfortunately this advice was not followed in Austria, where, in December 2017, the conservative party ÖVP not only formed a new coalition government with the extreme right FPÖ, but let this party take control of key ministries, such as defense, foreign affairs, and internal affairs.

37 It is telling that the Kremlin, which instrumentalizes populist movements abroad for its own geopolitical objectives, has a deep *angst* that such movements could develop in Russia. On this apparent paradox see Van Herpen, "Will Populism Come To Russia?" *The National Interest*, 20 September 2018. https://nationalinterest.org/feature/will-populism-come-russia-31602 (accessed 8 December 2017).

17

How to reduce economic inequality

Proposal #18: fight economic inequality and introduce a universal basic income

On Wednesday, 20 December 2017, the American House of Representatives voted on a new tax bill, which gave companies a massive permanent tax break and temporary tax breaks to individuals. On the same day, the bill was hailed by Trump in a tweet with the text: "We are delivering HISTORIC TAX RELIEF for the American people." The tweet was accompanied by a picture of a Christmas present box. When the box opened the text "TAX CUTS for CHRISTMAS" appeared. The American president was visibly proud of his new role as Santa Claus. The tax relief was indeed historic. Corporate tax had been lowered from 35 percent to 21 percent. But who was to benefit from Trump's generosity? The American people, as he pretended, or only a part of them? "It's a bill," wrote *Vox*, "that by almost every official analysis overwhelmingly benefits America's highest earners."[1]

The ideology behind the bill was the old "trickle down" theory, which runs as follows: if corporations pay less tax, they have more money to invest, and if they invest more, they create new jobs, which generate salaries for the newly employed. All this results in a "virtuous circle," leading to more prosperity for everyone and not just for the rich. It is interesting that this "trickle down" theory had already been criticized by William Jennings Bryan, a populist forerunner of Donald Trump who, in his famous "Cross of Gold" speech during the 1896 Democratic Convention, declared: "There are two ideas of government. There are those who believe that, if you will only legislate to make the well-to-do prosperous, their prosperity will leak through on those below. The Democratic idea, however, has been that if you legislate to make the masses prosperous, their prosperity will find its way up through every class which rests upon them."[2] More than 120 years later Bryan's remarks are still of great pertinence. While tax breaks could make sense in an economic slowdown, this economic sense was absent when the Trump administration adopted this new law.

The American economy was almost on the point of overheating and unemployment was at a historic low. One could predict where the money of the tax breaks would end up: in the pockets of the richest 10 percent. It was exactly the opposite of what should have been done.

We have seen that one of the drivers of populism is anger and increased anxiety about the future on the part of the citizens of Western democracies. Even if they are satisfied with their own economic situation, they are concerned about the prospects for their children, who, due to dramatic economic transformation processes, caused by globalization, robotization, and the introduction of artificial intelligence, have more problems entering the job market. The "new economy" with low-paid jobs and short-term contracts leads to economic insecurity and psychological stress, which, although not exclusively, hits in particular the younger generation. Neither anxiety, nor anger, is a good guide in politics. They tend to lead to an emotional vote – often for a populist party, which is able to instrumentalize the anxieties and disaffection of citizens for the promotion of its own illiberal agenda. According to John Kenneth Galbraith, "all of the great leaders have had one characteristic in common: it was the willingness to confront unequivocally the major anxiety of their people in their time."[3] Trump's tax break, however, by increasing economic inequality, will increase the anxieties and the anger of the average American citizen rather than confronting them. These negative emotions of citizens have to be taken seriously, because they are not unfounded.

Increasing inequality and the rise of the "1 percent": Lester Thurow's predictions

In his book *The Great Degeneration – How Institutions Decay and Economies Die*, the British historian Niall Ferguson quotes John Mack, former CEO of the investment bank Morgan Stanley, who, in 2009 – one year after the beginning of the financial crisis – almost desperately exclaimed: "We cannot control ourselves. You have to step in and control [Wall] Street."[4] It was a recognition by an insider that bankers' self-regulation of financial markets had failed and that capitalism needed control and regulation by governments. A market economy – if it is not politically controlled – may become a threatening, external power, kept in check by no one. The new, unbridled globalization not only undermined the stability of the international economic system, but was accompanied also by a steep increase in inequality in Western countries.

According to the economist and Nobel Prize laureate Simon Kuznets (1901–1985) increases in economic inequality are only temporary accompaniments of economic growth. In the long run, he argued, one could expect inequality to decrease. However, in the late 1970s this doctrine came under fire. One of the first to give a wake-up call was Lester Thurow, who, in his book *The Zero-Sum Society* (1980), predicted the advent of greater inequality in the United States. He considered two factors responsible for this phenomenon: in the first place the decline of the welfare state's transfer payments to the poor, and in the second place the fact that educated, middle-class women had begun to enter the labor market. "Labor force participation rates are now rising most rapidly for women who are married to men with higher incomes," wrote Thurow:

> Although income transfer payments have stopped the economic gap between the rich and the poor from rising since World War II, they cannot continue to rise as fast as they have over the past two decades. With income transfer payments slowing down and working wives contributing to inequality, the distribution of family income will start moving toward inequality in the 1980s and 1990s.[5]

Thurow wrote his book before the advent of Reaganomics in America and Thatcherism in Britain. However, he was already warning: "If the current demands for tax cuts on capital income to accelerating economic growth were to be met, this situation would become much worse."[6] Thurow's predictions came true: the welfare state became less generous for the poor, while educated women – increasingly inclined to "assortative mating," marrying high achievers – entered the labor market: two trends which augmented economic inequality.[7]

However, Thurow was not a prophet: he could not predict the revolutionary changes which would radically transform global society in the next three decades. These changes were threefold. First, there was the unfettered liberalization of the financial markets, ushered in by Reagan and Thatcher. Secondly, the high-tech revolution, leading to the computerization, automation, and robotization of labor processes and the development of the Internet economy. Thirdly, the process of globalization, which made it possible to move not only whole industries, but providers of sophisticated services also to low-wage countries.

These three revolutions, taken together, had a huge impact. They led to a radical change in the power relationship between capital and labor in the US and Europe, with enduring negative effects on economic equality. The liberalization of the financial markets, which made it possible to move capital flows around the world with little constraint, became a tool in the hands of the capital owners, pushing and sometimes blackmailing workers to accept lower wages if they wanted to avoid their production sites being moved abroad. The technological revolution amplified this process: through computerization and robotization not only did many low-qualified jobs disappear, but increasingly so did middle-class white-collar jobs.[8] On top of this came the Great Recession of 2008 which led governments to bail out banks that were "too big to fail" – leading to an unprecedented debt crisis which hit in particular the lower and middle classes, who had to pay the bill through higher taxes and reduced welfare benefits. Resulting high unemployment led to a further weakening of the positions of both blue-collar and white-collar workers. Factory workers in particular were trapped. In 2007 for instance – one year before the Great Recession – the base wage of an American autoworker was around $28 an hour. In 2014 new hires could expect only $15.[9] This means that in a short, seven-year period the wage was roughly halved.

The winners were the top 1 percent. In the United States "the income share of the top 1 percent of households rose from 9 percent in 1970 to 24 percent in 2007."[10] The income share of the top 1 percent thus almost *tripled*. This process was not even interrupted during the crisis years 2009–2010, when "for 99 percent of Americans, incomes increased by a mere 0.2 percent. Meanwhile, the incomes of the top 1 percent jumped by 11.6 percent."[11] The cumulative result of this development was, indeed, devastating. It was the finance industry in particular which created new opportunities for itself. The cost of its services has exploded since the subprime crisis. According to Paul Krugman "we're giving huge sums to the financial industry while receiving little or nothing – maybe less than nothing – in return."[12] Krugman, therefore, observed "a clear correlation between the rise of modern finance and America's return to Gilded Age levels of inequality."[13]

A new "Gilded Age"?

It was not only incomes that were characterized by a growing inequality – so was property ownership. This new inequality was reminiscent of the steep inequality which existed in the "Gilded Age" at the end of the nineteenth century. Brink Lindsey complained: "Despite the heaping riches that our economic system continues to pile up, millions remain trapped in a nightmare world of poverty, social exclusion, and despair."[14] And Thomas Piketty, a French economist, whose book *Capital in the Twenty-first Century* became a worldwide bestseller, asked the provocative question whether "the twenty-first century will be even more unequal than the nineteenth century."[15]

In his book Piketty made a detailed analysis of property relations in the last two centuries. He came to the conclusion that economic inequality peaked in the years before the First World War but was greatly reduced in the subsequent years. Three factors played a role here: in the first place the First World War, which worked as an "equalizer," because many property owners lost their property or saw it starkly reduced in value; secondly, redistribution by the emerging welfare state; and, thirdly, a change in tax policies which led to higher taxes for the rich. This period of "compressed inequality," which coincided with the emergence of the modern welfare state, however, ended in the 1980s, when an "Inequality Turn" took place.[16]

The main reason for the "Inequality Turn" was the introduction of new tax policies that benefitted the rich – and in particular the *super*-rich. In the US "Reagan slashed the highest marginal tax rate from 70 percent to 28 percent and reduced the maximum capital gains tax to 20 percent – reined in trade unions, cut social welfare spending, and deregulated the economy."[17] This new "Washington Consensus" was exported abroad and followed worldwide, not only in Western Europe but, after 1989, also in the former communist bloc.

The result was an immense concentration of wealth at the top which, in the US, had only been seen during the "Gilded Age" – the years between 1870 and 1900. The Gilded Age was known for its rich tycoons, such as the Morgans, Vanderbilts, Rockefellers, Carnegies, Harrimans, and Goulds. These so-called "robber barons" "were held to be uneducated and uncultivated, irresponsible, rootless and corrupt, devoid of refinement or of any sense of noblesse."[18] They were envied and despised, because "the new plutocracy had set standards of such extravagance and such notoriety that everyone else felt humbled by comparison."[19] The nineteenth-century "robber barons" have their modern equivalents in the "plutocrats" and "oligarchs": it is a new, international elite which lives in its own exclusive bubble – with luxurious yachts, private jets, sumptuous castles, private tennis courts and golf links, and a lifestyle of which normal citizens – simple millionaires included – can only dream.

Globalization created opportunities for property owners to escape taxes and circumvent the regulations of their home countries. Another cause was the voluntary retreat of politics from the economy, leaving it to the economy and to the markets to regulate themselves. "A self-regulating market demands nothing less than the institutional separation of society into an economic and a political sphere," wrote Karl Polanyi.[20] Through this separation the economic sphere was able to emancipate itself from political restrictions and obligations. However, in a democratic society the political sphere is the sphere in which each citizen – rich and poor – has equal voting rights. The principle of "one man, one vote" means that the majority has the chance to redress and correct inequalities which are experienced as unfair and unjust through the tax system and through the transfer payments of the welfare state. Joseph Stiglitz warned that "a so-called self-regulating market-economy may evolve into Mafia capitalism – and a Mafia political system – a concern that has unfortunately become all too real in some parts of the world."[21]

The super-rich tend to consider the political constraints of liberal democracy as a threat to their interests. This tension between the class of the super-rich and political democracy can lead to two reactions. The first consists of attempts by the super-rich to roll back democracy and support more authoritarian forms of government which enable them to better protect their interests. The second reaction consists of active involvement of the property-owning class in politics through lobbying, media influence, and party funding, to achieve the desired results. Their huge wealth gives them unequaled influence. "Just 158 families, along with companies they own or control, contributed $176 million in the first phase of the [2016 presidential] campaign," wrote the *New York Times*, adding, "not since before Watergate have so few people and businesses provided so much early money in a campaign, most of it through channels legalized by the Supreme Court's Citizens United decision five years ago."[22] According to the paper, "the families investing the most in presidential politics overwhelmingly lean right, contributing tens of millions of dollars to support Republican candidates who have pledged to pare regulations; cut taxes on income, capital gains and inheritances; and shrink entitlement programs."[23] Through investments in the media the super-rich also have the opportunity to influence public opinion. Rupert Murdoch's influence on British and American politics is proverbial.

It is telling that even Alan Greenspan, who was chairman of the Federal Reserve, told the Senate Banking Committee that he was concerned about the negative impact of the growing inequality on democracy. "I think that the effective increase in the concentration of incomes ... is not desirable in a democratic society," he said.[24] The problem is that the "self-regulating markets" which have dominated the global economy since the 1990s suffer from "not enough state."

What should be done?

In their book *The Spirit Level – Why Equality is Better for Everyone*, Richard Wilkinson and Kate Pickett come up with a series of concrete measures. "One approach to tackling runaway pay rates at the top," they write, "might be to plug loopholes in the tax system, limit 'business expenses', increase top tax rates, and even legislate to limit maximum pay in a company to some multiple of the average or lowest paid."[25] It is clear that the system of taxation in particular should be changed. In the US, for instance, in the period 1950 to 1979 the top tax rate on earned income averaged 75 percent. In the next thirty years, from 1980 to 2009, it averaged 39 percent,[26] which means that the top tax rate was almost halved. The same process could be observed in other countries. In 1979 in the UK, for instance, Thatcher lowered the top rate on earned income from 83 percent to 60 percent. In 1980 it was further reduced to

40 percent.[27] At the same time the rich profited handsomely from the welfare state. In the UK, for instance, research by the Fabian Society showed that generous tax breaks have created a "shadow welfare" for the UK's wealthiest 20 percent, who received almost as much from the state as the poorest 20 percent.[28]

What is necessary today is a new "New Deal," in which the tendency to install regressive top tax rates on earned income is reversed. According to Anthony Atkinson a top tax rate of 65 percent would be feasible without negative consequences for the tax base.[29] It is clear that this will be a task for the progressive parties: the social democratic parties in Europe and the Democratic Party in the US. However, moderate conservatives and liberals equally should be concerned, because an increasing inequality and growing economic insecurity of a large part of the population threatens to undermine the liberal democratic order. It is telling that the International Monetary Fund, which one can accuse neither of anti-capitalist fervor, nor of a revolutionary mindset, opened in October 2017 its publication, the *IMF Fiscal Monitor*, with the announcement of a new report, titled "Tackling Inequality." The authors write that "while some inequality is inevitable in a market-based economic system, excessive inequality can erode social cohesion, lead to political polarization, and ultimately lower economic growth."[30] The report discusses how inequality could be reduced by fiscal measures, including raising the top rates of income tax, the introduction of a wealth tax, and the adoption of a universal basic income.

A universal basic income: a means to reduce inequality and anxiety?

The last proposal in particular is interesting, because the present situation asks for bold, innovative approaches. A universal basic income is an income paid by the state to every individual resident without further conditions. The idea seems revolutionary, but is it? In fact the system exists already in many countries for some categories of the population, such as children and pensioners, who receive handouts, respectively as child benefits and state pensions. A universal basic income would make this system universal and extend it to all adult residents of a country.[31]

It is interesting that variants of this system have been proposed by progressive, as well as conservative economists. In 1953 the Dutch economist and Nobel Prize laureate Jan Tinbergen was probably the first to use the expression "basic income."[32] The idea cropped up again in the book, *Capitalism and Freedom*, of another Nobel Prize laureate, the conservative monetarist Milton Friedman, who called it a "negative income tax."[33] Friedman's idea was that people below a threshold would receive money rather than paying tax. However, the latter measure was still targeted at a certain category of the population, not the population as a whole. The idea behind a "universal basic income" is to pay a monthly grant to *all* residents. This system has the following benefits:

- Because it is universal, there is no stigma (one of the reasons why people entitled to receiving benefits sometimes don't apply).
- The bureaucracy, tasked with controlling jobseekers and means-testing, becomes superfluous, which saves money.
- There is no poverty trap. Jobseekers don't run the risk of being financially worse off by accepting a job, as is often the case in the existing system.
- Basic incomes paid to rich residents would be clawed back by the tax system.
- It would enhance the freedom of the least well off individuals, who would be certain of receiving a fixed amount of money each month.
- It would enable citizens in a period of economic transformation, characterized by robotization, the introduction of artificial intelligence, underemployment, and wage stagnation, to earn a decent living by "topping up" the basic income with an earned salary.
- There is no "workfare" pressure: citizens are free to take a paid job, to set up their own business, do creative work, to work as a volunteer, or even to do nothing.

However, the most important benefit of this system would be that it would reduce the anxiety of citizens, especially of young adults, a point that is emphasized by different authors. An article in the *Atlantic*, titled "America's Workers: Stressed Out, Overwhelmed, Totally Exhausted," explains that "more young people don't see a way to combine work and family in a rational way, so are choosing not to have families."[34] This phenomenon is not restricted to America. Also in Japan, writes *Le Monde*, the "casualization pushes many couples to abandon having a child, out of fear that they cannot afford an education which is always expensive."[35]

A recent survey in the Netherlands showed an important increase in the number of burnout cases. In November 2017 15 percent of Dutch women reported having or having had a burnout, an increase of more than 30 percent compared with 2015, when this percentage was 9.4. For men there was an increase in the same period from 6 to 9 percent. A major cause that was mentioned was "the mushrooming of temporary labor contracts." According to a researcher, the results "show that people with a permanent labor contract have less risk of having a burnout. The greater the insecurity about income, the higher the burnout risk."[36] In France the situation is even worse. In a survey conducted in 2016, a quarter of the respondents claimed to have had in their career a depression or burnout. Stress levels had almost doubled in one year and the young 18–25 age cohort in particular reported high stress levels.[37]

Rutger Bregman writes that a comparison of 269 studies conducted between 1952 and 1993 led to the conclusion that "the average child living in early 1990s North America was more anxious than psychiatric patients in the early 1950s. According to the World Health Organization, depression has even become the biggest health problem among teens and will be the number-one cause of illness worldwide by 2030. It's a vicious circle. Never before have so many young adults been seeing a psychiatrist. Never before have there been so many early career burnouts."[38] As Colin Crouch makes clear, "modern work problems are not just confined to the bottom third. Throughout the occupational structure people are finding that their jobs are taking up more and more of their lives and bringing them unreasonable stress ... For a large number of employees, working hours have been rising. Since both men and women now work within the formal economy, there is less overall time for leisure and family life."[39]

One of the main functions of the introduction of a basic income would be to reduce this anxiety. In the modern economy permanent labor contracts are becoming increasingly replaced by temporary contracts. Providing a basic income would be, therefore, not only a question of redistributive justice, but also a question of mental and physical health of the population. Unlike a worker or an employee with a permanent contract, a young worker with a temporary contract lives in constant uncertainty about his or her future work prospects. In the United States the mortality rates of the white population have been steadily rising. "A likely root cause for despair," writes *The Economist*, "is the absence of a security net for swathes of Americans, particularly in health care," adding that financial insecurity is such that "40% of Americans say they could not cover an unexpected $400 expense."[40] "Uncertainty," writes Guy Standing, "undermines resilience – the ability to cope with, compensate for and recover from shocks (unchosen adverse events) and hazards (normal life-cycle events that bring costs and risks, such as marriage, birth of a child, or death) ... A basic income would provide a modicum of ex ante security, reducing the stress of uncertainty and the probability that a shock or hazard would precipitate a financial crisis for the person or family."[41]

Is a universal basic income a pipe dream or a real possibility?

However, there are some pertinent questions about the introduction of a universal basic income. In the first place: how high should it be and can we afford it? Secondly, will it not take away the incentive to seek (or create) work? Thirdly, what about newly arrived residents, should they have the same rights as established residents?

As concerns the first question, proposed amounts vary between $600 and $1,100 a month.[42] Such an amount would be affordable in a developed economy. According to *The Economist* the US could pay $10,000 a year "if it began collecting about as much tax as a share of GDP as Germany (35%, as opposed to the current 26%) and replaced all other welfare programmes (including social security, or pensions, but not including health care) with the basic-income payment."[43] The implicit message here is that it is not too expensive, but that there will not be enough public support in the US to raise higher taxes. This may be true. The United States, a notorious welfare laggard, will certainly not be among the first countries to adopt such a system nationwide.

However, the US is not as monolithic as it appears. In 2017 Hawaii's Congress voted in a law to look into the idea of introducing a universal basic income, because a large number of the state's jobs – mostly in the tourist industry, such as waiters, cooks, and cleaners – are likely to be replaced by automated technology in the near future. The bill declares that all families in Hawaii are entitled to "basic financial security."[44] In the Californian city of Oakland a nonprofit group, Y Combinator, launched the biggest basic-income research project of the US. The project, which started in 2018, intends to pay a group of 1,000 low- and moderate-income people, selected at random, $1,000 a month for three to five years, with no strings attached, nor restrictions on how the money will be spent. The results will be compared with a control group of 2,000 people who get $50 a month.[45] Many Americans are not aware that a system of universal basic income already exists in Alaska. In 1976 Alaska established a Permanent Fund which collected revenue from oil and mineral leases. In 2017 the Fund had collected about $600 billion. This wealth fund enables the state to send each resident each year in the month of October a dividend check of up to $2,072.[46] North of the US border, the Canadian province of Ontario started a pilot in 2017, giving 4,000 citizens a basic income from about C$750 a month (approximately US $600) to assess how it affects their health, wellbeing, earnings and productivity.[47] "Many of those who are receiving payments," wrote the *Independent*, "say their lives have already been changed for the better."[48]

In Europe also different pilot projects have been initiated, such as in the city of Utrecht in the Netherlands, and in Finland, where Prime Minister Juha Sipilä introduced a project to pay in 2018 and 2019 2,000 unemployed Finns €560 a month. In a report with the preliminary results, published in February 2019, the authors wrote, "the experiment did not increase the employment level of the participants in the first year of the experiment. However, at the end of the experiment the recipients of a basic income perceived their wellbeing as being better than did those in the control group."[49] This experiment was targeted at unemployed people and was, as such, not an example of a *universal* basic income. However, one of the outcomes was that those who received the basic income did not work less than the control group, but on average one half-day more. According to Minna Ylikännö, the lead researcher of the project, "The recipients of a basic income had less stress symptoms as well as less difficulties to concentrate and less health problems than the control group. They were also more confident in their future and in their ability to influence societal issues."[50] In the summer of 2017, the German federal state Schleswig-Holstein announced that it would also start a pilot project. The project was supported by a broad coalition of conservatives (CDU), liberals (FDP), and Greens.[51] Critics fear that this free money will be a disincentive for work. Studies show however that this is not the case.[52] Others fear that the money will be spent on alcohol, tobacco, or luxury goods. In a report of the World Bank, the authors write that the results of their research "provide strong evidence that concerns that transfers will be used on alcohol and tobacco are unfounded."[53]

A more serious objection is the third one: that a system of basic income will attract unwanted migrants. "A basic income would make it almost impossible for countries to have open borders," writes *The Economist*. "The right to an income would encourage rich-world governments either to shut the doors to immigrants, or to create second-class citizenries without access to state support."[54] These concerns seem, however, exaggerated. In the first place it would be counterproductive for countries to "shut the doors" to immigrants, because they often need both highly qualified as well as low-qualified immigrants. Migrants who have work permits have globally the same rights of social protection (unemployment insurance, health insurance, etc.) as permanent residents. However, they should be eligible to receive the basic income only after becoming a permanent resident, which should imply the obligation to learn the country's language and pass a language test. This implies for the new resident a long-term commitment and would avoid "welfare shopping." Also a "waiting period" could be imposed, as is the case in Alaska[55] or in Brazil. In the latter a "citizen's income law," introduced in 2004, restricts entitlement to non-Brazilians to people who have been living in Brazil for at least five years.[56]

It is clear that before adopting a universal basic income one should analyze carefully the results of the pilot studies that are taking place in different countries. However, it seems that in this period, in which economic inequality has reached new heights, a universal basic income can play an important role – not only as a means of redistribution, but also as an instrument which can diminish the feelings of insecurity, anxiety, and anger of the population, not least of the younger generation. It is these negative feelings which are exploited by populist parties.

Notes

1. Tara Golshan, "4 winners and 4 losers from the Republican tax bill," *Vox*, 20 December 2017. www.vox.com/2017/12/20/16790040/gop-tax-bill-winners.
2. Bryan, "You Shall Not Crucify Mankind," pp. 382–383.
3. John Kenneth Galbraith, *The Age of Uncertainty* (London: British Broadcasting Corporation, 1977), p. 330.
4. Ferguson, *The Great Degeneration*, p. 59.
5. Lester C. Thurow, *The Zero-Sum Society – Distribution and the Possibilities for Economic Change* (Harmondsworth: Penguin Books, 1980), pp. 156–157.
6. Ibid., p. 171.
7. "If family income doubles at each step of the economic ladder," wrote Jerry Z. Muller, "then the total incomes of those families higher up the ladder are bound to increase faster than the total incomes of those further down" (Jerry Z. Muller, "Capitalism and Inequality – What the Right and the Left Get Wrong," *Foreign Affairs*, Volume 92, No. 2, March/April 2013, p. 39).
8. Carl Frey and Michael Osborne spoke in this context about "the current trend toward labour market polarization, with growing employment in high-income cognitive jobs and low-income manual occupations, accompanied by a hollowing-out of middle-income routine jobs" (cf. Carl Benedikt Frey and Michael A. Osborne, "The Future of Employment: How Susceptible Are Jobs to Computerisation?" 17 September 2013. www.oxfordmartin.ox.ac.uk/downloads/academic/The_Future_of_Employment.pdf (accessed 12 December 2017).
9. Cf. Joseph E. Stiglitz, *The Price of Inequality* (London: Penguin Books, 2013), pp. 71–72.
10. Ferguson, *The Great Degeneration*, p. 4.
11. Gar Alperovitz, *America Beyond Capitalism – Reclaiming Our Wealth, Our Liberty, and Our Democracy* (Hoboken: John Wiley & Sons, 2005), p. 5.
12. Paul Krugman, "Three expensive milliseconds," *International New York Times*, 15 April 2014.
13. Ibid.
14. Brink Lindsey, *Human Capitalism – How Economic Growth Has Made Us Smarter – and More Unequal* (Princeton: Princeton University Press, 2013), p. 2.
15. Thomas Piketty, *Le capital au XXIe siècle* (Paris: Éditions du Seuil, 2013), p. 596.
16. The term "Inequality Turn" is coined by Anthony B. Atkinson in his book *Inequality – What Can Be Done?* (Cambridge, Mass., and London: Harvard University Press, 2015), pp. 3, 20.
17. Chrystia Freeland, *Plutocrats – The Rise of the New Global Super-rich* (London: Penguin Books, 2012), p. 17.
18. Hofstadter, *Age of Reform*, p. 141.
19. Ibid., p. 147.
20. Karl Polanyi, *The Great Transformation: The Political and Economic Origins of Our Time*, with a new introduction by Fred Bloch (Boston: Beacon Press, 2001), p. 74.
21. Joseph E. Stiglitz, foreword in Polanyi, *The Great Transformation*, p. xv.
22. Nicholas Confessore, Sarah Cohen, and Karen Yourish, "The families funding the 2016 presidential election," *New York Times*, 10 October 2015. www.nytimes.com/interactive/2015/10/11/us/politics/2016-presidential-election-super-pac-donors.html (accessed 12 December 2017).

23 Ibid.
24 Nell Henderson, "Greenspan says workers' lack of skills lowers wages," *Washington Post*, 22 July 2004.
25 Richard Wilkinson and Kate Pickett, *The Spirit Level – Why Equality is Better for Everyone* (London: Penguin Books, 2010), p. 254.
26 Cf. Atkinson, *Inequality*, p. 61.
27 Ibid., p. 181.
28 Cf. Heather Stewart, "Top UK earners to receive as much in handouts as poorest by 2020," *Guardian*, 1 April 2016. www.theguardian.com/politics/2016/apr/01/top-uk-earners-to-receive-as-much-in-benefits-as-poorest-by-2020 (accessed 13 December 2017).
29 Atkinson, *Inequality*, p. 185.
30 "IMF Fiscal Monitor: Tackling Inequality, October 2017," *Fiscal Monitor*, October 2017. www.imf.org/en/Publications/FM/Issues/2017/10/05/fiscal-monitor-october-2017 (accessed 13 December 2017).
31 To all residents, not to all citizens, because the latter would include paying the basic income to diaspora living abroad.
32 Quoted in Philippe Van Parijs, *Real Freedom for All – What (If Anything) Can Justify Capitalism?* (Oxford: Clarendon Press, 1995), p. 243.
33 Milton Friedman, *Capitalism and Freedom* (Chicago: University of Chicago Press, 2002), p. 192. The first edition was in 1962. In 1980 Friedman was still defending the idea in the book *Free to Choose*, which he wrote together with his wife Rose. "An attractive alternative to the present welfare system," they wrote, "is a negative income tax. This proposal has been widely supported by individuals and groups of all political persuasions. A variant has been proposed by three Presidents; yet it seems politically unfeasible for the foreseeable future" (Milton Friedman and Rose Friedman, *Free to Choose – A Personal Statement* (Harmondsworth and New York: Penguin Books, 1980), p. 125).
34 Rebecca J. Rosen, "America's Workers: Stressed Out, Overwhelmed, Totally Exhausted," *Atlantic*, 25 March 2014. www.theatlantic.com/business/archive/2014/03/americas-workers-stressed-out-overwhelmed-totally-exhausted/284615/.
35 Philippe Mesmer, "Le Japon confronté à un rude déclin démographique," *Le Monde*, 10 January 2018.
36 Jonathan Witteman, "Aantal burn-outs zeer sterk gestegen – en dat komt deels door al die tijdelijke contracten," *De Volkskrant*, 15 November 2017. https://www.volkskrant.nl/wetenschap/aantal-burn-outs-zeer-sterk-gestegen-en-dat-komt-deels-door-al-die-tijdelijk e-contracten~a4537868/ (accessed 13 December 2017).
37 Cf. François Desnoyers, "Malades du travail," *Le Monde*, 3 May 2016. www.lemonde.fr/emploi/article/2016/05/03/malades-du-travail_4913040_1698637.html (accessed 14 December 2017).
38 Rutger Bregman, *Utopia for Realists and How We Can Get There* (London, Oxford, and New York: Bloomsbury, 2017), p. 18.
39 Crouch, *Post-Democracy*, p. 66.
40 "Deaths of despair," *The Economist*, 25 March 2017. www.economist.com/news/finance-and-economics/21719428-new-research-shows-mortality-middle-aged-whites-continues-rise-economic (accessed 14 December 2017).
41 Guy Standing, *Basic Income – A Guide for the Open-Minded* (New Haven and London: Yale University Press, 2017), p. 88.
42 On 5 June 2016, the Swiss voted on a referendum proposing a universal basic income. Although no amount was specified in the text of the referendum, campaigners proposed

2,500 Swiss francs ($2,560) per month for adults and 625 francs for children. The proposal was rejected by 77 percent of the electorate. It could be that these unrealistic amounts contributed to the rejection. Cf. Raphael Minder, "Guaranteed income for all? Switzerland's voters say no thanks," *New York Times*, 5 June 2016. www.nytimes.com/2016/06/06/world/europe/switzerland-swiss-vote-basic-income.html (accessed 14 December 2017).

43 "Basically flawed – Proponents of a basic income underestimate how disruptive it would be," *The Economist*, 4 June 2016. www.economist.com/news/leaders/21699907-proponents-basic-income-underestimate-how-disruptive-it-would-be-basically-flawed (accessed 15 December 2017).

44 Ben Kentish, "Hawaii considering universal basic income after positive trials in Europe," *Independent*, 5 September 2017. www.independent.co.uk/news/world/americas/universal-basic-income-hawaii-introduction-minimum-salary-a7931221.html (accessed 15 December 2017).

45 Cf. Kathleen Pender, "Oakland group plans to launch nation's biggest basic-income research project," *San Francisco Chronicle*, 1 September 2017. www.sfchronicle.com/business/networth/article/Oakland-group-plans-to-launch-nation-s-biggest-12219073.php (accessed 18 December 2017).

46 Cf. Michael J. Coren, "Alaska shows even people in the most conservative states prefer a basic income to lower taxes," *Quartz*, 30 June 2017.

47 Ben Kentish, "Canadian province trials basic income for thousands of residents," *Independent*, 29 November 2017. www.independent.co.uk/news/world/americas/canada-universal-basic-income-ontario-trial-citizens-residents-poverty-unemployment-benefits-a8082576.html (accessed 18 December 2017).

48 Ibid.

49 "Preliminary results of the basic income experiment: self-perceived wellbeing improved, during the first year no effects on employment," Press Release, Kela and the Ministry of Social Affairs and Health, 8 February 2019. www.epressi.com/tiedotteet/hallitus-ja-valtio/preliminary-results-of-the-basic-income-experiment-les-resultats-preliminaires-de-lexperience-du-revenu-de-basepredvariteljnye-rezuljtaty-eksperimentaljnoj-koncepcii-bezuslovnogovorlaufige-ergebnisse-des-experiments-zum-grundeinkommen.html (accessed 15 February 2019).

50 Ibid.

51 Cf. "Bundesland will das bedingungslose Grundeinkommen als erstes testen," *Focus*, 28 June 2017. www.focus.de/finanzen/news/arbeitsmarkt/bedingungsloses-grundeinkommen-in-schleswig-holstein-jamaica-koalition-schreibt-umsetzung-neuer-absicherungsmodelle-vor_id_7290471.html (accessed 18 December 2017).

52 A study of the effects of the introduction in 2011 of cash transfers in Iran comes to the conclusion that "the program did not affect labor supply in any appreciable way" (cf. Djavad Salehi-Isfahani and Mohammad H. Mostafavi-Dehzooei, "Cash Transfers and Labor Supply: Evidence from a Large-Scale Program in Iran," Economic Research Forum, Working Paper No. 1090, May 2017. http://erf.org.eg/wp-content/uploads/2017/05/1090.pdf (accessed 19 December 2017).

53 Cf. David K. Evans and Anna Popova, "Cash Transfers and Temptation Goods: A Review of Global Evidence," The World Bank, *Policy Research Working Paper* 6886, May 2014. http://documents.worldbank.org/curated/en/617631468001808739/pdf/WPS6886.pdf (accessed 20 December 2017).

54 "Basically flawed."

55 In Alaska dividends of the Permanent Fund are paid to residents who have lived within the state for a full calendar year (1 January to 31 December). If someone became a resident on 2 January 2017, he or she wouldn't receive their dividend in October 2018, but in October 2019.

56 Cf. Philippe Van Parijs and Yannick Vanderborght, "Basic Income, Globalization and Migration," in Sustainable Utopia and Basic Income in a Global Era, Proceedings of the Basic Income International Conference, Seoul, 27–28 January 2010. https://cdn.uclouvain.be/public/Exports%20reddot/etes/documents/2010.BIGlobalizationMigrationdraft4.pdf (accessed 20 December 2017).

18

Toward an economic democracy

Proposal #19: enhance economic democracy

Political democracy is often considered something which stands apart from the rest of society. As citizens of the state people have equal rights and equal power. However, as inhabitants of civil society – the place where they live and work – they are not equal and they do not have the same power. Of course, a society of completely equal individuals would not be possible. It would not even be desirable, because such a utopia would soon turn out to be a communist dystopia. However, one cannot deny that there exists a lot of what I would call "unnecessary surplus-inequality" in civil society, particularly in the sphere of the economy.

Power in the economy resides almost exclusively within the property-owning class, and even here power is skewed in favor of the super-rich. One hears a lot of talk about a "shareholder democracy," which is based on the principle of "one share one vote," but in practice even this principle doesn't apply fully. "Democracy is in decline around the world," writes *The Economist*. "Only 45% of countries are considered free today, and their number is slipping. Liberty is in retreat in the world of business, too. The idea that firms should be controlled by diverse shareholders who exercise one vote per share is increasingly viewed as redundant or even dangerous."[1]

This trend had already begun before the Great Recession of 2008. In 2005 two-thirds of the big European firms included in the FTSE Eurofirst 300 index operated a rule of one share one vote, which meant that "in the other third of firms, power tends to be concentrated in the hands of a minority of big shareholders who control a majority of voting rights."[2] At that time the "one share one vote" principle was applied in 97 percent of the companies in Germany and in 88 percent in Britain, but only in 14 percent in the Netherlands and 25 percent in Sweden.[3]

However, one can ask oneself whether even such a "shareholder democracy" should be the ultimate goal of a democratic governance of the economy. Because the economy is based not only on the capital factor, but also on the labor factor. Why shouldn't those who work in the factories, the laboratories, and offices, those whose lives depend on their workplace, not have a say in how the economy is run? This is a pertinent question. Not only in itself, but also for another reason: the organization of civil society has an impact on political democracy.

German "co-determination": a model?

Can political democracy be promoted and strengthened by introducing more democratic procedures in civil society, outside the realm of politics? This was one of the questions asked by Willy Brandt, when he became German chancellor in 1969. Expectations were high when, in October of that year, he entered the Bundestag building of the German parliament in Bonn to read the official government declaration of his new coalition government of social democrats and liberals. Brandt's speech was, indeed, a watershed. He famously promised his audience that his government wanted to "dare [to introduce] more democracy" (in German: *Wir wollen mehr Demokratie wagen*).[4] "Daring to introduce more democracy" included not only the promise to introduce more transparency and to lower the voting age from twenty-one to eighteen, but also a democratization of civil society. "We want the democratic society," he explained, "to which all should contribute with their ideas in order to bring about greater co-responsibility and codetermination."[5]

It was his successor, the social democratic chancellor Helmut Schmidt, who would realize these reforms. In 1976 the German parliament adopted the Co-determination Act (*Mitbestimmungsgesetz*), which required limited liability corporations (GmbH) with more than 500 employees, and stock corporations (AG) with more than 2,000 employees, in Germany to have a supervisory board, half of which consisted of representatives of the personnel. For stock corporations with between 500 and 2,000 workers the employee representation was one-third.[6] The chairman or -woman, elected by the shareholders, had an extra casting vote in the event of a tie. The German initiative was, ironically, based on an already existing model of co-determination in the coal and steel industry, imposed on Germany after the Second World War by the British occupying authorities to prevent a remilitarization of the country.

The new German co-determination law led to similar initiatives in other countries. In the same period, in the UK, Harold Wilson's Labour government appointed a "Committee of Inquiry on Industrial Democracy," headed by the Oxford historian Sir Alan Bullock. In January 1977 the committee published two reports. The majority report was in favor of adopting a compulsory system of employee representation on the board of directors[7] of companies with 2,000 employees or more.[8] This proposal would see the board of directors consist of two groups of equal size: one representing the shareholders, one representing the employees, and a third, smaller group of co-opted "neutral experts," who were acceptable to both. These plans, however, were shelved, when neither the employers' organization the CBI, nor the radical unions would back them. The window of opportunity was definitively closed when massive strikes during the "Winter of Discontent" of 1978–1979 led to the fall of the Labour government and the return, in May 1979, of the Conservatives under Prime Minister Margaret Thatcher.

However, in other countries these new forms of industrial democracy met with more success. In Denmark companies with more than thirty-five employees can appoint one-third of the members of the board, while in Norway this was the case for companies with more than fifty employees. In 1987 Sweden followed suit and granted employees of companies with more than twenty-five employees the right to appoint about a third of the representatives on the board of directors.[9] Because of the low threshold, in these Scandinavian countries the impact of co-determination is even greater than in Germany. In Denmark, for instance, 60 percent of employees work in companies with co-determination.[10] At the moment thirteen of the twenty-eight EU member states have provisions for employee representation on the boards of companies.[11]

Enhancing trust and feelings of self-esteem and dignity

The introduction of employee representation on the boards of companies was an important innovation. A higher-educated workforce will ask for more autonomy and more influence, not only on investment decisions, but also on the appointment and payment of managers. Although critics argued that participation of employee representatives on the board could make the decision-making process slower and therefore less effective, there are no clear examples to prove this is the case. On the contrary, economists found that "the move to almost parity after 1976 seems to increase productivity slightly in the affected firms ... There is certainly no suggestion of the negative effects predicted by opponents in both industry and academia."[12] Others emphasized that co-determination made it possible "to base labor relations on trust. The higher the premium which an advanced industrial society puts on the art of cooperative organization, the more ... the benefits of co-determination will exceed its costs."[13] Another positive consequence was the fact that "inside companies co-determination helps *to overcome hierarchies* and to diminish the social distance between those at 'the bottom' and 'the top.' Thereby it contributes to the *social integration of society as a whole*."[14]

Participation in the decision-making process of the company will enhance workers' feelings of self-esteem and dignity. The sociologists Richard Sennett and Jonathan Cobb wrote about the craving of the common man for dignity. "Dignity," they wrote, "is as compelling a human need as food or sex, and yet here is a society which casts the mass of its people into limbo, never satisfying their hunger for dignity … and revolt against the society [is] the only reasonable alternative."[15] Introducing forms of economic democracy has a positive effect not only on man's feeling of dignity, but also on the functioning of political democracy. This aspect was emphasized by Carole Pateman, who wrote:

> The existence of representative institutions at national level is not sufficient for democracy; for maximum participation by all the people at that level socialisation, or "social training", for democracy must take place in other spheres in order that the necessary individual attitudes and psychological qualities can be developed. This development takes place through the process of participation itself.[16]

In the same vein Harry Eckstein wrote that "a government will tend to be stable if its authority pattern is congruent with the other authority patterns of the society of which it is a part."[17] Robert Dahl similarly emphasizes that "democracy within firms would improve the quality of democracy in the government of the state by transforming us into better citizens and by facilitating greater political equality among us,"[18] adding that "if democracy is justified in the government of our state, then it is also justified in the governments that make decisions *within* firms."[19]

However, ideas of promoting the democratization of firms are, as a rule, not met with much enthusiasm. "I have no doubt," writes Dahl, "that many people will immediately reject the idea of extending the democratic process to business firms as foolish and unrealistic. It may therefore be helpful to recall that not long ago most people took it as a matter of self-evident good sense that the idea of applying the democratic process to the government of the nation-state was foolish and unrealistic."[20] Dahl added: "If the question were merely whether employees are as qualified on the whole to run their firms as the stockholders, the answer is, I think, that they are a good deal more qualified."[21] It is telling that Jürgen Schrempp, the CEO of DaimlerChrysler, declared in an interview that overall he had had a "very good experience with [the system of] co-determination," adding that on the employee side there were "very competent people, who were committed to the company and its success."[22]

Co-determination enhances economic equality

But co-determination has more benefits. Felix Hörisch of Mannheim University, who used the Gini coefficient to analyze the influence of co-determination on income distribution in thirty-two OECD member states, wrote that "it is fair to conclude that states with codetermination inhabit a more equal distribution of incomes than states without employee representation in the board of companies in the private sector."[23] He found that a "higher level of codetermination leads to a significantly lower income share for the highest decile of income."[24]

This trend is also visible in the recompense of CEOs. The American magazine *Fortune* published an article titled "Why do American CEOs make twice as much as German CEOs?"[25] It tried to explain why, on average, a German CEO of a large company made about $5.9 million in 2013, while his US counterpart in the S&P 500 made on average $12.3 million, making the average CEO-to-worker pay ratio for the US 354-to-1, while for Germany this was 147-to-1. "The lack of a say on CEO pay among workers has played a major part in the sky high pay of American CEOs," wrote the magazine, explaining the difference by the fact that "representation on German corporate boards is split between labor and shareholders through an executive board and a non-executive board. This has given workers the ability to raise employee pay along with overseeing CEO salaries."[26]

Co-determination seems an idea whose time has come. Even in the US there are positive comments. the *Washington Post* published an article titled "In Germany, workers help run their companies. And it's going great!"[27] Although the paper conceded that "obviously, the United States and Germany are very different countries and a policy that worked with one might not pan out in another," it concluded that "giving workers more control over their firms seems to help both them and the companies."[28] Even employers and conservatives begin to see its benefits. What about, for instance, Theresa May, who in the summer of 2016, when she became prime minister, announced her intention to put employees on the boards of major companies? "With her pledge to put worker representatives on the boards of big British companies," wrote the *Financial Times*, "Theresa May seems to be reaching for inspiration to Germany."[29] This inspiration, unfortunately, didn't last long. One year later the *Guardian* wrote in an editorial that "plans to put employee representatives on company boards have been abandoned. Now the appointment of a non-executive director 'to represent employees' will suffice."[30] It is a sign of the deep reluctance to embrace these reforms in the Anglo-Saxon corporate world.

Will co-determination make populist parties less attractive?

Projects to adopt co-determination are attractive for yet another reason: co-determination seems to reduce the attractiveness of populist parties. In a survey conducted in 2017 by the German Hans Böckler Stiftung, one of the findings was that workers who were more concerned than others about the future for themselves and their children and who generally felt a loss of control, were more inclined to vote for the populist extreme right party Allianz für Deutschland (AfD). The researchers found that people "in firms with fewer than 10 employees vote AFD significantly more often than those in companies with more than 1,000 employees."[31] This result was interpreted as being a consequence of the fact that feelings of powerlessness were more widespread in these small firms, where there is no system of co-determination, than in larger firms where co-determination is in place.[32] Although these results must be interpreted with caution (for instance, the mere size of the company in which one works could give the worker more certainty), the fact that the worker has a say in the way the firm is managed could be one of the elements that reduce feelings of being totally powerless.

Notes

1   "Shareholder democracy is ailing," *The Economist*, 9 February 2017. www.economist.com/news/business/21716654-snaps-refusal-hand-out-any-voting-shares-part-wider-trend-towards-corporate (accessed 9 January 2018).
2   "What shareholder democracy? Europe's unfair voting rights," *The Economist*, 23 March 2005. www.economist.com/node/3793305 (accessed 9 January 2018).
3   Ibid.
4   "Regierungserklärung von Bundeskanzler Willy Brandt vor dem Deutschen Bundestag in Bonn am 28. Oktober 1969." www.willy-brandt.de/fileadmin/brandt/Downloads/Regierungserklaerung_Willy_Brandt_1969.pdf (accessed 10 January 2018).
5   Ibid.
6   In Germany two-tier boards exist; these are the board of directors (*Vorstand*) and the supervisory board (*Aufsichtsrat*).
7   Unlike Germany, the UK has a unitary system of governance with only a board of directors.
8   Cf. Paul Davies, "The Bullock Report and Employee Participation in Corporate Planning in the U.K.," *Journal of Comparative Corporate Law and Securities Regulation*, 1 (1978). http://scholarship.law.upenn.edu/cgi/viewcontent.cgi?article=1012&context=jil (accessed 10 January 2018).
9   Cf. Board Representation Act ("Lag om styrelserepresentation för de privatanställda"). www.government.se/4ac877/contentassets/af2a3399726a445ea0e6655d58ac9508/19871245-board-representation-private-sector-employees-act (accessed 10 January 2018).

10 Cf. Felix Hörisch, "The Macro-economic Effect of Codetermination on Income Equality," Mannheimer Zentrum für Europäische Sozialforschung, *Arbeitspapiere*, No. 147, 2012, p. 12. https://www.mzes.uni-mannheim.de/publications/wp/wp-147.pdf.
11 These countries are Austria, the Czech Republic, Denmark, Finland, France, Germany, Hungary, Luxembourg, the Netherlands, Poland, the Slovak Republic, Slovenia, and Sweden.
12 Felix R. FitzRoy and Kornelius Kraft, "Co-determination, Efficiency, and Productivity," Institute for the Study of Labor (IZA), Bonn, *Discussion Paper* No. 1442, December 2004, p. 19.
13 Wolfgang Streeck and Norbert Kluge, "Vorwort," in Wolfgang Streeck and Norbert Kluge (eds), *Mitbestimmung in Deutschland – Tradition und Effizienz* (Frankfurt am Main and New York: Campus Verlag, 1999), p. 13.
14 "Anhang I – Kommission Mitbestimmung: Die Entwicklung der Mitbestimmung als Institution," in Streeck and Kluge, *Mitbestimmung in Deutschland*, p. 246.
15 Richard Sennett and Jonathan Cobb, *The Hidden Injuries of Class* (New York: Vintage Books, 1973), p. 191.
16 Carole Pateman, *Participation and Democratic Theory* (Cambridge: Cambridge University Press, 1970), p. 42.
17 Harry Eckstein, "A Theory of Stable Democracy," Appendix B in Harry Eckstein, *Division and Cohesion in Democracy* (Princeton: Princeton University Press, 1966), p. 234.
18 Robert A. Dahl, *A Preface to Economic Democracy* (Berkeley and Los Angeles: University of California Press, 1985), p. 94.
19 Ibid., p. 94.
20 Dahl, *Democracy and Its Critics*, p. 328.
21 Ibid., p. 331.
22 "Schrempp-Interview, 'Was der Kanzler macht, finde ich gut'," *Stern*, 19 October 2004. www.stern.de/politik/deutschland/schrempp-interview--was-der-kanzler-macht--finde-ich-gut--3548832.html (accessed 12 January 2018).
23 Hörisch, "Macro-economic Effect," p. 18.
24 Ibid., p. 19.
25 Ryan Derousseau, "Why do American CEOs make twice as much as German CEOs?" *Fortune*, 4 November 2014. http://fortune.com/2014/11/04/why-do-american-ceos-make-twice-as-much-as-german-ceos/ (accessed 12 January 2018).
26 Ibid.
27 Dylan Matthews, "In Germany, workers help run their companies. And it's going great!" *Washington Post*, 7 October 2012. www.washingtonpost.com/news/wonk/wp/2012/10/07/in-germany-workers-help-run-their-companies-and-its-going-great/?utm_term=.04459033463b (accessed 12 January 2018).
28 Ibid. Cf. also Bennet Berger and Elena Vaccarino, "Codetermination in Germany – a role model for the UK and the US? *Bruegel*, 13 October 2016. http://bruegel.org/2016/10/codetermination-in-germany-a-role-model-for-the-uk-and-the-us/ (accessed 13 January 2018).
29 Guy Chazan, "Theresa May looks to Germany for board reform," *Financial Times*, 11 July 2016. www.ft.com/content/3d70421e-4759-11e6-b387-64ab0a67014c (accessed 12 January 2018).
30 "The Guardian view on corporate governance reform: Be stronger, not weaker," *Guardian*, 29 August 2017. www.theguardian.com/commentisfree/2017/aug/28/the-guardian-view-on-corporate-governance-reform-be-stronger-not-weaker (accessed 15 January 2018).

31 Richard Hilmer, Bettina Kohlrausch, Rita Müller-Hilmer, and Jérémie Gagné, "Einstellung und soziale Lebenslage – Eine Spurensuche nach Gründen für rechtspopulistische Orientierung, auch unter Gewerkschaftsmitgliedern," Hans Böckler Stiftung, *Working Paper Forschungsförderung*, No. 044, August 2017, pp. 47–48. www.boeckler.de/pdf/p_fofoe_WP_044_2017.pdf (accessed 15 January 2018).

32 Working in a small firm was not the only indicator of the propensity to vote for the AfD. Short-term contracts and the absence of collective labor agreements were also mentioned as factors which favored an AfD vote.

19
Solving the knotty problem of migration

Proposal #20: Toward a humane and sustainable immigration policy

Last but not least there is the question of migration. While left-wing populists mainly focus on economic inequality, extreme right populist parties mainly target migration policies (or the lack of these). Migration plays therefore a central role in the electoral victories of these parties. Whether it is the Swiss People's Party, the Dutch Freedom Party, the French Rassemblement National (former Front National), or Donald Trump, they all consider immigration, particularly from Islamic countries, a major threat to the Western way of life. To attract followers they use all kinds of arguments: not only economic and ethnic arguments, but sometimes also "liberal" arguments – as the Dutch populists Pim Fortuyn and Geert Wilders, who accused Muslim immigrants of attacking the rights of gay people.

How should one react? In the first place, one should avoid falling into the trap of countering appeals to close the frontier with appeals to open the doors wide to migrants. In December 1989, the French socialist prime minister Michel Rocard, someone whom no one could accuse of being a xenophobe, famously declared: "I believe that we cannot take in all the world's misery, that France should remain what she is, a land of exile … nothing more."[1] At that time Rocard was heavily criticized for this rather narrow definition of France's immigration policy. And certainly France – as well as other Western countries – can afford a more generous immigration policy than one which is restricted to granting political asylum. The question is: how generous?

Migration: push and pull factors

International migration is a phenomenon characterized by pull and push factors. In the case of the former, migrants are recruited in the countries of origin, because in the countries of destination there is a labor shortage. This was the case in the 1960s, when workers from Southern Europe – and later Turkey and Morocco – came to Northern Europe. These migrants were called "guest workers," because they were supposed to be temporary "guests" who would return to their home countries as soon as they were no longer needed. However, the majority stayed where they were, which led to a second wave of migration, this time a "push wave," of family reunions, when spouses, children, and eventually other members of the workers' families came over.

Although the "pull" migration did not disappear – qualified personnel were still needed in businesses, hospitals, universities, and research centers, and also unskilled labor was still required in agriculture and construction – this became an increasingly smaller portion of the immigrant population. Because apart from family reunions there were two other "push" factors which played a role. In the first place there was a steadily growing flow of refugees fleeing war zones, and, secondly, the exponential growth of undocumented economic migrants – mostly Mexicans in the United States and Africans in Europe. Migration became a process which was less and less characterized by pull factors and more and more by push factors, or, as the French say: *une immigration choisie* (a chosen immigration) became increasingly *une immigration subie* (an imposed immigration). It is particularly this change in the nature of immigration which has led to a populist backlash exploited by populist extreme right parties.

Debunking the populist arguments

The central argument of populist parties is that governments have given up their sovereignty and are not capable or not willing to stem the tide. The keyword used in Germany is *Überfremdung*, which means that the original population is being "swamped" by foreigners. In France the extreme right ideologue Renaud Camus coined the term "the great replacement" (*le grand remplacement*), a conspirationist theory, accusing the French political and business elites of wanting to replace the French population with immigrants from Africa.[2]

As a rule, populist parties are using two kinds of argument: economic, as well as identity arguments. The economic argument is, in essence, that immigrants take away the jobs of the original population and that their competition on the labor market leads to lower wages. These arguments, despite their *prima facie* validity, do not seem to hold water, or contain only a partial truth, because immigrants do not only take existing jobs, but also create – directly or indirectly – new jobs.

A good way to measure the impact of immigrants on wages and the labor market is to analyze the consequences of a sudden immigration stop or of a sudden rise in immigration. The first was done by the French economist Alfred Sauvy, who "showed that in the United States the immigration stop of 1923, far from reducing unemployment, increased it by diminishing the number of consumers."[3] Another economist, David Card, analyzed the impact of the "Mariel boatlift," the sudden arrival in Florida of about 120,000 relatively unskilled Cubans, expelled by Fidel Castro between April 1980 and June 1981. Although their arrival increased the labor force in the Miami metropolitan area by 7 percent, this had, according to the author, "virtually no effect" on the wage rates of less-skilled non-Cuban workers. There was also "no evidence of an increase in unemployment."[4] Anthony Edo analyzed a similar case of a sudden arrival of a big group of immigrants in France. This time it concerned the repatriation of French citizens from Algeria after its independence in 1962. The sudden arrival in France of about 800,000 people had only a temporary impact. Edo concluded that "for massive, poorly anticipated migration flows, wage rates can be negatively influenced in the short term, before self-adjusting themselves in the longer term."[5]

However, more important than economic reasons to oppose immigration are identitarian reasons, put forward by populists. Because openly racist arguments have become taboo, these are replaced by cultural arguments. The problem with migrants would not be their race, but rather their culture, their habits, and their religion. The last point in particular has been put forward after the terror attacks of 9/11 and the wars against Al Qaeda, the Taliban, and ISIS. Immigrants are not only perceived as a threat to Western identity, but also as a security threat. These arguments have to be taken seriously. It is true that Islam is being used as the ideological cover for terrorist movements and sometimes recently arrived immigrants have been involved in terrorist attacks. However, more often these attacks were perpetrated by people born and educated in the West. The question is whether one should close the border for a whole group of migrants because some individuals pose a risk. For the Dutch populist Pim Fortuyn this was obvious. The Netherlands is full, was his conclusion, therefore we have to close the frontiers.[6] Trump came to a similar conclusion, wanting to build a wall along the Mexican frontier and signing, in January 2017, an executive order temporarily barring people from seven Muslim-majority countries from entering the US.[7]

Four approaches toward immigration

As concerns migration, there are four possible approaches:

- The populist approach: close the frontiers.
- The assimilationist approach: put pressure on immigrants to adapt to the culture and traditions of their new homeland.

- The multicultural approach: enable immigrants to keep their own language, culture, and traditions.
- The constitutional approach: expect immigrants to adhere to the principles of a liberal democratic polity.

Closing the frontiers and declaring that the country is "full" is the populist solution. This is not only contrary to the 1951 United Nations Convention relating to the Status of Refugees and other international conventions, but it has also negative economic consequences for the country which closes the frontier. Another approach is the assimilationist approach. In 2000 the German conservative parties CDU/CSU proposed introducing the principle of a *Leitkultur*, a "guiding culture" of Christian inspiration. This concept led to deep controversy when socialists and Greens accused the conservatives of lacking tolerance of diversity, aiming at the complete assimilation of newcomers. In 2017 interior minister Thomas de Maizière came up with this idea again, proposing a "ten-point catalogue." One of the points on this catalogue was that "Germany is part of the West" and that "our freedom is protected by NATO."[8] This may be true for the majority of Germans, but does it make sense to formulate such explicit political statements as a condition of accepting migrants? The concept of a "guiding culture" confers the idea that the culture of the indigenous population is not only superior to other cultures and that migrants should adapt themselves, but "culture" is also perceived as something immutable and given, instead of something that changes over time.

A quite different approach is multiculturalism, a model practiced in the US, Britain, and the Netherlands. The Dutch case in particular is an extreme example of this approach. The Netherlands, said Sniderman and Hagendoorn, "has awarded special influence to minority community leaders; established a separate state-funded school system for minorities; funded and organized housing projects designed to accommodate their religious practices; dedicated a significant portion of public radio and television media broadcasting time to minority interests; and in a variety of ways increased the power of spokesmen for the Muslim community who pride themselves on rejecting Western European values."[9] The Netherlands is an exemplary case of paternalistic pampering of immigrants in the name of "tolerance of diversity." The government and the political parties hoped that the newly arrived minorities would reciprocate and embrace the tolerance of their new home country. This policy, however, completely backfired:

> Dutch governments have made a broad commitment to preserving, indeed, promoting, a Muslim way of life – or more exactly, one version of a Muslim way of life … one that holds sway in rural and remote areas. The commitment of the government to

multiculturalism was a good-faith commitment. No one anticipated that liberal values would be used to legitimize illiberal practices. But so they have.[10]

The Dutch approach was to give rights to minority groups and to treat immigrants primarily as members of a group. This was different from the German approach, where foreign workers and immigrants were not treated as group members, but as individuals who, as individual persons, could claim certain rights. Dutch "liberal tolerance" was, in the end, incompatible with liberal individualism. For example, how should one react to cases in which the autonomy of the individual to choose his or her own life collided with the minority's group norms, which was evident in the case of Muslim women?[11] It is clear that one should not accept uncritically or tolerate cultural and religious habits that are at odds with basic Western values. From the beginning of the 1990s Dutch multiculturalism, which had led to social segregation and high unemployment among minorities, was increasingly criticized. In 1996 the Dutch government changed course, introducing mandatory language and integration courses for new immigrants. In 2003 the Dutch migration expert Han Entzinger could say: "Current policy can be labelled as quasi-assimilationist. The Dutch flirtation with multiculturalism is over."[12]

This brings us to the last approach to immigrant integration: the constitutional approach. Jürgen Habermas distinguishes two levels of acculturation. The first is the level of political socialization, which means that the immigrant accepts the principles of the constitution; the second is "the further level of a willingness to become acculturated, that is, not only to conform externally but to become habituated to the way of life, the practices, and customs of the local culture."[13] Habermas concludes that "a democratic constitutional state that is serious about uncoupling these two levels of integration can require of immigrants only the political socialization described ... above (and practically speaking can expect to see it only in the second generation)."[14]

Habermas is right that the receiving country can expect that immigrants respect the laws and the constitution of their new home country. But maybe it may expect a bit more. As Alan Wolfe rightly argues: "Once a society admits new members, those members are also under an obligation to open themselves to their new society ... There is a liberal bargain with respect to immigration ... Its basic premise is this: we will be open to you if you are open to us."[15] This commitment to openness, asked in particular of Muslim immigrants, includes abstaining from wearing the burqa, which shuts a woman off from everyone around her. It includes also that she does not refuse to shake hands with men or to consult a male doctor. Habits which emphasize mutual separation and apartheid should be avoided. This does not mean that these minorities should give up their own traditions. Nor should they be forced to give up habits or religious traditions which do not violate the law or fence them off from the outside world. It means that new immigrants should learn the language and accept the overarching political and democratic values of their new home country. When the religious or cultural traditions of immigrants come into conflict with these basic values, immigrants have a clear choice: "either they must accommodate themselves or yield, or if the espouser of them cannot do either, he must give up membership of the liberal society and seek a place where he can live according to his alternative values."[16]

The question of the "absorption capacity" of receiving countries

An important question in the immigration debate is the "absorption capacity" of the receiving country. We have already seen how French prime minister Michel Rocard argued that France could not "take in all the world's misery." Similar observations have been made for other countries. One author wrote that "refugee settlement in the United States has ceased to be a practical option. In an overpopulated world, the capacity to unleash disasters and to inflict suffering far exceeds this nation's capacity to absorb the victims."[17]

In 1995 the American sociologist Immanuel Wallerstein predicted that "by 2025 or so, in North America, the EC, and (even) Japan, the population socially defined as being of 'Southern' origin may well range from twenty-five to fifty percent."[18] And Samuel Huntington warned, in the same alarmist vein, that "cultural America is under siege,"[19] adding that "no society is immortal ... Even the most successful societies are at some point threatened by internal disintegration and by more vigorous and ruthless external 'barbarian' forces."[20] Unlike Huntington, Francis Fukuyama, himself a third-generation Japanese American, didn't believe that the "barbarians" should be stopped, nor could be stopped, but that the real issue was their assimilation, writing: "The real fight, the central fight, then, should not be over keeping newcomers out: this will be a waste of time and energy. The real fight ought to be over the question of assimilation itself: whether we believe that there is enough to our Western, rational, egalitarian, democratic civilization to force those coming to the country to absorb its language and rules."[21]

Recently, climate change has also entered the discussion. There are alarming articles in the press on how global warming could affect future refugee flows. One study predicted that in the case of an increase in global temperature of 4.5 to 5 degrees Celsius, asylum requests in Europe could increase by 188 percent before the year 2100.[22] These doom-laden scenarios are compounded by predictions concerning demographic developments in Africa: "More than 1 billion inhabitants in 2017, more than 2 billion in 2050," which means that "there will be a strong migratory push toward Europe."[23]

In 2015 the wars in Syria, Iraq, and elsewhere led to the sudden arrival in Europe of almost 1.3 million people, who applied for asylum. German chancellor Angela Merkel pleaded for an open-door policy, famously declaring "We will manage" (*Wir schaffen das*). Germany received 441,800 first-time applicants, which was more than one-third of the 1,255,640 first-time asylum applications made that year in the EU28.[24] Many Germans, however, did not agree, and in the parliamentary elections of September 2017 the Allianz für Deutschland, the extreme right anti-immigration party, won ninety-four seats in parliament and became the country's third largest party.

Because of this unexpected boost in the number of refugees 2015 was a special year. The French migration expert Jean-Claude Barreau speaks in this context of "tolerance rhythms." "If the flow of arrivals is slow," he writes, "we have perfectly accepted immigration."[25] In this case there is "reinforcement immigration." "However, if the flows of arrivals are too fast, we are confronted with uncontrollable movements which scare the natives."[26] Populists then call for "taking back control." However, when these calls lead to impulsive measures they can be expected to backfire. As Saskia Sassen rightly remarks: "If a government has, for instance, a very liberal policy on asylum, public opinion may turn against all asylum seekers and close up the country totally; this in turn is likely to promote an increase in irregular entries."[27]

Merkel's decision to open the frontier was not inspired exclusively by pure altruism: it also served clear German interests. In a report of an independent experts' commission on immigration headed by Rita Süssmuth, a former speaker of parliament, the authors wrote that "the German population is aging and will clearly decline in the twenty-first century." They warned that "without further immigration and with the number of children per woman staying the same, the German population will decrease from 82 million to less than 60 million, up to 2050." This would cause huge problems for the German economy, they indicated, "because it is already impossible to fill many high and low qualified jobs."[28]

There exists, therefore, a clear economic rationale for the fact that over the last few decades Germany has become one of the world's major immigration countries. In 2017 14.8 percent of the German population was made up of immigrants, which is only slightly different from the United States, where the percentage is 15.3.[29] It is interesting that in 2016 the demographic predictions of the Süssmuth commission seemed to be confirmed. In that year the demographic balance (live births minus deaths) of the German population was negative. Without immigration the population would have declined by 150,000 people.[30] According to the French economist Philippe Askenazy, in Germany "one would need a yearly net immigration of 400,000 persons during the two coming decennia to compensate the natural decline of the working age population."[31] The need for manpower can only partially be satisfied by robotization and artificial intelligence. The need to attract immigrants will remain. It is against this background that immigration policies must be judged.

Another example is Canada, where the government is boosting its immigration. It plans to bring in 310,000 new permanent residents in 2018, 330,000 in 2019, and 340,000 in 2020.[32] In a country which, in 2016, had just over 35 million inhabitants, this means that it will increase its population through immigration by about 1 percent a year. The reasons are the same as in Germany: a rapidly aging population. By 2036 the number of senior citizens in Canada will be more than double what it was in 2009. Immigration minister Hussen declared that "if we are going to be able to keep our commitments for health care and pensions and all our social programs and to continue to grow our economy and meet our labour market needs in the decades to come, we must respond to this clear demographic challenge."[33] One percent net immigration a year seems to be a good estimate of an optimal "absorption capacity." The Canadian approach is a mix of economic and humanitarian considerations, combining 58 percent "pull" immigration (i.e. economic immigrants of which 40 percent are highly skilled) and 42 percent "push" immigration (27 percent family reunions and 15 percent refugees and protected persons).

How information reduces anxiety, particularly among conservative voters

Despite the clear benefits for both immigrants and the receiving countries, immigration continues to cause fear as well as anger, and both negative emotions are exploited by far-right populists. How can people's anxiety and anger be reduced? In the first place by implementing a sustainable immigration policy. This means an immigration policy that neither closes the door, nor throws the door wide open, but prudently combines a humane approach with the country's legitimate economic interests. This includes fast-track asylum procedures, possibly taking no more than two months for initial procedures. It means also that rejected asylum-seekers are returned to their countries of origin (these countries could be made more cooperative by granting its nationals quotas for work permits and/or legal immigration).[34]

Last but not least, it means giving the population clear and reliable information on immigration. It is telling, for instance, that estimates of the number of undocumented migrants are often greatly exaggerated. Donald Trump said that there could be 30 million undocumented migrants in the United States,[35] while different reliable sources estimate the number at about 11 million.³⁶ Of course, it is difficult to convince a prejudiced audience. However, it is interesting that giving detailed factual information can change attitudes. In a survey conducted in the United States, the researchers observed that most respondents had exaggerated ideas about the number of immigrants. When respondents were confronted with the real numbers, they were ready to review their attitudes. "People who self-identify as Republican," wrote the authors,

> respond more strongly to the information treatment than people who identify as Democrat or as neither Republican nor Democrat. Indeed, we observe that Republicans are more likely than other political groups to change their beliefs about immigrants, to become more supportive of policy reforms favoring immigrants, and to accept to sign a pro-immigrant petition.³⁷

These results were a real surprise, not least because the researchers also found that respondents "who favoured Trump or Cruz in the Republican primary respond more strongly to the information treatment."³⁸ They concluded: "The government could disseminate information about immigrants in order to reduce people's biases," because "targeting individuals with the most negative views on immigration would be the most effective way of changing people's attitudes towards immigrants."³⁹

These findings in the US are confirmed by a survey conducted in the Netherlands by the University of Utrecht. "In every political party," write Sniderman and Hagendoorn,

> there is a faction especially ready to respond negatively to minorities. Paradoxically, it is the one that most easily can be influenced to respond positively to them. They can most easily be influenced because they attach the most importance to the value of conformity: and the more importance people attach to conformity, the more susceptible to influence they are. Hence the paradox: those who are most likely to respond negatively to immigrant minorities are most susceptible to influence to respond positively to them. Ironically, the intolerant afford politicians an extra margin to maneuver in favor of tolerance.⁴⁰

It is, paradoxically, the *conformity* of the populist voter which could provide governments with a handle on how to change prejudiced attitudes.

Very interesting also are the results of a British panel survey on attitudes toward immigration, conducted before and after the Brexit referendum. The researchers observed "a recent softening of attitudes toward immigration among Britons."⁴¹ What was surprising was that reacting to the statement "Immigration [is] good for the economy," *both* Remain voters and Leave voters had become more positive after the Brexit referendum. As concerns a statement about incoming workers from EU countries, "it is the Leavers who had the greater shift towards becoming more pro-immigration ... a large number of Leavers shifted from an unfavourable to a neutral position." The authors argued that the factors which could have played a role in this change "include the decline in net migration, which received news coverage."[42] Which means that after the Brexit campaign with its populist slogans had passed even Leave voters let themselves be influenced by the hard facts.

Notes

1 Interview Michel Rocard, 3 December 1989, *Le Monde*, Dictionnaire des citations. http://dicocitations.lemonde.fr/citations/citation-76371.php (accessed 29 January 2018).
2 Cf. Marc de Boni, "Le théoricien du 'grand remplacement' rejoint la galaxie FN," *Le Figaro*, 23 November 2015. www.lefigaro.fr/politique/le-scan/coulisses/2015/11/23/25006-20151123ARTFIG00204-le-theoricien-du-grand-remplacement-rejoint-la-galaxie-fn.php (accessed 29 January 2018).
3 Barreau, *De l'immigration*, p. 53.
4 David Card, "The Impact of the Mariel Boatlift on the Miami Labor Market," *Industrial and Labor Relations Review*, Vol. 43, No. 2, January 1990, p. 256. http://davidcard.berkeley.edu/papers/mariel-impact.pdf (accessed 29 January 2018).
5 Anthony Edo, "Migrations et salaires: Le cas des rapatriés d'Algérie," *La Lettre du CEPII*, No. 383, December 2017. www.cepii.fr/PDF_PUB/lettre/2017/let383.pdf (accessed 30 January 2018).
6 Fortuyn, *Islamisering van onze cultuur*, p. 101.
7 "Trump's executive order: Who does travel ban affect?" BBC, 10 February 2017. www.bbc.com/news/world-us-canada-38781302 (accessed 30 January 2018).
8 "German interior minister speaks out in favor of 'Leitkultur' for immigrants," *Deutsche Welle*, 30 April 2017. www.dw.com/en/german-interior-minister-speaks-out-in-favor-of-leitkultur-for-immigrants/a-38643836 (accessed 30 January 2018).
9 Sniderman and Hagendoorn, *When Ways of Life Collide*, pp. 132–133.
10 Ibid., p. 130.
11 Cf. Seyla Benhabib, who writes that "because the right of autonomous individuals to develop for themselves their idea of a good life [and] to strive for this good ... is one of the primary premises of political liberalism, merging individual legal claims into group rights is clearly a violation of the tenets of political liberalism" (Seyla Benhabib, *Kulturelle Vielfalt und demokratische Gleichheit – Politische Partizipation im Zeitalter der Globalisierung* (Frankfurt am Main: Fischer, 1999), p. 57).
12 Han Entzinger, "The Rise and Fall of Dutch Multiculturalism," Lecture in the conference "Migration – Citizenship – Ethnos. Incorporation Regimes in Germany, Western Europe and North America," Toronto, 2–4 October 2003.
13 Jürgen Habermas, "Struggles for Recognition in the Democratic Constitutional State," in Amy Gutmann (ed.), *Multiculturalism – Examining the Politics of Recognition* (Princeton: Princeton University Press, 1994), p. 138.
14 Ibid., p. 139.
15 Wolfe, *Future of Liberalism*, p. 205.
16 A. C. Grayling, "Isaiah Berlin and Liberty," in Grayling, *Liberty in the Age of Terror*, p. 166.
17 Gerda Bikales, "The Golden Rule in the Age of the Global Village," in Nicolaus Mills (ed.), *Arguing Immigration – Are New Immigrants a Wealth of Diversity ... or a Crushing Burden?* (New York and London: Simon & Schuster, 1994), p. 209.

18 Wallerstein, *After Liberalism*, p. 34.
19 Huntington, *Who Are We?*, p. 12.
20 Ibid., p. 11.
21 Francis Fukuyama, "Immigrants and Family Values," in Mills (ed.), *Arguing Immigration*, p. 164.
22 Simon Roger, "Le climat entraînera un afflux de migrants en Europe," *Le Monde*, 23 December 2017.
23 Alain Frachon, "La peur de l'Afrique," *Le Monde*, 9 February 2018.
24 Eurostat, "Asylum in the EU Member States," News Release 44/2016, 4 March 2016. http://ec.europa.eu/eurostat/documents/2995521/7203832/3-04032016-AP-EN.pdf/ (accessed 9 February 2018).
25 Barreau, *De l'immigration*, p. 82.
26 Ibid., p. 83.
27 Saskia Sassen, *Losing Control – Sovereignty in an Age of Globalization* (New York: Columbia University Press, 1995), p. 79.
28 "Zuwanderung gestalten – Integration fördern," Report of the Independent Commission "Zuwanderung," 2001. www.fluechtlingsrat.org/download/berkommzusfas.pdf (accessed 9 February 2018).
29 Migration Data Portal, IOM. http://gmdac.iom.int/migration-data-portal (accessed 9 February 2018).
30 "Population and population change statistics," *Eurostat*, July 2017. http://ec.europa.eu/eurostat/statistics-explained/index.php/Population_and_population_change_statistics (accessed 10 February 2018).
31 Philippe Askenazy, "Robots ou travailleurs immigrés," *Le Monde*, 16 November 2018.
32 Dakshana Bascaramurty, "Canada aims for immigration boost to buttress economy as population ages," *Globe and Mail*, 1 November 2017. www.theglobeandmail.com/news/politics/canada-to-admit-40000-more-immigrants-a-year-by-2020-under-liberals-new-three-year-plan/article36800775/ (accessed 11 February 2018).
33 Ibid.
34 Cf. John Gibson, "The removal of failed asylum seekers: International norms and procedures," New Issues in Refugee Research, Research Paper No. 145, UNHCR, Policy Development and Evaluation Service, December 2007. www.unhcr.org/research/working/476651262/removal-failed-asylum-seekers-international-norms-procedures-john-gibson.html (accessed 11 February 2018).
35 Linda Qiu and Amy Sherman, "Donald Trump repeats Pants on Fire claim about '30 million' illegal immigrants," *Politifact*, 1 September 2016. www.politifact.com/truth-o-meter/statements/2016/sep/01/donald-trump/donald-trump-repeats-pants-fire-claim-about-30-mil/ (accessed 12 February 2018).
36 Robert Stribley, "There is no illegal immigrant crisis," *Huffington Post*, 22 August 2016. www.huffingtonpost.com/entry/there-is-no-illegal-immigrant-crisis_us_57acc15ae4b0ae60ff01fed2 (accessed 15 February 2018).
37 Alexis Grigorieff, Christopher Roth, and Diego Ubfal, "Does Information Change Attitudes Towards Immigrants? Representative Evidence from Survey Experiments," IZA, *Discussion Paper* No. 10419, December 2016, pp. 17–18.
38 Ibid., p. 18.
39 Ibid., p. 24.
40 Sniderman and Hagendoorn, *When Ways of Life Collide*, p. 136.

41 Dr. Scott Blinder and Dr. Lindsay Richards, "UK Public Opinion toward Immigration: Overall Attitudes and Level of Concern," The Migration Observatory of the University of Oxford, 7 June 2018. https://migrationobservatory.ox.ac.uk/resources/briefings/uk-public-opinion-toward-immigration-overall-attitudes-and-level-of-concern/ (accessed 1 September 2018).
42 Ibid.

Conclusion

Is populism a transitory phenomenon? Some say so. The conservative Spanish prime minister Mariano Rajoy, for instance, said that "populism is a conjunctural phenomenon" which would disappear with economic recovery.[1] However, even when economic recovery was apparent, populism did not disappear. On the contrary, in the last decade populism has conquered the world's largest democracies, including Brazil and the United States.

What many people forget is that populism is a child of liberal democracy, a "problem child" admittedly, but a child nevertheless. Or, to put it differently, populism is the shadow of liberal democracy. Like a shadow, which follows a person who is walking in the sun, populism follows liberal democracy wherever it goes – at one moment surreptitiously, without anyone noticing, at other moments its presence overwhelming, dark, threatening. The reason for this is that populism feeds off an inbuilt contradiction in liberal democracy: on the one hand it proclaims that "the people" are the ultimate sovereign; on the other hand it defends the rights and freedoms of the individual and minorities against majority decisions, limiting the power of government. According to C. B. Macpherson,

> Liberal theory proper – the theory of individual rights and limited government – goes back, of course, to the seventeenth century. But until the nineteenth century, liberal theory, like the state, was not at all democratic; much of it was specifically anti-democratic. Liberal-democratic theory thus came as an uneasy compound of the classical liberal theory and the democratic principle of the equal entitlement of every man to a voice in choosing government and to some other satisfactions. It was an uneasy compound because the classical liberal theory was committed to the individual right to unlimited acquisition of property, to the capitalist market economy, and hence to inequality, and it was feared that these might be endangered by giving votes to the poor.[2]

The idea that government should be limited one can already find in John Locke (1632–1704), who, in his *Second Treatise of Government*, wrote that "the great and

Conclusion

chief end, therefore, of men's uniting into common-wealths, and putting themselves under government, *is the preservation of their property*."[3] No government, said Locke, had the right to infringe this right. Governments, therefore, should be limited. The idea that liberalism and democracy form an uneasy combination was also expressed by Norberto Bobbio, who wrote "liberalism and democracy are antithetical in the sense that democracy pushed to its furthest limits ends in the destruction of the liberal state."[4]

Macpherson called liberal democratic theory an "uneasy compound" and Bobbio called it "antithetical." And indeed, that is the case. For this reason populism will highly likely always be with us in one way or another, as long as we live in liberal democratic states. Although populism will be quasi absent in certain periods, it will sooner or later raise its head again and pop up in unexpected places. Populist revolts are the symptoms of popular disaffection and are, as such, an indication of real problems that exist in society. The point is that populist parties which pretend to offer solutions to these problems, instead of solving these problems, rather tend to deepen them.

Edward Luttwak's warning: a fascist America

This is particularly true of right-wing populist parties, which are often characterized by nationalism, racism, and xenophobia. "By 'nationalism'," wrote George Orwell, "I mean the habit of identifying oneself with a single nation or other unit, placing it beyond good and evil and recognizing no other duty than that of advancing its interests … Nationalism … is inseparable from the desire for power. The abiding purpose of every nationalist is to secure more power and more prestige, *not* for himself but for the nation or other unit in which he has chosen to sink his own individuality."[5] Extreme nationalism was a characteristic feature of the fascist regimes of the interbellum. Its resurgence in right-wing populist movements has led to accusations that these parties are a prelude to a re-emerging fascism, if not themselves already embodiments of a modern "fascism lite."

As early as 1994 the American political scientist Edward Luttwak warned of such a development. In a remarkable article, titled "Why Fascism is the Wave of the Future,"[6] Luttwak wrote:

> [T]hat structural change can inflict more disruption on working lives, firms, entire industries and their localities than individuals can absorb, or the connective tissue of friendships, families, clans, elective groupings, neighbourhoods, villages, towns, cities or even nations can withstand, is another old-hat truth more easily recognised than *Gemeinschaft* and *Gesellschaft* can be spelled. What is new-hat about the present

situation is only a matter of degree, a mere acceleration in the pace of structural changes that accompany economic growth, whatever its rate ... The engine turns, grinding lives and grinding down established human relationships, even when the car is stopped ... One obvious cause of the increased destructiveness of the capitalist process is the worldwide retreat of public ownership, central planning, administrative direction and regulatory control, with all their rigidities inimical to innovation, structural change, economic growth, individual dislocation and social disruption alike.[7]

Luttwak observed that the process of "creative destruction," touted by Schumpeter, led to an unbridled competition and destabilizing acceleration, which, deepened by globalization, led to a situation in which "once-secure enterprises face the perils of the market, and employees once equally secure no longer are so."[8] This analysis is not, of course, new. But what is interesting is that Luttwak already in 1994 observed that "neither the moderate Right nor the moderate Left even recognises, let alone offers any solution for the central problem of our days: the completely unprecedented personal economic insecurity of working people."[9] He concluded that "a vast space is thus left vacant" by these parties, "and this is the space that remains wide open for a product-improved Fascist party, dedicated to the enhancement of the personal economic security of the broad masses of (mainly) white-collar working people. Such a party could even be as free of racism as Mussolini's original was until the alliance with Hitler, because its real stock in trade would be corporativist restraints on corporate Darwinism, and delaying if not blocking barriers against globalisation."[10] Luttwak was not the first who warned against an American variant of fascism. Thomas Mann, in a lecture titled "War and Democracy," delivered on 3 October 1940 at Claremont College, Los Angeles, warned his audience with the words: "Let me tell you the whole truth: if ever Fascism should come to America, it will come in the name of freedom."[11]

The election of Donald Trump as president of the United States has put this question even higher up the agenda. It is clear that Luttwak's prediction that alongside the Republican Party and the Democratic Party a Fascist Party would develop, didn't materialize. We could rather observe a process in which the Republican Party morphed into a party which has become the party of Trump. The question is: Is Trump a fascist?

One of the first commentators to ask this question was Jeffrey Tucker, who followed Trump during the Republican primaries in 2015. "I just heard Trump speak live," he wrote. "The speech lasted an hour, and my jaw was on the floor most of the time. I've never before witnessed such a brazen display of nativistic jingoism, along with a complete disregard for economic reality. It was an awesome experience, a perfect repudiation of all good sense and intellectual sobriety."[12] Tucker continued:

Conclusion

"His speech was like an interwar séance of once-powerful dictators who inspired multitudes, drove countries into the ground and died grim deaths ... Since World War II, the ideology he represents has usually lived in dark corners, and we don't even have a name for it anymore. The right name, the correct name, the historically accurate name is fascism. I don't use that word as an insult only. It is accurate."[13]

This was before Trump's election. After his election the commentaries became even more alarming. The neoconservative publicist Robert Kagan, for instance, published an article in the *Washington Post* titled "This is how fascism comes to America." What Trump offers his followers, Kagan wrote,

> are not economic remedies – his proposals change daily. What he offers is an attitude, an aura of crude strength and machismo, a boasting disrespect for the niceties of the democratic culture that he claims, and his followers believe, has produced national weakness and incompetence. His incoherent and contradictory utterances have one thing in common: They provoke and play on feelings of resentment and disdain, intermingled with bits of fear, hatred and anger. His public discourse consists of attacking or ridiculing a wide range of "others" – Muslims, Hispanics, women, Chinese, Mexicans, Europeans, Arabs, immigrants, refugees – whom he depicts either as threats or as objects of derision.[14]

Kagan's conclusion was clear: "This is how fascism comes to America, not with jackboots and salutes (although there have been salutes and a whiff of violence) but with a television huckster, a phony billionaire, a textbook egomaniac 'tapping into' popular resentments and insecurities and within an entire national party ... falling in line behind him."[15] The political commentator Michael Kinsley was also quite clear. "Donald Trump is actually a fascist," he wrote.[16] In an interview, the Holocaust historian Timothy Snyder didn't even exclude regime change: "The general circumstances are when an unusual figure is elected by way of normal mechanisms at a time when for other reasons the system is under stress."[17] He warned that "things can go in all kinds of directions ... We're in a long-term relationship with disaster."[18] It is clear that in the time of the COVID-19 crisis these dangers have only increased.

Trump is not the only populist leader who has been accused of being a fascist. In the Netherlands, for instance, Rob Riemen, a philosopher, attacked Geert Wilders's Freedom Party for being fascist. "In Europe there exists a taboo on using the word 'fascism,'" he wrote, "insofar as it is related to contemporary political phenomena. There is right extremism, radical right, populism, rightwing populism, but fascism ... no, that doesn't exist: that cannot be true, such a thing does no longer exist in our societies, we live in a democracy, please, don't sow panic and insult people."[19] Riemen argued that "in the body of mass democracy the bacillus [of] fascism will always be virulently present. To deny this fact or to give the bacillus a different name will not make us resistant."[20]

Using the infamous f-word: is it legitimate?

Is using the infamous f-word to characterize contemporary populist phenomena not exaggerated? The Italian historian Enzo Traverso tried to relativize these criticisms, putting them in perspective. "Trump has been labeled a fascist," he said. "However, these analyses are often superficial and are focused on the personality of the republican candidate."[21] "In fact behind Trump there is no fascist movement. Trump is not the leader of a mass movement; he is a TV star. From this point of view one could compare him with Berlusconi rather than with Mussolini. He doesn't threaten to let his blackshirts (or brownshirts) march on Washington, for the simple reason that he has no organized troops behind him."[22] And, he continued: "He is at the same time protectionist and neoliberal … wanting to cut taxes in a radical way … Well, the classical fascisms were not neoliberal, they were very statist and imperialist, in favor of policies of military expansion. Trump is anti-statist and rather isolationist."[23]

Traverso is right to stress the differences between contemporary right-wing populist parties and the fascist regimes of the interbellum. He insists that one should not cry wolf too early. But this caution shouldn't make us blind to tendencies that are really worrying. Modern populism may lack the mysticism of the fascist regimes and not organize torch-lit parades at twilight, nor quasi-religious mass ceremonies. However, there exist important similarities, such as the reverence for the leader and the leader's central role in the organization. Both movements are examples of what Max Weber called the "charismatic" leadership model.[24] Charismatic leadership means authoritarian leadership, because the worshipped and venerated leader is considered to possess a unique wisdom and insight and doesn't need to take anyone else's advice. His followers are, therefore, in the strictest sense of the word "followers."

These movements purport to transcend the left–right divide and to represent the interests of the whole nation and not only of certain classes or groups. Although these populists play according to the established democratic rules, they tend to circumvent and change these rules, while galvanizing their audience by using vulgar language and conducting attacks *ad hominem* by unfounded demagogical accusations. Like the fascists of the interbellum these populists refer to the past, suggesting that everything was better in the past and that they are the harbingers of a "national rebirth." The only difference is that the "past" of the populists is less distant than

Conclusion

the "past" of the fascists. When Trump speaks of "Making America Great Again," he doesn't refer to the American Revolution or the era of the Founding Fathers, but rather to the recent post-Second World War period. When the Italian Fascists or the Nazis referred to the past, this was to a distant, mythological past, respectively the Roman Empire and a pre-Christian, "Aryan" civilization. However, in both cases this celebration of the past is the celebration of a *national* glorious past: a past which belongs exclusively to the "original" inhabitants of the country, who have lived in the country since time immemorial. Recent newcomers, such as refugees and immigrants – certainly when they come from regions with different religions and habits – don't fit into this national picture. Minorities also don't fit in.

Equally, on the level of ideology there are many striking similarities. Right-wing populists share fascism's objective of the creation of a strong state. For fascists this was a necessary precondition for their imperialist goals. Only a strong state could build a strong army. Populists don't share these imperialist goals. They need a strong state in order to protect the citizen from the forces of globalization. For fascists the strong state is an offensive state: a precondition for the conquest of the world. For right-wing populists a strong state is a defensive state: a precondition to protect the national frontiers against the "enemy from without": terrorists, illegal immigrants, Islam, cheap labor, cheap foreign products, dangerous viruses and other supposed health threats.

Racism is an inherent element of the fascist creed. Modern right-wing populists, however, are talking less about "race," a term which has become politically incorrect, but have developed a "cultural" variant: emphasizing the incompatibility of certain cultures and religions, in particular Islam, with Western Christian culture.

Both fascists and right-wing populists regard politics as a zero-sum game: it is a political fight in which the gains of the one are the losses of the other. Political opponents are not treated as contenders in fair elections, with whom one should sometimes cooperate or make compromises, but rather as irreconcilable enemies – in the tradition of Carl Schmitt.

Although right-wing populism lacks fascism's violent, putschist, militaristic, and imperialistic dimension, it is fascism's "junior partner" in many other dimensions. Between right-wing populism and fascism there seems to exist what Germans call a *Wahlverwandtschaft*, an elective affinity of mutual attraction and resemblance.

This affinity can be observed also in fascism's country of origin: Italy, where on several occasions right-wing populist leaders have openly praised the benefits of Benito Mussolini's regime. Silvio Berlusconi repeatedly praised the *Duce*. In 2003 he said in an interview that "Mussolini never killed anyone. Mussolini used to send people on vacation in internal exile," an association of Italian Fascism with "holidays" which was already popular in Mussolini's time.[25] In a speech in 2013 on Holocaust Memorial Day he said that "the racial laws were the worst fault of Mussolini as a leader, who in so many other ways did well."[26] In the 1980s Berlusconi was a paid-up member of Licio Gelli's secret Masonic lodge "Propaganda 2" (P2), an organization which had links with the members of the junta in Argentina. P2 was, according to an Italian Parliamentary Commission of Inquiry, a secret Masonic lodge which "made internal use of illegal and criminal methods against the law and the constitutional state."[27] Berlusconi was the first European politician who, in 1994, invited a neo-fascist party, the MSI, to become a coalition partner in his first government. He has been accused of being a fascist.[28]

More recently Lega leader Matteo Salvini followed in Berlusconi's footsteps, heaping praise on Mussolini, declaring that "in the twenty years before the foolish alliance with Hitler and the racial laws he has certainly done good things."[29] According to Rino Genovese, "Fascism in Italy hasn't been, like elsewhere in Europe, a temporary totalitarian solution … to the problems of mass society … In Italy it has become much more: the sediment of a diffuse historical psychology that eventually has been condensed in the anthropological DNA of the country."[30] And Paul Ginsborg emphasized the "particular role for Italy in the modern world: that of inventing from time to time new dictatorial models. In the 1920s fascism was the first example of a contemporary mass tyranny, which was copied on a large scale and developed further in the next twenty years. Today one admits that the years that Silvio Berlusconi was in power are not simply a passing spectacle, but are founded on the creation of a new type of regime, which is formally democratic, but in reality controlled from above."[31]

Does this mean that a fascist takeover is imminent? Not really. One may expect that old, long-established European democracies will contain the populist upheaval. The problem is rather whether the young democracies in Central and Eastern Europe are strong enough to resist. These countries, the heirs of autocratic regimes, lack a long experience with liberal democracy. In Poland Jarosław Kaczyński's Law and Justice Party and in Hungary Viktor Orbán's Fidesz party attack the liberal foundations of their states. Southern Europe is equally a region at risk. Four countries in this region: not only Italy, but equally Spain, Portugal, and Greece had in the twentieth century fascist regimes. Salazar founded his Estado Novo in 1933. Franco came to power in 1939 through a military coup. The Portuguese Estado Novo came to an end in 1974 through a coup organized by military officers. Franco died in 1975 and with him his regime. Both regimes outlived their German and Italian counterparts by about thirty years.

Conclusion

For a long time Germany has been considered to be "immune" to extreme right populism – due to its rigorous policy of *Vergangenheitsbewältigung* (coming to terms with its past). However, this is changing. The emergence of the AfD in Germany is a matter of concern. In the 2019 regional elections the AfD got almost one-quarter of the votes in four *Länder* of eastern Germany, where it became the second largest party. In Latin America it is not only right-wing populist movements which are a threat to democracy, but equally left-wing populist movements. The regimes of Hugo Chávez and Nicolas Máduro in Venezuela and Evo Morales in Bolivia stand out as examples of corrupt, autocratic rule.

And what about the United States? The British historian Eric Hobsbawm said that "ultimately, it does not matter much who is president of the United States: since 1865, seven presidents have been killed or forced to withdraw before the end of their terms, and they were replaced by persons not selected to run the country. Yet the history of America was not significantly changed by these traumas. In the United States the rails along which the train of power runs are so stable that whoever is driving can do it without derailment."[32] Is this true? One might hope so. Hobsbawm made this remark sixteen years before the arrival of Donald Trump. Much depends on the strength of the American institutions. And even these institutions provide no automatic guarantee. They depend for their effectiveness on the active support of the citizens. Rather than impenetrable dams these institutions are like river dikes: they suffice in normal times to contain the stream, but run the risk of overflowing in extreme circumstances. We have, therefore, many reasons to remain vigilant.

Notes

1. Quoted in Jorge Alemán and Germán Cano, *Del desencanto al populismo – Encrucijada de una época* (Barcelona: Ned Ediciones, 2016), p. 169.
2. C. B. Macpherson, "Post-Liberal-Democracy?" in Macpherson, *Democratic Theory*, pp. 172–173.
3. John Locke, *Second Treatise of Government*, edited by C. B. Macpherson (Indianapolis and Cambridge: Hackett Publishing Company, Inc., 1980), § 124, p. 66. In case their property rights are not respected, Locke even grants the people the right of revolution.
4. Bobbio, pp. 48–49.
5. George Orwell, *Notes on Nationalism* (London: Penguin Books, 2018), p. 2.
6. Edward Luttwak, "Why Fascism is the Wave of the Future," *London Review of Books*, Vol. 16, No. 7, 7 April 1994. www.lrb.co.uk/the-paper/v16/n07/edward-luttwak/why-fascism-is-the-wave-of-the-future (accessed 19 February 2018).
7. Ibid.
8. Ibid. This phenomenon that economic growth doesn't lead to more happiness, but, on the contrary, may lead to less happiness, is called by Carol Graham the "paradox of unhappy growth." She found "strong negative effects for the first stages of growth in

'miracle' growth economies, such as Ireland and South Korea during their take-off stages" (cf. Carol Graham, *Happiness around the World – The Paradox of Happy Peasants and Miserable Millionaires* (Oxford and New York: Oxford University Press, 2009), p. 148).
9   Luttwak, "Wave of the Future."
10 Ibid.
11 Quoted in Rob Riemen, *De eeuwige terugkeer van het fascisme* (Amsterdam and Antwerp: Atlas, 2010), p. 39.
12 Jeffrey A. Tucker, "Is Donald Trump a Fascist?" *Newsweek*, 17 July 2015. www.newsweek.com/donald-trump-fascist-354690 (accessed 20 February 2018).
13 Ibid.
14 Robert Kagan, "This is how fascism comes to America," *Washington Post*, 18 May 2016. www.washingtonpost.com/opinions/this-is-how-fascism-comes-to-america/2016/05/17/c4e32c58–1c47–11e6–8c7b-6931e66333e7_story.html?utm_term=.fdbc37c61aee (accessed 20 February 2018).
15 Ibid.
16 Michael Kinsley, "Donald Trump is actually a fascist," *Washington Post*, 9 December 2016. www.washingtonpost.com/opinions/donald-trump-is-actually-a-fascist/2016/12/09/e193a2b6-bd77–11e6–94ac-3d324840106c_story.html?utm_term=.e43bd9b191e2 (accessed 21 February 2018).
17 Quoted in Sean Illing, "'Post-truth is pre-fascism': A Holocaust historian on the Trump era," *Vox*, 9 March 2017. www.vox.com/conversations/2017/3/9/14838088/donald-trump-fascism-europe-history-totalitarianism-post-truth (accessed 22 February 2018).
18 Ibid.
19 Riemen, *De eeuwige terugkeer*, p. 8.
20 Ibid., p. 9.
21 Enzo Traverso, *Les nouveaux visages du fascisme,* Conversation avec Régis Meyran (Paris: Les éditions Textuel, 2017), p. 25.
22 Ibid., p. 26.
23 Ibid., p. 27.
24 Cf. Max Weber, "Die drei reinen Typen der legitimen Herrschaft. Eine soziologische Studie," in Weber, *Schriften 1894–1922*, pp. 725–733.
25 Quoted in "Mussolini non ha mai ammazzato nessuno," *Corriere della Sera*, 11 September 2003.
26 "Berlusconi praises Mussolini on Holocaust Memorial Day," BBC, 27 January 2013. www.bbc.com/news/world-europe-21222341 (accessed 24 February 2018).
27 Commissione Parlamentare d'Inchiesta sulla Loggia Massonica P2 (Legge 23 settembre 1981, n 527), *Camera dei Deputati / Senato della Repubblica*, Roma, 1984, p. 176.
28 Antonio Gibelli writes that "in 2002, a group of Italian and foreign historians, professors of universities of high prestige, participated in a conference explicitly dedicated to the meaning and the limits of a comparison between berlusconism and fascism; all came to the conclusion that such a comparison was completely legitimate" (Gibelli, *Berlusconi*, p. 14).
29 Quoted in Sergio Rame, "Salvini loda Mussolini: Fece tante cose buone," *Il giornale*, 16 February 2016. www.ilgiornale.it/news/politica/salvini-loda-mussolini-fece-tante-cose-buone-1225808.html (accessed 24 February 2018).
30 Genovese, *Che cos'è il Berlusconismo*, p. 90.
31 Ginsborg, *Salviamo l'Italia*, p. 102. Italian Fascism was not only a model for Europeans to emulate. In 1938 Colonel Juan Perón (1895–1974) was sent to Italy and Germany in an

Conclusion

army training delegation to study the fascist systems. He stayed two years and returned in early 1941 to Argentina, where he became one of the instigators of the Grupo de Oficiales Unidos, a secret military lodge which organized a *coup d'état* in 1943. Perón would introduce an authoritarian populist regime in Argentina, which was inspired by Mussolini's model.

32 Hobsbawm, *Edge of the New Century*, p. 109.

Bibliography

Achen, Christopher H., and Bartels, Larry M., *Democracy for Realists: Why Elections Do Not Produce Responsive Government* (Princeton and Oxford: Princeton University Press, 2016).
Ackerman, Bruce, *The Future of Liberal Revolution* (New Haven and London: Yale University Press, 1992).
Albertazzi, Daniele, and McDonnell, Duncan, *Populists in Power* (Oxford and New York: Routledge, 2015).
Alemán, Jorge, and Cano, Germán, *Del desencanto al populismo: Encrucijada de una época* (Barcelona: Ned Ediciones, 2016).
Almond, Gabriel A., and Bingham Powell Jr., G., *Comparative Politics: A Developmental Approach* (Boston: Little, Brown and Company, 1966).
Almond, Gabriel A., and Verba, Sidney, *The Civic Culture: Political Attitudes and Democracy in Five Nations* (Princeton: Princeton University Press, 1963).
Alperovitz, Gar, *America Beyond Capitalism: Reclaiming Our Wealth, Our Liberty, and Our Democracy* (Hoboken: John Wiley & Sons, 2005).
Andersen, Jorgen Goul, "Nationalism, New Right, and New Cleavages in Danish Politics: Foreign and Security Policy of the Danish People's Party," in Christina Schori Liang (ed.), *Europe for the Europeans: The Foreign and Security Policy of the Populist Radical Right* (Aldershot: Ashgate, 2007).
Arendt, Hannah, *The Origins of Totalitarianism* (New York and London: Harcourt Brace Jovanovich, 1973).
Arendt, Hannah, "At Table with Hitler," in Hannah Arendt, *Essays in Understanding 1930–1954: Formation, Exile, and Totalitarianism* (New York: Schocken Books, 1994).
Arendt, Hannah, "Truth and Politics," in Hannah Arendt, *The Portable Hannah Arendt*, edited by Peter Baehr (New York and London: Penguin Books, 2000).
Aron, Raymond, *Démocratie et totalitarisme* (Paris: Gallimard, 1965).
Atkinson, Anthony B., *Inequality: What Can Be Done?* (Cambridge, Mass., and London: Harvard University Press, 2015).
Baldacchino, Adeline, *La ferme des énarques* (Paris: Michalon, 2015).
Barreau, Jean-Claude, *De l'immigration en général et de la nation française en particulier* (Paris: Le Pré aux Clercs, 1992).
Bartels, Larry M., *Presidential Primaries and the Dynamics of Public Choice* (Princeton: Princeton University Press, 1988).
Bauman, Zygmunt, *Wasted Lives: Modernity and Its Outcasts* (Cambridge: Polity Press, 2004).
Beck, Ulrich, *Democracy without Enemies* (Cambridge: Polity Press, 1998).

Bibliography

Beer, Samuel, *Modern British Politics: A Study of Parties and Pressure Groups* (London: Faber and Faber, 1969).
Bell, Daniel, *The End of Ideology* (Glencoe: The Free Press, 1960).
Bell, Daniel, *The Coming of Post-Industrial Society: A Venture in Social Forecasting* (New York: Basic Books, 1976).
Bell, Daniel, *The Cultural Contradictions of Capitalism* (London: Heinemann, 1979).
Bellah, Robert N.; Madsen, Richard; Sullivan, William M.; Swidler, Ann; and Tipton, Steven M.; *Habits of the Heart: Individualism and Commitment in American Life* (Berkeley, Los Angeles, and London: University of California Press, 1996).
Benhabib, Seyla, *Kulturelle Vielfalt und demokratische Gleichheit: Politische Partizipation im Zeitalter der Globalisierung* (Frankfurt am Main: Fischer, 1999).
Berger, Bennett, and Vaccarino, Elena, "Codetermination in Germany – A Role Model for the UK and the US?" *Bruegel*, 13 October 2016.
Bikales, Gerda, "The Golden Rule in the Age of the Global Village," in Nicolaus Mills (ed.), *Arguing Immigration: Are New Immigrants a Wealth of Diversity ... or a Crushing Burden?* (New York and London: Simon & Schuster, 1994).
Birch, A. H., *Representative and Responsible Government: An Essay on the British Constitution* (Toronto: University of Toronto Press, 1964).
Bischof, Günter, "'Watschenmann der europäischen Einigung'? Internationales Image und Vergangenheitspolitik der Schüssel/Riess-Passer-ÖVP /FPÖ-Koalitionsregierung," in Michael Gehler, Anton Pelinka, and Günter Bischof (eds), *Österreich in der Europäischen Union: Bilanz seiner Mitgliedschaft, Austria in the European Union – Assessment of Her Membership* (Vienna, Cologne and Weimar: Bohlau Verlag, 2003).
Blair, Tony, *A Journey: My Political Life* (New York and Toronto: Alfred A. Knopf, 2010).
Blanc, Hélène, and Lesnik, Renata, *Les prédateurs du Kremlin (1917–2009)* (Paris: Seuil, 2009).
Bloom, Allan, *The Closing of the American Mind: How Higher Education has Failed Democracy and Impoverished the Souls of Today's Students* (New York and London: Simon & Schuster, 1987).
Bobbio, Norberto, *Il futuro della democrazia* (Turin: Einaudi, 1995).
Bobbio, Norberto, *Liberalism and Democracy* (London and New York: Verso, 2005).
Bobbio, Norberto, *Contro i nuovi dispotismi: Scritti sul berlusconismo*, with an introduction by Enzo Marzo (Bari: Edizione Dedalo, 2008).
Body-Gendrot, Sophie, *Les États-Unis et leurs immigrants: Des modes d'insertion variés* (Paris: La Documentation Française, 1991).
Boeri, Tito, *Populismo e stato sociale* (Bari and Rome: Editori Laterza, 2017).
Breger, Marshall J., and Edles, Gary J., *Independent Agencies in the United States: Law, Structure, and Politics* (Oxford and New York: Oxford University Press, 2015).
Bregman, Rutger, *Utopia for Realists and How We Can Get There* (London, Oxford, and New York: Bloomsbury, 2017).
Bryan, William Jennings, "You Shall Not Crucify Mankind Upon a Cross of Gold," in Brian MacArthur (ed.), *The Penguin Book of Historic Speeches* (London: Penguin Books, 2017).
Buffon, Bertrand, *Vulgarité et modernité* (Paris: Gallimard, 2019).
Carens, Joseph H., "Immigration and the Welfare State," in Amy Gutmann (ed.), *Democracy and the Welfare State* (Princeton: Princeton University Press, 1988).
Case, Anne, and Deaton, Angus, "Mortality and Morbidity in the 21st Century," *Brookings Papers on Economic Activity*, BPEA Conference Drafts, 23–24 March 2017.
Cassese, Sabino, *La democrazia e i suoi limiti* (Milan: Mondadori, 2017).

Chan, Tak Wing, and Clayton, Matthew, "Should the Voting Age be Lowered to Sixteen? Normative and Empirical Considerations," *Political Studies*, Vol. 54, 2006.

Chaplin, Ari, *Chávez's Legacy: The Transformation from Democracy to a Mafia State* (Lanham, Boulder, and New York: University Press of America, 2014).

Chayes, Sarah, "Kleptocracy in America – Corruption is Reshaping Governments Everywhere," *Foreign Affairs*, Vol. 96, No. 5, September/October 2017.

Chubarov, Alexander, *The Fragile Empire: A History of Imperial Russia* (New York and London: Continuum, 2001).

Cockcroft, Laurence, and Wegener, Anne-Christine, "An Enemy to Democracy? Political Party Finance and Corruption in the West," *Cicero Foundation Great Debate Paper*, No. 17/01, January 2017.

Cockcroft, Laurence, and Wegener, Anne-Christine, *Unmasked: Corruption in the West* (London and New York: I. B. Tauris, 2017).

Cohen, Joshua, "Deliberation and Democratic Legitimacy," in James Bohman and William Rehg (eds), *Deliberative Democracy: Essays on Reason and Politics* (Cambridge, Mass., and London: The MIT Press, 1999).

Cox, Archibald, *The Warren Court: Constitutional Decision as an Instrument of Reform* (Cambridge, Mass.: Harvard University Press, 1968).

Crick, Bernard, *The Reform of Parliament* (London: Weidenfeld and Nicolson, 1970).

Crick, Bernard, *In Defence of Politics* (London and New York: Penguin, 1992).

Crouch, Colin, *Post-Democracy* (Cambridge: Polity Press, 2004).

Crozier, Michel, *Le mal américain* (Paris: Fayard, 1980).

Dahl, Robert A., *Dilemmas of Pluralist Democracy: Autonomy vs. Control* (New Haven and London: Yale University Press, 1982).

Dahl, Robert A., *A Preface to Economic Democracy* (Berkeley and Los Angeles: University of California Press, 1985).

Dahl, Robert, *Democracy and Its Critics* (New Haven and London: Yale University Press, 1989).

Dahl, Robert A., *On Democracy* (New Haven and London: Yale University Press, 1998).

Dahl, Robert A., *Intervista sul pluralismo: A cura di Giancarlo Bosetti* (Rome and Bari: Editori Laterza, 2002).

Dahl, Robert A., *How Democratic Is the American Constitution?* (New Haven and London: Yale University Press, 2003).

Dahrendorf, Ralf, "Anmerkungen zur Globalisierung," in Peter Kemper and Ulrich Sonnenschein (eds), *Globalisierung im Alltag* (Frankfurt am Main: Suhrkamp, 2002).

Dahrendorf, Ralf, *Die Krisen der Demokratie* (Munich: C. H. Beck, 2002).

Dal Lago, Alessandro, *Populismo digitale: La crisi, la rete e la nuova destra* (Milan: Raffaello Cortina Editore, 2017).

Damhuis, Koen, *Wegen naar Wilders: PVV-stemmers in hun eigen woorden* (Amsterdam and Antwerp: De Arbeiderspers, 2017).

Dayen, David, "The California Ballot Is an Epic Joke," *New Republic*, 23 September 2016.

De Lange, Sarah L., *From Pariah to Power: The Government Participation of Radical Right-Wing Populist Parties in West European Democracies* (Antwerp: Universiteit van Antwerpen Faculteit Politieke en Sociale Wetenschappen, 2008).

Dewey, John, *Democracy and Education*, edited by Jim Manis (Hazleton: Pennsylvania State University Press, 2001).

Bibliography

Downs, William M., "How Effective is the Cordon Sanitaire? Lessons from Efforts to Contain the Far Right in Belgium, France, Denmark, and Norway," *Journal of Conflict and Violence Research*, Vol. 4, No. 1, 2002.

Drucker, Peter F., "New Political Alignments in the Great Society," in Bertram M. Gross (ed.), *A Great Society?* (New York and London: Basic Books, 1968).

Drysch, Thomas, *Parteienfinanzierung: Österreich, Schweiz, Bundesrepublik Deutschland* (Wiesbaden: Springer, 1998).

Dworkin, Ronald, *Is Democracy Possible Here? Principles for a New Political Debate* (Princeton and Oxford: Princeton University Press, 2008).

Eatwell, Roger, and Goodwin, Matthew, *National Populism: The Revolt Against Liberal Democracy* (London: Pelican, 2018).

Eckstein, Harry, "A Theory of Stable Democracy," Appendix B in Harry Eckstein, *Division and Cohesion in Democracy* (Princeton: Princeton University Press, 1966).

Elchardus, Mark, and Spruyt, Bram, "Populism, Persistent Republicanism and Declinism: An Empirical Analysis of Populism as a Thin Ideology," *Government and Opposition*, Vol. 51, No. 1, January 2016.

"Elitist Britain," Report from the Social Mobility and Child Poverty Commission and the Social Mobility Commission, London, 28 August 2014.

Entzinger, Han, "The Rise and Fall of Dutch Multiculturalism," Lecture in the conference "Migration – Citizenship – Ethnos. Incorporation Regimes in Germany, Western Europe and North America, Toronto, 2–4 October 2003.

Erikson, Erik H. "Growth and Crises of the Healthy Personality," in Erik H. Erikson, *Identity and the Life Cycle* (New York and London: W. W. Norton & Company, 1994).

Eulau, Heinz, "Political Science and Education: The Long View and the Short," in Klaus von Beyme (ed.), *Theory and Politics – Theorie und Politik – Festschrift zum 70. Geburtstag für Carl Joachim Friedrich* (The Hague: Martinus Nijhoff, 1971).

Fassin, Eric, *Populisme: Le grand ressentiment* (Paris: Éditions Textuel, 2017).

Ferguson, Niall, *The Great Degeneration: How Institutions Decay and Economies Die* (London and New York: Penguin Books, 2013).

Ferguson, Niall, and Zakaria, Fareed, *The End of the Liberal Order?* (London: Oneworld, 2017).

Fishkin, James S., *The Voice of the People: Public Opinion and Democracy* (New Haven and London: Yale University Press, 1997).

Fishkin, James S., *When the People Speak: Deliberative Democracy and Public Consultation* (Oxford and New York: Oxford University Press, 2011).

FitzRoy, Felix R., and Kraft, Kornelius, "Co-determination, Efficiency, and Productivity," Institute for the Study of Labor (IZA), Bonn, *Discussion Paper* No. 1442, December 2004.

Formenti, Carlo, *La variante populista: Lotta di classe nel neoliberalismo* (Rome: Comunità Concrete, 2016).

Fortuyn, Pim, *De islamisering van onze cultuur: Nederlandse identiteit als fundament* (Uithoorn: Karakter Uitgevers B. V., 2002).

Freeland, Chrystia, *Plutocrats: The Rise of the New Global Super-rich* (London: Penguin Books, 2012).

Friedman, Milton, *Capitalism and Freedom* (Chicago: University of Chicago Press, 2002).

Friedman, Milton, and Friedman, Rose, *Free to Choose: A Personal Statement* (Harmondsworth and New York: Penguin Books, 1980).

Fukuyama, Francis, "Immigrants and Family Values," in Nicolaus Mills (ed.), *Arguing Immigration: Are New Immigrants a Wealth of Diversity ... or a Crushing Burden?* (New York and London: Simon & Schuster, 1994).

Fukuyama, Francis, "Social Capital," in Lawrence E. Harrison and Samuel P. Huntington (eds), *Culture Matters: How Values Shape Human Progress* (New York: Basic Books, 2000).
Fukuyama, Francis, "The End of History?" *The National Interest*, No. 16, Summer 1989.
Fukuyama, Francis, "The Populist Surge," *The American Interest*, Vol. XIII, No. 4, March/April 2018.
Galbraith, John Kenneth, *The Age of Uncertainty* (London: British Broadcasting Corporation, 1977).
Galston, William A., *Anti-pluralism: The Populist Threat to Liberal Democracy* (New Haven and London: Yale University Press, 2018).
Gauchet, Marcel, *La démocratie contre elle-même* (Paris: Gallimard, 2002).
Genovese, Rino, *Che cos'è il Berlusconismo: La democrazia deformata e il caso italiano* (Rome: Manifestolibri, 2011).
George, Robert P., *Making Men Moral: Civil Liberties and Public Morality* (Oxford: Clarendon Press, 1995).
Gibelli, Antonio, *Berlusconi ou la démocratie autoritaire* (Paris: Éditions Belin, 2011).
Ginsborg, Paul, *Salviamo Italia* (Turin: Giulio Einaudi Editore, 2010).
Goodhart, David, *The Road to Somewhere: The Populist Revolt and the Future of Politics* (London: C. Hurst & Co., 2017).
Graham, Carol, *Happiness around the World: The Paradox of Happy Peasants and Miserable Millionaires* (Oxford and New York: Oxford University Press, 2009).
Grayling, A. C., *Liberty in the Age of Terror: A Defence of Civil Liberties and Enlightenment Values* (London, Berlin, and New York: Bloomsbury, 2009).
Griffin, Roger (ed.), *International Fascism: Theories, Causes and the New Consensus* (London: Arnold, 1998).
Grigorieff, Alexis; Roth, Christopher; and Ubfal, Diego; "Does Information Change Attitudes Towards Immigrants? Representative Evidence from Survey Experiments," IZA, *Discussion Paper* No. 10419, December 2016.
Grofman, Bernard, "Introduction to the Term Limits Debate: Hypotheses in Search of Data," in Bernard Grofman (ed.), *Legislative Term Limits: Public Choice Perspectives* (Boston, Dordrecht, and London: Kluwer Academic Publishers, 1996).
Gross, Bertram M, "Some Questions for Presidents," in Bertram M. Gross (ed.), *A Great Society?* (New York and London: Basic Books, 1968).
Guiso, Luigi; Herrera, Helios; Morelli, Massimo; and Sonno, Tommaso; "Demand and Supply of Populism," Centre for Economic Policy Research, *Discussion Paper*, Series DP11871, 22 February 2017.
Habermas, Jürgen, "Struggles for Recognition in the Democratic Constitutional State," in Amy Gutmann (ed.), *Multiculturalism: Examining the Politics of Recognition* (Princeton: Princeton University Press, 1994).
Hakhverdian, Armen, and Schakel, Wouter, *Nepparlement: Een pleidooi voor politiek hokjesdenken* (Amsterdam: Amsterdam University Press, 2017).
Hamilton, Alexander; Madison, James; and Jay, John; *The Federalist Papers*, with an introduction by Clinton Rossiter (New York and Scarborough, Ontario: New American Library, 1961).
Hart, H. L. A., *Law, Liberty, and Morality* (Stanford: Stanford University Press, 1963).
Hayek, F. A., *The Constitution of Liberty* (London and Henley: Routledge & Kegan Paul, 1976).
Hayek, F. A., *The Road to Serfdom* (London and Henley: Routledge & Kegan Paul, 1979).
Hayek, F. A., *The Fatal Conceit: The Errors of Socialism*, The Collected Works of Friedrich August Hayek, Vol. I, edited by W. W. Bartley, III (London: Routledge, 1990).

Bibliography

Hegel, Georg Wilhelm Friedrich, "Vorlesungen über die Philosophie der Geschichte," in G. W. F. Hegel, *Werke*, Vol. 12 (Frankfurt am Main: Suhrkamp Verlag, 1970).

Held, David, *Democracy and the Global Order: From the Modern State to Cosmopolitan Governance* (Stanford: Stanford University Press, 1995).

Herz, Rachel, *That's Disgusting: Unraveling the Mysteries of Repulsion* (New York and London: W. W. Norton & Company, 2012).

Hirschman, Albert O., "The Changing Tolerance for Income Inequality in the Course of Economic Development," in Albert O. Hirschman, *Essays in Trespassing: Economics to Politics and Beyond* (Cambridge, London, and New York: Cambridge University Press, 1984).

Hirschman, Albert O., *The Essential Hirschman*, edited and with an introduction by Jeremy Adelman, afterword by Emma Rothschild and Amartya Sen (Princeton: Princeton University Press, 2015).

Hitler, Adolf, *Mein Kampf* (Munich: Verlag Franz Eher Nachfolger, 1933).

Hobsbawm, Eric, *On the Edge of the New Century*, Eric Hobsbawm in conversation with Antonio Polito (New York: The New Press, 2000).

Höffe, Otfried, *Ist die Demokratie zukunftsfähig?* (Munich: Verlag C. H. Beck, 2009).

Hofstadter, Richard, *The American Political Tradition and the Men Who Made It* (New York: Vintage Books, 1948).

Hofstadter, Richard, *The Age of Reform: From Bryan to F.D.R.* (New York: Vintage Books, 1955).

Howell, Susan E., and Day, Christine L., "Complexities of the Gender Gap," *Journal of Politics*, Vol. 62, August 2000.

Huntington, Samuel P., *The Third Wave: Democratization in the Late Twentieth Century* (Norman: University of Oklahoma Press, 1993).

Huntington, Samuel P., *Who Are We? The Challenges to America's National Identity* (New York: Simon & Schuster, 2005).

Inglehart, Ronald, and Welzel, Christian, *Modernization, Cultural Change, and Democracy: The Human Development Sequence* (Cambridge and New York: Cambridge University Press, 2005).

Jaschke, Hans-Gerd, "Streitbare Demokratie," *Bundeszentrale für politische Bildung*, 19 September 2006.

Johnson, Harry M., *Sociology: A Systematic Introduction* (London: Routledge & Kegan Paul Ltd., 1964).

Judis, John B., *The Populist Explosion: How the Great Recession Transformed American and European Politics* (New York: Columbia Global Reports, 2016).

Kant, Immanuel, *Political Writings*, edited by H. S. Reiss (Cambridge and New York: Cambridge University Press, 1991).

Kaplan, Andee; Hare, Eric; Hofmann, Heike; and Cook, Dianne; "Can You Buy a President? Politics After the Tillman Act," *Chance*, no date.

Katz, Richard S., and Mair, Peter, "Changing Models of Party Organization and Party Democracy: The Emergence of the Cartel Party," *Party Politics*, Vol. 1, No. 1, 1995.

Katz, Richard S., and Mair, Peter, "The Cartel Party Thesis: A Restatement," *Perspectives on Politics*, Vol. 7, No. 4, December 2009.

Kennedy, Paul, *Preparing for the Twenty-first Century* (London: Fontana Press, 1994). Keynes, John Maynard, "Am I a Liberal?" in John Maynard Keynes, *Essays in Persuasion* (London: Macmillan and Co., 1931).

King, Anthony, "Distrust of Government: Explaining American Exceptionalism," in Susan J. Pharr and Robert D. Putnam (eds), *Disaffected Democracies: What's Troubling the Trilateral Countries?* (Princeton: Princeton University Press, 2000).

Kirchgässner, Gebhard, "Direkte Demokratie und Menschenrechte," Center for Research in Economics, Management and the Arts (CREMA), *Working Paper* No. 2009-18.

Kolnai, Aurel, *Ekel, Hochmut, Haß: Zur Phänomenologie feindlicher Gefühle*, with a postscript by Axel Honneth (Frankfurt am Main: Suhrkamp, 2007).

Koole, Ruud, "Cadre, Catch-All or Cartel? A Comment on the Notion of the Cartel Party," *Party Politics*, Vol. 2, No. 4, 1996.

Kretschmer, Kelsey; Mikolajczak, Gosia; Ruppanner, Leah; and Stout, Christopher; "Why white married women are more likely to vote for conservative parties," *The Convention*, 17 October 2019.

Kritzinger, Sylvia, and Zeglovits, Eva, "Wahlen mit 16 – Chance oder Risiko?" in Jörg Tremmel and Markus Rutschke (eds), *Politische Beteiligung junger Menschen: Grundlagen, Perspektiven, Fallstudien* (Wiesbaden: Springer, 2016).

Kuhn, Thomas S., *The Structure of Scientific Revolutions* (Chicago and London: University of Chicago Press, 2012).

Kupchan, Charles A., *The End of the American Era: U.S. Foreign Policy and the Geopolitics of the Twenty-first Century* (New York: Alfred A. Knopf, 2002).

Laclau, Ernesto, *On Populist Reason* (London and New York: Verso, 2007).

Lasch, Christopher, *The Revolt of the Elites and the Betrayal of Democracy* (New York and London: W. W. Norton & Company, 1995).

Le Bon, Gustave, *Psychologie des foules* (Paris: Félix Alcan, 1930).

Le Bras, Hervé, *Une autre France: Votes, réseaux de relations et classes sociales* (Paris: Odile Jacob, 2002).

Lenk, Kurt, and Neumann, Franz, "Einleitung," in Kurt Lenk and Franz Neumann, *Theorie und Soziologie der politischen Parteien* (Neuwied am Rhein and Berlin: Luchterhand, 1968).

Lijphart, Arend, *Democracy in Plural Societies: A Comparative Exploration* (New Haven and London: Yale University Press, 1977).

Lindsey, Brink, *Human Capitalism: How Economic Growth Has Made Us Smarter – and More Unequal* (Princeton: Princeton University Press, 2013).

Locke, John, *Second Treatise of Government*, edited by C. B. Macpherson (Indianapolis and Cambridge: Hackett Publishing Company, Inc., 1980).

Lord, Christopher, "Source the Crowd, Don't Rouse the Rabble: Crowdsourcing as a Modest Response to Populism," *The Progressive Post*, No. 4, Spring 2017.

Lukacs, John, *At the End of an Age* (New Haven and London: Yale University Press, 2002).

Lukacs, John, *Democracy and Populism: Fear and Hatred* (New Haven and London: Yale University Press, 2005).

Luyendijk, Joris, *Kunnen we praten* (Amsterdam and Antwerp: Atlas Contact, 2017).

MacArthur, Brian (ed.), *The Penguin Book of Historic Speeches* (London: Penguin Books, 2017).

Macpherson, C. B., *Democratic Theory: Essays in Retrieval* (Oxford: Oxford University Press, 1979).

Macpherson, C. B., "Post-Liberal-Democracy?" in C. B. Macpherson, *Democratic Theory: Essays in Retrieval* (Oxford: Oxford University Press, 1979).

Macpherson, C. B., *The Life and Times of Liberal Democracy* (Oxford: Oxford University Press, 1979).

Mannheim, Karl, *Man and Society in an Age of Reconstruction* (London and Henley: Routledge & Kegan Paul, 1980).

Bibliography

McGhee, Eric (with contributions from Daniel Krimm), *At Issue: Open Primaries* (San Francisco: Public Policy Institute of California, February 2010).

McWhinney, Edward, *Comparative Federalism: States' Rights and National Power* (Toronto: Toronto University Press, 1965).

Mead, Walter Russell, "The Jacksonian Revolt – American Populism and the Liberal Order," *Foreign Affairs*, Vol. 96, No. 2, March/April 2017.

Menninghaus, Winfried, *Ekel: Theorie und Geschichte einer starken Empfindung* (Frankfurt am Main: Suhrkamp, 1999).

Merton, Robert K., *Social Theory and Social Structure* (New York: The Free Press, 1965).

Michaels, Jon D., "Trump and the 'Deep State' – The Government Strikes Back," *Foreign Affairs*, Vol. 96, No. 5, September/October 2017.

Mill, John Stuart, *Autobiography of John Stuart Mill*, with a preface by John Jacob Coss (New York: Columbia University Press, 1960).

Miller, William Ian, *The Anatomy of Disgust* (Cambridge, Mass., and London: Harvard University Press, 1997).

Mills, Nicolaus (ed.), *Arguing Immigration: Are New Immigrants a Wealth of Diversity ... or a Crushing Burden?* (New York and London: Simon & Schuster, 1994).

Minogue, Kenneth R., *The Liberal Mind: A Critical Analysis of the Philosophy of Liberalism and its Political Effects* (New York: Vintage Books, 1968).

Mitch, David, "Education and Skill of the British Labour Force," in Roderick Floud and Paul Johnson (eds), *The Cambridge Economic History of Modern Britain, Vol. I: Industrialisation, 1700–1860* (Cambridge: Cambridge University Press, 2004).

Moffitt, Benjamin, *The Global Rise of Populism: Performance, Political Style, and Representation* (Stanford: Stanford University Press, 2016).

Mols, Frank, and Jetten, Jolanda, "Why Trump and Brexit are Not Working-Class Revolts," *ABC Religion & Ethics*, 15 November 2016.

Montesquieu, "De l'esprit des lois," in Montesquieu, *Œuvres Complètes* (Paris: Éditions du Seuil, 1964).

Mounk, Yascha, *The People vs. Democracy: Why Our Freedom Is in Danger and How to Save It* (Cambridge, Mass., and London: Harvard University Press, 2018).

Mudde, Cas, "Europe's Populist Surge – A Long Time in the Making," *Foreign Affairs*, Vol. 95, No. 6, November/December 2016.

Mudde, Cas, and Kaltwasser, Cristóbal Rovira, *Populism: A Very Short Introduction* (Oxford: Oxford University Press, 2017).

Müller, Jan-Werner, *Was ist Populismus?* (Berlin: Suhrkamp Verlag, 2016).

Muller, Jerry Z., "Capitalism and Inequality – What the Right and the Left Get Wrong," *Foreign Affairs*, Vol. 92, No. 2, March/April 2013.

Nagel, Thomas, *The View from Nowhere* (Oxford and New York: Oxford University Press, 1989).

Neiman, Susan, *Why Grow Up? Subversive Thoughts for an Infantile Age* (London: Penguin Books, 2016).

Nevis, Allan, and Steele Commager, Henry, *A Pocket History of the United States* (New York: Washington Square Press, 1981).

Nichols, Tom, "How America Lost Faith in Expertise and Why That's a Giant Problem," *Foreign Affairs*, Vol. 96, No. 2, March/April 2017.

Norris, Pippa, *Democratic Phoenix: Reinventing Political Activism* (Cambridge and New York: Cambridge University Press, 2002).

Nozick, Robert, *Examined Life: Philosophical Meditations* (New York and London: Simon & Schuster Inc., 1989).
Nussbaum, Martha C., *Hiding from Humanity: Disgust, Shame, and the Law* (Princeton and Oxford: Princeton University Press, 2004).
Nussbaum, Martha C., *The New Religious Intolerance: Overcoming the Politics of Fear in an Anxious Age* (Cambridge, Mass., and London: The Belknap Press of Harvard University Press, 2012).
Nye, Russell B., and Grabo, Norman S. (eds), *American Thought and Writing, Volume Two: The Revolution and the Early Republic* (Boston: Houghton Mifflin Company, 1965).
Orwell, George, *Notes on Nationalism* (London: Penguin Books, 2018).
Ostiguy, Pierre, "The High and the Low in Politics: A Two-Dimensional Political Space for Comparative Analysis and Electoral Studies," The Helen Kellogg Institute for International Studies, *Working Paper* #360, July 2009.
Pascal, Blaise, *Pensées and Other Writings* (Oxford and New York: Oxford University Press, 1999).
Pallaver, Günther, and Gärtner, Reinhold, "Populistische Parteien an der Regierung – Zum Scheitern Verdammt? Italien und Österreich im Vergleich," in Frank Decker (ed.), *Populismus: Gefahr für die Demokratie oder nützliches Korrektiv?* (Wiesbaden: Verlag für Sozialwissenschaft, 2006).
Pasquino, Gianfranco, and Valbruzzi, Marco, "Still an Outlier: Italy in a Southern European Comparative Perspective 1," *Journal of Modern Italian Studies*, Vol. 15, Issue 2, 2010.
Pateman, Carole, *Participation and Democratic Theory* (Cambridge: Cambridge University Press, 1970).
Paxton, Robert O., *The Anatomy of Fascism* (New York: Vintage Books, 2005).
Pehle, Heinrich, "Die Finanzierung der Parteien in Deutschland," *Bundeszentrale für politische Bildung*, 20 May 2015.
Pestritto, Ronald, and Kempema, Taylor, "The Birth of Direct Democracy: What Progressivism Did to the States," The Heritage Foundation, Report Political Process, 25 February 2014.
Piccio, Daniela R., and Van Biezen, Ingrid, "Political Finance and the Cartel Party Thesis," in Jonathan Mendilow and Eric Phélippeau (eds), *Handbook of Political Party Funding* (Cheltenham and Northampton, Mass.: Edward Elgar Publishers, 2018).
Piketty, Thomas, *Le capital au XXIe siècle* (Paris: Éditions du Seuil, 2013).
Pipes, Richard, *Russia under the Old Regime* (London and New York: Penguin, 1995).
Polanyi, Karl, *The Great Transformation: The Political and Economic Origins of Our Time*, with a new introduction by Fred Bloch (Boston: Beacon Press, 2001).
Potter, Allen M., *American Government and Politics* (London: Faber and Faber Limited, 1969).
Pozsgai, Joseph, "A Systems Model on Corruption and Anticorruption Reform – International, Domestic Pressure, and Government Strategies to Preserve the Status Quo," *Air and Space Power Journal*, Vol. 8, No. 3, 3d Quarter 2017.
Price, Don K., "Science in the Great Society," in Bertram M. Gross (ed.), *A Great Society?* (New York and London: Basic Books, 1968).
Prinz, Jesse J., *Gut Reactions: A Perceptual Theory of Emotion* (Oxford and New York: Oxford University Press, 2006).
Putnam, Robert D., *Bowling Alone: The Collapse and Revival of American Community* (New York, London, and Toronto: Simon & Schuster, 2000).
Pye, Lucian W., *Aspects of Political Development* (Boston and Toronto: Little, Brown and Company, 1966).

Rawls, John, *A Theory of Justice* (London, Oxford, and New York: Oxford University Press, 1973).
Rawls, John, *Political Liberalism* (New York: Columbia University Press, 1993).
Revelli, Marco, *Populismo 2.0* (Turin: Giulio Einaudi Editore, 2017).
Riemen, Rob, *De eeuwige terugkeer van het fascisme* (Amsterdam and Antwerp: Atlas, 2010).
Rooduijn, Matthijs; De Lange, Sarah L.; and Van der Brug, Wouter; "A Populist *Zeitgeist*? Programmatic Contagion by Populist Parties in Western Europe," *Party Politics*, Vol. 20, No. 4, 2014.
Rosanvallon, Pierre, *Le sacre du citoyen: Histoire du suffrage universel en France* (Paris: Gallimard, 1992).
Rosanvallon, Pierre, *Le peuple introuvable* (Paris: Gallimard, 1998).
Rosanvallon, Pierre, *La contre-démocratie: La politique à l'âge de la défiance* (Paris: Éditions du Seuil, 2006).
Rosanvallon, Pierre, *La légitimité démocratique: Impartialité, réflexivité, proximité* (Paris: Éditions du Seuil, 2008).
Rosanvallon, Pierre, *Le bon gouvernement* (Paris: Éditions du Seuil, 2015).
Rothwell, Jonathan, and Diego-Rosell, Pablo, "Explaining Nationalist Political Views: The Case of Donald Trump," Draft Working Paper, Gallup, 2 November 2016.
Rozin, Paul, "Food is Fundamental, Fun, Frightening, and Far-Reaching," *Social Research*, Vol. 66, Spring 1999.
Rozin, Paul; Haidt, Jonathan; and McCauley, Clark R.; "Disgust," in Michael Lewis and Jeannette M. Haviland-Jones (eds), *Handbook of the Emotions* (New York and London: The Guilford Press, 2004).
Saby, Olivier, *Promotion Ubu Roi*, with the collaboration of Christophe Quillien (Paris: Flammarion, 2012).
Sarkozy, Nicolas, *Témoignage* (Paris: XO Éditions, 2006).
Sassen, Saskia, *Losing Control – Sovereignty in an Age of Globalization* (New York: Columbia University Press, 1995).
Schlesinger, Arthur M. Jr., *The Disuniting of America: Reflections on a Multicultural Society* (New York and London: Norton, 1992).
Schmitt, Carl, *Völkerrechtliche Großraumordnung mit Interventionsverbot für raumfremde Mächte: Ein Beitrag zum Reichsbegriff im Völkerrecht* (Berlin: Duncker & Humblot, 1991).
Schmitt, Carl, *Der Nomos der Erde im Völkerrecht des Jus Publicum Europaeum* (Berlin: Duncker & Humblot, 1997).
Schmitt, Carl, *Der Begriff des Politischen* (Berlin: Duncker & Humblot, 2002).
Schrag, Peter, *Paradise Lost: California's Experience, America's Future* (Berkeley and Los Angeles: University of California Press, 2004).
Schumpeter, Joseph A., *Capitalism, Socialism, and Democracy* (New York and London: Harper and Brothers Publishers, 1947).
Schuyt, C. J. M., and Taverne, Ed, *1950. Welvaart in zwart-wit* (The Hague: SDU Uitgevers, 2000).
Seldon, Anthony, *Blair* (London: The Free Press, 2005).
Seligman, Adam B., *The Problem of Trust* (Princeton: Princeton University Press, 2000).
Sennett, Richard, *The Fall of Public Man: On the Psychology of Capitalism* (New York: Vintage Books, 1978).

Sennett, Richard, *The Culture of the New Capitalism* (New Haven and London: Yale University Press, 2006).

Sennett, Richard, and Cobb, Jonathan, *The Hidden Injuries of Class* (New York: Vintage Books, 1973).

Serfaty, Simon, "Trump's Moment in History," *The National Interest*, No. 152, November/December 2017.

Siegried, André, *Tableau politique de la France de l'ouest sous la troisième république* (Paris: Librairie Armand Colin, 1913).

Simmel, Georg, "Das Ende des Streits," in Georg Simmel, *Aufsätze und Abhandlungen 1901–1908*, Vol. I (Frankfurt am Main: Suhrkamp, 1995).

Simone, Raffaele, *Come la democrazia fallisce* (Milan: Garzanti, 2015).

Skenderovic, Damir, "Das rechtspopulistische Parteienlager in der Schweiz: Von den Splitterparteien zur Volkspartei," *Traverse: Zeitschrift für Geschichte – Revue d'histoire*, Vol. 14, No. 1, 2007.

Skocpol, Theda, *Diminished Democracy: From Membership to Management in American Civic Life* (Norman: University of Oklahoma Press, 2003).

Skocpol, Theda, "United States – From Membership to Advocacy," in Robert D. Putnam (ed.), *Democracies in Flux: The Evolution of Social Capital in Contemporary Society* (Oxford and New York: Oxford University Press, 2004).

Sniderman, Paul M., and Hagendoorn, Louk, *When Ways of Life Collide: Multiculturalism and Its Discontents in The Netherlands* (Princeton and Oxford: Princeton University Press, 2009).

Standing, Guy, *Basic Income: A Guide for the Open-Minded* (New Haven and London: Yale University Press, 2017).

Starink, Laura, *Slag om Oekraïne: Referendum over een land in opstand* (Amsterdam and Antwerp: Uitgeverij Augustus, 2016).

Stenner, Karen, *The Authoritarian Dynamic* (Cambridge and New York: Cambridge University Press, 2005).

Stiglitz, Joseph E., *The Price of Inequality* (London: Penguin Books, 2013).

Streeck, Wolfgang, and Kluge, Norbert, "Vorwort," in Wolfgang Streeck and Norbert Kluge (eds), *Mitbestimmung in Deutschland: Tradition und Effizienz* (Frankfurt am Main and New York: Campus Verlag, 1999).

Taguieff, Pierre-André, *Le nouveau national-populisme* (Paris: CNRS Éditions, 2012).

Thurow, Lester C., *The Zero-Sum Society: Distribution and the Possibilities for Economic Change* (Harmondsworth: Penguin Books, 1980).

Tilly, Charles, *Democracy* (Cambridge and New York: Cambridge University Press, 2008).

Tocqueville, Alexis de, *De la Démocratie en Amérique*, Part I, edited by François Furet (Paris: Garnier Flammarion, 1981).

Traverso, Enzo, *Les nouveaux visages du fascisme*, conversation with Régis Meyran (Paris: Les éditions Textuel, 2017).

Trump, Donald J., *How to Get Rich*, with Meredith McIver (New York: Ballantine Books, 2004).

Trump, Donald J., *Great Again: How to Fix Our Crippled America* (New York and London: Threshold Editions, 2015).

Tuchman, Barbara W., *A Distant Mirror: The Calamitous 14th Century* (Harmondsworth: Penguin, 1984).

Van den Brink, H. M., *Koning Wilders: Een wintersprookje* (Amsterdam and Antwerp: Atlas Contact, 2017).

Bibliography

Van Herpen, Marcel H., "Rousseau en de 'Sturm und Drang' – de vroegste receptie van Rousseau's cultuurkritiek in Duitsland," *De Gids*, Vol. 142, 1979.
Van Herpen, Marcel H., *Putinism: The Slow Rise of a Radical Right Regime in Russia* (Houndmills, Basingstoke, and New York: Palgrave Macmillan, 2013).
Van Herpen, Marcel H., *Putin's Wars: The Rise of Russia's New Imperialism* (Lanham and London: Rowman & Littlefield, 2015).
Van Herpen, Marcel H., *Putin's Propaganda Machine: Soft Power and Russian Foreign Policy* (Lanham and London: Rowman & Littlefield, 2016).
Van Herpen, Marcel H., "The Rise of Kremlin-Friendly Populism in the Netherlands," *Cicero Foundation Great Debate Paper*, No. 18/04, June 2018.
Van Leeuwen, Maarten, "Systematic Stylistic Analysis: The Use of a Linguistic Checklist," in Bertie Kaal, Isa Maks, and Annemarie van Elfrinkhof (eds), *From Text to Political Positions: Text Analysis Across Disciplines* (Amsterdam and Philadelphia: John Benjamins Publishing Company, 2014).
Van Parijs, Philippe, *Real Freedom for All: What (If Anything) Can Justify Capitalism?* (Oxford: Clarendon Press, 1995).
Van Reybrouck, David, *Against Elections: The Case for Democracy* (London: The Bodley Head, 2016).
Verba, Sidney, and Nie, Norman H., *Participation in America: Political Democracy and Social Equality* (New York: Harper & Row, 1972).
Voltaire, *Philosophical Dictionary* (London and New York: Penguin, 2004).
Wallerstein, Immanuel, *After Liberalism* (New York: The New Press, 1995). Walzer, Michael, *Spheres of Justice: A Defense of Pluralism and Equality* (New York: Basic Books Inc., 1983).
Walzer, Michael, *Thick and Thin: Moral Argument at Home and Abroad* (Notre Dame and London: University of Notre Dame Press, 1994).
Weber, Max, *Wirtschaft und Gesellschaft*, first half-volume, edited by Johannes Winckelmann (Cologne and Berlin: Kiepenheuer & Witsch, 1964).
Weber, Max, "Die 'Objektivität' sozialwissenschaftlicher und sozialpolitischer Erkenntnis," in Max Weber, *Gesammelte Aufsätze zur Wissenschaftslehre*, edited by J. Winckelmann (Tübingen: J. C. B. Mohr-Paul Siebeck, 1968).
Weber, Max, "Die drei reinen Typen der legitimen Herrschaft. Eine soziologische Studie," in Max Weber, *Schriften 1894–1922* (Stuttgart: Alfred Kröner Verlag, 2002).
Weber, Max, "Die protestantische Ethik und der 'Geist' des Kapitalismus," in Max Weber, *Schriften 1894–1922* (Stuttgart: Alfred Kröner Verlag, 2002).
Weber, Max, "Parlament und Regierung im neugeordneten Deutschland. Zur politischen Kritik des Beamtentums und Parteiwesens," in Max Weber, *Schriften 1894–1922* (Stuttgart: Alfred Kröner Verlag, 2002).
Weber, Max, "Politik als Beruf," in Max Weber, *Schriften 1894–1922* (Stuttgart: Alfred Kröner Verlag, 2002).
Weitz, Eric D., *Weimar Germany: Promise and Tragedy* (Princeton and Oxford: Princeton University Press, 2007).
Wilkinson, Richard, and Pickett, Kate, *The Spirit Level: Why Equality is Better for Everyone* (London: Penguin Books, 2010).
Winkler, Günther, *Zeit und Recht* (Vienna and New York: Springer Verlag, 1995).
Winock, Michel, *Histoire de l'extrême droite en France* (Paris: Éditions du Seuil, 1994).
Winock, Michel, *La Droite: Hier et aujourd'hui* (Paris: Perrin, 2012).

Bibliography

Wolfe, Alan, *The Future of Liberalism* (New York: Vintage Books, 2010).
Zakaria, Fareed, *The Future of Freedom: Illiberal Democracy at Home and Abroad* (New York and London: W. W. Norton & Company, 2004).
Zakaria, Fareed, *The Post-American World* (New York and London: W. W. Norton & Company, 2008).

Index

Acemoglu, Daron 67
Achen, Christopher H. 74, 82–84, 89, 91, 92, 118, 124, 270
Ackerman, Bruce 131, 134–136, 199, 206
Adorno, Theodor 55
Advisory Committee on Business Appointments (ACOBA) 177
Africa 249
African Americans 40, 42, 104
Aichholzer, Julian 203, 208
Alaska 234, 235, 238, 239
Albertazzi, Daniele 154, 270
Alemán, Jorge 267, 270
Algeria 250, 257
Allianz für Deutschland (AfD) 43, 46, 152, 224, 245, 247, 254, 267
Almond, Gabriel A. 91, 204, 209, 270
Alperovitz, Gar 236, 270
Al Qaeda 250
alternative facts 213, 214, 216, 217, 222 *see also* fake news and post-truth
American People's Party 7, 10 *see also* Populists, the
Andersen, Jorgen Goul 270
ANEL Party (Greece) 154
Annemans, Gerolf 30
anti-corruption 133, 136, 142, 156–160, 167
 watchdogs 159, 171, 172
 pledge 171
anti-elite feelings 127
anti-immigrant policy 148, 150
anti-Islam policy 148
anti-Semitism 8, 10, 107
anxiety, economic 36, 37, 61, 232, 233
Apol, David J. 172, 173
Arendt, Hannah 29, 32, 214, 215, 222, 270
Argentina 164, 266, 269

Aron, Raymond 36, 44, 270
Ataka (Bulgaria) 221
Atkinson, Anthony 231, 236, 237, 270
Austria 5, 68, 110, 120, 146, 149, 153, 202, 203, 224, 246
authoritarianism 10, 12, 14, 25, 41, 132, 200, 221
 and disgust sensitivity 54–56, 58

backstop 94 *see also* Brexit
Baldacchino, Adeline 182, 189, 270
Balladur, Édouard 189
Barreau, Jean-Claude 181, 189, 254, 257, 258, 270
Barroso, Manuel 176, 179
Bartels, Larry M. 74, 82–84, 89, 91, 92, 118, 119, 124, 270
Barter, Joe 175
Baudet, Thierry 41
Bauman, Zygmunt 66, 270
Bayrou, François 158, 181
Beck, Ulrich 125, 270
Beer, Samuel 92, 271
Belgium 9, 35, 104, 145, 150, 166, 215
Bell, Daniel 186, 187, 191, 271
Bellah, Robert N. 15, 271
Benhabib, Seyla 257, 271
Berger, Bennett 271
Berlusconi, Silvio 17, 25, 182, 264, 265, 268
Bettencourt, Liliane 158
Biden, Joe 220
Bikales, Gerda 257, 271
Bingham Powell Jr., G. 91, 270
Bipartisan Campaign Reform Act (BCRA) 162
Birch, Anthony 105, 113, 271
Bischof, Günter 153, 271

283

Index

Blair, Tony 85–87, 91, 92, 121, 176, 271
Blanc, Hélène 167, 271
Blocher, Christoph 108, 111
Bloom, Allan 184, 190, 271
Bobbio, Norberto 28, 31, 72, 75, 139, 144, 200, 206, 207, 261, 267, 271
Body-Gendrot, Sophie 271
Boeri, Tito 177, 271
Bolivia 267
Bolsonaro, Jair 2, 5, 15, 68
Bonapartism 93
Boulanger, Georges 9, 10, 24, 49, 56
boulangism, 8, 10, 28
Brandt, Willy 241, 245
Brazil, 2, 5, 15, 68, 201, 235, 260
Breger, Marshall J. 133, 136, 271
Bregman, Rutger 233, 237, 271
Breitbart 217, 223
Brexit 13, 42, 46, 93, 144, 202, 205, 214, 222, 256
  hard 95
  no deal 94–96, 105, 111 *see also* backstop
Britain 13, 85, 88, 105, 173, 175, 177, 183, 190, 193, 197, 202, 240
  see also United Kingdom (UK)
"bubbles" (of social media) 216, 218
Buffon, Bertrand 271
Bullock, Sir Allan 241, 245
Bündnis Zukunft Österreich (BZÖ) 146, 160
Burke, Edmund 48
Buruma, Ian 26, 30, 40, 46
Bush, George W. 163

California 13, 63, 88, 89, 92, 98, 99–102, 104, 110, 112, 113, 118, 141, 234
  popular initiatives 13
  Proposition 13, consequences of 99, 101, 112
  tax revolt in 99, 100
Cameron, David 93–95, 141
Camus, Renaud 39, 249 *see also* Great Replacement
Canada 89, 234, 238, 255, 258
Cano, Germán 267
Carens, Joseph H. 66, 271
cartel parties 152, 166, 169
Case, Anne 271
Cassese, Sabino 105, 113, 271
caste (political) 174, 180
Central Bank, 142
  European 127, 128

French 127, 128
German 127, 128
Chaplin, Ari 272
charismatic leadership 23, 24, 264
Chauprade, Aymeric 224
Chávez, Hugo 28, 31, 68, 267, 272
Chayes, Sarah 164, 169, 171, 177, 272
checks and balances, necessity of 129
China 1, 38, 45, 200, 204
Chirac, Jacques 158, 167, 189
Christlich Demokratische Union (CDU) 119, 157, 235, 251
Christlich Soziale Union (CSU) 251
Chubarov Alexander 15, 272
Citizens United (judgement) 162
Citrin, Jack 100, 101, 112
Clémenceau, Georges 215
climate change 253
Clinton, Bill 83, 91
Clinton, Hillary 42, 46, 50, 131, 162, 217
coalition formation 150
Cobb, Jonathan 243, 246
Cockroft, Laurence 161, 167, 168, 272
Cohen, Joshua 169, 272
common good 80, 81
Coney Barret, Justice Amy 136
Conservative Party 93, 95, 119, 158, 197
constitutional amendments 98, 99, 102
Conway, Kellyanne 214, 222
Corbyn, Jeremy 121, 124
cordon sanitaire 13, 145–155, 221
Costa Rica 164
Council of Europe 128
COVID-19 1, 2, 5, 14, 263
Cox, Archibald 130, 135, 272
Cox, Jo 111
Crick, Bernard 102, 113, 200, 207, 272
Crimea 220, 221, 224
Croatia 158
Crouch, Colin 24, 30, 158, 160, 167, 168, 233, 237, 272
Crozier, Michel 222, 272
Cubans 250
Cummings, Dominic 214, 222
Cuomo, Mario 168
Cyprus 120
Czechoslovakia 224
Czech Republic 28, 207, 246

Dahl, Robert A. 7, 16, 131, 135, 136, 139, 140, 144, 180, 189, 196, 197, 206, 243, 246, 272
Dahrendorf, Ralf 3, 15, 142, 144, 272

Index

Dal Lago, Alessandro 223, 272
Damhuis, Koen 41, 56, 272
Dansk Folkeparti (Danish People's Party) 148, 154
Darling, Alistair 176
Davis, Gray 100
Deaton, Angus 271
dédiabolisation 145 *see also* Front National and Rassemblement National
deep state 130, 135
De Gaulle, Charles 142
De Lange, Sarah 150, 154, 272, 279
Deliberation Day 89, 90, 192
De Maistre, Joseph 48
De Maizière, Thomas 251
democracy, demand-side 13, 79, 87
　supply-side 13, 79, 87, 116
democracy, direct 12, 72, 73, 98, 99, 101, 102, 104, 107, 110, 139–142, 144, 219
　deliberative 87, 89, 92
　representative 97, 102, 105
democracy, economic 240–247
　majoritarian 131, 132
　partnership 132, 136
　shareholder 240, 245
democracy, illiberal 5, 11, 128, 132, 142, 200, 221
　liberal 11, 13, 15, 133, 142, 197, 199, 200, 221, 260
Democraten 66 (D66) 96, 97, 111
democratic fundamentalism 105
Democratic Party (Italy) 37, 150
Democratic Party (US) 6, 7, 118, 124, 131, 197, 231, 262
Denmark 148, 154, 157, 242, 246
Derispaska, Oleg 158
De Villepin, Dominique 189
Dewey, John 13, 196, 197, 206, 272
Dewinter, Filip 30
Diego-Rosell, Pablo 279
Die Linke 221
disgust 31, 49–58
Donbas 224
Downs, William M. 154, 273
Drucker, Peter 7, 16, 273
Drysch, Thomas 169, 273
Duda, Andrzej 72
Duterte, Rodrigo 2, 5, 15
Dworkin, Ronald 132, 136, 206, 273

EADS 160, 168
Eatwell, Roger 15, 273

Eckstein, Harry 243, 246, 273
École Nationale d'Administration (ENA) 13, 181–183, 185, 188, 189, 190
Edles, Gary J. 133, 136, 271
education, democratic 192–209
Eisenhower, Dwight D. 163, 168
Ekman, Paul 57
Elchardus, Mark 273
elites, revolt against 120, 180, 181, 187, 189
Énarques 181, 189
England 94
Entzinger, Han 252, 257, 273
Enzensberger, Hans Magnus 120
Erdogan, Recep Tayyip 5, 11, 152
Erikson, Erik 60, 66, 273
Estado Novo 266
Ethics Committee of the House of Representatives 172
Eulau, Heinz 194, 205, 273
Europe 3, 8, 9, 63, 120, 140, 143, 146, 219 *see also* European Union
European Commission 129, 134, 176
European Convention on Human Rights 108, 109, 151
European Council 129
European Parliament 174, 203
European Union (EU) 94–97, 109, 113, 141, 146, 214, 220, 254 *see also* Europe
experts, distrust of 181, 187, 192

Fabius, Laurent 189
Facebook 216–218
fact checking 218
fake news 1, 142, 213, 214, 216, 217, 222 *see also* alternative facts and post-truth
family members, employed by deputies 174, 175
Farage, Nigel 31, 93, 95
Fascism, Italian 265, 266
fascism 14, 17, 194, 261–263
Fassin, Éric 56, 273
Faure, Olivier 178
Federal Corrupt Practices Act 161
Feingold, Russ 162
Ferguson, Niall 67, 205, 209, 226, 236, 273
Fidesz 71, 152
filibuster 131
Fillon, François 122, 158, 167, 175, 179
Finland 47, 149, 223, 234, 246
Finns Party 43, 47, 149
Fishkin, James 87, 88, 90, 92, 103, 112, 113, 192, 193, 273

Index

FitzRoy, Felix R. 273
Five Star Movement 26, 28, 35, 37, 68, 150, 166
Florida 250
Foa, Roberto Stefan 41, 205
focus groups 85
Ford, Henry James 117, 124
Formenti, Carlo 273
Fortuyn, Pim 25, 39, 41, 46, 248, 250, 257, 273 *see also* Lijst Pim Fortuyn
Forum voor Democratie 41, 43, 47, 111
Forza Italia 25
France 8, 10, 13, 24, 25, 28, 34, 38, 45, 48, 49, 75, 107, 119, 120, 122, 142, 154, 174, 175, 197, 202, 232, 248, 250
Franco, Francisco 266
Freedom Party (NL) 25, 48, 54, 248, 263 *see also* Partij voor de Vrijheid
Freeland, Chrystia 236, 273
Freie Demokratische Partei (FDP) 235
Freiheitliche Partei Österreichs FPÖ (Austrian Freedom Party) 68, 110, 111, 113–115, 146, 147, 149, 153, 160, 192, 221, 224
Fremskridtspartiet (Progress Party Denmark) 148, 154
Fremskrittspartiet (Progress Party Norway) 148
Friedman, Milton 231, 237, 273 *see also* negative income tax
Friedman, Rose 237, 273
Front National 25, 34, 38, 43, 47, 48, 56, 114, 122, 149, 154, 159, 167, 221 *see also* Rassemblement National
Fukuyama, Francis 3, 139, 156, 166, 253, 258, 273, 274

Gaddafi, Muammar 158, 167
Galbraith, John Kenneth 226, 236, 274
Gallagher, Mike 174, 178
Galston, William A. 190, 274
Gärtner, Reinhold 153, 278
Gauchet, Marcel 61, 66, 182, 189, 274
Gauck, Joachim 110, 114
GeenStijl 111
Gelli, Licio 266
Genovese, Rino 274
George, Robert 171, 177, 274
Georgia 220, 221
German Democratic Republic 176
Germany 9, 39, 43, 106, 110, 119, 152, 175, 200, 201, 215, 216, 234, 251, 254, 268

as a model for party financing 164
co-determination 240–243, 245, 246
Gibelli, Antonio 159, 268, 274
Gilded Age 14, 163, 228, 229
Ginsborg, Paul 159, 168, 266, 268, 274
Giscard d'Estaing, Valéry 189
Glistrup, Mogens 148, 154
Goethe, Johann Wolfgang 221
Golden Dawn 145
Goldman Sachs 176
Good Friday Agreement 94
Goodhart, David 274
Goodwin, Matthew 15, 273
Gorsuch, Justice Neil M. 131, 144
Gould, Philip 85, 86
Grabo, Norman S. 278
Graham, Carol 267
Graham, Lindsey 168
Grasser, Karl-Heinz 160
Grayling, A. C. 218, 223, 257, 274
great coalitions 152, 154
Great Recession 5, 228, 240
Great Replacement 39, 41, 249, 257 *see also* Camus, Renaud
Greece 5, 67, 68, 142, 145, 149, 150, 154, 176, 266
Green Party 147
Greenspan, Alan 230, 237
Griffin, Roger 17, 274
Grillo, Beppe 26, 28, 31, 35
Grofman, Bernard 174, 178, 274
Gros, Bertram 223, 274
Guttman, Amy 66

Habermas, Jürgen 252, 257, 274
Hagendoorn, Louk 151, 155, 251, 256–258, 280
Hague, William 176
Haider, Jörg 146, 153, 160
Haidt, Jonathan 53, 57, 58
Hakhverdian, Armen 74, 190, 274
Halla-Aho, Jussi 149
Hamilton, Alexander 274
Hamon, Benoît 123
Hart, H. L. A. 92, 274
Hawaii 234, 238
Hayek, Friedrich 68, 69, 74, 206, 215, 222, 274
health, bad 37
Hegel, G. W. F. 48, 139, 170, 177, 275
Held, David 73, 75, 275
Herz, Rachel 57, 275

286

Index

Hirschman, Albert O. 39, 40, 45, 275
Hispanics 42, 45, 63, 104, 263
Hitler, Adolf 32, 93, 128, 151, 194, 262, 266, 275
  disgust of 52, 54, 57
Hobsbawm, Eric 164, 169, 267, 268
Hofer, Norbert 147
Höffe, Otfried 182, 190, 275
Hofstadter, Richard 16, 105, 113, 117, 124, 236, 275
Hollande, François 122, 161, 181, 189
Holocaust 266, 268
Hong Kong 200
Hörisch, Felix 244, 246
Humphrey, Hubert 124
Hungary 2, 15, 68, 71, 75, 145, 200, 207, 246, 266
Huntington, Samuel 13, 63, 67, 139, 144, 253, 258, 275
  on third wave of democratization 139, 140
Huyse, Luc 166

Ibizagate 153
ideal type 12, 21, 22, 59 *see also* Weber, Max
identities, threatened 39, 61
ideology (of populism) 59
Immigration Act (US) 63
independent agencies, stabilizing role of 127–136, 142
Independent Parliamentary Standards Authority (IPSA) 173, 179
inequality, economic 14
  reduce 225–239
Inequality Turn 229, 236
Inglehart, Ronald 204, 209, 275
initiative, popular 12, 98, 99, 102, 103, 106, 109, 110, 141, 142
  minaret 108, 114 *see also* plebiscite and referendum
Iran 238
Iraq 121, 254
Ireland 268
ISIS 27, 250
Islam 250
Italy 5, 24, 35, 68, 104, 150, 159, 166, 177, 266, 268

Jackson, Andrew 112
Japan 66, 232, 253
Jarvis, Howard 99
Jay, John 274
Jennings Bryan, William 7, 16, 225, 236, 271

Jetten, Jolanda 40, 45
Jobbik 145, 221
Johnson, Boris 2, 14, 69, 74, 94–96, 111
Johnson, Harry 92, 129, 135, 275
Johnson, Lyndon B. 124
Jones, Erik 154
Jospin, Lionel 189
Judis, John B. 8, 17, 275
Juncker, Jean-Claude 176
Juppé, Alain 189

Kaczyński, Jarosław 17, 128, 266
Kagan, Robert 200, 207, 263, 268
Kaltwasser, Cristóbal Rovira 66, 133, 136, 277
Kammenos, Panos 154
Kant, Immanuel 170, 177, 206, 275
Kasich, John 168
Katz, Richard 152, 155, 166, 169, 275
Kavanaugh, Justice Brett 131, 136, 144
Kennedy, Paul 63, 67, 275
Kennedy, Robert 124
Keynes, John Maynard 128, 134
Khrushchev, Nikita 29
King, Anthony 10, 17, 276
Kirchgässner, Gebhart 276
Kjaersgaard, Pia 148
Kluge, Norbert 246
Know-Nothings 63
Koch, Charles 162
Koch, David 162
Kohl, Helmut 157
  scandal 157
Kok, Wim 177
Kolnai, Aurel 57, 276
Koole, Ruud 152, 155, 276
Kosovo 108
Kraft, Kornelius 273
Kritzinger, Sylvia 203, 208, 276
Krugman, Paul 228, 236
Kuhn, Thomas 222, 276
Kupchan, Charles 177, 276
Kuznets, Simon 226

Labour Party 85, 93, 95, 119, 120, 202, 208, 241
  New 85
La France Insoumise (LFI) 44
laissez faire, laissez aller 199
La République En Marche (LREM) 122, 197
Lasch, Christopher 180, 189, 276
Latin America 140, 267

287

Index

Latvia 120
Le Bon, Gustave 49, 56, 276
Le Bras, Hervé 34, 44, 276
Lega (Nord) 25, 28, 68, 104, 150, 266
Leitkultur 251
Le Maire, Bruno 182
Lenk, Kurt 112, 276
Le Pen, Jean-Marie 43, 44, 145
Le Pen, Marine 25, 43, 47, 122, 145, 149, 154, 159, 224
Lesnik, Renata 167, 271
Les Républicains 119, 122, 123
  see also Union pour un mouvement populaire (UMP)
LGBT community 29, 186, 248
"liberal", what does it mean? 197–201, 206, 207
  neoliberal 197, 198
  ultra-liberal 197, 198
Liberal Democratic Party (UK) 197, 202
liberalism, economic 200
Libya 158
Lijphart, Arend 114, 276
Lijst Pim Fortuyn 25 *see also* Pim Fortuyn
Lincoln, Abraham 55, 123, 215
Lindsey, Brink 236, 276
Lipset, Seymour Martin 17
lobbyists, influence of 161, 162, 164, 168, 173, 174, 176, 177
Locke, John 198, 206, 260, 261, 267, 276
lottocracy 186
Luhmann, Niklas 167
Lukacs, John 17, 56, 61, 62, 66, 276
Luther King, Martin 124
Luttwak, Edward 261, 262, 267, 268
Luxembourg 246
Luyendijk, Joris 179, 276

Macedonia 154
Macpherson, C. B. 73, 75, 124, 260, 261, 267, 276
McCain, John 162, 168
McConnell, Mitch 168
McDonnell, Duncan 154, 270
McGhee, Eric 118, 124, 277
McKinley, William 7
McWhinney, Edward 135, 277
Macron, Emmanuel 122, 149, 175, 182, 183, 189, 190, 197
Madison, James 70, 74, 103, 113, 170, 274
Maduro, Nicolás 5, 11, 152, 267
Mair, Peter 152, 155, 166, 169, 275

Major, John 176
Mamonova, Natalia 17
Mann, Thomas 262
Mannheim, Karl 142, 144, 276
manufactured will 13, 81, 82, 84
Maréchal, Marion 25
Mariel boatlift 250, 257
Matthijs, Matthias 154
May, Theresa 94, 244, 246
Mead, Walter Russell 61, 66, 277
Medvedev, Dmitri 220
Mélenchon, Jean-Luc 44, 205
Menninghaus, Winfried 57, 277
meritocracy 181, 182, 184, 188, 191
Merkel, Angela 65, 254
Merton, Robert 124, 277
Mexicans 27, 39, 62, 65, 249, 263
Michaels, Jon D. 277
migration 14, 248–259
  absorption capacity 253, 254
  push and pull factors 248, 249
  economic arguments against 249, 250
  identitarian arguments against 250
Miliband, Ed 120, 121
Mill, John Stuart 48, 49, 56, 75, 93, 277
millennials, rejecting democracy 193
Miller, William Ian 52, 57, 277
Mills, Nicolaus 277
Minogue, Kenneth 84, 91, 277
"mirroring" of electorate 185
Mitbestimmung 14, 241
Mitch, David 277
Mitterrand, François 157, 167
Modi, Narendra 5
Moffitt, Benjamin 30, 32, 277
Mohammed, Prophet 28
Mols, Frank 40, 45, 277
Montesquieu 70, 74, 170, 177, 277
moral charter 171
Morales, Evo 267
moralization (of politics) 170–179
Morocco 249
Moroccans 65
Mounk, Yasha 41, 205, 277
Movimento Sociale Italiano (MSI) 266
Mudde, Cas 67, 71, 75, 133, 136, 155, 277
Müller, Jan-Werner 70, 74, 277
Muller, Jerzy C. 236, 277
multiculturalism 14, 251, 252, 257
Muslims 27, 39, 55, 107, 108, 251, 253, 263
Mussolini, Benito 25, 140, 262, 264–266, 268

Index

Nagel, Thomas 215, 223
Napoleon Bonaparte 93, 111
Napoleon III (Louis Napoleon) 10, 93, 111
narodniki 6
Nastase, Adna 158
National Health Service (NHS) 141, 214, 222
nationalism 261
NATO 121, 219, 251
Navalny, Alexei 11
Nazi roots (of populist parties) 145, 146, 153
negative income tax 231 *see also* Friedman, Milton
Neiman, Susan 198, 206, 277
Netherlands, The 13, 25, 39, 41, 43, 46, 54, 58, 96, 97, 105, 116, 141, 144, 152, 171, 177, 185, 186, 197, 216, 223, 232, 234, 240, 246
   Ukraine referendum 13, 96, 141, 144
   multiculturalism in 250–252, 257
Neumann, Franz 112
Nevis, Allan 277
New Alliance (Finland) 149
New Deal 7, 129, 231
new rich 40
Nichols, Tom 187, 191, 192, 205, 277
Nie, Norman H. 208, 281
Nord Stream 176
Norris, Pippa 208, 277
Northern Ireland 94, 95
Norway 148, 154, 242
Nozick, Robert 87, 92, 278
NSDAP 151
Nussbaum, Martha 51, 57, 108, 114, 278
Nye, Russell B. 278

Obama, Barack 65, 162, 168, 218
Office of Congressional Complaint Review 172
Office of Congressional Ethics (OCE) 172
OMOV system 121–122
Ontario 234, 238
Orbán, Viktor 2, 17, 68, 71, 75, 129, 152, 266
Ortega y Gasset, José 207
Orwell, George 182, 261, 267, 278
Osborne, George 176
Ostiguy, Pierre 65, 67, 278
Österreichische Volkspartei (ÖVP) 111, 146, 224
Oxbridge 13, 183

Pallaver, Günther, 153, 278
Parti Socialiste 119, 120, 122

Partij voor de Vrijheid 25
   see also Freedom Party (NL)
party financing 156–158, 161, 165
   illegal 157, 158, 160, 161
   by the state 165
Pascal, Blaise 213, 222, 278
Pateman, Carol 243, 246, 278
Paxton, Robert 9, 17, 278
Penelopegate 175
Perón, Juan 268
personalization (of politics) 24, 25
pessimism-optimism divide 34
Pharr, Susan J. 17
Philippe, Édouard 189
Philippines 2, 5, 15
Philippot, Florian 149
Piccio, Daniela R. 166, 169, 278
Picket, Kate 230, 237, 281
Piketty, Thomas 228, 236, 278
Pipes, Richard 15, 278
PiS (Law and Justice Party) 72, 128, 129, 134, 152, 219
plebiscite 93, 111, 142 *see also* referendum and initiative, popular
plutocrats 15
Podemos 67, 133
Poland 5, 72, 120, 128, 129, 134, 152, 200, 207, 219, 246, 266
Polanyi, Karl 229, 236, 278
polarization 142
Political Action Committee (PAC) 162, 163
political parties 116–119, 124
   declining membership of 119, 120, 124
Populists, the 7, 8, 15, 36
   see also American People's Party
Portugal 266
post-truth 14, 213, 214, 216, 217, 222, 268
   see also alternative facts and fake news
Potter, Allan M. 135, 278
Poujade, Pierre 36, 44, 107
poujadist movement 44
Pozsgai, Joseph 167, 278
Price, Don K. 16, 278
primaries 143, 116–119
   open 13, 143, 118–124
Prinz, Jesse J. 58, 278
Propaganda 2 (Masonic lodge) 266
property, private 198, 199
protection, need for 59
public opinion, raw 88–90
   refined 88–90
purity, quest for 51

289

Index

Putin, Vladimir 10, 17, 28, 29, 50, 121, 159, 168, 223, 224
Putnam, Robert D. 17, 33, 44, 104, 113, 276, 278
Pye, Lucian 182, 190, 278

racism 265
Rajoy, Mariano 260
Rassemblement National 25, 35, 64, 145, 149, 192, 248
  see also Front National
Rawls, John 136, 188, 191, 199, 206, 279
Reagan, Ronald 227, 229
recall (of elected officials) 98, 99, 112, 117
referendum 12, 72, 88, 96, 97, 99, 105, 106, 116, 141, 142, 144, 202, 205, 208, 219 see also plebiscite and initiative, popular
  advisory 96–98
  binding 97, 98
refugees 251, 255, 263
Republican Party 6, 25, 197, 262
resentment 48
Restrepo, Pascual 67
retrospective accountability 82, 83
Revelli, Marco 166, 279
revolving-door practices 175, 176
Riemen, Rob 263, 268, 279
Robertson, William 198
Rocard, Michel 248, 253, 257
Rockefeller, Nelson 163
Romania 158
Rooduijn, Matthijs 279
Roosevelt, Franklin Delano 7, 129, 163
Roosevelt, Theodore 7, 161
Rosanvallon, Pierre 17, 23, 30, 44, 51, 57, 75, 91, 92, 125, 132, 136, 279
Rothwell, Jonathan 279
Roudinesco, Elisabeth 27
Rozin, Paul 57, 279
Rubio, Marco 28, 50, 168
Ruding, Onno 177
Russia 6, 10, 15, 17, 67, 97, 163, 179, 193, 200, 219–221
  as sponsor of populist parties 219, 221
  meddling in US presidential election 173
Rutte, Mark 141

Saby, Olivier 181, 189, 279
Salvini, Matteo 5, 25, 32, 150, 266
Sandar, Ivo 158

Sanders, Bernie 184, 190
Sarkozy, Nicolas 122, 158, 167, 279
Sassen, Saskia 254, 258, 279
Saudi Arabia 108, 157
Schakel, Wouter 74, 190, 274
Schlesinger, Arthur M. 62, 66, 279
Schmidt, Helmut 241
Schmitt, Carl 70, 74, 220, 223, 265, 279
  fiend-foe opposition 70, 74
Schrag, Peter 99, 100, 103, 104, 112, 113
Schrempp, Jürgen 243, 246, 279
Schröder, Gerhard 176, 179
Schumpeter, Joseph 13, 80–82, 90, 91, 262
Schüssel, Wolfgang 146, 153
Schuyt, C. J. M. 223, 279
Schwarzenegger, Arnold 100
Schweizerischer Volkspartei (SVP) 107, 111, 114, 248
scientific revolution 213
Scotland 94, 95, 201, 205
Seldon, Anthony 91, 279
Seligman, Adam 156, 166, 167, 279
Senate Ethics Committee 172
Sennett, Richard 24, 30, 63, 67, 243, 246, 279, 280
Serfaty, Simon 280
Shaub, Walter M. 172, 173, 178
Siegfried, André 280
Simmel, Georg 201, 207, 280
Simone, Raffaele 280
Sipilä, Juha 234
Skenderovic, Damir, 107, 114, 280
Skocpol, Theda 33, 44, 280
Slovak Republic 246
Slovenia 246
Smith, Adam 198
Sniderman, Paul M. 151, 155, 251, 256–258, 280
Snyder, Timothy 263
social capital 33, 44
soft money 161
solidarity, erosion of 103
South Korea 268
Soviet Union 215, 219, 224
Sozialdemokratische Partei Deutschlands (SPD) 119
Sozialdemokratische Partei Österreichs (SPÖ) 147, 153
Spain 67, 166, 266
Spruyt, Bram 273
Stalin, Joseph 31, 215
Standing, Guy 233, 237, 280

Index

Starink, Laura 96, 112, 280
Steele Commager, Henry 277
Stenner, Karen 54, 55, 58, 104, 113, 280
Stiglitz, Joseph E. 236, 280
Strache, Heinz-Christian 147, 153
Streeck, Wolfgang 246, 280
subprime crisis 176
Supreme Court (US) 130–132, 135, 142, 144
  activist 129, 130
  self-restraint of 129, 130
Süssmuth, Rita 254
Sweden 240, 242, 246
Swedish Democrats (Sverige Demokraterna) 145
Switzerland 13, 105, 106–110, 114–116, 141, 237, 238
Syria 254
Syriza 67, 68, 150, 154

Taguieff, Pierre-André 15, 56, 145, 153, 280
Taverne, Ed 223
Tea Party 30, 40
term limits (for office holders) 173
Thatcher, Margaret 85, 227, 242
Thurow, Lester 226, 227, 236, 280
Tillman Act 161, 169
Tilly, Charles 156, 166, 169, 280
Timmermans, Frans 129
Tocqueville, Alexis de 49, 131, 280
Transparency International 157, 159, 161
Traverso, Enzo 264, 268, 280
"trickle down" theory 189, 199
Trotsky, Leon 215
Trump, Donald 2, 5, 12, 14, 17, 24, 25, 30, 31, 35–40, 42, 45, 46, 62, 63, 65, 68, 70, 74, 130, 131, 135, 142, 163, 164, 168, 169, 172, 173, 178, 182, 214, 217, 222, 280
  and disgust 49–57
  a fascist? 262–264
  and migration 248, 255–257
  simple language used by 26, 27
  tax cuts of 225
  vulgar language of 27, 28
trust 215
  depletion of 156, 157, 167, 188
Tsipras, Alexis 154
Tuchman, Barbara 6, 15, 280
Turkey 5, 11, 108, 152, 159, 249
Twitter 216, 217

Ukraine 13, 96, 121, 141, 220, 221, 224
Union pour un movement populaire (UMP) 119
  see also Les Républicains
United Kingdom (UK) 13, 94, 95, 105, 116, 119, 120, 213, 214, 230, 241, 245
  See also Britain
United Kingdom Independence Party (UKIP) 93–95, 111
United Nations High Commissioner for Refugees (UNHCR) 258
United States 3, 5, 6, 8, 10, 13, 36–38, 42, 51, 54, 55, 62, 63, 68, 90, 106, 116–120, 140, 142, 156, 157, 161, 164, 184, 185, 187, 194, 200, 201, 204, 213, 227, 231, 232, 234, 244, 249, 250, 253, 254, 260, 267
universal basic income 14, 91, 225, 231–238
US Office of Government Ethics (OGE) 172

Vaccarino, Elena 271
Valls, Manuel 123
Van Biezen, Ingrid 166, 169, 278
Van den Brink, H. M. 74, 280
Van der Bellen, Alexander 147
Van der Brug, Wouter 279
Van Grieken, Tom 151
Vanhecke, Frank 30
Van Herpen, Marcel H. 17, 31, 167, 223, 224, 281
Van Leeuwen, Maarten 281
Van Parijs, Philippe 237, 239, 281
Van Reybrouck, David 186, 191, 281
Venezuela 5, 11, 28, 68, 152, 267
Verba, Sidney 204, 208, 209, 281
Verhagen, Maxime 28, 31
Vlaams Belang 17, 104, 145, 151, 154, 221
  see also Vlaams Blok
Vlaams Blok 30, 114, 145, 151, 154
  see also Vlaams Belang
Voltaire 281
Von Hindenburg, Paul 93
voting age, lowering of 201
vulgarity 27, 28, 31 *see also* Trump, Donald
Volkspartij voor Vrijheid en Democratie (VVD) 197

Wales 94
Walker, Scott 168
Wallerstein, Immanuel 66, 253, 258, 281
Walzer, Michael 143, 144, 182, 190, 281
Warner, Daniel M. 144
Warren, Chief Justice Earl 130

Washington Consensus 229
Washington, George 71, 74
Watson, Tom 121
Weber, Max 12, 21, 30, 91, 116, 117, 124, 142, 144, 179, 180, 189, 268, 281 *see also* ideal type
Wegener, Anne-Christine 167, 168, 272
Weimar Republic 128, 134
Weitz, Eric D. 134, 281
Welzel, Christian 204, 275
Wilders, Geert 4, 25–27, 30, 41, 48, 54, 56, 65, 70, 74, 190, 248, 263
Wilkinson, Richard 230, 237, 281
Wilson, Harold 241
Wilson, Woodrow 7

Winkler, Günther 74, 281
Winock, Michel 17, 28, 31, 281
Wolfe, Alan 16, 252, 257, 282
World Health Organization (WHO) 2, 14, 233
Wyplosz, Charles 198, 206

xenophobia 10, 55, 107, 142, 248

Yeltsin, Boris 28

Zakaria, Fareed 123, 126, 205–207, 209, 282
Zeglovits, Eva 203, 208, 276
Zeman, Miloš 28, 31